8/94

BIO WILS

D0898994

The
Stranger
Wilde

GARY SCHMIDGALL

The Stranger Wilde

Interpreting Oscar

Yours in Oscar!

Gary Schmidgall

A WILLIAM ABRAHAMS BOOK

DUTTON

DUTTON

Published by the Penguin Group
Penguin Books USA Inc., 375 Hudson Street, New York, New York 10014, U.S.A.
Penguin Books Ltd, 27 Wrights Lane, London W8 5TZ, England
Penguin Books Australia Ltd, Ringwood, Victoria, Australia
Penguin Books Canada Ltd, 10 Alcorn Avenue, Toronto, Ontario, Canada M4V 3B2
Penguin Books (N.Z.) Ltd, 182–190 Wairau Road, Auckland 10, New Zealand

Penguin Books Ltd, Registered Offices:
Harmondsworth, Middlesex, England

First published by Dutton,
an imprint of Dutton Signet,
a division of Penguin Books USA Inc.
Distributed in Canada by McClelland & Stewart Inc.

First Printing, April, 1994

1   3   5   7   9   10   8   6   4   2

 REGISTERED TRADEMARK—MARCA REGISTRADA

LIBRARY OF CONGRESS CATALOGING-IN-PUBLICATION DATA:
Schmidgall, Gary, 1945–
The stranger Wilde : interpreting Oscar / Gary Schmidgall.
p.   cm.
ISBN 0-525-93763-3
1. Wilde, Oscar, 1854–1900—Biography.   2. Authors, Irish—19th century—
Biography.   3. Gay men—Great Britain—Biography.
I. Title.
PR5823.S35   1994
828'.809—dc20

[B]   93-39638
                                                                           CIP

Printed in the United States of America
Set in Goudy and Helvetica Condensed

DESIGNED BY STEVEN N. STATHAKIS

For Tom Tanselle

Contents

☆ ☆ ☆ ☆ ☆ ☆ ☆ ☆ ☆ ☆ ☆ ☆ ☆ ☆ ☆ ☆ ☆ ☆

Illustrations　　*ix*

Foreword　　*xi*

Chapter One　SEEING OSCAR　　*1*

Chapter Two　TRESPASSER　　*27*

Chapter Three　*PUNCH* V. OSCAR I　　*43*

Chapter Four　*ARBITER ELEGANTIARUM*　　*65*

Chapter Five　"MOTHERS ARE DARLINGS"　　*81*

Chapter Six　A WIFE'S TRAGEDY　　*97*

Chapter Seven　"MY GOOD PAPA!"　　*127*

Chapter Eight　TALES OF A PRODIGAL BABY　　*145*

Chapter Nine　ASS-THETE: LOVER OF YOUTH　　*169*

Chapter Ten　*PUNCH* V. OSCAR II　　*199*

Chapter Eleven　THE MAN WILDE: HIS CRIME　　*213*

Chapter Twelve　WHY HE STAYED　　*233*

Chapter Thirteen　TRAGEDIAN: *AMOR FATI*　　*255*

The Stranger Wilde

Chapter Fourteen   FALLEN EAGLE: DEVILS AND ANGELS   *271*

Chapter Fifteen   CLOSET PHILOSOPHER   *295*

Chapter Sixteen   PARIAH-DOG   *331*

Chapter Seventeen   WILDESHAWSHOW   *345*

Chapter Eighteen   OSCAR TODAY   *375*

Chapter Nineteen   PERFECT PESSIMIST, CHILD OF SUNSHINE   *393*

Chronology   *411*

Notes   *419*

Select Bibliography   *475*

Index   *481*

Illustrations

(exclusive of Punch *drawings in Chapters 3 and 10)*

Portrait of Wilde by Harper Pennington *(p. xii)*

Portrait of Wilde by Toulouse-Lautrec *(p. xiii)*

Caricature of Wilde from Beerbohm's A *Peep into the Past* (p. 2)

Wilde in costume as Salome *(p. 8)*

Cartoon of Wilde from the *New York Daily Graphic* (p. 67)

Masculine attire for ladies, *Punch* drawing *(p. 71)*

Caricatures of Sir William and Lady Wilde *(p. 85)*

Wilde's wife, Constance Mary Lloyd, before marriage *(p. 99)*

Haberdasher's advertisement featuring Wilde,
Chicago 1882 *(p. 170)*

Wilde with two Oxford classmates *(p. 173)*

Clyde Fitch as Lydia Languish in *The Rivals* (p. 179)

Six portrait drawings of participants in the trials *(pp. 186–187)*

Lord Alfred Douglas and Maurice Schwabe (*p. 189*)

Henry Labouchere caricature by Beerbohm (*p. 216*)

Frank Harris caricature by Beerbohm (*p. 242*)

Newspaper drawing of Wilde's arrest (*p. 272*)

Newspaper drawing of Queensberry's assault on his son (*p. 282*)

Walter Sickert drawing of "Sebastian Melmoth" on release from prison (*p. 333*)

"Mr Wilde of Borneo" cartoon, *Washington Post* (*p. 339*)

Bernard Shaw at the time his novel
Immaturity was published (*p. 349*)

Foreword

It is a popular superstition that in America a visitor is invariably addressed as "Stranger." I was never once addressed as "Stranger."
—"Impressions of America"

Picture, if you will, Oscar Wilde.

Imagine the amiable giant loping in his "odd elephantine gait" over the links of a golf course on the Norfolk coast, clubs slung over his shoulder. "I find Cromer excellent for writing, and golf still better," he reported to Beerbohm Tree in 1892. Ah! to have teed off in a foursome with Oscar. Out on the fairway, might he have quipped, with his usual euphonious alliteration, about the improbable in full pursuit of the unplayable?—just as, in the play he was writing at Cromer, he quipped about the English country gentleman galloping after a fox: "the unspeakable in full pursuit of the uneatable." Now picture Oscar winning the hearts of a band of Leadville, Colorado, silver miners by quaffing something they called a cocktail without flinching and being pronounced by them "a bully boy with no glass eye." Then summon the vision of Oscar as an exuberant papa, building the most excellent sandcastles for his two boys, Cyril and Vyvyan, on the beach near Brighton. Or picture him, in his last year, sitting contentedly in Rome's Borghese gardens looking at the daisies, drinking (so he said) *milk* . . . and pursuing his new hobby: "Can you photograph cows well? I did one of cows in the Borghese. . . . Cows are very fond of being photographed, and, unlike architecture, don't move." Picture, finally, Oscar's corpse lying in his

Oscar Wilde as he looked in 1881, by Harper Pennington (1855–1920). The portrait (seventy by thirty-six inches) was bought by Robert Ross at the sale of Wilde's possessions in 1895 and bequeathed to Christopher Millard in 1918. Millard advertised it for sale at £200 in 1921; his hope that it would "find a permanent home in some great Library or Museum in the United States where the foundation of Wilde's fame was laid" was realized.

room in the little hotel in the Rue des Beaux-Arts where he died and Edouard Dupoirier, his humane and generous hotelier, leaning over to extract one of the few valuables that might diminish his guest's arrears: Oscar's gold-laced dentures.

Picture, indeed, the lone formal portrait ever painted of Oscar. A wedding gift from the American artist Harper Pennington, it hung in the drawing room of Oscar and Constance Wilde's Tite Street house for eleven years, until it was sold at the sheriff's sale after Oscar's arrest. Now, its varnish blackened by time, the painting hangs in very poor light on the wall of a back stairwell in the Clark Library in Los Angeles.

Or—speaking of portraits—imagine instead Oscar, out on bail and in hiding between his trials, receiving a visit from Toulouse-Lautrec. Lautrec asked Oscar whether he would sit for him. Knowing how wickedly satiric Lautrec's brush could be, Oscar refused. As he did so, did he recall a highly pertinent passage he had written in *Dorian Gray*? He might well have, for this passage was also in *Oscariana*, the anthology of his aphorisms that his wife, Constance, had compiled and published just a few months before: "Sin is a thing that writes itself across a man's face. It cannot be concealed," says the artist Basil Hallward; "If a wretched man has a vice, it shows itself in the lines of his mouth, the droop of his eyelids, the moulding of his hands." Lautrec took the refusal in stride, but obviously left with a splendid mental picture of the vain pariah. Oscar's artist friend Will Rothenstein said of Lautrec, "He was a frank, indeed brutal, cynic. Human weakness lay naked and unprotected before his eyes." And the portrait he produced

Portrait of Oscar Wilde by Henri de Toulouse-Lautrec (Dortu catalogue P.574, twenty-four by twenty inches), probably executed in 1894 or early 1895 and now in the Roger–Viollet collection, Paris.

certainly gives us an old sinner for whom time was running out. Big Ben in the background is perhaps Lautrec's acerbic little *jeu*.

The point of gathering together here so many glimpses of unfamiliar Oscars is the point of my title—which of course, given the title of his most famous play, required some kind of pun. This point is to suggest that there is more to the man than one would guess from the caricature who appears to inhabit the common memory nowadays. The common memory, as always, prefers simplicity. It prefers primary colors . . . colors that Oscar and his Aesthetic Movement cohorts so deplored. The resulting portrait is a blatant one indeed: an ignominious fate for one who proclaimed that "a colour-sense is more important . . . than a sense of right and wrong" and who doted on all the unprimary colors . . . like sage green, heliotrope, and lavender. But *not* mauve: "Never trust a woman who wears mauve," he wrote.

This gaudy caricature-Oscar is almost always caught in one

or the other of his two most famous poses. He is either "the most famous pederast in the world's history" or—in the words of his fatal boyfriend, Lord Alfred Douglas—"the greatest talker who ever lived, not excepting Socrates who lacked Wilde's sense of humor." No one celebrated this latter Oscar more eloquently or succinctly than Dorothy Parker, who was surely the most Oscarian American woman of our century:

> *If, with the literate, I am*
> *Impelled to try an epigram,*
> *I never seek to take the credit;*
> *We all assume that Oscar said it.*

Titillating and entertaining though these two prominent features of Oscar's life are, they obscure much else, indeed distort our perceptions of what he did, thought, and wrote. His son Vyvyan made this point a half-century after his father's death, when he collected his memories in a loving, generous-spirited though sadness-laden book called *Son of Oscar Wilde*. He expressed dismay at how the common memory—like the timeworn varnish of the Pennington portrait—had obscured his father's identity: "As people recede further and further into the past, they are apt to assume the aspect of effigies from which all humanity has departed." Oscar the Wit and Wilde the Convict have become such effigies, exceedingly familiar, unthreatening, convenient ones, and my purpose in the following chapters will be to discover a more dubious, perplexing, and inconvenient Oscar.

That is, the Oscar who has become a stranger to us . . . and who is also more profoundly strange than most delighted visitors to *The Importance of Being Earnest* could ever imagine. At the heart of this strangeness, I believe, lies the fact that made him in many ways a stranger in his own world: the fact of his homosexuality. "The degree and kind of a person's sexuality," wrote Friedrich Nietzsche, "reach up into the ultimate pinnacle of his spirit," and this study is predicated on this assumption. Though by no means hostage to that merely more newfangled and fashionable effigy, Oscar the Gay Martyr, several of the following chapters take some aspect of his sexual identity as a point of departure or arrival.

Since his death, great forests have been decimated for books about Oscar and his homosexuality, but few have been of much value. In 1973 a Modern Language Association bibliographer could even summarize that "the relationship between Wilde's homosexuality, creative writing, and aesthetic theorizing has been wearisomely but largely profitlessly discussed." The atmosphere for more candid and free-ranging approaches to the subject has, in fact, not existed for very long. In 1967, two years before the Stonewall riot and the genuine dawn of the gay liberation movement, Rupert Croft-Cooke could write in his racy Wilde book, *Feasting with Panthers*, "We have had more than enough of every kind of literature dealing with homosexuality, which is not a subject in itself of remarkable interest and nearly always a bore in fiction." Three years later, in 1970, Timothy d'Arch Smith, introducing his study of gay poets in England between 1889 and 1930, averred that he was living "in an age saturated in adult homosexuality." Oh? The Gutenberg-like explosion of gay and lesbian writing and publication in the two and a half decades since 1969 would doubtless boggle Croft-Cooke's and d'Arch Smith's minds: emphatically, the subject has now been voted not boring—or unprofitable—at all.

And yet . . . the ramifications of Oscar's gay identity have still not been fully and satisfyingly explored. Even the massive—and by many accounted definitive—1987 biography by Richard Ellmann strikes one as being a product of the older, more genteel and discreet biographical dispensation. For all his candor in discussing sexual matters, shrewd and sly eloquence, and comprehensiveness, Ellmann left unpursued many fascinating traces. Ed Cohen made something like this point in a 1988 review: "In Ellmann's account . . . Wilde's life is not radical but 'disguised'—hidden by the various 'masks' that he self-consciously donned throughout his life." Even Jonathan Dollimore, in his *Sexual Dissidence* of 1991, judged Oscar's "transgressive aesthetic" to be "still largely excluded from consideration" and "still subjected to the judgment of [the] older vision." The present book, I hope, will prove to be but one of many efforts to discover more about the "radical" behind the masks . . . and more about the transgressive implications of the masks themselves.

To be sure, one is daunted a little by Oscar—or is "taunted" the better word?—when one speaks of trying to retrieve his "real" or "historical" personality. He thought any such effort ultimately illusory, once calling history "an unattractive form of fiction." He even accounted it the "proper occupation" of the historian as well as the artist to "give an accurate description of what has never occurred." And another remark strikes me as a warning to anyone looking at the 1890s with post–Stonewall Revolution eyes: "We cannot re-write the whole of history for the purpose of gratifying our moral sense of what should be." This caveat makes very clear how fraught with danger is any attempt to breathe something like life back into the effigial Oscar. The danger, however, makes the attempt all the more worthwhile, as Oscar—who feasted with panthers and toyed with tigers—demonstrated in his own life.

The first chapter considers the challenges of addressing Oscar in the figurative sense. A few words are necessary about addressing him in the literal sense. In his "Impressions of America" lecture, Oscar added, after the words in the epigraph, "When I went to Texas I was called 'Captain'; when I got to the centre of the country I was addressed as 'Colonel,' and, on arriving at the borders of Mexico, as 'General.' On the whole, however, 'Sir,' the old English method of addressing people, is the most common." What to call my protagonist, Oscar Fingal O'Flahertie Wills Wilde, has not been weighed lightly. Authors who assume first-name familiarity with their subjects have always irked me, and yet I have obviously chosen to do so myself. This is in part because he is *the* Oscar: history's quintessential and only Oscar, a few Scandinavian kings and a much-coveted statuette aside. In fact, he was jealous of the name. After visiting the Cambridge don Oscar Browning, he wrote to a friend: "I wish he was *not* called Oscar." Also, this man always retained something of the child—Walt Whitman justly called him "a great big, splendid boy"—and surnames fit youngsters a bit awkwardly.

Besides, Oscar had become for the late Victorian age—as for *Punch* magazine—"Our Oscar." He was obliged to point this out himself when an American friend took him to his club and signed him in as O. Wilde: "O. Wilde! Who is O. Wilde? Nobody knows 'O. Wilde,' but 'Oscar Wilde' is a household word!" When a drama critic harshly attacked *Lady Windermere's Fan*, Oscar focused the ire of his letter to the critic's editor entirely on having been erroneously given the name of "the most charming of all the Disciples": "John is not amongst the many delightful names given to me at my baptism. . . . [Your critic's] attempt to falsify one of the most important facts in the History of Art must be checked at once." When a rich vein of silver in Leadville was named in his honor, it was of course not "The Wilde" but "The Oscar."

Nor do I desire to conceal my affection for the fellow, flawed though his character was and atrocious his behavior on many occasions. As Oscar himself said, when the prosecutor at his trial asked him whether he called the young men he consorted with by their Christian names: "Yes. I always call by their Christian names people whom I like. People I dislike I call something else." My preference for "Oscar" over "Wilde" became fixed, though, when I came upon a letter he wrote shortly after being released from prison: "I am in the Public Press sometimes 'the ex-convict,' which is too obvious: sometimes '*le poète-forçat*' [the convicted poet], which I like, as it puts me into good company: sometimes I am 'Mr Oscar Wilde,' a phrase I remember: sometimes 'the man Wilde,' a phrase I don't."

How, incidentally, did Oscar come by his name? The story told by his son Vyvyan is that Sir William Wilde, a prominent eye surgeon, was away in Sweden when his second son was born, successfully removing a cataract that had long afflicted King Oscar. The King consented to act as godfather. Sir William also operated on the father of Bernard Shaw, who amusingly described a less happy outcome: "Wilde . . . operated on my father to correct a squint, and overdid the corrections so much that my father squinted the other way all the rest of his life. To this day I never notice a squint; it is as normal to me as a nose or a tall hat."

☆ ☆ ☆

THE SOURCES FOR ALL quotations are given in the endnotes; particularly relevant matter I have raised into footnotes. I would like to acknowledge the invaluable assistance of Michael Halls and Suzanne Tatian at the Clark Library, Gregory Gallagher of the Century Club library, the Huntington Library and its staff, and the extraordinary resources and always amazingly efficient staff of the New York Public Library. I am also grateful for the generous assistance of Thomas Hellie; Mary Hyde, Viscountess Eccles; John Lancaster; Thomas Lange; Dan H. Laurence; Kim Marra; Lucy McDiarmid; Shoki Plummer; Rosanna Schmidgall; Timothy Toohey; and Joseph Wittreich. For permission to quote from letters under copyright and unpublished manuscripts—and for saving me from several factual oversights—I am grateful to Oscar Wilde's grandson, Merlin Holland.

Finally, I must recall to mind Arthur Davis Schmidgall (1906–1989). My Uncle Art, who lost his job in the Postal Service in the 1940s when his homosexuality was discovered, was the sole and astonishing cultural mentor of my youth. He introduced me, among many other joys, to Ruth Draper and Bea Lillie, McCracken's Otello and Schwarzkopf's Marschallin, my first Shakespeare (Bert Lahr as Bottom), my first ballet ("Gaîté Parisienne" by the Ballets Russes), the music of Scott Joplin and Carl Orff and Turk Murphy, Jacques Tati's *Mon Oncle* and Fellini's *La Dolce Vita*, Saki, Shaw, his beloved Noël Coward (when Art moved into a home for the infirm, he sent me a tape of "The Party's Over Now"), the Oscar Wildes of Micheál MacLiammóir and Vincent Price . . . and to the importance of being earnest about aesthetic response. How pleased he would be to know that my idle preoccupations with Shakespeare have ceased, and that my inheritance from him gave me the opportunity to write this book.

Chapter One

SEEING OSCAR

His detractors . . . an imperfectly warm-blooded race, apparently conceive him as a great white caterpillar.

—JAMES JOYCE

Before I first met Oscar . . . I had been told he was like a giant with the wings of a Brazilian butterfly, and I was not disappointed.

—ADA LEVERSON

EVERYONE WHO LAID EYES on Oscar agreed on at least one fact: he was about six feet, three inches tall.

Beyond that, almost every aspect of his physique and physiognomy ignited controversy. As one would expect, the tenor of most sketches of him depended upon the extent to which the observer had fallen under the spell of his charm. Joyce's allusion to Oscar, one of several in *Finnegans Wake*, records a famous insult of the day, as Bernard Shaw recalled: "Oscar was an overgrown man, with something not quite normal about his bigness—something that made Lady Colin Campbell, who hated him, describe him as 'the great white caterpillar.'" Ada Leverson, one of

1

his best friends, naturally chose a more Aesthetic lepidopterous image. One guesses she was alluding to the brilliantly colored silk linings of the cloaks he sported: in a letter to the editor of the *Daily Telegraph* he once assured his dour compatriots that "bright-coloured linings are delightful, and fanciful and gay."

Clearly, the physical man evoked reactions just as various as the celebrity and social satirist. Taken at their most merciless, the descriptions of Oscar in his heyday by his enemies (and some of his more candid friends) produce an appalling composite, one that makes Max Beerbohm's several wicked caricatures or Lautrec's sarcastic image of a slack-jowled, epicene old coquette seem utterly plausible. One soon understands how Lady Campbell came by her caterpillar image. An Oxford classmate recalled his face as "colourless, moonlike, with heavy eyes and thick lips; he had a perpetual simper and a convulsive laugh. He swayed as he walked, and lolled when at table. I never saw him run." Mrs J. Comyns Carr said his features "were heavy, his mouth was loose and large, his face was of an unwholesome pallor, and on each side of it hung long strands of straight, lank hair." (Oscar often took appropriate action on his hair. Richard Le Gallienne said it was sometimes "unashamedly curled and massively modeled to his head,"

Detail of the title page for Max Beerbohm's short essay *A Peep into the Past,* first published in 1923 but written for the inaugural issue of *The Yellow Book* in 1894.

2

and Louise Jopling told of Oscar accosting her in a new hairdo and saying: "I took my *coiffeur* to the Louvre and showed him the head of the youthful Antinous. 'Make me like that,' I said; and here is the result!") Le Gallienne's feelings, like those of many others, were mixed: though he found Oscar "in a way handsome," he felt "something grotesquely excessive about his whole appearance." Vincent O'Sullivan expressed the latter view in terms that would have mortified Oscar: "The best tailor in London could not have made Wilde look well dressed . . . he had neither the build, nor the knack of wearing clothes, to appear the dandy he aspired to be." Perhaps the same view led the *Milwaukee Sentinel* to call him, on his American lecture tour, "a great ungainly crane."

We come even closer to Lautrec's portrait in Edith Cooper's recollection of a face like "a rich yet ungainly fruit" and an Oxford undergraduate's unsparing sketch of him as he was in 1893 at age thirty-nine: "He was by then a heavy, rather gross figure, with a massive head. His face . . . was marred by a rabbit-mouth, which gave an impression of greed and weakness." Irene Vanbrugh, the first Gwendolen in *Earnest*, also noticed a "rather badly shaped mouth of which he appeared to be conscious because in conversation he covered it with his eloquent, finely shaped hands." But O'Sullivan called the hands, usually moving in "slow episcopal gestures" amid wafting cigarette smoke, "ugly."

Those whose friendly instinct was to put the best possible face on Oscar had to be diplomatic: rather than eliminating the negative, as the Arlen–Mercer song goes, they tended to selectively accentuate the positive. Most went for his eyes, which Edith Cooper called "china blue"—the consummately "utter" Aesthetic hue, as we will see. (Even here lay controversy: his great friend Robert Ross reported, discreetly without taking sides: "M. Joseph-Renaud recently described Wilde's eyes as being *blue*, while Lord Alfred Douglas affirms that they were *green*.") Michael Field wrote of "his courteous eyes, where vivacity springs up round heaviness," and Lillie Langtry made the same point more emphatically: "The plainness of his face was redeemed by the splendour of his great, eager eyes." One French acquaintance remembered how "the eyes smiled," another how a "pure blue light, almost like that of a child's eyes . . . shone in his look." Some did find his hands beautiful. Langtry noticed their "pointed fingers and perfectly shaped filbert nails indicative of his artistic disposition" (though she regretted to record they "rarely received the attention they deserved"). Nor could the Oxford undergraduate quoted above help noticing the art with which they were deployed: "His hands were large and beautifully shaped, and he made a great play with them, and with enormous showy cuffs, while he talked."

Though there was a division of the house as to the hands, wide agreement prevailed over an invisible part of Oscar's physique: the vocal cords. "Exquisitely musical," recalled Renaud. "A mezzo voice," said Beerbohm, "uttering itself in a leisurely fashion, with every variety of tone." Le Gallienne recalled a "wonderful golden voice . . . modulated with elaborate self-consciousness," and to Langtry it was "one of the most alluring voices I have ever listened to, round and soft, and full of variety." All in all, Oscar seems very like his own Lord Henry in *Dorian Gray*, who speaks in a "low, musical voice . . . with that graceful wave of the hand that was always so characteristic of him."

What is more, the voice seems to have worked a kind of alchemical magic on the surrounding physical dross. "His appearance was not in his favour, heavy and sensual," Chartres Biron wrote, "but directly he spoke his whole face lit up, the aspect of the man changed and he seemed a different personality." Nellie Melba, of famously ravishing voice herself, said "a strange, almost *macabre* element" in his presence made her feel uneasy, and yet she too was swept away by the "fiery-coloured chain of words [that] fell from his coarse lips."

Somehow, Oscar pulled off a physiognomic coup in spite of the odds. It was a curious feat, as O'Sullivan suggested: "He had not a single good feature; but his face taken altogether was unusual and striking." The face offered a disconcerting combination of traits, youthfully endearing to some, macabre to others; ingratiating in certain details, in others repellent. No wonder the *Courier Journal* declared him, on his visit to Louisville, Kentucky, "a gentleman altogether worthy to be stared at." It seems to have been nearly impossible to remain objective in Oscar's physical presence. Indeed, I have encountered only one thumbnail sketch of him in which unbiased calm seems to predominate. The oddity of it—as well as the place it appeared (the *Daily Record-Union* of Sacramento, California)—makes it worth recording:

> His clean-shaven face is long, broadest at the lower jaw, with a full, round and oversized chin; a large and well-developed nose, a broad mouth, with full lips opening over large, prominent teeth, the upper lip a shade too short, and eyes very full, large and handsome and an apology between gray and blue, are arched by delicately lined eyebrows. His forehead is high, narrows as it ascends, and on either side [is] his straight brown hair.

This is accurate, perhaps, but distinctly uninformative, even tedious . . . as Oscar himself might have predicted. More than once he asserted, "An unbiassed opinion is always absolutely valueless."

IT IS, THEN, ALMOST universally tempting—even fun (whether amiable or vindictive)—to let bias affect one's description of Oscar. The result, though, is that, if we had no photographs or pictures of him, we might be in a genuine quandary as to how to picture him. The purpose of my elaborately pictorial opening paragraphs is in part to begin replacing the "effigy" Oscar with the one who actually lived. More important, this is also a way to suggest that Oscar is in *many* important respects difficult to "see"

clearly. Oscar the philosopher, the celebrity behaver, the out-of-joint Victorian, the satirist, the sexual renegade . . . these Oscars are all as difficult to "fix" clearly in the mind as the actual Oscar of the blue (or green? or gray?) eyes, the beautifully shaped (or ugly?) hands, the broad (or rabbit?) mouth . . . and the "simpering," "half-fatuous" (or "wholly charming"?) smile which played upon it.

An eloquent measure of this difficulty of pinning down the great Brazilian butterfly lies in the numerous ways that exquisitely mixed feelings about him have been expressed, in his lifetime and since. One acquaintance found him "a contented ogre." "I have a kind of sneaking affection for the fellow at bottom," confessed one woman of his acquaintance, for example, "though I detest him at top." Oscar had much the same ambiguous effect on an Oxford scholar named Campbell Dodgson, it seems. In February 1893, Lady Queensberry hired Dodgson to tutor her son Bosie, who was ensconced with Oscar and his boys at Babbacombe Cliff. This was the splendid house of Lady Mount-Temple, a distant cousin of Constance Wilde, who was conveniently traveling in Italy at the time. Dodgson stayed in this *ménage* a week and reported being equally appalled and delighted:

> Our life is lazy and luxurious; our morals are lax. . . . Oscar implores me, with outspread arms and tears in his eyes, to let my soul alone and cultivate my body for six weeks. . . . We do no logic, no history, but play with pigeons and children and drive by the sea.
>
> Oscar sits in the most artistic of all the rooms called "Wonderland," and meditates on his next play [*A Woman of No Importance*]. I think him perfectly delightful with the firmest conviction that his morals are detestable. He professes to have discovered that mine are as bad. . . . I am going back on Saturday. I shall probably leave all that remains of my religion and my morals behind me.

Delightful and detestable: this charming anecdote captures, in essence, the curious way Oscar was embraced by late-Victorian England in general.

In this, he was like the several Oscarian characters he invented who utter the most subversive ideas with irresistible charm, as for instance Ernest does in "The Critic as Artist." "You are quite delightful," says Gilbert to him, "but your views are terribly unsound." Lady Hunstanton says to Lord Illingworth in *A Woman of No Importance*, "Everything you have said to-day seems to me excessively immoral. It has been most interesting, listening to you." (Could she in fact *be* Campbell Dodgson?) Lady Hunstanton says she has "the dim idea" that Illingworth is "always on the side of the sinners." So, too, was Oscar, as we will see. Le Gallienne put his finger on the disturbing subversion of his friend's "entertainment" in his shrewd observation that Oscar "made dying Victorianism laugh at itself, and it may be said to have died of the laughter." Shaw, too, perceived that the implications of Oscar's powerful wit were not fully comprehended by the public at large: "English society is not in the least witty, and always runs curiously to see a wit like Wilde's exactly as it sits down to *look at* a man playing the piano."

To put the way Victorians embraced Oscar in a darker light, it might be said that he played an outrageous Salome to the British public's fascinated Herod. The expatriate American poet Stuart Merrill suggested as much in his remark that Oscar "used to entertain the public at the same time as he frightened them." After Salome charms Herod with her dance of the seven veils and exults over the head of Jokanaan, Herod is suddenly revulsed and orders, "Kill that woman!" A similar ecstasy of revulsion was to occur across Britain when Oscar emerged from the cistern of London gay life at his trials. In the event, the phrase "to give head" takes on a piquant pertinence.

Oscar's friends and gay admirers, as well, left some remarkably mixed memorials of him. George Ives was one of the day's most fervent though closeted gay activists (this paradox was com-

Oscar Wilde in costume as Salome. Photograph in the Roger–Viollet collection, Paris.

mon then), and in 1905 he entered in his diary this rueful and contradictory retrospect on his former acquaintance: "Oscar *meant* well, to all. He had not the gift of responsibility, he could

not estimate consequence. . . . I looked up to him as to a superman (and still do, while utterly disagreeing with his written philosophy, and even with his life, on many sides)." Le Gallienne's
summary judgment in his memoirs is also a masterpiece of fence-
sitting: "Doubtless, he was weak as well as strong, and wrong as
he was right, but, if there was evil in him, there was also a great
good. His success developed a dangerous arrogance, and he lost
the captainship of his soul, but that his soul was essentially pure
and his heart tender, no one who knew him well could for a moment doubt." Nobody was more mercilessly candid about Oscar's
faults than Shaw, loathing him as a "prime specimen" of a "Dublin snob," appalled by his "stupendous laziness" and the "humbug" of his gadding about as an Apostle of Art, even repelled by
"the sort of skin that never looks clean." In the end, though,
even Shaw relented: "I should have made a far sterner summing
up. I am sure Oscar has not found the gates of heaven shut
against him. He is too good company to be excluded." In 1948,
when the ever-sprightly curmudgeon had reached the age of
ninety-two, he was asked what famous man of the past he would
most like to meet. Shaw replied, "If I craved for entertaining conversation by a first-class raconteur I should choose Oscar Wilde."

Paradoxical strategies for describing Oscar have continued
apace. Auden called him a "serious playboy"; a Gide scholar
termed him a "genuine counterfeiter"; and a recent study of him,
by Norbert Kohl, is titled *The Works of a Conformist Rebel*. The
disconcertingly contradictory Oscar who emerges from all this
eddying of opinion was perhaps never more gracefully acknowledged than by Robert Ross, in his preface to *De Profundis*: "He
was . . . a man with many facets to his character; and he left in
regard to that character, and to his attainments, both before and
after his downfall, curiously different impressions on professsing
judges of their fellowmen." As if to underscore the point, *De Profundis* itself, like so many of Oscar's writings, has produced "curiously different impressions." Oscar thought he was composing it
in the tragic mode. But Ellmann called it "a love letter," and

The Stranger Wilde

Shaw asserted that "no other Irishman has yet produced as masterful a comedy as *De Profundis*."

☆   ☆   ☆

PRESENTED WITH SUCH A blurred image of the man, our perhaps natural tendency is to close one eye, as it were, and simplify. The history of pontification about Oscar is strewn with marvels of simplification. Some are obvious, others surprising; some are kindly, others grudging. Much depends on the "Oscar mood" at the time they were uttered. Oscar wrote from prison, "The gibbet on which I swing in history now is high enough." But the gibbet has a way of turning into a cross (as may be happening currently), and its height has varied considerably. In 1946 Oscar's gibbet was all but dismantled, at least in Buenos Aires. Jorge Luis Borges then declared, "The pleasure we derive from his company is irresistible and constant," and even ventured to assert "the provable and elementary fact that Wilde is almost always right." (There was a time when Oscar would have eagerly agreed, but late in life he confessed, "I was all wrong, my dear boy, in my life.") The next year, in 1947, the gibbet was up again, at least for James Agate and Mary McCarthy. Agate, in his seventieth and last year, groused that "apart from his wit, he was bogus"—something akin to saying that, apart from deathless iambic pentameter, Shakespeare's plays are pure fudge. McCarthy took the breath away by finding "this fellow really insufferable" and suggesting, "There is something *outré* in all of Wilde's work that makes one sympathize to a degree with the Marquess of Queensberry." In 1961 the gibbet vanished again, and Colin MacInnes told us, "Now, of Oscar Wilde it is impossible, in most senses, to write with other than total admiration." And so it goes.

Sir Francis Bacon long ago noticed that the human understanding is "prone to suppose the existence of more order and regularity in the world than it finds." This tendency has produced a plethora of lavish simplifications—like the ones just sampled—

designed to embrace Oscar's disorderly, contradictory oeuvre and personality. This has in turn produced several convenient simulacrums, or puppets of Oscar. There is not a little irony in this, for *Punch* magazine chided Oscar's first theatrical success, *Lady Windermere's Fan*, precisely for its puppetry. In its 5 March 1892 issue appeared a skit mimicking the blasé curtain speech he had made at the premiere: "I must tell you I think my piece was excellent. And all the puppets that have performed in it have played extremely well."

Most of the puppet Oscars have also played extremely well, not least because they represent undeniably significant truths about him. Each one is "classic" in its way. There is Oscar the Master Farceur,

QUITE TOO-TOO PUFFICKLY PRECIOUS!!

Being Lady Windy-mère's Fan-cy Portrait of the new dramatic author, Shakespeare Sheridan Oscar Puff, Esq.

["He addressed from the stage a public audience, mostly composed of ladies, pressing between his daintily-gloved fingers a still burning and half-smoked cigarette." —*Daily Telegraph*.]

author of *The Importance of Being Earnest*. This personage tempts us to view him simply as the quintessence of (as Algy says to Jack Worthing) an "absolutely trivial nature." He is perhaps the best-known and least edifying Oscar puppet of them all. To suggest that it represents the man is not a little akin to suggesting, as Ada Leverson once jestingly did, that the first act of *Earnest* is about cucumber sandwiches. Max Beerbohm loved the play (saw it again after Oscar died and said, "It still seems perfect"), yet he retained a clear sense of how tangential it and its brethren were to the whole man: "It was by way of a brilliant afterthought that Oscar Wilde began to be a playwright." Bernard Shaw offered another reason to become restive when this Oscar puppet is allowed to steal the stage: "As a matter of fact, I am overrated as an author," he admitted; "most great men are." I shall be suggesting in various ways, later on, that paying too much heed to the *Earnest* side of Oscar is a certain way to allow his greatness to escape us.

Another highly popular and convenient puppet is the conventionalized Tragically Flawed Hero smote by the gods from his pinnacle of fame. "Is there another life story to compete with it?" W. H. Auden asked. A rival, for sheer police-court melodrama, does not come readily to mind. This vividly theatrical way of seeing Oscar was impossible for the man himself—and countless latecomers—to resist. Nor will it be resisted in the following pages: a chapter is devoted to the subject. But this approach, too, takes risks. The most important one is explained, curiously enough, by Oscar's suggestion of an unusual way to go about book reviewing:

> There is a great deal to be said in favour of reading a novel backwards. The last page is, as a rule, the most interesting, and when one begins with the catastrophe or the *dénouement* one feels on pleasant terms of equality with the author. It is like going behind the scenes of a theatre. One is no longer taken in. . . . One knows the jealously-guarded secret, and one can afford to smile at the quite unnecessary anxiety that the puppets of fiction always consider it their duty to display.

Oscar's trial and conviction were the catastrophe of his life, his imprisonment and years of exile merely an extended anticlimax . . . the sixth act that his Lord Henry Wotton accuses women of always wanting "as soon as the interest of the play is entirely over." "Reading" Oscar's life backwards from its catastrophe—and knowing his "jealously-guarded secret" at the outset—is indeed "pleasant," for it imposes yet another form of convenient "order and regularity" upon Oscar's life, enabling us to treat it as if it were carefully composed according to some author's intentions (Oscar's? the gods'?).

But this approach ruins some marvelous suspense; little can as effectively provoke concentration and curiosity as being "taken in." Knowing the plot beforehand makes nearly impossible our being swept up in the tangle of motivations, follies, and coincidences that lead to the great denouement. As Oscar said, starting at the terminus tempts us to turn credibly human characters into puppets, distance ourselves from emotional and psychological transactions. Besides, life is never as tidy and artistic as this puppet Oscar would require us to believe it is. He made this point before he fell, with prophetic accuracy: "Life is terribly deficient in form. Its catastrophes happen in the wrong way and to the wrong people. . . . Things last either too long or not long enough." And in the aftermath he candidly admitted the "artistic" vulgarity of his tragic fall: "My tragedy has lasted far too long: its climax is over: its end is mean."

The most entrancing, purely enjoyable puppet Oscar is surely the Colorful Talker. "Imagine a wilderness of Wildes!" said a writer in the *Idler* of May 1882. "It would be like a sky all rainbows." This is Oscar "the conversationalist and behaver," whom Auden accounted the really "significant figure." And no wonder, since so many contemporaries sought to make clear that his writings were decidedly inferior to his *in vivo* improvisations. "The best of his writing is but a pale reflection of his brilliant conversations," said André Gide, and Ross, who knew Oscar better than anyone, was inclined to agree that "his personality and conversation were far more wonderful than anything he wrote." Several years after Oscar's death, Ross reminisced with an Aesthetic glow: "You could not tell what flowers were at your feet or what fantastic architecture was silhouetted against the purple atmosphere of his conversation." Doubtless his friends were always telling him, as Mr Erskine tells Lord Henry Wotton in *Dorian,* "You talk books away . . . why don't you write one?"

William Butler Yeats recalled his first meeting with Oscar as "an astonishment. I never before heard a man talking with perfect sentences." The creator of Sherlock Holmes remembered him as no "monologue man": "He took as well as he gave, but what he gave was unique. He had a curious precision of statement, a delicate flavour of humour, and a trick of small gestures . . . peculiar to himself." Conan Doyle added, alas, "The effect cannot be reproduced." No one's praise of Oscar's conversational virtuosity, however, is more impressive or worthy of respect than Max Beerbohm's, offered at the age of eighty-two on the centennial of Wilde's birth in 1954:

> I suppose there are now few survivors among the people who had the delight of hearing Oscar Wilde talk. Of these I am one.
>
> I have had the privilege of listening also to many other masters of table-talk—Meredith and Swinburne, Edmund Gosse and Henry James, Augustine Birrell and Arthur Balfour, Gilbert Chesterton and Desmond MacCarthy and Hilaire Belloc—all of them splendid in their own way. But assuredly Oscar in *his* way was the greatest of them all—the most spontaneous and yet the most polished, the most soothing and yet the most surprising.
>
> That his talk was mostly monologue was not his own fault. His manners were very good; he was careful to give his guests or his fellow-guests many a conversational opening; but seldom did anyone respond with more than a very few words. Nobody was willing to interrupt the music of so magnificent a virtuoso. To have heard him consoles me for not having heard Dr Johnson or Edmund Burke.

The trouble with this Oscar, of course, is that—like those great nineteenth-century opera singers whose voices we can only wistfully imagine—he must remain a figment of our imagination. He had, as Nellie Melba among many others regretted, no Boswell to save the extemporal treasure for posterity. It has vanished as surely as the echoes of the old divas.

Except, of course, for the one large and one slender volume of his letters, which sparkle often enough to give a tantalizing indication of his conversational style. And a few anecdotes tell us that the real-life Oscar can now and then be discerned in his writings. Though Ada Leverson thought him "quicker in repartee and conversation than in his writing," she did remark that "he constantly made use in his work, afterwards, of things he had improvised." One of his actors, Beerbohm Tree, confirmed this habit: "Many, many times I have inserted things in his plays that he said off-hand. Once he asked me to do something in a play at rehearsal and I replied that I could not afford to do it. 'By all means then you must,' he said. 'Extravagance is the luxury of the poor.' So that line went into the play." We get a glimpse of the procedure from Oscar himself, in a letter he wrote a few days after coming out of prison: "Nowadays everybody is jealous of everyone else, except, of course, husband and wife. I think I shall keep this last remark of mine for my play." Alas, no more plays were destined to appear and upstage *Earnest*. For some reason, Ross described this plagiarism from actual conversation as a matter of great secrecy in his touching postmortem letter to Oscar's devoted friend Adela Schuster: "I stayed with him in '87 for two months and used then to write down what he said, but to tell you a *great secret* which I ought not to do, I gave him my notes and he used a great deal of them for one of his later plays which was written in a great hurry and against time as he wanted money. This of course is *private*."

As with the other versions of Oscar, too strong an affection for Oscar, Champion Dinner-party Divo, courts danger, too. Too easily, he can lull us into a thoroughly happy, carefree mood, as though the last word on Oscar is Le Gallienne's assertion of the "unfailing gaiety of his mind" or Holbrook Jackson's remark that he had "no purpose in life save play." In this highly agreeable, narcotized mood, we are bound to forget what a serious and refrigerating intellect Oscar also possessed. In this respect, a Shavian *obiter dictum* is particularly apt: "After all, nothing requires so much gravity as joking." It is not wise to submit so sybaritically to the larks of Oscar in his Falstaffian mask. For he is also capable of doffing it all of a sudden and replacing it with the mask of Hamlet, whose lavish joking also derives from extraordinary gravity.

☆ ☆ ☆

CATERPILLAR OR BUTTERFLY? FALSTAFF or Hamlet? Superman or snob? Bogus or brilliant? Seeing Oscar seems scarcely a matter of making fine Jamesian distinctions: quandaries are blatant and constant with him. This raucous ambiguity delighted him in life and would do so now. For he habitually behaved in several ways calculated to cause the eye to squint, the head to cock in bemusement, and the mind to boggle. Two of the most significant Oscarian modes of disconcerting his audience bear pausing over before we plunge into the following chapters.

Alliteration was much beloved by Oscar, and the stately London *Times* once identified his famed mode of expression with a fine burst of it, marveling at his "passion for paradox, persiflage, and proverbial perversity." Oscar was indeed Prince Paradox— Dorian calls Lord Henry this—as befits a man whose very life was in so many ways paradoxical. As Ross observed, "It was natural to Wilde to be artificial." The *Times* was responding to the premiere of *A Woman of No Importance*, and the play spangles with paradoxes. Lady Hunstanton observes, "All Americans do dress well. They get their clothes in Paris." Lord Illingworth professes outrage at the monstrous way people go about "saying things against one behind one's back that are absolutely and entirely true." And Mrs Allonby declares women have a "much better time" than men because "there are far more things forbidden to us than are forbidden to them."

Charming even in their mildest guise, as in the above, Oscar's paradoxes were nevertheless only part of a very serious arsenal that included witty petards, satirical grenades, and whatever rhetorical siege tools were necessary to tunnel underneath Victorian complacencies. Still, the swiftly skewering paradox was his weapon of choice. "You fence divinely," says Lord Illingworth to Mrs Allonby, "but the button has come off your foil." Oscar's skill lay in not allowing that to happen, in scoring his points without drawing blood. Remarks upon the gentility and kindness of Oscar's wit are almost unanimous, and instances of cruelty or violence in this wit are very rare. Nonetheless, against several classes of Oscar's enemies the paradox was to prove very successful, notably the literal-minded and the unimaginative. Against the paradox, mere pugilists—literalists, that is—like Queensberry hadn't a chance. As Henry James, who was grudgingly impressed by Oscar's "cheeky paradoxical wit," shrewdly noticed, "Everything Oscar does is a deliberate trap for the literalist." Against the merely unimaginative, too, the paradox was a perfect weapon. "Consistency is the last refuge of the unimaginative," said Oscar, which perhaps is all the explanation we need for his delight in the paradox.

But we should know a bit more about the paradoxer's strategy. Oscar made the paradox not only the centerpiece of his own manly art of self-defense, but also a brilliant mode of assertion. Now, the dictionary defines "paradox" as a "seemingly contradictory statement that may nonetheless be true," but Oscar defined it more keenly, calling it a "dangerous" thing. In his dialogue of 1889, "The Decay of Lying," Cyril (playing the literalist) asks, "But you don't mean to say that you seriously believe that Life imitates Art, that Life in fact is the mirror, and Art the reality?" To which Vivian replies: "Certainly I do. Paradox though it may seem—and paradoxes are always dangerous things—it is none the less true." Oscar refined and made his definition more poetic the next year, when *Dorian Gray* appeared: "The way of paradoxes is the way of truth. To test Reality we must see it on the tight-rope. When the Verities become acrobats we can judge them." Oscar was the wittiest and harshest judge of late-Victorian verities. They were unexercised, awkward, flabby verities, and made poor acrobats. Few survived a passage over the tightrope of Oscar's paradoxing wit. They were also often hypocritical verities, and there is hardly a better rhetorical device for exposing hypocrisy than the paradox.

The paradox was a perfect vehicle for Oscar, many of whose pursuits were trivial but whose mind was strangely serious. Le Gallienne was close enough to him to see how the paradox bridged these two distinct traits: "As I once said, paradox with him was merely 'truth standing on its head to attract attention.' Behind all his humorous fopperies there was a serious philosophy." Lord Goring, in a stage direction of *An Ideal Husband*, is described as "fond of being misunderstood. It gives him a post of vantage." This is a paradox . . . but also the Paradoxist's Credo. For out of the temporary misunderstanding that a paradox induces comes a fresher understanding of what, the dictionary says, is "nonetheless true." Oscar occupied a fine post of vantage on his age, and by virtue of his humorous paradoxical fopperies he was able to insinuate in his behavings and writings a philosophy that was serious indeed. Purveying, as Percival Almy phrased it in 1894, "a counter-glitter of words," he enticed a reluctant public to confront the elderliness of verities long taken for granted. In regard to the paradox, Oscar was therefore of one mind with a great theatrical contemporary, August Strindberg. For in his preface to *Miss Julie* (1888) Strindberg wrote: "I am proud to say that this complicated way of looking at things is in tune with the times. . . . I am proud that I am not alone in my paradoxes, as all new discoveries are called."

OSCAR LIKED VERITIES TO be acrobats. He also liked acrobats:

> A good circus is an oasis of Hellenism in a world that
> reads too much to be wise, and thinks too much to be

beautiful. . . . Circus proprietors . . . give us acrobats, and the acrobat is an artist. The mere fact that he never speaks to the audience shows how well he appreciates the great truth that the aim of art is not to reveal personality but to please. The clown may be blatant, but the acrobat is always beautiful.*

This remark reminds us yet again of its author's paradoxical nature, for he was both a clown and—in every sense except the literal one—an acrobat. But it also introduces the second confusing Oscarian penchant, namely, his delight in concealment, in masking, in acting. His friends noticed this in him with some delight. His wife, just weeks before her death, was in no mood to be amused by this characteristic, however: "Oscar is so pathetic and such a born actor." Oscar once quipped to Ada Leverson about Max Beerbohm, "When you are alone with him, Sphinx, does he take off his face and reveal his mask?"—but, as we shall see, he was a brilliantly masked man himself. (This perhaps explains the poorness of his poetry. Auden flatly asserted that Oscar was "totally lacking in a poetic voice of his own"—a lacking not surprising in a "born actor.")

As with the paradox, Oscar made something of a science out of the topsy-turvy notion of concealment being a "great truth," which he expressed in his remark on acrobats. In the opening "Credo" section of *Oscariana* (Constance Wilde's compilation of her husband's aphorisms), the second entry is: "To reveal art and conceal the artist is art's aim." Best known, perhaps, is his assertion in "The Critic as Artist" that "Man is least himself when he talks in his own person. Give him a mask, and he will tell you the truth." And Oscar rightly observed that acting is really the human condition. "Anybody can act," he informed the editor of the

---

*Oscar even received love letters from acrobats, if a Gide anecdote is true. Oscar told him that a London friend forwarded to him in Paris only "serious letters—the love-letters. . . . Oh! this one is from a young . . . what do you call it? . . . acrobat? yes; acrobat; absolutely delicious. . . . It's the first time he has written to me, so he doesn't like to spell properly."

Daily Telegraph; "Most people in England do nothing else. To be conventional is to be a comedian."

But then Oscar adds this sentence: "To act a particular part, however, is a very different thing, and a very difficult thing as well." This Oscar did, and to spectacular effect. What was Oscar's role? The role he *thought* he was playing is, I believe, suggested by the butler in *An Ideal Husband*. A stage direction tells us, "The distinction of Phipps is his impassivity. He has been termed by enthusiasts the Ideal Butler. The Sphinx is not so incommunicable. He is a mask with a manner. Of his intellectual or emotional life, history knows nothing. He represents the dominance of form." Phipps certainly suits Oscar's dogmatic insistence that the personality of the artist is of no consequence ... and his insistence that the more the public is interested in the artist, the less it can be interested in art. In some quarters, it appears, Oscar succeeded in being like Phipps. For *The Theatre* magazine, in March 1894, complained that the playwright "never allows us to see the real emotions of his heart; his object seems to be to cast a glamour over us with the brilliance of his mind."

The irony of Phipps's appearance on the London stage, though, is that within weeks the privacy of his creator was blown sky high: soon history was to be informed of *everything* about his emotional life. Scandalous substance obliterated the dominance of Oscar's social and artistic "form." This happened, one might say, because Oscar was not in fact playing a butler's comprimario role, but a more virtuoso one of his own choosing. It was a comic role to be sure, but profoundly *un*conventional. So much so that—by virtue of a surreal scene change from drawing room to courtroom—he suddenly found himself playing the hero's role in a different genre altogether. "I thought life was going to be a brilliant comedy ... I found it to be a revolting and repellent tragedy," he wrote later from prison.

Role-playing and concealment were more than "artistic principle" for Oscar, as the debacle of 1895 made clear. He quipped about an author once, "Mr James Payn is an adept in the art of concealing what is not worth finding," but Oscar of course had something very worthwhile to conceal: his homosexuality. Years of experience hiding this fact doubtless served to strengthen his dedication to this method of impersonation in other realms . . . and honed his skills as a speaker through masks. I have found only one passage in Oscar's pretrials correspondence that conveys something of the soul-destroying pressure of concealing one's true identity. Not surprisingly, it comes in 1894, when that pressure was probably becoming increasingly hard to cope with, in a letter to a young artist named Philip Houghton. I suspect that Houghton had somehow made his sexual preference clear to Oscar. Oscar's reply is carefully oblique, but there is eloquence (and desire?) between the lines:

> Your letter has deeply moved me. To the world I seem, by intention on my part, a dilettante and dandy merely—it is not wise to show one's heart to the world—and as seriousness of manner is the disguise of the fool, folly in its exquisite modes of triviality and indifference and lack of care is the robe of the wise man. In so vulgar an age as this we all need masks.
>
> But write to me about yourself; tell me your life and loves, and all that keeps you wondering. Who are you? (what a difficult question for any one of us to answer!) I, at any rate, am your friend OSCAR WILDE

Perhaps there is even a hint in this letter of growing weariness of the mask . . . and a corollary instinct to play more boldly a role that he, rather than that great comic author, Society, had chosen for himself.

An observation made by André Gide just a year later renders it all the more tempting to think so. Gide happened upon Oscar and Bosie on their reckless trip to Algiers in early 1895, and recorded in his memoir *If It Die*: "Wilde covered over his sincerest feelings with a cloak of affectation which many people found intolerable. He would never cease from acting—could not, no doubt." Gide was referring to the "dandy" persona that Oscar admitted he had long been serving up "by intention." But Gide spoke as an insider, of course. To close gay friends, like Ross, and gay acquaintances, like young Gide or Houghton, Oscar was more willing to show his heart. Thus, Gide was able to add to his observation this remarkable insight: "But the character he played was his own; the role itself, which his everlasting demon kept prompting him, was a sincere one." This of course raises the question—to which we will later return—whether Oscar may have consciously chosen to play the role of a gay man with ever more reckless abandon and, thus, test the limits of his Victorian audience's willing suspension of disbelief. It is just the sort of risk—and Oscar was enamored of risk—that boredom, disgust, arrogance, or all three might have driven him to.

Oscar seems to have been in a confessional mood when he wrote to Houghton. The same month, a young man named Ralph Payne wrote him a fan letter about *Dorian Gray* and asked the title of the "poisonous" book, bound in yellow, that so ruins Dorian's moral fiber. In his reply, Oscar made the most informative autobiographical confession of his pretrial life. He made it clear, I think, that his skillful playing of multiple roles was part of deeper strategies of gay concealment and (albeit disguised) gay assertiveness:

The book that poisoned, or made perfect, Dorian Gray does not exist; it is a fancy of mine merely.

I am so glad you like that strange coloured book of mine: it contains much of me in it. Basil Hallward is what I think I am: Lord Henry what the world thinks me: Dorian what I would like to be—in other ages, perhaps.

Will you come and see me?

I am writing a play, and go to St James's Place, number *10*, where I have rooms, every day at 11.30. Come on Tuesday about 12.30, will you? But perhaps you are busy? Still, we can meet, surely, some day. Your

handwriting fascinates me, your praise charms me. Truly
yours   OSCAR WILDE

Oscar thought he was—and *was* indeed—like Hallward. He, too,
was an artist hopelessly and ruinously infatuated with beautiful
young men. The world thought him the witty, cynical, risqué
dandy Lord Henry. And like all gay men he longed to be—in another age!—an irresistibly gorgeous object of desire like Dorian. It
is ironic that, this not being possible at Oscar's advanced age, he
turned the letter into a proposal of what might (who knows?)
turn into an assignation. His famous charm might work in lieu of
conventional Dorian beauty.

BEHIND ALL OF OSCAR'S paradoxical persiflage and playing with
masks lay a more fundamental devotion to uncertainty. It was an
age of many appalling certainties, among them the Queen's certainty that such a thing as lesbians could not exist in the world.
(Lawmakers couldn't imagine it either; lesbians are not mentioned in the statute Oscar fell afoul of.) Oscar, being an instinctive contrarian, turned champion of those who have the courage
of their lack of conviction. Thus, he praised his Aesthetic elder,
Walter Pater, as an "intellectual impressionist" who "does not
weary us with any definite doctrine." A few years later Lord
Henry Wotton abjures talk about "politics" by saying, "I like persons better than principles, and I like persons with no principles
better than anything else in the world."

Lord Illingworth says on Oscar's behalf, "One should never
take sides in anything. . . . Taking sides is the beginning of sincerity, and earnestness follows shortly afterwards, and the human being becomes a bore." This elaborately negligent pose made Oscar
hopeless as a political animal, which infuriated the veteran platform haranguer Shaw. But it would have pleased Nietzsche: "Men
of conviction are not worthy of the least consideration in fundamental questions of value and disvalue. Convictions are prisons."

It would be a serious mistake, however, to assume Oscar lacked political consciousness. On the contrary, as Jonathan Dollimore has concluded, Oscar's aesthetic embraced "an acute political awareness and often an uncompromising political commitment." Oscar simply preferred to filter these through the logical mazes of paradox and personal theatrics. His lapses from this style were rare. One notable instance before his fall was on the occasion of the Haymarket Riots in Chicago in 1886; Shaw drew up a petition in support of the anarchists, and Oscar was the only person to sign it immediately. After his imprisonment, his only publications besides *The Ballad of Reading Gaol* were letters on prison reform that carried strong conviction indeed.

Oscar's mockery of earnestness and sincerity, however, must also be viewed at least in part as an ironically appropriate mode of homosexual response. Sincere and earnest public expression of his sexual identity was denied him: he would therefore deny it to others in general. Denied the "maturity" of his sexual personality, he would exalt the callow carelessness, the polymorphic perversity allowed to "youth."

And to youths. Oscar's devotion to uncertainty joined amiably with his love of risk ... and of older boys and young men. He became an increasingly promiscuous sexual predator. Gay gathering places like the bar of the St. James's, the skating rink in Knightsbridge, the Alhambra Theatre,* the perfumed rooms of Alfred Taylor near Westminster Abbey must have become regular places of haunt. There is in *Dorian Gray* a passage that strongly implies how—as often among the promiscuous—love of uncertainty encouraged this ever more reckless philandering. The

---

*The hero of Bernard Shaw's first novel—*Immaturity*, written during Oscar's first London year—hears the Alhambra is "a wicked place" and so pays a visit. "Dissipated loungers" abound in its lobbies. "There were many old men present and many young ones, who looked on their seniors with that intolerance of dissipation which depraved youth exhibits when it perceives its own weaknesses reflected in old age." He also overhears a conversation about the evening's ballet between a "courtly old man in black silk stockings" and a young officer. Shaw added, in a 1921 footnote, that about 1890 the "moral atmosphere" of the Alhambra improved under the municipal control of the new London County Council. He also recalled that "Alhambra ballets ranked with other Leicester Square entertainments of that day as pornographic."

pretty young Duchess of Monmouth, married to a jaded man of sixty, has fallen for Dorian. Alone with her, Lord Henry asks, "Are you very much in love with him?" "I wish I knew." Lord Henry shakes his head and says, "Knowledge would be fatal. It is the uncertainty that charms one. A mist makes things wonderful."

> "One may lose one's way."
> "All ways end at the same point, my dear Gladys."
> "What is that?"
> "Disillusion."

Spoken like a true Don Giovanni. Here, too, Oscar was perhaps divulging feelings about his own life, which by the 1890s had become one of ever more frenetic pursuing and conquering. The two letters to young Houghton and Payne suggest that, by 1894, he had become an old hand at this pastime.

As with so much that Oscar wrote, the passage from *Dorian Gray* anticipates later events with eerie accuracy. He did lose his way in the mists of London's homosexual underground . . . and mists of "wild adoration" and many a "wild longing." (Oscar's tragedy is artfully strewn with numerous puns on his name, some of them perhaps even conscious.) And, as a letter he wrote a few weeks after release from prison suggests, his end was just as Lord Henry predicts, disillusion: "I used to be utterly reckless of young lives: I used to take up a boy, love him 'passionately,' and then grow bored with him, and often take no notice of him. That is what I regret in my past life."

☆ ☆ ☆

JOYCE CAROL OATES HAS said of *The Picture of Dorian Gray*, "One feels about it as one feels about the most profoundly haunting works of art—that it has not been fully understood." One is now inclined to say the same thing about Oscar's life. This would doubtless please the man who believed that the only acceptable alternative to wearing a work of art is to be one—and preferably, of course, a haunting work of art. He would also like the "profoundly" part, for the mystery of concealed depths appealed to him greatly: "Only the shallow know themselves," he said. Oscar was, decidedly, one of those people who have, as Samuel Johnson phrased it, "made themselves *publick*, without making themselves *known*."

Assessing the stranger Wilde—or rather stranger *Wildes*—is thus a by no means easy task. One might predict as much about a man who defended insincerity as "a method by which we can multiply our personalities" . . . and who urged the "true critic" to "realise himself in many forms, and by a thousand different ways." As with so many enduringly memorable and haunting figures, seeing him also means being forced to see ourselves. And that, though rewarding, can often prove a disagreeable experience.

The last words on the difficulty of seeing Oscar—fixing him in the mind's eye—might most fittingly be left to Walt Whitman, another seer who challenged the vision of his age. One day he said to his friend Horace Traubel, "Everybody's been so in the habit of looking at Wilde cross-eyed, sort of, that they have charged the defect of their vision up against Wilde as a weakness of *his* character." The following chapters, I hope, will serve to correct this defect of vision, or rather—to return to an appropriate image from *Dorian Gray*—to remove some of the presumptions and prejudices that, a *fin de siècle* later, have come to obscure his disturbingly equivocal portrait.

Chapter Two

☆ ☆ ☆ ☆ ☆ ☆ ☆ ☆ ☆ ☆ ☆ ☆ ☆ ☆ ☆

TRESPASSER

His writing was huge and sprawling—somewhat like himself . . . four words to a line was his normal allowance, and he took no notice of lines.
—G. T. ATKINSON

IN MARCH OF 1899 Oscar sojourned at the villa of Harold Mellor, an acquaintance he had met on the Riviera the year before. It was located on Lake Geneva, he reported to his close London friend More Adey, amid "much beauty of an obvious, old-fashioned kind—snow-capped mountains, blue sky, pine trees, and the like." But the houseguest was not happy, though the free hospitality was a boon to his purse. Mellor was—much to Oscar's annoyance—gay but uncomfortable with the fact, wealthy but tightfisted. "I don't like my host," Oscar said, and then compared young Swiss men quite invidiously with those of other climes: "At Nice I knew three lads like bronzes, quite perfect in form.

English lads are chryselephantine [i.e., made of gold and ivory]. Swiss people are carved out of wood with a rough knife, most of them; the others are carved out of turnips." To escape from Mellor and his villa and to cheer himself, Oscar became at long last a real hiker . . . usually to the gardens of Prince Napoleon's Château de Prangins, with its own consoling bronze statues, or to a village three miles away for a bock and French newspapers. Of these excursions Oscar told Adey, "There are lovely walks here by the Lake, through the grounds of others: but I am a born trespasser."

Born trespasser indeed. Just as he ignored the lines of his university examination books in his youth and Swiss property lines in the year before his death, Oscar chose to ignore—often with flagrant glee—many other "lines" of his day. Who else but Oscar could have transformed so mundane a thing as the cigarette into a battering ram for use against hoary Victorian ramparts: insisting on tipping it with gaudy gold; smoking one, to universal stupefaction, during a curtain speech at the St. James's Theatre; even venturing with a lighted one into the *dining room*. "My father did actually smoke in the dining-room," recalled his son Vyvyan. "This was considered to be very daring and *fin de siècle.*" As we shall see later, Oscar ignored the lines of fashion to spectacular effect: succeeded, indeed, in defining vulgarity as "the conduct of others" and the unfashionable as "what other people wear."

As with all expert trespassers, Oscar was always testing the security of the boundaries presented to him—"pushing the envelope" being the recently chic phrase for such exertion. "He had a way of looking at one to see how much nonsense one would believe," recalled Helena Sickert, and he looked similarly on the world around him. Of course, most of what Oscar dispensed made very good sense; only those as clever and daring as Polonius were disposed to call it nonsense. These dullards, failing to see the method in Oscar's madness, simply laughed and condescended, as if to a harmless *enfant terrible*. Yeats was among those thus taken in: "One took all his words for play." Robert Buchanan was another: "You seem to me like a holiday maker throwing pebbles into the sea," he wrote to Oscar in 1891. "You are simply joking at your own expense." Those who *did* sense aggression behind the witty method were threatened by it, became furious, and retaliated with humorless attacks that sometimes astonished Oscar and his friends by their intensity.

Oscar admired—and in some ways modeled himself after— other great trespassers in history. Lord Alfred Douglas many years later called him "a Heresiarch, and a most powerful and convincing one," and this captures him perfectly, though a more buoyant, mannerly, and suave Savonarola could hardly be imagined. Oscar's heresies were presented much more in the ingratiating style of Socrates. One who believed that Art worthy of the name is "usually in direct opposition" to its age was bound to become a partisan of Socrates, and "The Decay of Lying," "The Critic as Artist," and several chapters in *Dorian Gray* are fashioned as Socratic dialogues. The grimmer parallels between the confrontations of Socrates and Wilde with the law were certainly noticed by many . . . and especially by Oscar himself (as will be seen in Chapter 12, "Why He Stayed").

Oscar called Benvenuto Cellini the "supreme scoundrel of the Renaissance," and the "story of his splendour and his shame" especially appealed to him. Shrewdly judging his audience of miners in Leadville, Colorado, he chose to read passages from Cellini's *Autobiography* to them, to very agreeable effect: "They seemed much delighted. I was reproved by my hearers for not having brought him with me. I explained that he had been dead for some little time which elicited the enquiry 'Who shot him?' " Yeats's remark that he could only compare Oscar to Benvenuto Cellini would have delighted our skillful trespasser. However, one melancholy point of comparison between the two was unwittingly made by Oscar himself four years before prison doors opened to receive him. In a passage in "The Soul of Man Under Socialism" on the various kinds of tyranny, Oscar observed, "There is danger in Popes . . . It was a Pope who thrust Cellini into prison, and kept him there till he sickened with rage, and created unreal vi-sions for himself, and saw the gilded sun enter his room, and grew so enamoured of it that he sought to escape, and crept out from tower to tower, and falling through dizzy air at dawn, maimed himself." Oscar wrote that Popes merely tyrannize the soul; the despot who "tyrannizes over soul and body alike" he identified as "the People." True enough, the People's law, the Criminal Law Amendment Act of 1885, thrust him into prison to suffer precisely Cellini's fate. And he did leave prison maimed in spirit, if not in body ... nor maimed in the conviction with which he would subsequently maintain his sexual preference.

Another, more contemporary artist-*isolé* greatly admired by Oscar is worth mentioning, that most heroically inconvenient and trespassing of nineteenth-century novelists, Honoré de Balzac. "I can't travel without Balzac," Oscar wrote from Augusta, Georgia, to Julia Ward Howe, and he told Vincent O'Sullivan that when he was a boy his "two favourite characters were [Balzac's] Lucien de Rubempré and [Stendhal's] Julien Sorel. Lucien hanged himself, Julien died on the scaffold, and I died in prison." In his review of a new English edition, he called *La Comédie humaine* "really the greatest monument that literature has produced in our century." He quoted with approval Baudelaire's remark that "every mind [in Balzac's characters] is a weapon loaded to the muzzle with will," and he quoted with admiration Balzac's own response to the charge of being immoral: "Whoever contributes his stone to the edifice of ideas, whoever proclaims an abuse, whoever sets his mark upon an evil to be abolished, always passes for immoral." Oscar would, in later years, often defend himself in this wise. Near the end of his life he could still assert that "all Balzac's heroes" still dominate "our age."

The great French reveler in expatriates from Society especially delighted Oscar in the form he took under the chisel of Auguste Rodin. Rodin created a heroic figure that itself trespassed boldly across lines drawn in the sand by Philistines. Oscar adored it, telling his publisher in London, "You must really come over and see me and also look on Rodin's wonderful statue of

Balzac—a superb work of genius." The (possibly) unwitting implication that Oscar and the monumental statue were the two notable sights of Paris is suggestive. For, while Balzac's imperious, beetling expression is utterly unlike Oscar's, one is still tempted to see in his descriptions of the statue Oscar's view of himself as a heroic but sadly fallen immoralist: "Rodin's statue of Balzac is superb—just what a *romancier* is, or should be. The leonine head of a fallen angel" . . . "an astonishing masterpiece, a gorgeous leonine head, stuck on the top of a cone-shaped dressing-gown." His admiration was heightened, needless to add, by the fury over Rodin's trespasses upon notions of "proper" form for sculpture celebrating cultural heroes: "People howl with rage over it" . . . "the Philistines are mad with rage about it."

Oscar shared affinities not only with eminent trespassers of the past like Socrates, Cellini, and Balzac, but also with the great ones of his own age. He, Bernard Shaw, and James Joyce comprised the devastating troika of liberating Irish immoralists (that is, antimoralists) . . . all of whom had to leave Ireland to perform their variously obliterating agendas. Oscar and Shaw both had their first London premieres in 1892, and afterward the former wrote to the latter, joking that these two plays were Opus 1 and Opus 2 of "the great Celtic school." If so, it was, Michael Holroyd has pointed out, "a school of truancy" in which—as the tutor Campbell Dodgson found under Oscar's spell at Babbacombe Cliff—trespassing was in order, out-of-bounds was "in," and "bad" boys succeeded. Which, by the way, Oscar did when he achieved a First in "Greats" at Oxford: "The dons are 'astonied' beyond words," he preened in a letter to a classmate, "the Bad Boy doing so well in the end!" (More on these two brilliant, blandishing Irishmen in Chapter 17, "Wildeshawshow.")

Oscar can also be associated with two supreme Continental trespassers of the day. Entirely unwittingly, he was a remarkable soul mate of Friedrich Nietzsche. Nietzsche's enemies were principally "the prigs, the priests, the virtuous"; those he nominated to fight them were "we ourselves, we immoralists." Oscar fought the same enemies, as he made caustically and wittily clear in the following remark about a friend who came to displease him: "The comic thing about him is the moral attitude he takes up. To be either a Puritan, a prig, or a preacher is a bad thing. To be all three at once reminds me of the worst excesses of the French Revolution." Both Wilde and Nietzsche were wonderfully adept at disguising their trespasses upon received values with paradoxical turns of the table, like this of the German's: "Morality, insofar as it *condemns* for its own sake, and *not* out of regard for the concerns, considerations, and contrivances of life, is . . . an *idiosyncrasy* of *degenerates* which has caused immeasurable harm." No other aim is more tirelessly pursued in Oscar's writings than this one of transforming the despotic moral majority into an impotent and foolish-looking minority. (We will return to Nietzsche in Chapter 15, "Closet Philosopher.")

The Frenchman who would in time write *L'Immoraliste* and several other boundary-crashing titles like *Les Nourritures terrestres* and *Corydon* practically took his first lessons in trespassing from Oscar, who, he said in his unpublished notes, was "always trying to instill into you *a sanction for evil.*" André Gide also made the Wilde–Nietzsche connection, saying he was subsequently less astonished by Nietzsche because he had first known Oscar. Oscar's induction of Gide into active homosexuality is discussed in a later chapter.

HOW DID THE GREAT IRRESPONSIBLE (as he was called by William Archer, a leading drama critic of the day) chiefly operate in his role as trespasser? First of all, by invariably and perversely preferring the exception to the general rule. As his Lady Markby wistfully declares to Lady Chiltern, "Your husband is an exception. Mine is the general rule, and nothing ages a woman so rapidly as having married the general rule." Oscar became, in other words, professionally and exuberantly iconoclastic. Shaw, in a review of Nietzsche's *Zarathustra,* said of iconoclasm that it is "perhaps the one pursuit that is as useful as it is amusing," and Oscar certainly

made it so. No small part of his fame derived from his eager sub-
versions of universally respected cultural icons. Like all English
Bad Boys worthy of the name, he could thumb his nose at Shakespeare on occasion. In 1894 an interviewer discovered that he
"likes Ford and Marlowe, and Jonson and Massinger, and the Eliz-
abethan dramatists generally, but he does not rave over Shakespeare." And he was capable of writing that he was "inclined to
say" that Ophelia is a "more difficult part" than Hamlet. He was
surely pleased when, after the premiere of *Earnest,* a cartoon of
him in Shakespearean pose and attire as "The Bard of St. James"
appeared. He also rattled Victorian taste by professing himself unimpressed by two of the century's most popular novelists. "Dickens has influenced only journalism," he said. He turned to
Trollope and found him "admirable . . . undoubtedly" for "rainy
afternoons and tedious railway journeys." But "from the point of
view of literature he is merely the perpetual curate of Pudlington
Parva." The manly Kipling he cordially reviled as "our first authority on the second-rate, [who] has seen marvellous things
through keyholes." Even Mother Nature was not immune. He
complained that "the mountains of California are so gigantic that
they are not favorable to art or poetry" and gibed famously about
"that disappointing Atlantic Ocean."

Such innocuous utterances were mere pranks. Oscar, however, was capable of committing more serious—though still thoroughly amusing—misdemeanors and felonies against Victorian
values. Only the Queen herself, it seems, was above his barbed
jests. At a luncheon party he declared there was nothing on
which he could not speak at a moment's notice. Another guest
suggested "The Queen"—to which he instantly replied, "The
Queen is *not* a subject." Shaw identified "Comedy: the criticism
of morals and manners *viva voce,*" as Oscar's "real forte," and
comedy—whether extemporized in a drawing room or rigged up
for a West End stage—was certainly the main arena for his most
trenchant trespasses. He became a brilliant harrier of "the seven
deadly virtues," as well as all the "domestic virtues" (they "are
not the true basis of art"), useful professions (it is "tragic" how

many young men with "perfect profiles" adopt them), and the appalling habit of industry: "We live in an age . . . in which people are so industrious that they become absolutely stupid." The rigidity of the class system is his target in the magnificently stiff Lady Bracknell—"On this point, as indeed on all points, I am firm"— and in Lord Illingworth's taste in fiction: "You should study [Burke's] Peerage, Gerald. It is the one book a young man about town should know thoroughly, and it is the best thing in fiction the English have ever done."

One of Oscar's most frequent trespasses on fundamental Victorian verities was to step on the toes of philanthropic doers of "good." In a little essay on the best books to give away, he observed that "charity is largely on the increase" because "people are so fond of giving away what they do not want themselves." This is the moral of his fairy tale "The Devoted Friend." Gilbert, in "The Critic as Artist," says "the desire to do good to others produces a plentiful crop of prigs" and ridicules "these philanthropists and sentimentalists of our day, who are always chattering to one about one's duty to one's neighbour." Lord Henry informs his uncle in *Dorian Gray*, "Philanthropic people lose all sense of humanity. It is their distinguishing characteristic." Oscar resented do-gooders because the good they proposed to do was of the doer's own devising. He resented being accosted by the eager philanthropist who attempts to impose missionary positions upon him, directly or through a more powerful instrument: "In an evil moment the Philanthropist made his appearance, and brought with him the mischievous idea of Government." Governments, for instance, that would pass such laws as the Criminal Law Amendment Act of 1885, under which he was eventually prosecuted.

To Oscar, the doers of good were at heart despotically inclined moralists, and he resisted their impositions with passion. As Mrs Cheveley says in his *An Ideal Husband*, "Morality is simply the attitude we adopt towards people whom we personally dislike." Oscar believed that trying to make other people good was a "silly occupation . . . a mere waste of energy." The *true* immorality was "interfering with the individual." The dilemma he wished to force upon his audience was precisely the one he had forced upon Gide: "to be moral or to be sincere." On this point, he was in perfect agreement with Nietzsche, who said: "An 'altruistic' morality—a morality in which self-interest wilts away—remains a bad sign under all circumstances." No wonder Oscar made such fun of good-conduct prizes, and those who won them. Mrs Cheveley reminisces about the saddest character in *An Ideal Husband*, "I have a distinct recollection of Lady Chiltern always getting the good conduct prize!"

Inevitably, the class responsible for the morality that so aggravated him—the middle class—often felt his withering scorn. "Fortunately, in England," he wrote in 1889, "thought is not catching," and the next year appeared this exchange in "The Critic as Artist":

> ERNEST: The English public always feels perfectly at its
>   ease when a mediocrity is talking to it.
> GILBERT: Yes: the public is wonderfully tolerant. It for-
>   gives everything except genius.

In *Dorian Gray* Oscar had called England "the native land of the hypocrite," but after his release from prison, he suggested to Frank Harris that the problem was even more ghastly than mere hypocrisy: "Isn't it comic, Frank, the way the English talk of the 'open door' while their doors are always locked and barred and bolted, even their church doors? Yet it is not hypocrisy in them; they simply cannot see themselves as they are; they have no imagination." This dismal view also extended to the English sense of humor: "The English type and symbol of a joke [is] the jug on the half-opened door, or the distribution of orange-peel on the pavement of a crowded thoroughfare."

Part of what made Oscar such a brilliant trespasser is that—for all his reputation as a darling jester to the upper crust and highly successful fixture in the best Mayfair drawing rooms and for all his exquisitely clubbable manners—he was Not One of Us. No class in Victorian society unreservedly embraced him. His

Irishness, the sheer magnitude of his idiosyncrasy ("He had a reputation of being something out of the common," said a Magdalen classmate), and eventually his homosexuality were in large part responsible for his alienation. A British aristocrat could thus tell Le Gallienne that he "had always thought there was something 'foreign' about Wilde," and another friend, O'Sullivan, admitted, "I never could make out just where Wilde considered himself to rank in the social hierarchy of England."

Shaw, in his memories of Oscar, perhaps summarized this social apartness best in his usual unminced terms. He thought "vulgar snobbery" hampered him and pointed to his insistence on being "Oscar" to his intimates and "Mr Wilde" to others as preventing him from establishing "that fortifying body of acquaintance among plain men in which a man must move as himself a plain man, and be Smith and Jones and Wilde and Shaw and Harris instead of Bosie and Robbie and Oscar and Mister. That is the sort of folly that does not last forever in a man of Wilde's ability; but it lasted long enough to prevent Oscar laying any solid social foundations." Shaw concluded that Oscar "made the mistake of not knowing his place." But then, this is a mistake that constitutional trespassers (and despisers of plainness and plain men) are wont to make. Oscar declined to accept any "place" offered to him. He preferred to be an interloper.

☆ ☆ ☆

As OSCAR HAD MADE a science of the paradox and impersonation, he also became a practiced tactician in the art of cultural guerrilla warfare, the essence of which is to keep one's adversary off-balance, disoriented, uncertain. Everyone on the path toward good-conduct prizes was subject to Oscarian incursions that had these disconcerting effects. Upon practicers and keepers of Victorian morality he wished to have precisely the kind of success he had with young Gide in their first few weeks of acquaintance: "I think that Wilde did me nothing but harm. In his company I had forgotten how to think. I had more varied emotions, but could no longer get them in order." But "harm" that evokes self-discovery was the supreme good in Oscar's topsy-turvy universe; "varied emotions" were precisely the joy of life; and getting one's emotions "in order" was not virtuous but vicious if the "order" was not of one's own creation. These were the golden theorems in the ideal world Oscar envisioned. Only he could have managed to turn what Gide perceived (before he shed his bourgeois morality) as a "sanction for evil" into the true Christian message: " 'Know Thyself' was written over the portal of the antique world. Over the portal of the new world, 'Be thyself' shall be written. And the message of Christ to man was simply 'Be thyself.' That is the secret of Christ."

Oscar's delight in disorientation manifested itself years earlier. One particularly telling instance of this trait can be seen in an 1885 review of a play called *Olivia*, starring Henry Irving and Ellen Terry. His reaction to this play's Bad Boy was, characteristically, just a little narcissistic: "Mr Terriss's Squire Thornhill was an admirable picture of a fascinating young rake. Indeed, it was so fascinating that the moral equilibrium of the audience was quite disturbed, and nobody seemed to care very much for the virtuous Mr Burchell. I was not sorry to see this triumph of the artistic over the ethical sympathy." Oscar then added the characteristic topper, saying he hoped this would encourage "a reaction in favor of the cultured criminal." Maybe unconsciously, Oscar was here admiring himself and—yet one more time— anticipating his own future brilliantly. For his regular habit was to upset the moral equilibrium of his 1890s audiences. Nothing gave him greater pleasure. And he became easily the supreme "cultured criminal" of his day.

Oscar called himself once a "perverse and impossible person," and the courage of his perversity led to an almost systematic outrageousness, a kind of intellectual slapstick with which he harassed Britannia rather as Groucho Marx harassed Margaret Dumont in the movies. Oscar's eye for arresting rhetoric produced such war-cries as "No crime is vulgar" and "All art is immoral."

And it led him to such categorical tweakings of propriety as in this brief sampling:

> [The] abnormal . . . is the only thing in Life that stands in normal relations to Art.

> How different [from politicians is] . . . the true liar, with his frank, fearless statements, his superb irresponsibility, his healthy, natural disdain of proof of any kind!

> Never attempt to reform a man . . . men never repent.

> To have been well brought up is a great drawback now-a-days. It shuts one out from so much.

An interviewer questioned Oscar and reported that he "loves true ignorance. He has not much faith in our modern system of educating everybody: 'A truly ignorant and unsophisticated man is the noblest work of God.' "

These are all vintage Oscarian larks. But on other occasions he could be, for lack of a better word, far more earnest. Indeed, behind most of his larks there is, if one considers carefully, a serious and profound implication. Max Beerbohm, in his very first published work, an essay on Oscar, shrewdly observed, "To say Mr Wilde is not in earnest is manifestly false." Ford Madox Ford agreed: "When Oscar Wilde wandered down Bond Street in a mediaeval costume, bearing in his hand a flower, he was doing something not merely ridiculous. It was militant." What Oscar knew thoroughly well was, simply, the importance of not seeming earnest.

In 1910, a year before Ford expressed his view about Oscar's militancy, G. K. Chesterton also remarked on the core of confrontational truculence in Oscar's behavior on the late-Victorian scene. Chesterton first sketched this scene in evocative fashion: "The years from 1885 to 1898 were like the hours of af-

ternoon in a rich house with large rooms; the hours before tea-
time. They believed in nothing but good manners; and the essence of good manners is a concealed yawn." Into these staid
environs came rambunctious and Irish Oscar with his philosophy
of individualism (which Chesterton did not like) and a style that
extorted admiration nevertheless: "His philosophy (which was
vile) was a philosophy of ease, of acceptance, and luxurious illusion; yet, being Irish, he could not help putting it in pugnacious
and propagandist epigrams. . . . This armed insolence, which was
the noblest thing about him, was also the Irish thing: he challenged all comers." "Armed insolence"—a splendid phrase for Oscar's romp through the musty corridors of the late-Victorian age.
Oscar's "philosophy" was also certainly one of "acceptance";
whether it was merely a vile one of "ease"—or whether his illusions were only "luxurious"—we shall have occasion to consider
later.

As Ford and Chesterton suggested, Oscar did not bother to
shroud in secrecy his insolent eagerness to upset and revolt. This
was risky, of course, but, as he had written in "The Critic as Artist," "An idea that is not dangerous is unworthy of being called
an idea at all." Oscar's trespasses upon propriety were often
phrased and fraught with danger, notably in his most extreme political utterance, "The Soul of Man Under Socialism" (1891).
There he praised a "fine thinker" for asserting that the person
"who would be free must not conform." In this essay he also observed, "Art is Individualism, and Individualism is a disturbing
and disintegrating force"; that "Disobedience, in the eyes of any
one who has read history, is man's original virtue"; and that "ag-
itators are so absolutely necessary." Had such bold and threatening beliefs been unaccompanied by the dazzling circus calliope of
the Oscarian style, the Victorian age would have been even more
shocked by them than by the "gross indecency" of which the
mere Law finally convicted him.

The great expression of the trespasser's credo, however, was
to come in *Dorian Gray*. In 1888, Nietzsche happened to observe

that "for the English morality is not yet a problem." Just two years later, with *Dorian Gray's* appearance in *Lippincott's Magazine*, Oscar made morality a problem in spectacular fashion with such passages as the following, which comes as near to expressing his view of the world as any he ever wrote. The novel's Oscar-surrogate, Lord Henry, is the speaker:

> To be good is to be in harmony with one's self. . . . Discord is to be forced to be in harmony with others. One's own life—that is the important thing. As for the lives of one's neighbours, if one wishes to be a prig or a Puritan, one can flaunt one's moral views about them, but they are not one's concern. Besides, Individualism has really the higher aim. Modern morality consists in accepting the standard of one's age. I consider that for any man of culture to accept the standard of his age is a form of the grossest immorality.

This is vintage, pugnacious Oscar, turning the tables on those so eager to label the behavior of others "evil" or "wicked" or "perverted." (It is a potent irony, given his last phrase, that Oscar would several times be accused of "gross indecency and immorality" in Queensberry's Plea of Justification at his libel trial.)

Oscar adopted as his own "useful profession" the pursuit of this philosophy of individualism in many of his essays, journalistic pieces, and plays. He became a brilliant apologist for The Other in all its guises. He praised the impractical: "There is no country in the world so much in need of unpractical people as this country of ours," says Gilbert in "The Critic as Artist." He praised the poisoner Thomas Wainewright for his "extremely artistic temperament." He invented the notorious green carnation and made green his signature color, praising it as the color of The Other: "Believe me, love the green, love Hell," he admonished; "the colour green and Hell are both made for thieves and artists." And in *The Chameleon*, the ill-starred Oxford undergraduate magazine with unmistakable homosexual content that was to figure in his downfall, he even demystified wickedness: "Wickedness is a myth invented by good people to account for the curious attractiveness of others."

SUCH DIABLERIE OBVIOUSLY CHARMED and delighted his late-Victorian public, but only so long as that public remained complacently convinced that he was talking deliberate "nonsense" intended to be taken, in Yeats's phrase, "for play." To the ubiquitous question "Can he possibly be serious?" the public blithely answered "No" and continued to laugh. They laughed in particular at Lord Illingworth, that expert at discovering how one's "most glaring fault" is really one's "most important virtue." Mrs Allonby says to him, "There is one thing I shall always like you for," and he replies in mock dismay, "Only one thing? And I have so many bad qualities." Until the scandal and trials of 1895, only a few shrewd observers had recognized that Oscar was a Lord Illingworth who was quite serious. (To Beerbohm Tree, the first Lord Illingworth, he declared that the character was "myself.") Beneath all the witty exuberance was a most earnest professor of "bad qualities"—his homosexuality being, if not the only, surely the seminal one. This "most glaring fault" imaginable in Victorian England he turned, by means of witty rhetorical alchemy, into his "most important virtue." The trials, however, forced Victorian England to confront the reality behind the elaborate *roman à clef* of his real life that Oscar had so virtuosically foisted upon it.

As soon as the light went on across London, Oscar truly became "the perverse and impossible person." Overnight, the charming guest became the repugnant trespasser. His true colors revealed, the vindictive retaliation for intimacies formerly granted was striking and to be expected. Mary McCarthy, also distinctly unamused by Oscar, caught exactly the flavor of the public's final reaction to the trespasser when she accused him of "making himself too much at home" and complained that "he ensconces himself with intolerable freedom." Such is the fate of all trespassers when they are discovered.

Chapter Three

PUNCH v. OSCAR I

Oscar Wilde! I wonder to how many of my readers the jingle of this name suggests anything at all? Yet, at one time, it was familiar to many and if we search back among the old volumes of Punch, *we shall find many a quip and crank at its owner's expense.*

—MAX BEERBOHM, *A PEEP INTO THE PAST*

THUS BEGINS ONE OF Beerbohm's most delightful *jeux d'esprit,* first published in 1923. In this little essay, we pay an imaginary visit to an aged Oscar at his house in Tite Street. Here the now retired "old gentleman" solaces himself with memories of "the friends of his youth" and leaves "his better-known brother, William" to perpetuate the family name. He sports a "nut-brown Georgian wig" and amuses visitors "by the delightfully old-fashioned way in which he rolls out his well-rounded periods." Most of Oscar's indolent habits are turned deliciously topsy-turvy: "the old journalist"—Max knew how Oscar despised journalists—now rises at 4:30 a.m. every day and is "still the glutton for work that he always was." The inveterate cab-rider, we are told, now walks the length of King's Road for an hour each afternoon, and he has become "something of a martinet about punctuality," which accounts "for the constant succession of page-boys, which so startles the neighborhood."

The hilarity of the piece, though, lies in the fact that it was not written in the 1920s, but just as Oscar was nearing the zenith of his career . . . and also nearing a terrible abyss. Beerbohm wrote it for the inaugural April 1894 issue of *The Yellow Book*, the preeminent Aesthetic/Decadent magazine of the nineties, but it was held back in favor of his notorious "Defence of Cosmetics." "A Peep into the Past" was never used, almost certainly because unintended ironies in it came into play as the months of 1894 passed and Oscar behaved ever more recklessly with a "constant succession of page-boys" and his page-boy-in-chief, Bosie. Beerbohm wrote of Oscar "pleasantly . . . reading Ruskin" to his sons in Tite Street, and that is where he *should* have been, rather than bankrupting his family by his lavish secret life in Piccadilly. What Beerbohm or the editors of *The Yellow Book* must have sensed as they peeped into the future was that the public personality Oscar and the English press had conspired to create over the preceding decade and a half was in the process of vanishing from the scene. Someone else—a Mr Hyde of some kind?—was taking his place, and this made Beerbohm's clever premise increasingly awkward and (for most everyone close to Oscar) painful.

The emerging new celebrity will much concern us in following chapters, but what of the old celebrity? Who was this departing figure who had so amused and benignly outraged the English public for years, and how did the great middle class in particular perceive him during his London career? As Beerbohm hinted, a very good way to answer these questions is to follow Oscar's fortunes in the pages of *Punch*, the supreme humor magazine of the day and incubator of Victorian middle-class morality and artistic tastes, from his arrival in London in 1878. What larks the two institutions had! On one side, the intrepid rooter-out of cant and pretense, manned notably by its editor Frank Burnand from 1880 to 1906 and the wicked cartoonist George Du Maurier, whose thirty years at *Punch* began in 1864. On the other side, the complaisant comic butt Oscar, a master of that best shortcut to fame: self-advertisement. Whistler once ran into Du Maurier and Oscar on the street and slyly suggested the symbiosis by inquiring, "Which of you two discovered the other?"

Oscar and his fellow Aesthetes were skewered in *Punch* under several pseudonymous composites, most famously the poet Postlethwaite and the painter Maudle (from "maudlin" and a punny reference, perhaps, to Oscar's Oxford college, Magdalen). Later his own name would provoke zany exertions from *Punch* writers: he became, at various times, Oscuro Wildegoose, Drawit Milde, Ossian Wilderness, His Aesthetic Two-Twoness Oscar, Mr Wild Hoskar, The O'scar, and The O'Wilde. A few years before he became "the man Wilde" of the police news, he finally arrived in Mr Punch's cherishing heart as simply "Our Oscar." Many of *Punch's* thrusts are in this exuberant, harmless vein. And while much of the wit lies dead on the page now, palpable hits are now and then scored. There is the occasional witty verse—

The drowse of the dreary aesthetical Canter,
Absorbed in bad dreams and poetical flummery,
Is no more like life than sour milk is like Pommery.

—and sometimes a clever parody like "Racine, with the Chill Off," an Oscarian rewrite of *Phèdre*, in French, in the style of *Salome*. One of the best skits, "An Afternoon Party," was written by Oscar's dear friend Ada Leverson, whom he nicknamed Sphinx. Her party is attended by such celebrities as Madame Santuzza from Mascagni's opera, Charley's Aunt (the Brandon Thomas play had premiered the previous year), Sardou's Dora, and several Oscarian characters. Someone asks who are the two men "smoking gold-tipped cigarettes and talking epigrams." They

are Lord Illingworth from *A Woman of No Importance* and Lord
Henry Wotton from *Dorian Gray;* they "always say exactly the
same things. They are awfully clever and cynical." Salome appears
at the hors d'oeuvre table and utters this perfect send-up of her
play's verbal style:

> Is that mayonnaise? . . . I think it is mayonnaise. I am
> sure it is mayonnaise. It is mayonnaise of salmon, pink
> as a branch of coral which fishermen find in the twi-
> light of the sea, and which they keep for the King. It is
> pinker than the pink roses that bloom in the Queen's
> garden. The pink roses that bloom in the garden of the
> Queen of Arabia are not so pink.

Then there was the steady run of trenchant cartoons. At the beginning Oscar and his Aesthetic cohorts were brilliantly made fun
of by Du Maurier, as in "An Aesthetic Midday Meal" (17 July
1880). Much later, J. Bernard Partridge was to make merry over
Oscar the haughty, paradoxing playwright in a "Fancy Portrait" of
5 March 1892. There is also much that fascinates and astonishes
in the prose of *Punch's* hundred or so sallies against Oscar. Considered altogether, as a kind of continuing saga, the modes and
details of this satirical campaign against Oscar now seem strikingly forthright, occasionally even blatant, in typecasting him not
merely as a social subversive but also as an insidious effeminizer
of British youth. Indeed, the pages of *Punch* go far in explaining
the most curious fact about Oscar's eventual fall from his pinnacle, namely, that while much outrage and horror erupted when
the news broke, there was virtually *no* expression of real surprise.
Rather, one senses the relief of long suspense finally ended: gleeful comeuppance visited upon one who had long insouciantly
evaded it by a hairsbreadth. It is certainly hard to believe that
any regular and careful reader of *Punch* over the years could have
been much shocked at the activities exposed in the trials.

☆ ☆ ☆

AN ÆSTHETIC MIDDAY MEAL.

At the Luncheon hour, Jellaby Postlethwaite enters a Pastrycook's and calls for a glass of Water, into which he puts a freshly-cut Lily, and loses himself in contemplation thereof.

Waiter. "SHALL I BRING YOU ANYTHING ELSE, SIR?"

Jellaby Postlethwaite. "THANKS, NO! I HAVE ALL I REQUIRE, AND SHALL SOON HAVE DONE!"

A REFINED ÆSTHETIC EXQUISITE.

BEFORE WE LOOK AT Oscar's early appearances in *Punch*, it is important to emphasize that the Aesthetic Movement had been a part of the London scene several years before he became its most notable, rather dilettantish exponent (Shaw thought "Oscar knew no more about pictures than anyone of his general culture and with his opportunities can pick up as he goes along"). All the important founding figures of the movement were of the preceding generation and had been prominent since the late 1860s: Rossetti (1828–1882), Burne-Jones (1833–1898), Morris (1834–1896), Swinburne (1837–1909), and Pater (1839–1894). Before Oscar appeared on the scene, *Punch* only infrequently trained its satire upon this first generation of Aesthetes, a fairly proper, unflamboyant set that did not lend itself easily to satire. Oscar's great hero, Walter Pater, for example, was an extraordinarily closeted homosexual (he lived most of his adult life with his two sisters). The *Dictionary of National Biography* says his career "was exceedingly quiet and even monotonous," and a recent biographer has even written that the "most dramatic event" of his life was the heart attack that killed him. A Du Maurier cartoon that appeared several months before Oscar moved to London, "A Refined Aesthetic Exquisite," shows how little the prim Paterian demeanor gave humor to work with. Another cartoon published in September 1878, also pre-Oscar, emphasizes the personal stylelessness of Aesthetes. The stooped, heavy-lidded, shaggy, frumpily dressed "young geniuses" are contrasted with a trio of sleek, buttonholed conventional dandies. (How these swells achieved their hourglass figures may be suggested by an advertisement that appeared in *Punch*.) Soon, though, the buttonhole would make a spectacular transit into the other camp of fashion. In fairly short order, a cadre of young Aesthetic turks—with Oscar to the fore—began to wrest the movement from their dour, retiring elders and flutter their colorful butterfly wings.

Ye Æsthetic young Geniuses!...

Ye Gorgeous young Swells!

Mr Punch's interest was piqued, and he immediately began to take more notice of what was perceived, I think it is fair to say, as a more overt homosexualization of the Aesthetic Movement. What *The Echo* said Oscar did at Magdalen College—"He cultivated dilettante eccentricity to the amusement of his healthy, sinewy, and athletic fellow undergraduates"—he was later to do to the Aesthetes. The very month Oscar set up London housekeeping began a serial attack on the movement called "The Rise and Fall of the Jack Spratts: A Tale of Art & Fashion," which chronicled the initial weakening of Aesthetic sinews (see p. 58). Here is one of

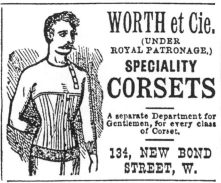

many Aesthetes posed by *Punch* cartoonists in what might be called a Gay Contrapposto, the legs no longer nerdily knock-kneed but femininely graceful. In due course hats obscuring lavish hair are doffed, and the hands of Aesthetes become more delicate and slender; they also find repose in graceful, womanly ways . . . as with the boy in a September 1879 cartoon who informs his mother of the rarefied clique he is joining. Is the clique in question alluded to by the potted flower and the two androgynous, long-locked figures holding hands in the background? In an issue the next month, the same boy appears to be back at school ("A Promising Young Aesthetic"): the feminine lips, languid eyelids, long hair, and young-odalisque pose are notable in this face-off with the manly Philistine . . . which ends with a nice touch of manly violence.

In a little poem called "An Aesthetic Rondeau," one of the chosen grants that his enemies may say,

ÆSTHETIC PRIDE.

Fond Mother. "YOU LIVE TOO MUCH ALONE, ALGERNON!"
Young Genius (Poet, Painter, Sculptor, & c.). " 'TIS BETTER SO, MOTHER! BESIDES I ONLY CARE FOR THE SOCIETY OF MY EQUALS, AND—A—SUCH BEING THE CASE—A—MY CIRCLE IS NECESSARILY RATHER LIMITED."
Fond Mother. "BUT SURELY THE SOCIETY OF YOUR SUPERIORS——"
Young Genius. "MY *WHAT*, MOTHER? MY SUPERIORS! WHERE ARE THEY !!!"

*That I'm limp from
        crown to shoe-tie;
That my taste's mad fad
        full-blown,
That my talk is maudlin
        splutter;
But the Philistines must
        own
I am Utter!*

A PROMISING YOUNG AESTHETIC.

Old Boy. "ULLO! WHAT'S YOUR NAME?"

New Boy. "DANTE MICHAEL ANGELO SALVATOR ROSA NUPKINS!"

Old Boy. "IS THAT ALL? WHAT'S YOUR FATHER?"

New Boy. "POET, PAINTER, SCULPTOR, ARCHITECT, AND MUSICIAN."

Old Boy. "CRIMINI! IS HE GREAT?"

New Boy. "THE GREATEST THAT EVER LIVED."

Old Boy. "I NEVER! AND WHAT ARE YOU GOING TO BE?"

New Boy. "THE SAME AS MY FATHER, ONLY GREATER."

Old Boy. "OH MY!"   *Kicks Young Nupkins, and exit.*

The Stranger Wilde

The confrontation of limp, effeminate Aesthetes and sinewy, upright Philistines was a regular feature in *Punch* at this time, notably in a series of cartoons called "Nincompoopiana" that appeared in late 1879 and 1880, from which three examples are shown. Posture was clearly one of *Punch's* ways of separating virile men from tainted Aesthetic boys.

Perhaps the most unsubtle instance of this before Oscar's first appearance in the magazine was the "Nincompoopiana" cartoon of 20 December 1879 featuring seven or eight figures. In addition to the graceful hand and contrapposto of the pontificating central figure in this all-male salon and the long hair all around, the three members of his "chorus" of admirers, elaborately seated in feminine postures, are remarkable. The flowers are by now usual Aesthetic furniture. Rather more daring is the inclusion of the bust of Antinous to preside over the salon, Antinous being the gorgeous Bithnyian youth who became the favorite of Emperor Hadrian. Late in life Oscar was to write from Naples of spending "my days with Heliogabalus, and my nights with Antinous."

When, then, did Oscar make his *Punch* debut? Some think on 30 October 1880, in a cartoon of a newly married Aesthetic couple admiring a piece of blue china (see p. 54), presumably because Oscar had made a famous remark while at Oxford, "I find it harder and harder every day to live up to my blue china." The husband does not look much like Oscar, though, and his marriage was still four years off. Besides, there was much longing at this time, in W. S. Gilbert's phrase, "for all one sees / That's Japanese." In the Jack Spratts tale, probably the most elaborate send-up of Aestheticism *Punch* published Before Oscar, the Aesthetic couple has a studio "full of blue china." There was even a popular poetry book on the scene called *Ballades in Blue China.*

Though some glimmers and shards of Oscar's personality may be scattered in earlier issues of *Punch*, his first full-blown entrance must have been on 12 February 1881, a few months before his first London publication, the *Poems*, appeared and gave satirists

NINCOMPOOPIANA.

something to bite into. This was a Du Maurier cartoon in which Maudle acquired an Oscarian physique and physiognomy (his pose clearly owes something to figures in the "Nincompoopiana" cartoons on page 53). Most of the themes of *Punch*'s ridicule of Oscar-as-Aesthete are on display here: the long hair, the heavy-lidded eyes, the fleshly body. The gush, the association of Aesthetes with effeminacy, the diction of connoisseurship . . . all were to become satiric staples. The words "consummate," "utter," and "too too" were made special fun of by *Punch* (in May 1881 it asserted the "most Aesthetic line in Shakespeare is, 'Oh, that this Too Too, solid flesh' &c"). Oscar's later assertions of the importance

THE SIX-MARK TEA-POT.

Aesthetic Bridegroom. "IT IS QUITE CONSUMMATE, IS IT NOT?"

Intense Bride. "IT IS, INDEED! OH, ALGERNON, LET US LIVE UP TO IT!"

of *being* rather than *doing* are also foreshadowed here. But mainly what is striking about the cartoon is its homosexual innuendos: the set of the hands, the crooked knee, the interest in Mrs Brown's "lovely" son.

In several issues Postlethwaite and Maudle become something of an "item" on the *Punch* social scene. In a December 1880 sketch, Postlethwaite speaks of "the tender companionship of my Maudle" and calls him "Consummately Supreme." On one occasion they attend a salon in identical limp wrists, flowing

54

MAUDLE ON THE CHOICE OF A PROFESSION.

Maudle. "HOW CONSUMMATELY LOVELY YOUR SON IS, MRS. BROWN!"

Mrs. Brown (a Philistine from the country). "WHAT? HE'S A NICE, MANLY BOY, IF YOU MEAN THAT, MR. MAUDLE. HE HAS JUST LEFT SCHOOL, YOU KNOW, AND WISHES TO BE AN ARTIST."

Maudle. "WHY SHOULD HE BE AN ARTIST?"

Mrs. Brown. "WELL, HE MUST BE SOMETHING!"

Maudle. "WHY SHOULD HE BE ANYTHING? WHY NOT LET HIM REMAIN FOR EVER CONTENT TO EXIST BEAUTIFULLY?"   [*Mrs. Brown determines that at all events her Son shall not study Art under Maudle.*

locks, and costume (in the caption Postlethwaite is described as having a "Slender Willowy Frame, as yielding and fragile as a Woman's"). On another occasion, having learned they "exist only in Mr Punch's vivid imagination," they solace each other emotionally over their "Frustrated Social Ambition." Their artistic collaboration is also risqué in its flamboyant indulgence in the confusion of gender. The picture of a nymph's love agony is published, along with "Verses by Jellaby Postlethwaite, who is also said to have sat for the picture." An appearance by Postlethwaite six months later in exactly the same posture wryly ratifies the rumor.

☆ ☆ ☆

As the fashionable contretemps between "unmanly, unwholesome" Aesthetes and "sinewy, athletic" Swells played out in the early 1880s, *Punch* regularly showed itself friendly to the latter. For "Swelldom is friends with horses and dogs, and guns and fishing-rods, which are easier to master than pictures and poems, and the intellectual problems of the day, and do not wrinkle the brow, nor waste the cheek, nor sap the youthful frame." An eighty-line poem published in the October 1879 issue, "From the Philistine Point of View," amusingly epitomizes the magazine's own profoundly conservative reaction to Oscar and the Aes-

thetes. All their "very low spirits and very high Art" are ridiculed, all their poems and essays "Beginning in doldrums and ending in doubt," all their "finical flam" and "emotional gush." Disgust is several times reiterated at the Aesthetic tendency to delve beneath the surface and find unpleasantness and ambiguity. Much preferable is a life

> Neat and not nubilistic, I think you will say,
> Which is just what we want in our fog-flustered day.
> Clear sense and no clouds! That's my maxim all round . . .
> Life's a plant, say the seers; well, don't poke at its roots,
> But let the thing grow, and look out for its fruits . . .
> It's all this confounded new fad for analysis,
> This poking and prying that ends in paralysis . . .

The irony, of course, is that *Punch* had been quite happy to poke about the roots of Aestheticism, looking, as it were, for the fruits. There is indeed something prurient in the wicked stare of Mr Punch as he attends a performance of Jack Spratt (a nice leg points in his victim's direction). "Clear sense and no clouds" rather accurately describes much of the obvious sexual innuendo of the period when *Punch* pursued its attacks under the cover of such composite caricatures as Maudle, Postlethwaite, and Milkington Sopley. This *modus operandi* was pretty much captured in the Marquess of Queensberry's response when Oscar much later asked him pointblank whether he was accusing him of a homosexual relationship with his son: "I do not say that you are it, but you look it."

By late 1880, however, Oscar had decidedly come into his own as a London personality. In November opened a satirical play, *Where's the Cat?*, featuring a character that spoofed him, and by this time Gilbert and Sullivan were already at work on *Patience* (it premiered in September 1881). On 2 February 1881, a play by Burnand himself, *The Colonel*, opened and had a great success; it featured an obviously Oscarian character. In the issue of 19 February, in a skit describing Mr Maudle and a Philistine at a performance, we learn of "a Professor of Aesthetics, a certain Lambert Streyke, who is, to the eyes of all but his dupes, a ghastly old humbug." The play "winds up merrily with the discomfiture of the Aesthete, and the triumph of common sense." Maudle is left "very angry." Understandably so, for Maudle was soon—in a mere few months, in fact—to be replaced by Oscuro Wildegoose and his numerous alter egos.

The official nomination of "The Sunflower Gentleman" (as the *Louisville Courier-Journal* was later to call him) to celebrity came in the issue of 25 June and was clearly a response to the collection of poems he had published at his own expense in May. This was Oscar's inclusion by *Punch* in its regularly featured series of "fancy portraits" (the equivalent, one might say, of being on the cover of *Mad* magazine). Edward Sambourne's drawing is cleverly detailed: the (presumably blue china) wastebasket into which the "ode" is likely to soon land, the hallmark cigarette case, the ivory-tipped walking stick. The unattractive set of the mouth, too, was to become standard among his caricaturists.

PUNCH'S FANCY PORTRAITS.—
No. 37.
"O. W."
"O, I feel just as happy as a bright Sunflower!"
Lays of Christy Minstrelsy.

Æsthete of Æsthetes!
What's in a name?
The poet is WILDE,
But his poetry's tame.

In the following six months or so, before Oscar left for his yearlong lecture tour of America and thus dropped from Mr Punch's menu, some fun was had at his expense. *Punch* was distinctly unimpressed by his verse. In a brief review titled

THE SLEEPING BEAUTY.

"Swinburne and Water," *Poems* was termed "a volume of echoes ... poor and pretentious stuff." Sarcasm was heaped on the book itself: "The cover is consummate, the paper is distinctly precious, the binding is beautiful, and the type is utterly too." The next month came "A Sonnet of Sorrow. By Oscuro Wildegoose" titled "Too-Too Awful!" It ends with a swipe at a favorite element of Aesthetic interior decoration, the dado (the lower portion of a wall, usually ornamented):

> *Life is nought*
> *Till Culture's crescent grows full plenilune.*
> *"What is a Dado?" Weep till all is blue,*
> *Ye who had hoped to see our planet soon*
> *Lapped in the Elysian Limbo of Too-Too!*

When a performance on 17 December of Oscar's first play, *Vera,* was canceled, Mr Punch assumed the worst in his "Mother Hubbard Fairy Tale Grin-away Christmas Cards." In one panel the play becomes the source of Sleeping Beauty's somnolence. When *Vera* was finally first produced, in New York in 1883, *Punch* reported gleefully: "Mr Oscar Wilde's Play, *Vera,* which the *Herald* dismissed as 'long-drawn dramatic rot'—(they have a neat style of criticism in New York)—was, from all accounts, except the Poet's own, Vera Bad."

Shortly after leaving for America, Oscar appeared in the magazine as Dickens's Harold Skimpole, and in March 1882 an amusing Ossian-style skit appeared. It reported how the "carborne Son of Erin" had "strung the harp in Bostona" and greeted sixty youths "bearing the Flower of the Sun" in "Fila-Delfia's Hall." All his friends in the East sit in "The Dadoed Hall and the Chamber of Yallery-green" awaiting his return. The accompanying drawing (see p. 62) shows him almost willowy and performing a rather graceful *jeté*.

Oscar Wilde as *Harold Skimpole*.

When he did return to England, Oscar went into hibernation as far as Mr Punch was concerned. He faded, quite literally, into the background, as he does in a large panel cartoon that appeared in June 1885: "At Burlington House. The 'Swarry'" (see detail at right). Several reasons account for this eclipse. Most notably, he began to jettison many of his earlier Aesthetic mannerisms (his knee-breeches, for

OSSIAN (WITH VARIATIONS).
THE SON OF IA-CULTCHA.

62

instance). He also avoided publishing further mediocre poetry that might incite satirical merriment. But perhaps most important was his becoming an apparently happily married man and the most respectable father of two sons: as surely a mortal wound to celebrity among the fashionable as can be imagined. *Punch* made light of the seemingly vanished celebrity when it reported this anecdote and titled it "And is this Fame?"

> We've just seen the wrapper of a newspaper addressed—
> "Oscar Wilde,
> Poet.
> London."
> And above is written "Not Known." Some very kind person had scribbled on it "Try No. 4, xxxxxx Place," but it had evidently been returned to St. Martin's with the fatal words, "Not Known."

Chapter Four

ARBITER ELEGANTIARUM

Fashion is what one wears oneself. What is unfashionable is what other people wear.

—LORD GORING IN *AN IDEAL HUSBAND*

I hope you will never lose the sense of style in life: it keeps the barbarians away.

—LETTER TO GEORGE IVES, 1900

VINCENT O'SULLIVAN SAID THERE were in Oscar's plays "two kinds of characters, and only two." One consisted of mere puppets of theatrical convention, paltry "phantoms arising from the dust of the stage." The other, more fascinating kind—and here O'Sullivan employed an anachronistic image from phonography—were the "discs which give forth their Master's voice." Oscar's plays (his fictions and dialogues, too) are mainly prized for these characters who seem to speak in his low musical mezzo-soprano voice and in his own style of scintillating badinage. Manifestly, he could not see his way clear to the suppression of his personality in his writings. It is hard, in fact, to find evidence that he ever tried seriously to do so.

Some theater critics accounted this a grave problem. If so, it was one he shared notably and brilliantly with Bernard Shaw. The great complaint of William Archer, the eminent critic and friend of Shaw, was that he could not "throw his characters outside himself," that he was simply a kind of "ventriloquist" who could "seldom or never disguise his own voice and accent." Such, too, is the splendid ignominy of the Wilde canon, for its most treasurable characters—the Lord Illingworths, Lady Allonbys, Algernon Moncrieffs, and Mrs Cheveleys—tend to be the ones who *sound* pure Oscar.

Rarer is the surrogate who *looks* pure Oscar. Perhaps the quintessential example of such a character is Lord Goring, the "flawless dandy" in *An Ideal Husband*. The second-act curtain rises on him in a most characteristic Oscarian pose: "dressed in the height of fashion" and "lounging in an armchair." But it is for his entrance in the third act that Oscar saves his sartorial *tour de force*:

> Enter Lord Goring in evening dress with a buttonhole. He is wearing a silk hat and Inverness cape. White-gloved, he carries a Louis Seize cane. His are all the delicate fopperies of Fashion. One sees that he stands in immediate relation to modern life, makes it indeed, and so masters it. He is the first well-dressed philosopher in the history of thought.

Oscar the philosopher will occupy us in later chapters, but now is the time to acquaint ourselves with the Oscar introduced to us in the person of Lord Goring. Indeed, this was the first and the most consistently and continuously celebrated of all his public personas: namely, Oscar the fashion plate and authority on Style, the *arbiter elegantiarum*. *The Echo*, in a "portrait" sketch that looked back on his career in 1892, emphasized with not a little sarcasm this earliest mode of Oscarian self-assertion: "Reaching

London at the mature age of twenty-three, and glancing round with a keen eye for some means of bringing himself before the public, the aesthetic craze, then in full blast, recommended itself to his notice, and with a sufficiency of assurance, placing himself at its head, he assumed the character of its apostle, and, with long locks and short breeches, preached its gospel in town and shire."

Of course, it was his preaching in the towns and shires of America on dress and interior decoration that crystallized his reputation as a pronouncer on good taste and a reveler in ele-

The Old Lady of Beacon Hill: "No, Sir. Shoddy New York may receive you with open arms, but we have an Aestheticism of our own." Drawing that appeared in the *New York Daily Graphic*, 19 January 1882.

gant luxuries. His notorious floral predilections were regularly flattered during his tour, notably when the epicurean *bon vivant* Sam Ward and a half-dozen "Aesthetic" gentlemen entertained him in Clinton Place. The *New York Times* reported on the table's centerpiece, "a magnificent floral bed of lilies of the valley, the edges being trimmed with large white calla lilies." All his public appearances were clearly preceded by the most scrupulous sartorial calculations; newspaper reporters rehearsed his mode of dress in painstaking detail in virtually every new city he visited. A few weeks after his arrival, *Lady's Pictorial* offered this poetical sketch of "His Dress": "smoking suit of dark brown velvet faced with lapels of red quilted silk. The ends of a long dark necktie floated over the facing like sea-weed on foam tinged by the dying sun. Dark brown nether garments, striped with red up the seam, and patent leather shoes." Helen Potter, a close student of public deportment, recorded another example of an ensemble à la Oscar: "A dark purple velvet sack coat, and knee-breeches; black hose, low shoes with bright buckles; coat lined with lavender satin, and frill of rich lace at the wrists and for tie-ends over a low turndown collar; hair long, and parted in the middle, or all combed over . . . a circular cavalier cloak over the shoulder."

Thirteen years later, at the premiere of *Earnest,* the effect of Oscar in full getup was not greatly different:

> He was dressed with elaborate dandyism and a sort of florid sobriety. His coat had a black velvet collar. He held white gloves in his small pointed hands. On one finger he wore a large scarab ring. A green carnation, echo in colour of the ring, bloomed in his buttonhole, and a large bunch of seals on a black moiré ribbon watch-chain hung from his white waistcoat. This costume, which on another man might have appeared perilously like fancy dress, and on his imitators was nothing less, seemed to suit him perfectly.

Ada Leverson's sketch of her dear friend in his finest theatrical hour highlights some of the most notable aspects of fashion on which he offered his magisterial opinions. A meticulously arranged buttonhole had long been one of his hallmarks. After a grueling four-day train ride from Omaha to San Francisco, the bedraggled tourist was noticed to sport in his coat-front a "withered bouquet of heliotrope, daisy, and tuberose." In 1891, in a letter to the editor of the *Daily Telegraph,* he lamented that the general dreariness of men's fashion was broken only by the buttonhole: "The little note of individualism that makes dress delightful can only be attained nowadays by the colour and treatment of the flower one wears. This is a great pity." One of the aphorisms he contributed to *The Chameleon* in 1894 suggested, "A really well-made buttonhole is the only link between Art and Nature."

The white gloves Leverson recalled had once been resolutely

lavender. Lillie Langtry remembered Oscar always having, though never wearing, a pair of lavender gloves. Leverson did not mention a cane, but doubtless he arrived at the St. James's Theatre with one. Ford Madox Ford recalled that he "possessed a walking-stick with an ivory head, to which he attached much affection"; perhaps it is the one that appears in the Pennington portrait. Leverson noticed many "tall canes of ebony with ivory tops" in the theater, doubtless sported in homage to the author by members of, or aspirants to, his stylish circle.

Surely a colorfully lined cloak of the kind that left the impression of a giant Brazilian butterfly figured in the occasion. Oscar was well known in his partisanship for this precious means of enlivening nineteenth-century male dress. Cloaks "in constant service" might be dark in color on the outside, he explained in the *Daily Telegraph*, but let them have "bright-coloured linings. . . . We must wear cloaks with lovely linings. Otherwise we shall be very incomplete."

Nor was he shy about pontificating on the "colour sense." He was—like all proper Aesthetes—much in love with dull greens, pale yellows, Venetian reds, peacock blues. But he was a sworn enemy of mauve . . . and all the primary colors (great fun is made of this in Gilbert and Sullivan's *Patience*). Green, however, he especially doted on. It was the color of the scarab ring Ada Leverson mentions and of the carnation blooming savagely in his buttonhole. It was also the favorite color of the poisoner Wainewright, the subject of one of Oscar's first journalistic "think" pieces, "Pen, Pencil and Poison" (it was subtitled "A Study in Green"): "He had that curious love of green, which in individuals is always the sign of a subtle artistic temperament, and in nations is said to denote a laxity, if not a decadence of morals." The love of green was thus perfectly suitable to the great demoralizer of the 1890s.

Oscar, in short, became a master at the peremptory aphorism defining taste, a skill that requires much chutzpah. He suggested as much, I think, when he allowed Lady Bracknell to say, "Style largely depends on the way the chin is worn." When the chin is worn in a sufficiently elevated fashion, one can get away with the most outrageous *obiter dicta*. And Oscar certainly did: "The essential thing for a necktie is style. A well-tied tie is the first serious step in life." "Dandyism is the assertion of the absolute modernity of Beauty." Or the remark made by Lord Goring in the epigraph, which could do service as the credo of any self-respecting *arbiter elegantiarum*.

☆ ☆ ☆

OSCAR'S PONTIFICATORY SKILLS, his long-standing Aesthetic credentials, and his presiding, with his wife, Constance, over a well-publicized "house beautiful" in Tite Street made him an obvious candidate in 1887 to take over the editorship of a year-old magazine called *Lady's World*. He balked, though, with laudable taste, at the name of the magazine, writing to the proprietor, Cassell's, that it had "a certain taint of vulgarity about it." The name would not, he said, be suitable "to a magazine that aims at being the organ of women of intellect, culture, and position." The publishing firm relented, and the issue of November 1887, the first with Oscar as editor, came out under the name *Woman's World*.

He had said the magazine he took over was "a most vulgar trivial production" and did his best to raise its tone, scouring both sides of the Atlantic for suitable contributions. From Julia Ward Howe he requested 4,000 words "on Concord, with sketches of Thoreau, the faun, and Alcott, the mystic, and Emerson, with his bright Attic mind . . . and Margaret Fuller, to whom Venus gave everything except beauty, and Pallas everything except wisdom." From Queen Victoria he asked, more modestly, for a poem: the unamused monarch harrumphed at the presumption that she had ever written one. Within a few months Oscar had succeeded in turning the magazine into something like the *Ms.*, *Vogue*, or *Elle* of the 1880s. Its "keynote," said Oscar's assistant editor, was "the right of woman to equality of treatment with man" and the presentation to view of "women who had gained high position by virtue of their skill as writers or workers in the world's great field of labour."

A typical forty-eight-page issue devoted about twenty pages to regular features like separate reports on London and Paris fashions, serialized fiction, and Literary Notes written "by the Editor." The remaining pages were devoted to special articles like "A Visit to a South African Ostrich Farm," "The Gymnasium for Girls," or an intriguing piece on "Women Wearers of Men's Clothes" (a phenomenon *Punch* had noticed several years before). Most every issue carried an essay on a political or social subject like Mrs Charles M'Laren's "The Fallacy of the Superiority of Man" or Lady Sandhurst's "On Women's Work in Politics." Each issue offered a historical essay on some object of the toilette or wardrobe.

"MAN OR WOMAN?"—A TOSS UP.
"Dresses are still universally cut en Coeur. A very dressy Toilette, and one, much worn now, for the Evening, is of black Broché or Cloth material cut en Habit d'Homme, with plain or kilted Skirt, very tight; for fair Ladies it is very becoming to omit a Tucker, and have the Black with no softening."
Journal des Modes, 1st April.

Constance herself contributed an essay on muffs, and other essays appeared titled "The Umbrella," "A Treatise of Hoops," and "The History of the Bonnets of Queen Victoria's Reign." Oscar's own rather exotic literary tastes were vigorously pursued, notably in Blanche Roosevelt's essay on Maupassant, an essay on Villiers de L'Isle-Adam, and one on "The American Girl in Fiction." In the magazine's pages he declared Balzac to be France's "one great genius" and Flaubert its "one great artist," while belittling Dickens and Trollope.

Nor did Oscar scruple at enlisting his mother's skills: he published her poem "Heroic Women" and asked her to discourse on "Irish Peasant Tales." Lady Wilde, in turn, did not forbear from complaining when her son failed to mention her in his review of a poetry anthology called *Woman's Voices*: "Why didn't you name *me* in the review of Mrs Sharp's book? Me, who hold such an historic place in Irish literature?" Perhaps the son made amends with his mention, in one of his Literary Notes columns, of Lady Wilde's translation of *Sidonia the Sorceress*, "my favourite romantic reading when a boy."

Oscar was of course subject to ridicule from the manly for his immersion in the world of women. Even some of his friends were a bit put off by a rather effusive style that obviously helped him to become a highly successful editor and habitué of women's weekday salons. O'Sullivan, for instance, expressed his dismay when Oscar purveyed among women a manner that was "overdone, loaded with crushing compliments, almost oily." Whenever O'Sullivan heard Oscar going on in this wise he thought "of Mr Turveydrop, Dickens's Professor of Deportment. Wilde often used this kind of talk with women. They seemed to like it. Perhaps it was a variation of his national 'blarney.'" Happily, there is little of this sort of patronizing *blague* in the pages of *Woman's World*, though now and again Oscar's Literary Notes manifest an air of condescension. For instance, he dismisses George Eliot's style as "too cumbrous" and Charlotte Brontë's as "too exaggerated" and then urges women writers to do what they are best at: employing "a light touch, a delicate hand, a graceful mode of treatment, and an unstudied felicity of phrase."

For the most part, however, Oscar treats the works and views of the women under his review with respect and candor. His bouquets are poised and eloquent—notably on Mrs Craik, "one of the finest of our women-writers"—but even where affection lay he was not inclined to pull his punches. Of Ouida he concluded that she "is fond of airing a smattering of culture, but she has a certain intrinsic insight into things and, though she is rarely true, she is never dull. *Guilderoy*, with all its faults, which are great, and its absurdities, which are greater, is a book to be read."

Inevitably, a substantial part of *Woman's World* was devoted to the ephemeral details of changing fashions, announcements of what was no longer chic and what was destined to be so ("the spring bonnet will be the Tosca bonnet, of coloured straw, lined with velvet and trimmed with faille ribbon") and of the establishments most apt to keep the reader abreast ("Liberty's is the chosen resort of the artistic shopper"). Thus, there is much talk in the long monthly fashion reports of such marvels of couture as "a daintily fine tea-gown . . . composed of white matelassé silk, opened slightly in a point in front, over a fichu of white crepon" and of mantilla cloaks "of pink peau de soie, covered with finely pleated écru lace and fastened with agrafes of steel passementerie." Two years of this—and perhaps a half-dozen years plying the book-chat trade—appear to have been enough for Oscar. On the second anniversary of assuming his post, he resigned *Woman's World* with the October 1889 issue (the magazine survived but one year more).

Oscar, of course, did not by any means cease to be a "man of taste"—and of very specific personal tastes—though he made it less and less his occupation to offer public pronouncements on the subject. There was a great toning down of the fripperies of his Aesthetic heyday, but exquisite clothes and luxurious accessories remained an important part of his life. One thinks, ominously, of the fancy, engraved silver cigarette cases purchased from jewelers in Bond Street that he began giving to the young objects of his desire . . . and of such gifts as the "dainty sleeve-links—four heart-shaped moonstones of silver mist, girdled by alternate ruby and diamond" that he himself designed for Bosie.

Not even two years in prison could extinguish the *arbiter elegantiarum* of old. His attachment to physical things was evidenced in his eagerness to be reunited with a favorite fur coat that his brother had unconscionably pawned: "I am anxious to trace it, and if possible get it back. I have had it for twelve years, it was all over America with me, it was at all my first nights, it knows me perfectly, and I really want it." And his letter to More Adey detailing his toilette and wardrobe needs on release showed no falling-off in his concern for style. He asked for a blue serge suit from his old tailor Doré, a dozen handkerchiefs "with coloured borders," neckties ("some dark blue with white spots and diapers"), shirts with turn-down collars and cuffs (both with colored borders), and mother-of-pearl studs ("by the way I want to make 'nacred' an English word"). He also desired "Peau d'Espagne" or "Sac de Laitue" soap from Pritchard's in King Street, some "Canterbury Wood Violet" cologne, and "Eau de Lubin" toilet water. He also noted that his hair had turned color ("I am under the impression that it is quite white") and asked that a "wonderful" hair tonic called Koko Marikopas be fetched at 233 Regent Street: "The name alone seems worth the money, so please get a large bottle." If "the dreadful people" (his brother and sister-in-law) wouldn't relinquish two of his old rugs, he asked for "a travelling Scotch rug, with a good fringe" ("*not* a tartan, of course . . . but the sort of fleecy striped thing").

A little self-conscious about making so many specific requests, Oscar added this explanation: "I want, for psychological reasons, to feel entirely cleansed of the stain and soil of prison life, so these things are all—trivial as they may sound—really of great importance."

OSCAR WAS, IN A deeper sense, right about these seemingly trivial things being in fact "of great importance." For the instinct that led him to wear suits of velvet ("the most beautiful dress for a man"), iridescent neckties of "fainting-green" Chinese silk, waistcoats with buttons of precious jewels, overcoats with braiding "broad enough for the pelisse of a Magyar," and shoes "varnished in three coats" and "pointed as the ace of spades" was the same instinct that made Oscar such a courageous contrarian and trespasser in his other walks of life. His seemingly flippant aphorism, "One should either be a work of art, or wear a work of art," is perhaps the best clue we have to the integral connections between Oscar's philosophies of dress and of life: they were, in fact, the same philosophy. Another aphorism (never published) drives the point home: "In the mode of the knotting of one's necktie or the conduct of one's cane there is an entire creed of life."

The exuberantly idiosyncratic taste for the sartorial Other was a piece with his relentless insistence, elsewhere, upon the right to express his own individual personality. The soul of man cannot exist apart from self-inventing and self-generating Style: the greatest felicity—and the rarest—was to create and achieve a harmony with one's own style, not the style imposed by all the world's self-appointed political, social, and aesthetic gurus of fashion.

Oscar was thus of Nietzsche's mind that the "one thing needful" in life was the "great and rare art" of "giving style" to one's life. In no cranny of life, he therefore believed, could the question of style be considered unimportant: style is a matter of personal choice, and choice is self-definition. Thus, he professed admiration for Wainewright, even though the fellow poisoned several people: "He recognised that Life itself is an art, and has its modes of style no less than the arts that seek to express it." Oscar articulated his devotion to self-definition-as-style in another of his subversive aphorisms for *The Chameleon*: "In all unimportant matters, style, not sincerity, is the essential. In all important matters, style, not sincerity, is the essential." He liked this point so much, in fact, that he recycled it a few months later in *Earnest*; Gwendolen says, "In matters of grave importance, style, not sincerity is the vital thing."

Oscar was one of the several great liberators Ireland has produced, and the leitmotif of freedom sounds constantly even in his utterances as a professor of fashion. In 1891 he wrote to the editor of the *Daily Telegraph* to urge that the very colorful evening dress worn by a character in Dion Boucicault's play *London Assurance* should usher in a new fashion:

The costume in question belongs to 1840 or 1841, and its charm resides in the fact that the choice of the colour of the coat is left to the taste and fancy and inclination of the wearer. Freedom in such selection of colour is a necessary condition of variety and individualism of costume. . . . The colour of the coat should be entirely for the good taste of the wearer to decide. This would give pleasure, and produce charming variety of colour effects in modern life.

Oscar's modest proposal, of course, fell on deaf ears ("the English dislike individualism," he said in the same letter), but what is remarkable about it, as we shall see, is that it sounds the essential notes of his entire philosophy of life and art: the primacy of freedom, the insistence upon individual "fancy," and the all-embracing eagerness for variety in "modern" life.

Oscar came down in favor of the controversial divided skirt or culotte (which, among other things, made bicycle riding possible for women) because it was based on the principles of "ease and liberty." The *super-totus*, or loose cloak, he especially admired, since its "principles are those of freedom and comfort." Likewise, he preferred the turned-down collar to the "strangling stock" and soft-leather boots to "stiff Hessian" ones because they "are more supple, and give consequently more freedom." Whatever is worn "on the extremities," he insisted, "should for the sake of comfort be made of a soft material and for the sake of freedom should take its shape from the way one chooses to wear it, and not from any stiff, stereotypical design of hat or boot maker." Pure Oscar, this antipathy to the stiff or stereotypical designs of one's fellow man.

As Oscar hated moralists of a religious or political stripe, so, too, he hated moralists of fashion. To one such nuisance, named Wentworth Huyshe, he recommended his sartorial Golden Rule: "I hope he consults his own comfort and wishes in everything which has to do with his dress, and is allowed to enjoy that individualism in apparel which he so eloquently claims for himself, and so foolishly tries to deny to others." Oscar had been called affected thousands of times in his life, but it was the mindless and timid affectation of *other* people's tastes that he accounted the truest and ignoblest affectation of all. In "The Soul of Man Under Socialism," he made just this point: "A man is called affected, now-a-days, if he dresses as he likes to dress. But in doing that he is acting in a perfectly natural manner. Affectation, in such matters, consists in dressing according to the views of one's neighbour, whose views, as they are the views of the majority, will probably be extremely stupid." A few pages later in this same essay, he added a corollary to this credo, ridiculing "the immoral ideal of uniformity of type and conformity to rule which is so prevalent everywhere, and is perhaps most obnoxious in England." Beneath all the fur-trimmed, floor-length ulsters, puce-colored ties, monster malmaisons in the buttonhole, frilly cuffs of *mousseline de soie*, and patent-leather slippers lay a very serious philosophy indeed.

OSCAR DIVULGED THIS PHILOSOPHY to Frank Harris one day precisely in terms of "taste." "There is no general rule of spiritual health; it is all personal, individual," he said; "I only demand that freedom which I willingly concede to others. No one condemns another for preferring green to gold. Why should any taste be condemned? Liking and disliking are not under our control. I want to choose the nourishment which suits *my* body and *my* soul." For several years Oscar nourished his body and soul (and a healthy appetite for publicity and the limelight) as an apostle for the Aesthetic Movement. When it died the inevitable death of all particularly flamboyant fashions, he passed easily on to other things. He came to recognize, as Dorian Gray does, that fashion ("by which what is really fantastic becomes for a moment universal") and its fopperies were only "half-serious"—that far more serious (and dangerous) forms of self-assertion remained to be ventured: forms like the essay "The Soul of Man Under Socialism" and the novel *The Picture of Dorian Gray*.

Indeed, Oscar seems, at the dawn of the 1890s, to have reached the same point that Dorian reaches at the midpoint of his novel, the point when "in his inmost heart he desired to be something more than a mere *arbiter elegantiarum*, to be consulted on the wearing of a jewel, or the knotting of a necktie, or the conduct of a cane. He sought to elaborate some new scheme of life that would have its reasoned philosophy and its ordered principles." The point came, in other words, when Oscar began to live in earnest his philosophy of self-assertion. *The Echo* ended its 1892 summary of Oscar's career with this witty conclusion: "Capable of considerable mental effort, he has succeeded in believing in himself." His many years as a leader and creator of fashion helped him to hone this rare skill and doubtless encouraged him to employ it, ever more recklessly, in more consequential aspects of his life. He elected to believe in himself.

Bernard Shaw, for one, saw Oscar's tendency to regard style as evidence of strength as the source of his vulnerability. Wilde, said Shaw, "was so in love with style that he never realized the danger of biting off more than he could chew. In other words, of putting up more style than his matter would carry. Wise kings wear shabby clothes, and leave the gold lace to the drum major." Shaw, however, was perhaps naive in his judgment: for Oscar loved risk, loved the danger of biting off more than he could chew, loved the dangers of artistry and thievery. This characteristic brings again to mind the dazzling green ring that became an Oscarian trademark—and which so many of his acquaintances commented on. "As his hand moved with a slow gesture," recalled Henri de Régnier, for example, "the *scarabaeus* of his ring threw off its green lights." Green was, for Oscar, the color of artists and thieves and Hell. It was for him the color of risk and self-assertion: his entire career, it might therefore be said, threw off its green lights.

The scarab, by the way, was also the Egyptians' symbol for the soul. The famous green scarab ring was thus the perfect accessory for a man whose constitutional habit was to nourish his soul by taking risks, whose byword in fashion was freedom, and whose destiny was to include two dreadful years in prison. "After all, even in prison, a man can be quite free," Oscar wrote a few years before his sentence was pronounced. Even there, "his soul can be free."

Chapter Five

☆ ☆ ☆ ☆ ☆ ☆ ☆ ☆ ☆ ☆ ☆ ☆ ☆ ☆ ☆ ☆

"MOTHERS ARE DARLINGS"

Fathers should be neither seen nor heard. That is the only proper basis for family life. Mothers are different. Mothers are darlings.
—LORD GORING IN *AN IDEAL HUSBAND*

ONE OF THE PLEASURES of *A Woman of No Importance* is the merry war of wits betwixt Mrs Allonby and Lord Illingworth. In a second-act scene comes this typical volley:

> Lord Illingworth: People's mothers always bore me to death. All women become like their mothers. That is their tragedy.
> Mrs Allonby: No man does. That is his.

Oscar must have admired the conceit enormously, for he recycled it verbatim two years later in *The Importance of Being Earnest*, giving both ends of it to Algy. Jack's needling response is to ask, "Is that clever?"—to which Algy replies, "It is perfectly phrased! and quite as true as any observation in civilized life should be."

Of the manifold ironies in this witticism two are particularly stunning—and may have been relished by the author himself. The first is that Oscar *did* become extraordinarily like his mother, Lady Wilde, born Jane Francesca Elgee but familiarly known by her assumed name, Speranza ("hope" in Italian). Just how alike they were can be conveniently suggested simply by glancing at the lengthy obituary accorded her in London's *Daily News* when she died in 1896 at the age of seventy-five. Though it begins by noting that a "strange, peculiar, picturesque figure" had passed from the scene, it offers a respectful, almost affectionate sketch of her life and character. Often it mirrors the salient qualities of her strangely picturesque younger son. She was "stately" and "very tall" and had become in later years "eccentric in dress." She had been "a very brilliant woman in her earlier working days." With thirteen books to her credit, she was even more industrious than her son. Like Oscar, "She retained her vivid conversational powers almost to the very end." Her writing, as Oscar's often was, is described as being "aflame with enthusiasm and rhetoric."

After the death of her husband, Sir William Wilde (described by the obituarist as "a man of great ability and position in his profession [and] surgeon-oculist to the Queen's Viceroys in Dublin"), Speranza emigrated to London to be near her son. There she reveled as Oscar did in the excitement of a well-stocked drawing room, becoming famous for a salon where "one met clever men and clever women belonging to every department in letters and in art." Also like Oscar, she was the focus of much town-talk: "She became, naturally, the subject of many an anecdote and story, and no doubt the anecdotes and stories were not all true." Finally, she seems, for all her satire-eliciting colorfulness, to have had Oscar's knack for ingratiation: "While one might occasionally smile at her, it is certain that everybody who knew her liked her well." These notable similarities—and several others—will require a further look, but the *Daily News* obituary can serve for the moment to suggest how strikingly alike were this mother and son.

The second impressive irony of Oscar's witticism is that this Gemini factor goes a considerable way toward explaining the "tragedy" he was eventually to suffer. He was much later to attribute his fall to "the nemesis of character," and much of this character seems to have been formed under the influence and example of Speranza. Indeed, the cliché of the mama's boy who grows up in a household with a strong-willed mother and an aloof, distant, often-absent father who has adopted a "useful profession" and whose son then issues a homosexual is splendidly ratified in the case of the Wildes.

Not a single show of affection by Oscar for his father survives. The one extant letter to Sir William, written at age nineteen, bears no salutation and is oddly signed, "Oscar O'F. W. Wilde." In a letter to Speranza from the same time, Oscar even refers to his father as "Sir William." And Sir William—an inveterate philanderer both before and after his marriage to Lady Wilde—was "away" from the family in an adulterous sense as well. In 1864, when Oscar was eight, his father was the focus of a lawsuit involving the charge of raping a patient under chloroform, which he lost to the tune of £2,000 in costs. Speranza, who had responded vehemently to the woman's charges, was sued by her for libel, and was the actual defendant. Coming to the "defense" of her husband, it seems clear, had more to do with her high self-regard and a taste for public posturing than with wifely loyalty. She was by nature given to such quixotic, heroic postures, and eventually came to accept her marriage as one of convenience. She—like Oscar—was an essentially self-delighting, if not precisely selfish, creature: Lord Goring's observation, "To love oneself is the beginning of a life-long romance," applied to both of them. Speranza was thus not about to let mere spousal treachery spoil her life. Her equanimity in the face of arrant extramarital betrayal for appearance's sake may well have encouraged Oscar to expect the same of his own wife later. Algy's pronouncement in *Earnest* that "in married life three is company and two is none" certainly applies to the mother and son's working theory of family values.

Sir William died in 1876 when Oscar was twenty-two. He was, by several accounts, an odd bird. The future dean of *Punch* cartoonists, Harry Furniss, met the Wildes in what he called their "large pretentious house" in Merrion Square, Dublin, and his verbal sketch is wicked: Sir William "resembled a monkey, a miserable-looking little creature, who, apparently unshorn and unkempt, looked as if he had been rolling in the dust." The Wildes must have made an odd couple indeed, for Furniss remembered Speranza as "a very tall and stoutishly inclined woman, with the appearance and air of a tragedy queen of the Mrs Crummles type. She might have walked out of the pages of *Nicholas Nickleby*." Furniss's two drawings certainly bear out his tart perceptions.

Oscar Wilde's Dantesque laureate mother, "Speranza." Drawing by Harry Furniss.

In any event, Sir William figures in Oscar's story just about as Lord Goring suggests in the epigraph a father should. Not much is seen or heard of him, and the same can be said of father figures among Oscar's *dramatis personae*. The entire lack of a proper one seems to have done wonders for Jack Worthing's self-esteem in *Earnest*. When fathers do appear briefly, it is as prime butts for comedy. Lord Goring's father, the Earl of Caversham, K.G., is a fine comprimario sketch of bluff British dullardry, "demming" this and "demming" that and especially "demming" his "good-for-nothing" son's "idle life." He trumpets the three banes of Oscar's real-life and fictional worlds: "high character, high moral tone, high principles." Cecil Graham's father, in *Lady Windermere's Fan,* must be of the same ilk, for he insists on talking morality after dinner. Says Cecil, "I told him he was old enough to know better. But my experience is that as soon as people are old enough to know better, they don't know anything at all."

☆   ☆   ☆

AH, BUT MOTHERS ARE darlings. And few come as quaintly colorful as flamboyant, eagle-beaked Speranza, who played at life as Algy says he plays the

Sir William and Lady Wilde. Drawing by Harry Furniss.

piano: "I don't play accurately—anyone can play accurately—but I play with wonderful expression." She preferred to think herself descended from Dante rather than Irish country ecclesiastics. Hence her name and her motto, *Fidanza, Speranza, Costanza* (happily for Oscar's future wife, she did not take this last word as her *nome di guerra*). Hence also her frequent salutations in letters to Oscar such as "Figlio mio caro" and "La Madre." She fudged her age downward—at one point making her father die in Bangalore two years before her birth—and went along with the same little habit of vanity when Oscar indulged it in later years. (The prosecutor at his trial, we'll see, was not so obliging.)

Also like her son, she favored scarlet . . . and her books were even read, though not always with pleasure. Of the three-decker novel she translated "extremely well" from the German, *The First Temptation*, the *Athenaeum* reviewer reported, "All the characters go more or less mad, and the reader will find himself inclined to follow their example." *The Cambridge History of English Literature* remembered her only as the author of "remarkable rhetorical verses upon the Irish potato famine," and one of her biographers, Horace Wyndham, implies that her wonderful passion tended to subvert accuracy in her work, speaking of her "verbose and turgid style" and an "undisciplined tendency to over-statement." He also refers to the one truly notable difference between Speranza and Oscar: "A sense of humour would also have been helpful. This, however, was denied her."

Humor aside, the large and small ways mother and son mimicked each other are invariably striking and suggestive. Their gregarious carelessness is apparent even in their handwriting: Speranza's is if anything more sprawling, more nearly illegible—and yet at the same time more authoritative-looking—than Oscar's. Both struck many observers as rather anachronistic in spirit. There was something nostalgically romantic, even Ossianic about Speranza's spirit. In fact, she chose Fingal as one of her son's names because it was "grand, misty, and Ossianic." I am convinced that Oscar praised the style of the novelist Ouida, about which he clearly felt some reservations, because she was so much in the style of his mother. Ouida, he said, "tries to make passion, imagination, and poetry part of fiction. She still believes in heroes and in heroines. She is florid and fervent and fanciful." A better thumbnail sketch of Speranza is hard to imagine. Oscar's appearance, too, struck many as well behind its time. Vincent O'Sullivan spoke about his face as "of the heavy type—rather an eighteenth-century face," and Oscar struck Le Gallienne as a "sort of caricature Dionysus disguised as a rather heavy dandy of the Regency period." Ada Leverson whimsically pictured him as "a Roman emperor who should have lived at the Pavilion at Brighton with George IV." Both mother and son, by the way, developed in their later years a belief in the exertions of palmists, astrologists, and the like.

Their most obvious and important shared trait was simply a fearlessness in the assertion of personality. Speranza aimed for grandeur in her prose and poetry: "I express the soul of a great nation," she exulted in 1864 while in one of her Volumnia moods. "Nothing less would satisfy me, who am the acknowledged voice in poetry of all the people of Ireland." And the same attitude caused her to paint her social presence in large brushstrokes as well, as Yeats found when he visited her modest flat in Chelsea. She announced to him, "I want to live on some high place, Primrose Hill or Highgate, because I was an eagle in my youth." Yeats, like many, seemed more charmed and bemused than annoyed, and so put her keen vanity in the kindest possible light, saying she "longed always perhaps, though certainly amid much self-mockery, for some impossible splendour of character and circumstance."

To her most recent biographer, though, Speranza was a woman who "never had her eyes off herself" and "queened it always." And she queened it long, as well. The obituarist tells us she "carried her height well" into old age, until bad health finally collapsed "her former erectness of bearing." Even then, in her dingy eight-by-eight-foot drawing room with its low light to flatter her features and dowdy maid serving tea badly, she could still impress the Comtesse de Brémont by how she "made her surroundings subservient to her personality" and amaze the visiting American novelist Gertrude Atherton with her massive and by no means meretricious dignity: "She might have been a queen graciously giving a private audience."

Oscar also queened it and ran the same risks as Speranza: the risk that one would be mistaken—or, indeed, *rightly* taken—for a snob and the risk that laughter *with* one would turn into laughter *at* one. If one's eyes are determinedly fixed upon oneself, of course, the chances are smaller that defections in one's audience will be noticed. This sort of blindness born of vanity certainly extended Speranza's social career well beyond its normal life span.

This same obliviousness induced by self-regard, I believe, encouraged Oscar to extend his own much more risky "social career" in the few years leading up to the winter of his discontent in 1895.

But mere eccentricity of deportment and bizarre costumes and jewelry could not have made this grande dame, as Atherton put it, "one of the London curios." A vivid Bohemianism of spirit was also necessary, and here we can see most distinctly the shadow of Speranza's son. She scrupled not at all over many proprieties, political or social. She expressed in impassioned though far from deathless verse the "romantic passion of 1848 in Ireland," and was splendidly blithe on more mundane occasions. When her Merrion Square house was temporarily seized by bailiffs for debt, she, quite unruffled, was to be found "lying on the sofa reading *Prometheus Vinctus* by Aeschylus, from which she began to declaim passages . . . with exalted enthusiasm." As in the trial over her husband's alleged rape, she—like Oscar's future Lord Illingworth—was not shy about taking the sinner's side. When Oscar arrived back at Oxford a month late from a trip to Greece, he lost his fellowship and was sent home. Any ordinary mother would have chidden her son; Speranza, instead, was furious at the stodgy old dons who had rusticated him. When she got wind of the title Oscar contemplated for his first London play—*A Good Woman*—her reaction was quintessentially Oscarian: "I don't like it. It is mawkish. No one cares for a good woman." Another anecdote reminds us perfectly of her son the contrarian. On being asked to receive a young woman said to be "respectable," she replied: "You must never employ that description in this house. Only tradespeople are 'respectable.'"

The would-be eagle of Highgate, like her aquiline son, flew particularly high above respectability on the subject of marriage. Oscar's satirical views on the institution must have been shaped to some degree by his mother, who certainly had reason to view it cynically. Her remark that "in the fatal intimacy of daily life illusions soon vanish" was, in fact, to be borne out by Oscar's own experience with Constance. And her prescription for happiness before the Hearth seems precisely what Oscar had imagined his marriage would be: "The best chance . . . of domestic felicity is when all the family are Bohemian, and all clever, and all enjoy thoroughly the erratic, impulsive, reckless life of work and joy." This is a fancifully unorthodox ideal, and, as we shall see, Constance proved particularly unsuited in intellect or personal style to rise to the challenge of it. Marriage was well enough for the general rule, but Speranza considered herself, and certainly her younger son, exceptional. Was marriage suitable for humanity's eagles? Her conclusion was vouchsafed in an essay on "Genius and Marriage": "Let all genius remain unwed."

Nevertheless, Speranza professed great pleasure in Oscar's announcement of his engagement to Constance Mary Lloyd, and some affectionate correspondence between the two took place ("My dear, darling Constance . . ."). There is extreme disagreement as to whether Constance and Speranza truly "got on." One of Speranza's biographers has said they were "very companionable . . . visited each other . . . and generally kept each other company." H. M. Hyde, though, has asserted that, "as Lady Wilde never went to Tite Street and Constance never visited her in Oakley Street, it may be concluded that the mother and daughter-in-law were not particularly drawn towards each other." Both women were sufficiently keen on polite social decorum to have made a pretense of civility, but clearly they possessed vastly different personalities.

The Comtesse de Brémont called Constance "a thoroughly womanly woman," and she does appear to have been a perfect example, one might say, of the woman who grows up to be like her mother. As an exemplar of the "general rule" she was much admired. Speranza, on the other hand, was an extrovert show-off, a "behaver." She was also rather more at home in the manly world of letters and politics, even as she wrote vigorously on the behalf of women. Her protofeminist essay "The Bondage of Woman," in particular, is an eloquent and wholly admirable performance. Its first sentence: "For six thousand years the history of woman has been a mournful record of helpless resignation to social prejudice and legal tyranny." In subsequent pages she ridiculed "this *Dalai*

Lama religion" of husband-worship, raged that "female education at present is mere dilettante-ism" ("female professorships might be founded"), and asked the marvelous question, "Why not vice-queens as well as queens?" And she admired the typical American woman for having the qualities she obviously believed she herself possessed. The American "revolts against social usages that would limit her bold originality and assertive self-manifestation. She is proud, conscious, strong-souled and self-reliant."

Speranza's feminism, though, was of a peculiarly romantic and self-vaunting kind. While she admired the "latter-half-nineteenth-century woman" as a "fine, high-spirited creature," she thought that romantic style was wanting in her: "Life used to be a temple where woman was priestess, or a court where woman was queen. . . . Now life is a school board, where woman takes the chair." Speranza preferred to hear and write about the "clank" of women's "fetters" through history, as if she were the heroine in a rescue opera. She believed "the age of splendour"—*her* fiery days of 1848, of course—"had passed" and that a "dreadful uniformity of homeliness and utility pervades all classes." Unfortunately, she was in all this criticizing the kind of diligent, hardworking, unprepossessing feminist activism that Constance herself was to dedicate much of her free time to.*

This attitudinizing urged her to cultivate a kind of female misogyny, which her son would in time hone into one of his principal satiric themes. "As a rule, I cannot stand girls or women," said she, "they are so flimsy, frivolous, and feeble of purpose—they so seldom achieve anything." Oscar betrayed a similarly schizophrenic attitude toward women, editing *Woman's World* with often remarkably forward-thinking concerns, for instance, while reaping laughter on the stage (and in his letters) with occasionally arrant sexism.

As between the "Hope" of his mother and the "Constancy"

---

* Still, who could fail to be charmed by a woman who wrote so agreeably of George Eliot's "fatal tendency to the insufferably prosey" and of her chief work, "*Middlemarch* especially exhausts our patience by page after page of pretentious commonplace; and probably no amount of bribery would induce anyone to read it through a second time."

of his wife, where did Oscar's heart finally lie? Perhaps there is a clue in their different responses to the publication of *Dorian Gray*. Constance observed that "since Oscar wrote *Dorian Gray*, no one will speak to us." Speranza called it "the most wonderful piece of writing in all the fiction of the day. . . . I nearly fainted at the last scene."

An obvious suggestion of Oscar's spiritual kinship with his mother is also revealed in the two women's highly divergent views about dress. Constance became a dedicated partisan for functional, simple, and rational dress—became, in fact, prominent in the Rational Dress Society. It was a characteristically sensible and down-to-earth endeavor. Speranza was concerned about so-called "rational" dress, too, but entirely in the Oscarian sense of allowing maximum freedom to assert one's (very vivid) personality. Here is her sketch of the proper attire for a woman writer:

> Literary dress should, in fact, be free, untrammelled and unswathed. . . . No stiff corselet should depress the full impulses of a passionate heart. There should be no false coils upon the head to weigh upon the brain, no fuzzy furze bush on the brow to heat the temples and mar the cool logic of some grand, deep thought. And the fewer frills, cuffs and cascades of lace the better, for inkspots do not improve Venetian point, and in moments of divine fury [!] or feverish excitement the authoress is often prone to overturn her ink-bottle.

In a different essay, Speranza brought her sartorial and moral philosophies together in a thoroughly Oscarian way:

> A woman . . . should first study her own personality, and consider well what she means to be, desires to be, and can be—either a superb Juno, or a seductive Aphrodite, or a Hebe, blooming and coquette, or a Pallas Athene, grand, majestic and awe-inspiring. And, when the style is discovered that best suits her . . . let her

keep to it as the symbol of her higher self, unchanged
by the frivolous mutations of fashion. For dress thus at-
tains a moral significance.

This exudes a buoyant self-vaunting gusto, a romantic apprehension, that were clearly passed on to her son. It could be called the
utterance of a woman whose head always seemed (in her biographer's phrase) "securely fixed in the clouds," yet there is in it the
same insistence upon self-definition that we have already seen in
the pronouncements of her son the *arbiter elegantiarum* . . . and
that we will see in her son the Philosopher.

"OSCAR REVERED HIS MOTHER," concluded Terence White, and his
letters certainly convey that impression. To a friend whose
mother was seriously ill, he wrote consolingly, "All poets love
their mothers, and as I worship mine I can understand how you
feel." He obligingly ornamented her Chelsea salon from time to
time, and when he reviewed a Yeats volume on Irish folklore in
Woman's World, he gallantly quoted Yeats's little bouquet for
Speranza: "The best book since Croker is Lady Wilde's *Ancient
Legends.* The humour has all given way to pathos and tenderness.
We have here the innermost heart of the Celt." He also published
in his magazine her essay on "Irish Peasant Tales" and a long
blank-verse paean to women whose "strong, splendid souls . . .
chafed at human wrong."

It was an indication of his deep affection for his mother that
Constance felt it necessary to travel from Italy specially to break
the news of her death to Oscar in Reading Prison. A few months
later, in a petition to the Home Secretary for early release, he
spoke of himself in the third person: "The despair and misery of
this lonely and wretched life [has] been intensified beyond words
by the death of his mother, Lady Wilde, to whom he was deeply
attached." The rhetoric was turned up considerably in *De profun-*

dis in order to excruciate Bosie for his callousness in not condoling Oscar at the time of Speranza's death:

> You knew, none better, how deeply I loved and honoured her. Her death was so terrible to me that I, once a lord of language, have no words in which to express my anguish and shame. Never, even in the most perfect days of my development as an artist, could I have had words fit to bear so august a burden, or to move with sufficient stateliness of music through the purple pageant of my incommunicable woe. She and my father had bequeathed me a name they had made noble and honoured not merely in Literature, Art, Archaeology and Science, but in the public history of my own country. . . . I had disgraced that name eternally. I had made it a low byword among low people. I had dragged it through the very mire.

Further on, he wrote of Speranza ranking "intellectually . . . with Elizabeth Barrett Browning" and (thinking of her fiery Young Ireland exploits) "historically" with the French Revolutionary heroine Madame Rolland. Finally, after release from prison, he wrote to an Irish Member of Parliament who was questioning the treatment of prisoners in Reading and expressed in passing his regret for a life "of senseless pleasure and hard materialism and a mode of existence unworthy of an artist, and still more unworthy of my mother's son."

One would like to take all of this protestation at face value, and perhaps one should. But it may be that he was too good and polite a son ever to utter less than totally admiring thoughts about Speranza in conversation or letters. Could he, sitting in prison, have thought that her utterly forbidding him to flee England and avoid trial derived more from her invincible *amour-propre*—"Woman is no coward fronting fate," she had clarioned in "Heroic Women"—than from concern for his own welfare? Would he have been angered if he could have overheard Speranza

hoping that "prison would do him good"? Could he have harbored resentment, recognizing, as he must have done, that so
much in her character contributed to the formation of his own
. . . and encouraged him to risk the disaster that befell him?
Could this be why, three months after his conviction, Speranza
wrote plaintively to Ernest Leverson, "I thought that Oscar might
perhaps write to me . . . but I have not had a line from him"?
Questions impossible to answer.

And yet . . . there is a remarkable scene in *A Woman of No
Importance* that tempts one to answer these tantalizing questions
yes. This scene may also shed some light on Oscar's feelings about
this woman of doubtless the greatest importance in his life. This
is the interview in Act Three between Lord Illingworth and Gerald Arbuthnot, who has been raised entirely by his mother. Unknown to Gerald, Lord Illingworth—the play's Oscarian
character—is his father.

> LORD ILLINGWORTH: You have missed not having a fa-
>   ther, I suppose, Gerald?
> GERALD: Oh, no; my mother has been good to me. No
>   one ever had such a mother as I have had.
> LORD ILLINGWORTH: I am quite sure of that. Still I
>   should imagine that most mothers don't quite un-
>   derstand their sons. Don't realise, I mean, that a
>   son has ambitions, a desire to see life, to make
>   himself a name. After all, Gerald, you couldn't be
>   expected to pass all your life in such a hole as [his
>   house in] Wrockley, could you?
> GERALD: Oh, no! It would be dreadful!
> LORD ILLINGWORTH: A mother's love is very touching,
>   of course, but it is often curiously selfish. I mean,
>   there is a good deal of selfishness in it.
> GERALD: (*slowly*) I suppose there is.

Slowly, indeed. This passage makes one wonder how much personal feeling might lurk in another snippet of dialogue Oscar

once jotted down but never used: "She looks on me as a son—women of that sort are extremely dangerous."

Ten days after Oscar was released from prison and crossed the Channel, his friends finally departed and he was alone for the first time. The next day he wrote a poignant letter to Robbie Ross in London that perhaps sheds further light on the subterranean tensions of his relationship with Speranza. He told of "moods of rage passing over my nature, like gusts of bitter wind," of visiting a chapel near Berneval-sur-Mer that was filled with "the most fantastic saints, so ugly and so Gothic." Then he told of falling asleep on the warm coarse sea-grass near the beach: "My dream was that my mother was speaking to me with some sternness, and that she was in trouble." Was it simply, as Oscar in fact thought, because she would have disapproved of the possible reunion with Bosie he was then agonizing over? Or was it something more profound: the tarnished family name he had mentioned before, or a genuine sense of guilt at the life of "senseless pleasure" he had allowed to be his ruin, or his spectacular failure to measure up to her romantic notion, as Yeats said, of a life "of impossible splendour of character and circumstance"?

The respective ends of Speranza and Oscar—inevitably for those who fancy themselves eagles—were rich in pathos. Though he was only something over half her age, they both had reason to feel they had lived well beyond their day. "She belonged to a time," said Speranza's obituary, "which had long since passed out of the range of living realities." Her mood became almost permanently retrospective. She "revered in age the dreams of her youth, as Schiller's line says every one ought to do." Oscar's time, too, had passed with spectacular fleetness beyond the "range of living realities." He, too, in his last three years, was obliged to live his life, as he put it in his last year, "in echoes." Even the memories they left behind were of a similar bittersweet kind. What Henriette Corkran remembered of Speranza applies perfectly to her *caro figlio*: "Her talk was like fireworks—brilliant, whimsical, flashy. She was most inconsistent, and in many ways foolish. But in great adversity she was brave, indeed heroic."

Bittersweet, too, is a poem of Speranza's called "Death Wishes," which was included in her 1864 volume of poems (dedicated, incidentally, "To my sons Willie and Oscar Wilde"). Its last stanza displays Speranza's usual romantic gesturing but also, it must be said, captures the flavor of the last years of both mother and son:

> *Thou wilt pass, but not till thy beauty is withered,*
> *Not till thy powers and hopes lie shivered:*
> *Silence and beauty are Nature's death-token;*
> *But the poor human heart, ere it die—must be broken!*

Speranza, by most accounts, was a woman of great, if sometimes foolish, heart. Did Oscar perhaps have her in mind when he had Lady Hunstanton say of mothers, "We are all heart, all heart"? Oscar, in his own miserable decline, chose not to pen such artful death wishes as she: his took the more palpable forms of cigarettes, champagne, absinthe, and young panthers. Yet he was like his mother in being great and foolish of heart. Though, as he admitted many times in prison and after, he discovered too late the fact that he had one. How like Mrs Erlynne, in *Lady Windermere's Fan*, Oscar was. She ruefully observes, "I thought I had no heart. I find I have, and a heart doesn't suit me. . . . Somehow it doesn't go with modern dress. It makes one look old. . . . And it spoils one's career at critical moments."

Yeats said that Speranza's "son lived with no self-mockery at all an imaginary life," and the same could be said of her. And one can also say the world is very apt to break the hearts of such people.

Chapter Six

A WIFE'S TRAGEDY

Leading a double life is the only preparation for marriage.
—UNPUBLISHED APHORISM

The Cloister or the Café—there is my future. I tried the Hearth, but it was a failure.
—LETTER TO ROBERT ROSS, 1900

PERHAPS THE MOST INTRIGUING item in the preeminent Wilde collection at the Clark Library in Los Angeles is a sheaf of twenty-eight leaves of foolscap filled with Oscar's rough draft for a play he never finished. Among the scraps of dialogue are some doodles, including a few fine "Greek" profiles. Perhaps they capture one of the young men he liked to have about him to inspire his theatrical muse. Could it have been Charlie Parker, a boy Oscar met in 1893, who was to be a damaging witness at his trials two years later? For the servant in this play (as in *Lady Windermere's Fan*) is named Parker. The play concerns the most unhappy marriage of a Mr and Mrs Lovel. An exotic comtesse and the inev-

97

itable Oscarian "lord"—Lord Mertoun—also figure in the cast. As do *A Woman of No Importance, An Ideal Husband,* and *The Importance of Being Earnest,* this play also bears a title that resonates with appalling irony in the light of what we know about the marriage of Oscar Wilde and Constance Mary Lloyd: *A Wife's Tragedy.* Among the possessions auctioned at the sheriff's sale while Oscar was in prison, reported *The Morning* on 25 April, was the manuscript of a "yet unproduced play." Perhaps this was *A Wife's Tragedy.*

Certain snippets of dialogue reflect, with almost neon portent, on Oscar's own spousal attitudes. Mrs Lovel is described (as Constance often was) as having "a noble nature" and being able to "suffer." Mr Lovel, who is, like Oscar, a poet, assumes Oscar's usual pose of anti-Respectability bonhomie and asserts:

"Of course I love my wife."
"You don't show it."
"It's very vulgar to show one's love for one's wife."

A separation finally comes, with Mrs Lovel feeling she is no longer "made of iron and of steel" and saying she is bitterly sorry that her husband has "starved me of love . . . never called me one sweet name" and has "withered whatever youth and joy I had." Lord Mertoun (like many who observed the Wilde marriage?) says to Mr Lovel, "I just don't understand what place your wife has in your life."

This was by no means the only time the real-life "plot" of Oscar's marriage emerged eerily in his writings . . . and not merely between the lines but *in* them. In February 1889, he had occasion to review a novel called *Faithful and Unfaithful* by Margaret Lee in *Woman's World.* Could he have described its plot without some shock of self-recognition? For in it "a very noble and graciously Puritanic" young woman marries a man who cannot bear the weight of so good a wife. "Her husband cannot live in the high rarefied atmosphere of idealism with which she surrounds him; her firm and fearless faith in him becomes a factor in his degradation." Something like this discomfort must have been at play behind Oscar's frequent jests at the expense of good wives and marital self-sacrifice. He quoted with approval a climactic speech that Lee's husband makes "in a finely conceived scene at the end of the book":

"You are too good for me. We have not an idea, an inclination, or a passion in common. I'm sick and tired of seeming to live up to a standard that is entirely beyond my reach and my desire. We make each other miserable! I can't pull you down,

Constance Mary Lloyd at twenty-five, the year before she married Oscar Wilde. Photograph from the Clark Library, Los Angeles.

and for ten years you have been exhausting yourself in vain efforts to raise me to your level. The thing must end!"

One wonders very much if such a speech was ever uttered by Oscar to Constance in the privacy of Tite Street as—five years later in 1894 (and about ten years after the wedding)—his marital status became more and more untenable to him. This speech would have suited the situation precisely.

A few months later, in May 1889, Oscar reviewed Ouida's novel *Guilderoy* for the *Pall Mall Gazette*. Ouida's plot included an element of adultery curiously pertinent to life in Tite Street. Ouida's hero Guilderoy marries "a provincial little Artemis" with "a Gainsborough face, with wide-opened questioning eyes and tumbled auburn hair." (Oscar had bragged to Lillie Langtry six years before that his fiancée was a "violet-eyed little Artemis, with great coils of heavy brown hair which make her flower-like head droop like a blossom.") But Guilderoy soon tires of "her shyness, her lack of power to express herself, her want of knowledge of fashionable life," and so returns to his "old passion for a wonderful creature called the Duchess of Soria." In his typical contrary spirit, Oscar admired the heartless husband's character most of all: "He is thoroughly weak, thoroughly worthless, and the most fascinating person in the whole story." Not for the first or last time, there was an element of narcissistic self-congratulation in this reaction: he was probably already beginning to behave like Guilderoy in his own marriage. In fact, the fate of Ouida's hero, as he described it, was to be his own: "At the end of the book Guilderoy is a pitiable object."

There is more than a whiff of the wayward husbands of the Lee and Ouida novels in a most astonishing scenario for a play that Oscar concocted while he was on vacation with his family at a cottage called "The Haven" at Worthing in that last mad summer of freedom in 1894. A "haven" indeed: he and his wife, the two boys, and a "horrid ugly Swiss governess" cramped in close quarters, with Bosie much in evidence to mitigate the domestic tedium. Oscar wrote to George Alexander, the actor-manager who was to produce *Earnest*, which he was just then completing:

> What do you think of this for a play for you? A man of rank and fashion marries a simple sweet country girl—a lady—but simple and ignorant of fashionable life. They live at his country place and after a time he gets bored with her, and invites down a lot of fashionable *fin-de-siècle* women and men. The play opens by his lecturing his wife on how to behave—not to be prudish, etc— and not to mind if anyone flirts with her.

Later the husband himself flirts, then indulges in a love scene that is interrupted by his wife. She soon leaves with a former admirer, also a guest at the party, and becomes his lover (and also pregnant by him). She refuses with disgust the notion that she should return and forgive her husband: "All this self-sacrifice is wrong, we are meant to live. That is the meaning of life." The play ends with the husband's suicide and the adulterous couple "clinging to each other as if with a mad desire to make love eternal."

Oscar was pleased with his handiwork: "I think it extremely strong. *I want the sheer passion of love to dominate everything.* No morbid self-sacrifice. No renunciation. A sheer flame of love between a man and a woman." Invented by a husband who was becoming ever more reckless in his passions, the subtext here is unambiguous: the wife of the scenario was acting out Oscar's own fantasy of escape from the marital yoke. As he was already doing in real life, the wife throws off the yoke in the name of a higher and more intense "passion." The "flame of love" burned, instead, between one man and another. Oscar would cling to Bosie (or someone) with "mad desire."

WHAT, THEN, WAS THE place Constance occupied in Oscar's life? And why, after a few apparently happy years, did their marriage decline inexorably into pain, misery, and cruelty . . . whether inflicted intentionally or not? Toward the end of Oscar's life, an acquaintance versed in palmistry pointed to the line of marriage in his hand, and he replied, "That, too, was a fatality." Why a fatality? Speculating about answers to these questions is more unpleasant than difficult; many plausible explanations for the sad demise leap immediately to view. Some take us back to the very beginning of their courtship.

The first meeting between Constance and Oscar appears to have taken place at the Wilde family's Dublin house in Merrion Square in May of 1881. Lady Wilde gave a party for Willie and Oscar, and Constance was invited (relatives of hers also lived in Merrion Square). Oscar—with his *Poems* just published and already famous enough to be satirized in two plays and the operetta

Patience—seems to have played the literary lion well. Constance was charmed, and an acquaintance was struck. On 7 June she wrote to her brother, Otho, "O.W. came yesterday [to an aunt's London house] and stayed for half an hour, begged me to come and see his mother again soon." And she added, "I can't help liking him, because when he's talking to me alone he's never a bit affected, and speaks naturally, except that he uses better language than most people do." In the next months they saw each other frequently. At this time, it is worth noting, Oscar was sharing digs near the Strand with a homosexual Oxford classmate, Frank Miles. When the *Poems* appeared Frank's father, Canon Miles, objected to what he perceived as their immoral tendencies, and Oscar was forced to move out. Constance appears not to have found the poetry objectionable, however, and they remained friendly for several months, until Oscar departed on 14 December 1881 for his yearlong American lecture tour.

After returning a financially secure and even more famous man and sojourning a few months in Paris, Oscar began lecturing around the British Isles. The occasion for the crucial reunion was a lecture on "The House Beautiful" in Dublin on 22 November 1883. In a few days' time, the courtship flared up and blazed in sudden glory. Oscar visited Constance for tea afterward, and the next day she attended a lecture on his impressions of America. She reported to her brother on the twenty-fourth that this lecture was not "as interesting as the former one"—though it did contain one of Oscar's earliest and most famous gibes at married life: "I was disappointed with Niagara. . . . Every American bride is taken there, and the sight of the stupendous waterfall must be one of the earliest, if not the keenest, disappointments in American married life." But she added that Oscar was "so improved in appearance, and he is certainly very pleasant."

Two days later Constance wrote, "My dearest Otho, Prepare yourself for an astounding piece of news! I am engaged to Oscar Wilde and perfectly and insanely happy." Oscar, for his part, showed himself ecstatic in his few letters from this time: "*Her* name is Constance and she is quite young, very grave, and mystical, with wonderful eyes, and dark brown coils of hair: quite perfect except that she does not think Jimmy [Whistler] the only painter that ever really existed." There is a line in the *Wife's Tragedy* manuscript that perhaps sets this whirlwind romance in perspective. At one point the early career of the heartless husband is described: "At Oxford he always declared he hated women—so of course he fell in love with the first girl that was civil to him." Though Oscar had one previous heartthrob (Florence Balcombe, who in 1878 married Bram Stoker, the author of *Dracula*), it does seem that he reveled in the generally misogynist university atmosphere that was typical of the time. And, like Mr Lovel, he certainly fell under the marital yoke with astonishing alacrity.

The engagement lasted exactly six months. It is doubtful Lady Bracknell would have approved of the term: "I am not in favour of long engagements," says she. "They give people the opportunity of finding out each other's character before marriage, which I think is never advisable." There are some hints that the six months were mildly revealing: Oscar's twice describing her as "grave" is full of portent. Still, it is unlikely that their marriage day was sullied by significant insight into each other's character. One can guess as much from Oscar's response when Louise Jopling asked him why he came to fall in love. He replied, wittily and cryptically, "She scarcely ever speaks. I am always wondering what her thoughts are like."

The much-publicized wedding took place in London on 29 May 1884. The bride wore a "rich creamy satin dress . . . of a delicate cowslip tint; the bodice, cut square and somewhat low in front, was finished with a high Medici collar [Oscar's choice]; the ample sleeves were puffed; the skirt . . . gathered by a silver girdle of beautiful workmanship, the gift of Mr Oscar Wilde." The bridegroom, according to the *Irish Times*, "looked less like George IV than usual . . . though his hair was fully curled." Whistler could not attend and sent a jaunty telegram: "Fear I may not be able to reach you in time for the ceremony— Don't wait."

After honeymooning in France, the couple settled in what was to be the sole family house, at 16 (now 34) Tite Street, Chelsea. Spirits were then very high. Aside from a few short notes, the only surviving published letter from Oscar to Constance (from Edinburgh in December 1884) is a loving if rather formula-romantic one: "Dear and Beloved, Here am I, and you at the Antipodes. O execrable facts, that keep our lips from kissing, though our souls are one." In the visitors' autograph book kept in Tite Street, Oscar inscribed a gallant poem "To My Wife, with a Copy of my Poems." Its first quatrain runs

> *I can write no stately proem*
> *As a prelude to my lay;*
> *From a poet to a poem*
> *I would dare say.*

The Wildes became a highly visible social couple: Burne-Jones, Sargent, Bernhardt, Langtry, Terry, Beerbohm Tree, Swinburne, Browning, and Ruskin all visited in Tite Street. The Comtesse de Brémont was impressed and left a glowing memoir, but even it contains certain melancholy premonitions. Constance she described as having "a youthful, almost boyish [!] face with its clear colouring and full dark eyes." And—as with the decidedly unmerry wives of Lee, Ouida, and Oscar's Worthing scenario—Brémont noticed that Constance displayed "an air of shy self-consciousness and restraint . . . that gave the impression of what is called stage fright" when in fashionable society. She also noticed a "secret weariness and effort" in Constance's bearing as she attempted to cope with the glare of publicity that Oscar so avidly courted.

Still, on the surface all seemed well. A year after the wedding, the first son, Cyril, was born; sixteen months later Vyvyan arrived. The charmingly outrageous jester had—like Benedick in *Much Ado About Nothing*—become, willy-nilly, a proper married man . . . and a family man, no less.

Oddly enough, in November 1885, Oscar happened to review for the *Pall Mall Gazette* a book titled *How to Be Happy Though Married,* by "A Graduate of the University of Matrimony." Oscar treated the book kindly, "in spite of its somewhat alarming title" (its author was really a Rev. E. J. Hardy). He ended up cheerfully recommending it as "a complete handbook to an earthly Paradise. . . . Its author may be regarded as the Murray of matrimony and the Baedeker of bliss." In the course of his review, Oscar observed, "In our day it is best for a man to be married." Unfortunately, the Rev. Hardy made several assertions that suggested Oscar was quite the wrong person to marry. He observed, "Like government, marriage must be a series of compromises," but Oscar was of a self-indulgent rather than a compromising nature. Hardy explained, "Satiety follows quickly upon the heels of possession," and this was to be spectacularly true of the highly restless Oscar, especially in his sexual escapades. Hardy also asserted, "A married pair should be all the world to each other." This was never to be: Oscar and Constance were too vastly different—she "grave," he boisterous and devil-may-care— for Hardy's pleasant notion to have survived for more than a few years.

And Oscar was a gay man. In England at the time it was also "best"—or at least prudent—for such men to assume a wife, though the good Reverend certainly did not address this arcane aspect of being "happy though married." The commonplace of a gay man marrying for society's sake may be the burden of the first line of an affectionate letter Oscar wrote to a male contemporary confirming the fact of his marriage: "Yes! my dear Waldino, yes! Amazing of course—that was necessary." It was *always* a necessity for Oscar to amaze, but perhaps he was here also acknowledging the social necessity of the marriage itself.

It was the common English procedure. Oscar was merely · doing what many gay men—John Addington Symonds, one of his Aesthetic elders, for instance—had done. Rather like Oscar, Symonds took "no part in school games," matriculated at Magdalen, and eventually married in his mid-twenties, fathering three daughters. With astonishing discretion, he timed his death for the day in 1893 when his quite candid appreciation of Walt Whitman was published.* One guesses there is something of the withering that the closeted married man can suffer in the *Dictionary of National Biography*'s description of Symonds as "one given up to morbid introspection, and disabled by physical and spiritual maladies."

Oscar did not go gentle into such closeted malaise as Symonds did . . . and also Walter Pater, who in his life "grew increasingly discreet" in his responses to "youthful male beauty." Oscar chose another strategy, one that was quite familiar to the preeminent early sexologist, Richard Krafft-Ebing, whose *Psychopathia Sexualis* had appeared in an English translation in 1893. This bolder strategy is remarkably paralleled in the sexual history of Krafft-Ebing's case number 112, which began at age thirteen and continued through several highly promiscuous pedophilic decades. Krafft-Ebing's informant estimated that he had sex with "at least six hundred" male partners and ended his sexual autobiography, "To this day, the sight of a youth of sixteen puts me into violent sexual excitement with painful erections." *And yet* . . . this man married and fathered four boys. His remark that "the boyish appearance of my wife was of effectual assistance" in achieving successful intercourse poignantly reminds us of the Comtesse de Brémont's remark about Constance's "almost boyish face."

In 1894, when Oscar's apparent urge to mimic the promiscuity of case number 112 grew increasingly reckless, Edward Carpenter was writing one of the very first apologias for the "intermediate sex." In this essay, "Homogenic Love" (published early in 1895), he based his discussion of gay men who marry and the difficulties they sometimes encounter on *Psychopathia Sexualis*:

> [Krafft-Ebing] goes on to say that many such men, notwithstanding their actual aversion to intercourse with the female, do ultimately marry—whether from ethical, as sometimes happens, or from social considerations.

* Symonds discusses the poet's "comradeship or . . . impassioned relation between man and man" very frankly for the time. There is even a long footnote about the young "baggage-master on the freight trains" who was "tenderly loved" by Whitman. Two years later, no publisher would have dared to print it.

But very remarkable—as illustrating the depth and tenacity of the homogenic instinct—and pathetic too, are the records that he gives of these cases; for in many of them a real friendship and regard between the married pair was still of no avail . . . to check the continual flow of affection to some third person of the same sex.

A few months later Carpenter would discover in London's newspapers that he was, unwittingly, writing here about the Wilde marriage.

How, then, did Oscar fare just after his marriage? Several years later, he accepted for publication in *Woman's World* an article titled "Being Married, and Afterwards." Its author asserts, "The first year of your married life is the first thing about which you must be very careful. The shadow of that year, if mismanaged, will darken all the rest." All the public signs of the Wildes' first year, we have seen, seemed auspicious. But a remarkable anecdote from this time has survived that suggests a shadow of some kind may have fallen on the marriage very early on. It was, admittedly, reported thirdhand by Ada Leverson in her memoir of Oscar and is impossible to verify. Still, it has the distinct ring of truth. "Oscar once told a friend," Ada remembered, "of a strange experience that he never forgot and later often thought of":

When first married, he was quite madly in love, and showed himself an unusually devoted husband. He never left his wife for an hour, and she adored him in return. A few months after their marriage, she went shopping, and Oscar accompanied her. He waited for her outside Swan and Edgar's while she made some long and tedious purchases.

As he stood there full of careless good spirits, on a cold sunny May morning, a curious, very young, but hard-eyed creature appeared, looked at him, gave a sort of laugh, and passed on. He felt, he said, "as if an icy hand had clutched his heart." He had a sudden presentiment. He saw a vision of folly, misery, and ruin.

A poignant and doomful moment for Oscar, one that throws a brilliant shaft of light on the next ten years of his life. The informant of Krafft-Ebing's case number 112 confessed, "I, who at the sight of the dirtiest ragamuffin had painful erections, could scarcely induce one with the most beautiful woman." Oscar's indelible memory of standing outside Swan and Edgar's suggests a sudden recognition that he was like case number 112: his innate sexual instincts were surfacing and could not be suppressed. The grotesque "creature" was *attractive* to him—had icily "clutched at his heart"—in spite of all the pressures on him to be more "respectable." And his presentiment was accurate: he would eventually follow his bliss, and this would lead him in the end to "folly, misery, and ruin."

THE MANSERVANT IN *EARNEST* observes, "In married households the champagne is rarely of a first-rate brand." The champagne in Tite Street could not have been first-rate, for finances were always very much of a tightness there. But there are several other explanations, aside from the main one, for why Oscar was to find marriage, as Algernon Moncrieff puts it, "so demoralising." One of them was offered by Oscar himself to Frank Harris, in rather brutal terms. It has to do with the spousal double standard that sometimes comes into play when a former object of desire is transformed by pregnancy into a mother:

> When I married, my wife was a beautiful girl, white and slim as a lily, with dancing eyes and gay rippling laughter like music. In a year or so the flower-like grace had all vanished; she became heavy, shapeless, deformed: she dragged herself about the house in uncouth misery with drawn blotched face and hideous body. . . . Oh, na-

ture is disgusting; it takes beauty and defiles it: it defaces the ivory-white body we have adored with the vile cicatrices of maternity.

Harris's detailed reconstruction of a conversation long past must, as usual, be taken with salt. An element of a gay man's rationalization for a desire to extricate himself from spousal duties may also be in play here. But one suspects there is a grain of truth in Oscar's revulsion. In any event, it appears that romance and sexual relations did not survive Constance's second pregnancy in 1886.

A more elaborate and compelling explanation, however, may lie in the huge discrepancies of their personalities. The giddily brief courtship produced a spectacular attraction of opposites, whose spell a six-month period of engagement did not break. Marriage is "a long conversation," Nietzsche wrote. "When marrying, one should ask oneself this question: Do you believe that you will be able to converse well with this woman into your old age? Everything else in marriage is transitory." In light of Nietzsche's prescription, Oscar's half-jest about marrying Constance because she never spoke takes on a melancholy truth. The disparity was obvious to most of their friends and acquaintances. Richard Le Gallienne visited the family in Tite Street and left a picture of Constance shared by most everyone who expressed a view of her:

> Mrs Wilde was a pretty young woman of the innocent Kate Greenaway type. They seemed very happy together, though it was impossible not to predict suffering for a woman so simple and domestic mated with a mind so searching and so perverse and a character so self-indulgent. It was hard to see where two such different natures could find a meeting-place, particularly as poor Mrs Wilde was entirely devoid of humour and evangelically religious. So sweet and pretty and good, how came she by her outrageously intellectual husband . . . ?

This was no recipe for the engaging and extended conversation Nietzsche had in mind.

One of the few extant letters from Constance to Oscar epitomizes vividly their different natures. Oscar's first play, *Vera*, had just failed at its New York City premiere, and he gave a privately printed copy of it to Constance for her reaction. She wrote to him from Dublin, just two weeks before he asked for her hand. If he had been attentive, he might have gleaned a first hint that failure before *her* hearth might be inevitable. She consoled him for the audience's unsympathetic response to his political views: "The world is surely unjust and bitter to most of us; I think we must either renounce our opinions and run with the general stream or else totally ignore the world and go on our own regardless of all." Oscar's instinct, we have seen, was for the latter course. Constance characteristically chose the safer, more conservative path: "There is not the slightest use in *fighting* against existing prejudices, for we are always worsted in the struggle." Then she added, "I am afraid you and I disagree in our opinions on art, for I hold that there is no perfect art without perfect morality." This to the man who, six years later, would write: "The fact of a man being a poisoner is nothing against his prose. The domestic virtues are not the true basis of art." Nor were domestic virtues the basis of Oscar's performance as a husband.

The willingness to "run with the general stream," the forthright simplicity, the, well, earnestness Constance displayed in her letter reflected her character and were to define her years as a housewife. Like the miserable husband in Lee's novel *Faithful and Unfaithful*, Oscar must have become increasingly uncomfortable, doomed as he was to the company of a spouse so ideal in all the conventionally respectable ways. Mr Lovel's remark about his wife in *A Wife's Tragedy* is thus particularly poignant: "Her life is self-contained, rounded off—she is so satisfied." The Comtesse Soria refers to Mrs Lovel as "that pale Octavia," and that noble, poised, selfless Shakespearean spouse is precisely what Constance became. Oscar began looking for his fatal Cleopatra in all the exotic "Alexandrian" venues of London's homosexual underground.

Throughout his writings are scattered shameless allusions to spousal discomfort. Lord Henry in *Dorian Gray* observes, "I am not a champion of marriage. The real drawback to marriage is that it makes one unselfish. And unselfish people are colourless. They lack individuality." Constance became an adoring wife, self-sacrificing mother, and gracious hostess of Oscar's "house beautiful." An interview and tour of the Tite Street house, "Mrs Oscar Wilde at Home," appeared late in 1894 in *To-day* magazine and shows her reveling charmingly in these roles. But Oscar, taking Lord Henry's view, may well have registered all this with regret or boredom . . . or both. Serious conversation between husband and wife must have dwindled, with Constance eventually becoming like Lord Henry's wife: "I always hear Harry's views from his friends. It is the only way I get to know of them."

In his 1893 play, *A Woman of No Importance*, droll Mrs Allonby is asked her view of the ideal husband: "The Ideal Husband? There couldn't be such a thing. The institution is wrong." On the ideal *man*, however, she elaborates: "He should encourage us to have caprices, and forbid us to have missions." But, again like the husband in Lee's novel, Oscar clearly failed to pull Constance down to the level of his caprices; she instead became devoted to several philanthropic missions. She became a protégée of the Dowager Baroness Sandhurst, a pillar of British church work, and was a leader in the Rational Dress Society, also the first editor of its *Gazette*. She belonged to the Chelsea Women's Liberal Association and was particularly concerned with the plight of the London poor. She even managed to drag an unwilling Oscar to a Hyde Park demonstration during the dock strikes in 1889. (In yet another telling parallel in *A Wife's Tragedy*, Mr Lovel complains that his wife would "sooner I wrote a report on the bedridden villagers than bring [Cleopatra's] Egypt and the Nile back to our common world.")

Her husband's frequent assaults on philanthropists, even when uttered with buoyant humor, could scarcely have pleased Constance. Le Gallienne recalls Oscar saying to her at a dinner party, "Don't you realize that missionaries are the divinely provided food for destitute and under-fed cannibals? Whenever they are on the brink of starvation, Heaven, in its infinite mercy, sends them a nice plump missionary." To which Constance "could only pathetically exclaim": "Oh, Oscar! you cannot surely be in earnest. You can only be joking." Goodness and wit were bound to cohabit uneasily, as Oscar's Lord Illingworth suggests in his remark, "Good women have such limited views of life, their horizon is so small."

Even more blatant allusions to the marriage occur in his play written to prove Mrs Allonby correct about the impossibility of ideal husbands. In the second act of *An Ideal Husband*, which had its premiere mere weeks before the marriage was finally obliterated, the sister of the seemingly ideal husband commiserates with his unhappy wife: "You married a man with a future . . . a genius, and you have a noble, self-sacrificing character. You can stand geniuses. . . . As a rule, I think they are quite impossible. Geniuses talk so much, don't they? Such a bad habit! And they are always thinking about themselves." Here Oscar was skating on very thin ice: guying himself, yet also not very subtly ridiculing his wife's goodness and years of forbearance over his extramarital extravagances. A bit later in the play, Lady Markby says, "Modern women understand everything, I am told," and Mrs Cheveley (whose acid, paradoxing view of life is pure Oscar) replies, "Except their husbands. That is the one thing the modern woman never understands." Can it be a wonder that Constance chose to absent herself from the felicity of the play's opening night? The illustrated weekly *Lika Joko* reported on 12 January that Oscar instead attended the premiere "in the presence of quite a large gathering of young people of the same sex" (Bosie among them).

Obviously lacking, then, in the marriage was something Oscar had on a much earlier occasion said was absolutely essential to him in his companions: "intellectual friction." While at Magdalen he wrote to a classmate about a charmingly nicknamed mutual friend who was beginning to wear upon him: "I am quite as fond of the dear Kitten as ever but he . . . never exerts my intellect or brain *in any way*. Between his mind and mine there is no *intellectual friction to rouse me up to talk or think.*" (Kitten went on to become a London stockbroker.) This complaint applies particularly to the later years of the Wilde marriage, as Oscar increasingly forsook the domestic scene, with its intrusive governesses, chattering boys, earnest wife, and all-around propriety.

Humor was not Constance's game, and there is scarce evidence of her being especially well attuned to Oscar's writings, except perhaps for the fairy tales. For she published two children's books herself, *There Was Once* (1889) and *A Long Time Ago* (1892). When, in what may have been conceived as a last-ditch effort to rekindle her marriage, she undertook in 1894 to make an anthology of Oscar's witticisms, she found herself reading much of his work for the first time. Oscar did not think she performed the task very well. Seeing the results of her culling, he wrote their publisher: "The book is, as it stands, so bad, so disappointing, that I am writing a set of new aphorisms, and will have to alter much of the printed matter. The plays are particularly badly done. Long passages are quoted, where a single aphorism should have been extracted." (He was equally frank, be it said, when Bosie showed him his wretched English translation of *Salome.*) Much later, from prison, Oscar wrote to Ross naming him his literary executor and reiterating his wife's estrangement from his life as a writer: "My wife does not understand my art, nor could be expected to have any interest in it." This eerily repeats a remark made by the poet Lovel in *A Wife's Tragedy*: "My wife doesn't care much, I think, for what I do."

☆　☆　☆

TO WHAT EXTENT—and for how long—did Constance fail to grasp her husband's art . . . and his supposedly concealed sexual identity and activities? It is now impossible to say. Even usually temerarious Frank Harris never dared to guess what the answers might be. Yet the question naturally fascinates and perplexes, not least because Oscar had for years been reaping comic rewards from the subjects of marital deceit and betrayal. Had he not proclaimed that the "proper basis for marriage is a mutual misunderstanding" and that, employing the image of a greenhouse, marriage is "a sort of forcing house [that] brings strange sins to fruit"? The horrible pun is hard to resist: in his case, marriage brought a strange fruit to sin. This is by no means to suggest that a happy and satisfying marriage between a homosexual man and a heterosexual woman is beyond imagination. The Wilde marriage, however, was not to be one.

There is a veritable chorus of misogamists in *Dorian Gray* and the plays. Lord Henry, for instance, opines, "The one charm of marriage is that it makes a life of deception absolutely necessary for both parties. I never know where my wife is, and my wife never knows what I am doing." And Algy in *Earnest*: "If ever I get married, I'll certainly try to forget the fact." Did Oscar assume that the Victorian age hadn't the courage, imagination, or stomach to take seriously all this airy raillery about marital infidelity? Were these iterations either reenforcements of or self-inducements to his personal philandering? Or were all these outrageous, not so subtle self-exposures of his own adulterous behavior part of the self-destructive "plot" he was, as a tragic hero, crafting for himself? Is the oddly terse inscription in the presentation copy of *Lord Arthur Savile's Crime and Other Stories*—"Constance, from Oscar. July 1891"—a melancholy hint of things to come?

The answers to these teasing questions are by no means clear. Very clear, though, is Oscar's inability to take his marriage vows seriously, as the facts disclosed in his trials were to show so elaborately. Several months before the trials, he had confessed this inability in the most ironic of contexts. From "The Haven" at Worthing, he wrote to Charles Spurrier Mason, a member of his London gay circle. It was to come out in the trials that Mason had actually been "married" to the doyen of this circle, Alfred Taylor. Pierre Louÿs, to whom Oscar dedicated *Salome*, heard about the event on a London visit, and reported on the amazing "gay scene" to Gide: "A few days before, they had celebrated a marriage—a real marriage—between two of them, with an exchange of rings and so on." In the cozy, racy style of his gay-circle letters, Oscar said to Mason, "When I come back to town do come and dine. What fun our dinners were in the old days! I hope marriage has not made you too serious? It has never had that effect on me." This in August 1894, just months before the fall.

Constance and his chattering boys must have been nearby as Oscar penned this letter to Mason. Had the light by then gone on for her? Her brother Otho later asserted that her first intimation came in 1895, just weeks before the calamity. This boggles belief. One of her biographers has asserted that "the truth became painfully obvious" in the summer of 1894. This seems a fair guess, but when did it become merely "obvious"? Edgar Saltus recalled in his memoirs that after the crash "Mrs Wilde said that [Oscar] was mad and had been for three years, 'quite mad,' as the poor woman put it." That is, sometime in 1892.

This seems more plausible. On one hand, Constance was then still very cordial to Bosie: on 18 September, hearing of his illness, she wrote to Oscar from Torquay, "I am so sorry about Lord Alfred Douglas, and wish I was at Cromer to look after him." Her offer to come if telegraphed, however, was *not* accepted. On 6 December she extended an invitation to Oscar's longtime gay friend Ross to come to them in Torquay and stay "as long as you will." And she wrote several very friendly letters to him in 1893–94. On the other hand, *Dorian* had already appeared in 1890. The *Scots Observer* accused its author of writing for "outlawed noblemen and perverted telegraph boys," and Constance did notice people snubbing Oscar and her thereafter. True, Oscar wrote in July 1890 to Arthur Fish, stating bluntly that Lord Henry's views on marriage "are quite monstrous, and I highly disapprove of them." But Fish was just about to marry, and Oscar obviously did not wish to throw a wet blanket on the event.

By 1891 André Gide had had his first traumatic encounter with Oscar, which set him on the road to his homosexual awakening. Being with Oscar, said Gide, who agonized greatly over his coming out, caused him "nothing but harm." On 20 February

1892 an event occurred that might well have inaugurated the three years of "madness" Constance spoke of. This was the night of Oscar's first great London theatrical success, *Lady Windermere's Fan*. Constance, Henry James, Le Gallienne, Lillie Langtry, and Harris, among many fashionable others, were present. After making his curtain speech, cigarette shockingly in hand, however, Oscar apparently did not escort his wife home to Tite Street. He was likely at the Albemarle Hotel with Edward Shelley, a teenager who worked in the office of his publisher (the Queensberry plea alleges February as the month of one assignation). Early in 1892 the young John Gray became a constant companion, and Oscar agreed in June to pay for the publication of a volume of Gray's poems. Soon, though, Gray was supplanted by Bosie, and on 3 July the two went alone to the chic German spa at Bad Homburg. Did Constance really believe, as she wrote to her brother, that Oscar was there, ill and under a strict regimen of early rising, massage, little smoking, and drinking the waters? By the fall of 1892 Alfred Taylor, Sidney Mavor, and Freddy Atkins—who would all figure in the trials—had entered Oscar's life. It is difficult to imagine a wife being so utterly blind as to survive such a year with the scales on her eyes intact.

In any event, it is hard to avoid seeing what took place on 19 April 1893 as clearly indicating an *entente*—cordial or not—between a philandering gay husband and his wife. This was the premiere of *A Woman of No Importance*. The Haymarket Theatre's box-office manager recalled this as the most difficult first night of his fifty years on the job, mainly because Oscar came to the manager, Beerbohm Tree, and asked for forty of the best seats in the house (to be paid for, of course). Tree demurred; Oscar insisted. Tree then demanded the names of his guests, and Oscar exploded. "Do you think, my dear Tree, that I'm going to submit the names of my friends for your approval?" Why was Tree suspicious? Surely because rumors were beginning to abound concerning Oscar's flamboyant circle, some of whom must have been among the forty. Several of the same fashionable young gents whom Oscar wished to invite must have been present two years later at the premiere of *Earnest*. Ada Leverson spotted them: "Most of the smart young men held tall canes of ebony with ivory tops; they wore white gloves with rows of black stitching and very pointed shoes."

One wonders whether Constance had read the script of the new play, with all its swipes at "good" married women. "One should always be in love," says Lord Illingworth, for example. "That is the reason one should never marry." That could not have pleased her any more than the shrewd suggestion in *Punch*, ten days later, that the Wilde "recipe" for playwriting required him to "shred into the mixture a wronged woman, a dull wife." And the sight of Oscar preening among his fashionable entourage must have produced in her decidedly mixed feelings.

☆　☆　☆

IN RETROSPECT, IT IS amazing that the marriage remained ostensibly intact for as long as it did. Some reasons for this artificial longevity come immediately to mind. The Victorian age in general, of course, vastly preferred a polite, normal-seeming veneer to the upsetting reality of anything morally out of the way. But specific family history may also have encouraged Oscar and Constance to live with rather than explode the lie. Both came from families in which unhappy marital relations had been put up with for respectability's sake. Oscar's father had three illegitimate children before he married Lady Wilde and was notorious as an adulterer afterward as well. Speranza acclimatized herself to this over time, even to the extent of allowing William Wilde's last mistress to visit him regularly at his deathbed. Constance's father—who, Harris once rumored, was himself homosexual—was also wayward, spending much of his time with the Prince of Wales's set in fashionable Continental spas like Bad Homburg. Her parents went their separate ways, leaving the children in the care of servants much of the time. Inured to such compromises, Oscar and Constance may have reached an "understanding" of a similar kind, if only out of concern for their two boys.

Alternatively, Constance may have come to a private recognition of the truth of her marriage without Oscar's knowing it. Following the advice of the Duchess of Berwick in *Lady Windermere's Fan*—"Don't make scenes, men hate them!"—perhaps she decided not to raise a fuss. Lord Darlington, in the same play, expresses disgust at such a cowardly tactic: "You are just the same as every other woman. You would stand anything rather than face the censure of a world whose praise you would despise.... You would endure anything rather than break with one blow this monstrous tie." Manifestly, Constance was not capable of this bold, jousting Oscarian pose. Choosing to go with the "general stream," she may have thought acceptance the only recourse for herself and her children. If so, she was hewing to an aphorism by Ouida that Oscar had cited with approval in his review of *Guilderoy:* "It is because men feel the necessity to explain that they drop into the habit of saying what is not true. Wise is the woman who never insists on an explanation."

If this supposition is correct, some of the things Oscar wrote in these years assume a decidedly unpleasant, taunting quality. Lord Henry, for instance, says that when his wife discovers his deceptions, "she makes no row at all. I sometimes wish she would; but she merely laughs at me." Like Lady Wotton, who finds her husband has seventeen photographs of Dorian Gray and pretends not to care, Constance may have chosen to greet as cordially as possible the many young men he brought round to Tite Street to dine. She would allow Oscar to think his charades were successful. She would allow him to think, as his Lord Goring thinks in *An Ideal Husband,* "Women have a wonderful instinct about things. They can discover everything except the obvious." If this is what she did, it must have been a bitter, melancholy, soul-destroying tactic . . . one bound to leave her in the end uttering the line that Oscar gave to Lady Windermere: "How alone I am in life! How terribly alone!"

There are enough vignettes of extraordinary pathos from Constance's last year as Mrs Wilde to do justice to the title of this chapter. Consider her sitting at her desk, surrounded by Oscar's writings, for instance. It must have been a rueful task to collect so many aphorisms for *Oscariana* that inscribed her own life:

> There's nothing in the world like the devotion of a married woman. It's a thing no married man knows anything about.

> Women are a decorative sex. They never have anything to say, but say it charmingly.

> How marriage ruins a man! It is as demoralising as cigarettes, and far more expensive.

> London is full of women who trust their husbands. One can always recognize them. They look so thoroughly unhappy.

Then there was the evening sometime in January 1895 when she was alone in Tite Street, Oscar either cozy with Bosie in his hotel in Piccadilly or on their trip to Algiers. That evening she fell down a full flight of stairs, causing a spinal injury that was in time to have serious consequences. Excruciating in an entirely different way must have been the evening of 7 March, a few days after Oscar broke the news to her of the imminent Queensberry libel trial. Constance allowed herself to be convinced, as a show of marital solidarity, to attend a performance of *Earnest* in the company of both Oscar and Bosie—a piece of effrontery which left everyone backstage aghast. Sitting in the St. James's Theatre—the cynosure of so much gossipy curiosity—and listening to the blithe gibes onstage about marriage and the illicit pleasures of secret lives must have been dreadful. Bosie later recalled her as being most distressed, and at evening's end she departed for Tite Street, alone, in tears. Five days later Oscar was Bunburying with Bosie in Monte Carlo, and Constance was embarrassingly obliged to write Ross: "I don't know Oscar's address. . . . If you write to him tell him . . . I am going to have an operation (not a serious one!) performed on me next week, and hope after that to be better."

April rained miseries: sending Cyril and Vyvyan across the Channel with their governess; the rack and ruin of "the house beautiful" at the sale to satisfy creditors on 24 April; the hasty dismissal of Arthur, their butler for all the Tite Street years, with money from her own purse (the poor man collapsed shortly after and ended his days in an asylum). If one letter from Constance expresses the pathos of this time, it is the one she wrote from hiding at Lady Mount-Temple's Babbacombe Cliff house to the fortune-teller she and Oscar had occasionally consulted:

> My dear Mrs Robinson, What is to become of my husband who has so betrayed and deceived me and ruined the lives of my darling boys? Can you tell me anything? You told me that after this terrible shock my life was to become easier, but will there be any happiness in it, or is that dead for me? And I have had so little. My life has all been cut to pieces as my hand is by its lines.
>
> As soon as this trial is over I have to get my judicial separation, or if possible my divorce in order to get the guardianship of the boys. What a tragedy for him who is so gifted.
>
> Do write to me and tell me what you can. Very sincerely yours.
>
> CONSTANCE WILDE
>
> I have not forgotten that I owe you a guinea.

☆ ☆ ☆

IF MRS ROBINSON HAD been an accurate and candid fortune-teller, she would have replied with very small comfort for the future. As before, the highlights of the marriage during and after Oscar's prison years—there was judicial separation but never a divorce—are all notable for pathos rather than heartsease. A month after his sentencing Constance wrote from Switzerland to a friend, "It is so terrible to be here free in the heavenly air, and to think of those four walls round him." In February 1896 she traveled from Genoa to London in order to be the one to tell Oscar his mother had died. She found him "an absolute wreck compared with what he was." It was the last time they were together, but not the last time Constance saw Oscar. That happened a year later, in February 1897, when Oscar's solicitor visited him to gain his signature on papers turning custody of the boys over to Constance and her cousin Adrian Hope. In London on a visit at the time, she asked to accompany the lawyer. The prison warder recalled the scene:

> The interview took place in the consultation room, and Wilde sat at a table with his head on his hands opposite the lawyer.
>
> Outside, in the passage with me, waited a sad figure in deepest mourning. It was Mrs Wilde—in tears ... [who] turned to me and begged a favour. "Let me have one glimpse of my husband," she said, and I could not refuse.
>
> So silently I stepped to one side, Mrs Wilde cast one long lingering glance inside, and saw the convict-poet, who, in deep mental distress himself, was totally unconscious that any eyes save those of the stern lawyer and myself witnessed his degradation. A second later, Mrs Wilde, apparently labouring under deep emotion, drew back, and left the prison.

A little more than a year later, on 7 April 1898, she died in Genoa after an unsuccessful operation on her spine. Her boys were away at school in Germany at the time.

There was much talk, toward the end of his sentence, of Constance's taking Oscar back. Bosie, in perhaps the most supercilious utterance of his entire life, wrote later, "If she had treated him properly and stuck to him after he had been in prison, as a really good wife would have done, he would have gone on loving her to the end of his life." Such talk of joining Oscar in Continental exile might have reminded Constance of the Duchess of Berwick telling Lady Windermere how to deal with husbands who "come back, slightly damaged": "Mind you don't take this little aberration of Windermere's too much to heart. Just take him abroad, and he'll come back to you all right."

The urgings to reconciliation might also have reminded her of an appalling speech—the most repellent Oscar ever penned—in *An Ideal Husband,* in which Lord Goring (that is, Oscar) urges Lady Chiltern to forgive her husband:

> Women are not meant to judge us, but to forgive us when we need forgiveness. Pardon, not punishment, is their mission. . . . A man's life is of more value than a woman's. It has larger issues, wider scope, greater ambitions. A woman's life revolves in curves of emotions. It is upon lines of intellect that a man's life progresses. Don't make any terrible mistake, Lady Chiltern. A woman who can keep a man's love, and love him in return, has done all the world wants of women, or should want of them.

Lady Chiltern does forgive her husband, and the play ends in a kind of fairy tale, she telling her husband that for them "a new life is beginning." Constance kept her wits and common sense amid such talk and refused for once to flow with the "general stream." A few months before Oscar's release she wrote to Otho from Italy, "I have again had pressure put upon me to persuade me to go back to Oscar, but . . . that is impossible. I am told that I would save a human soul, but I have no influence over Oscar. I have had none, and though I think he is affectionate I see no reason for believing that I should be able now to perform miracles."

How right she was in her self-protective instinct and cool view of Oscar's "love" is remarkably demonstrated, as it happens, in a letter he wrote the very same week to Ross to discuss legal matters. For in this letter he summarized his feelings about Constance and the marriage in shockingly callous terms: "Whether I am married or not is a matter that does not concern me. For years I disregarded the tie. But I really think it is hard on my wife to be tied to me. I always thought so. And, though it may surprise some of my friends, I am really very fond of my wife and very sorry for her. I sincerely hope she may have a happy marriage, if she marries again. She could not understand me, and I was bored to death with the married life. But she had some sweet points in her character, and was wonderfully loyal to me." Such airy flippancy tempts one to conclude there was more than a little truth in this sad epigram Oscar wrote but never published: "One can always be kind to people about whom one cares nothing. That is why English family life is so pleasant."

Oscar's confession to Ross makes it all the more plausible that, in a speech for Sir Robert near the end of *An Ideal Husband*, he was writing in fact about his own marriage:

> There is one thing worse than an absolutely loveless marriage. A marriage in which there is love, but on one side only; faith, but on one side only; devotion, but on one side only, and in which of the two hearts one is sure to be broken.

In the Wildes' case, there was apparently only one heart. Oscar was to admit in prison to the belated discovery that he had one, too. Indeed, it was precisely the heartlessness of *Earnest*—the play he wrote at the simultaneous height of his powers and the depths of his "Neronian hours"—that appalled Bernard Shaw when he first saw it. He called it Oscar's "first really heartless play. . . . Though extremely funny . . . essentially hateful. I had no idea that Oscar was going to the dogs, and that this represented a real degeneracy produced by his debaucheries."

No, it was Constance who had the heart, and it was most assuredly broken. She had married, it became clear in time, a devout misogamist . . . one in whom there ran a deep vein of misogyny as well. (When Oscar passed his manuscript of *De profundis* to Ross for copying, he urged him to "get Mrs Marshall to send down one of her type-writing girls—women are the most reliable, as they have no memory for the important.") It had been a painfully one-sided marriage, and yet in its awful aftermath Constance behaved with considerable poise and humanity. Her letters from this time show her capable of candid disgust at times, but it is sometimes blended with humane sympathy. This balance was struck early on, in a letter from October 1895: "My poor misguided husband, who is weak rather than wicked, repents most bitterly all his past madness and I cannot refuse to him the forgiveness that he has asked." Much later, on 4 March 1898, she wrote to Carlos Blacker from the more distanced standpoint she later came to: "All possibility of our living together has come to an end, but I am interested in him, as is my way with anyone that I have once known . . . if you do see him tell him that I think *The Ballad [of Reading Gaol]* exquisite, and I hope that the great success it has had in London at all events will urge him on to write more." A week later, her good nature having been tried by Oscar's financial desperation and importuning, she wrote Blacker again with poignant but still unhurtful resentment: "I know that he is in great poverty, but I don't care to be written to as though it were my fault. He says he loved me too much and that that is better than hate! This is true abstractedly, but his was an unnatural love, a madness that I think is worse than hate. I have no hatred for him, but I confess that I am afraid of him."

Characteristically, though, her charitable instincts had the last word. On 28 March Oscar told Blacker that he had received "a very nice letter from Constance yesterday." And the last letter she wrote to her son Vyvyan contains this moving admonition: "Try not to feel harshly about your father; remember that he is your father and that he loves you. All his troubles arose from the hatred of a son for his father, and whatever he has done he has suffered bitterly for." Though she did not seem to fear death from her impending operation, this letter does have the feeling of an ending. Within days she was lying in the Protestant cemetery in Genoa, under a gravestone that read

CONSTANCE MARY
DAUGHTER OF HORACE LLOYD, Q.C.*

☆　☆　☆

TWO SUBSEQUENT EVENTS PROVIDE an apt coda to this "tragedy" of a far-from-ideal husband and a woman of no importance . . . apt because they leave us disconcerted and perplexed.

When news of the death reached Oscar, he telegraphed Ross: "Come tomorrow and stay in my hotel. Am in great grief." To Otho Lloyd he telegraphed, "Am overwhelmed with grief. It is the most terrible tragedy." And to Blacker he wrote, "It is really awful. I don't know what to do. If we had only met once and kissed each other. It's too late. How awful life is." And yet . . . Ross did come as requested and reported to Oscar's publisher, "You will have heard of Mrs Wilde's death. Oscar of course did not feel it at all. . . . He is in very good spirits and does not consume too many. . . ." Ross was Oscar's closest and most loyal friend, but that "of course" is a terrible indictment. Not quite as terrible, though, as an assertion Ross was to make in a letter written just after his death: "He really did not understand how cruel he was to his wife, but I never expect anyone to believe that."

The profound contradictions of Oscar's relationship with Constance even displayed themselves strikingly when, traveling from Nice to Switzerland in 1899, he found himself in Genoa and visited her grave. He described this to Ross, who had fondly admired Constance: "The cemetery is a garden at the foot of the lovely hills that climb into the mountains that girdle Genoa. It was very tragic seeing her name carved on a tomb—her surname, my name not mentioned of course. . . . I brought some flowers. I was deeply affected—with a sense, also, of the uselessness of all

* Subsequently, in an unfortunately sentimental gesture, the words "Wife of Oscar Wilde" were added.

regrets. Nothing could have been otherwise, and Life is a very terrible thing."

Oscar had said he traveled to Genoa to visit the grave, but this was not entirely so. For later, from Switzerland, he wrote to another one of his London gay circle describing a quite different highlight of his sojourn in Genoa and not even mentioning the trip to the cemetery: "On my way I stopped at Genoa, where I met a beautiful young actor, a Florentine, whom I wildly loved. He has the strange name of Didaco. He had the look of Romeo, without Romeo's sadness: a face chiselled for high romance. We spent three days together." That "wildly" is the saddest pun Oscar ever invented.

☆ ☆ ☆

IN JANUARY 1884, Constance wrote to Oscar to report the demise of Jimmy, a pet that her husband-to-be had given her. She wondered in her letter, "Is it my fault that everything you give me has an untimely end?" Whether Constance was responsible for Jimmy's death is beyond our knowing, but it seems clear that the untimely end of her marriage and the love Oscar gave her was not her fault but his.

Chapter Seven

☆ ☆ ☆ ☆ ☆ ☆ ☆ ☆ ☆ ☆ ☆ ☆ ☆ ☆ ☆

"MY GOOD PAPA!"

*I remember one of his children running and calling at him: "My good papa!"
and I remember Wilde patting the boy and saying: "Don't call me that, it
sounds so respectable."*

—EDGAR SALTUS

ON 24 APRIL 1895, when Oscar was in Holloway Prison and
about to stand trial, a rowdy sheriff's sale of all his belongings
took place in Tite Street, everything from his 1,700-book library
to a "colossal bust of Apollo," a rabbit hutch, and the "linoleum,
as laid" on the third floor. The sale had legal sanction, though
the report in *The Morning* on 25 April that creditors claimed
debts mainly for cigarette cases may not have been entirely accurate. Robert Sherard wrote that the proceedings amounted to
"pillage of an unprotected house. People stole with the greatest
effrontery." The scene in the small drawing room, "crowded to
suffocation" with buyers, must have been appalling, and the prices

for such articles as did come to the hammer "were ridiculously low." A Whistler nude fetched £21; a parcel of manuscripts, £5.15s.; Carlyle's writing desk, "a wondrous piece of mechanism," sold for fourteen guineas; five volumes of *Dorian Gray* and the *Poems* went for sixty-three shillings. Oscar's Arundel prints did well, but, there being no nostalgic Aesthetes on hand, his "old blue china . . . did not excite connoisseurs to high bidding." Among the more mundane lots was number 237, "A very large quantity of toys." These brought a paltry six shillings.

These toys had hitherto been spread about on the top floor of the house, which consisted of a day and night nursery and a bathroom, all devoted to the use of Oscar's boys, Cyril and Vyvyan, then aged nine and eight. Oscar had occasion, a few weeks after the sale, to think—with what must have been paralyzing grief and regret—about these toys and the childish delight that transpired among them on that top floor. For when he was out on bail and in hiding for more than a week as a guest of Ada and Ernest Leverson, he was domiciled in their son George's nursery, "almost a flat in itself" and likewise at the top of the house. George had been sent to the country, but his toys remained: a rocking horse, some doll houses, a variety of golliwogs leaning against a blue-and-white dado painted with rabbits. A cot was brought in for Oscar, and Ada, recognizing the pain the toys might cause him, asked whether he wished them removed.

Well aware that he might never see his boys again, he thought for a moment and said they should not be disturbed. This painful request was perhaps a gesture of expiation, an acknowledgment that he was not suffering alone for the reckless, wretchedly selfish behavior that had led to the sale of Cyril and Vyvyan's toys for a pittance. The presence of the toys of the Leversons' son would be a fitting goad to his remorse of conscience.

And suffer the boys most certainly did over the loss of their toys. "For months afterwards," wrote Vyvyan, "my brother and I kept asking for our soldiers, our trains and other toys, and we could not understand why it upset our mother." Besides not sparing himself the reminder of the toys, Oscar at this time seems to have steadfastly shouldered the entire blame for the collapse of the family's life: "I never heard a recrimination pass his lips," reported Sherard; "his moral attitude was splendid." And many times thereafter he confessed his entire responsibility for the dreadful life he had fashioned for his wife and children. "I have brought such unhappiness on her and such ruin on my children," he admitted to Ross after a year in prison.

As his sentence neared its end, anguish over the likely separation from his boys obviously began to mount. Explaining to Bosie in *De profundis* why he preferred to reserve for family business the first letter he had been allowed to receive in prison, he wrote: "I could not bear the idea of being separated from Cyril, that beautiful, loving, loveable child of mine, my friend of all friends, my companion beyond all companions, one single hair of whose little golden head should have been dearer and of more value to me than . . . the entire chrysolite of the whole world: was so indeed to me always, though I failed to understand it till too late." In a letter to More Adey two months before his release, Oscar addressed the practical details of his future life:

As regards my children, I sincerely hope I may be recognised by the Court as having some little, I won't say right, but claim to be allowed to see Cyril from time to time: it would be to me a sorrow beyond words if I were not. I do hope the Court will see in me something more than a man with a tragic vice in his life. There is so much more in me, and I always was a good father to both my children. I love them dearly and was dearly loved by them, and Cyril was my friend. And it would be better for them not to be forced to think of me as an outcast, but to know me as a man who has suffered . . . it is a terrible responsibility for the Law to say to a father that he is unfit to see his own children: the consciousness of it often makes me unhappy all day long.

The Law, in the end, eagerly embraced the "terrible" responsibility; he never did see Cyril or Vyvyan again. Stuart Merrill, in a Parisian obituary essay on Oscar, referred to secret visits with them in Geneva, but these are never mentioned in Oscar's letters or by anyone else. And Vyvyan himself wrote that "after 1895 I never saw him again."

☆   ☆   ☆

OSCAR TO THE CONTRARY, he was not "always" a good father; nor was he a good father for the appropriate duration of time. But he did commence as a father satisfactorily enough, boasting proudly to a friend after Cyril was born on 5 June 1885, "The baby is wonderful: it has a bridge to its nose! which the nurse says is a proof of genius! It also has a superb voice, which it quite freely exercises: its style is essentially Wagnerian." Constance and Oscar recorded Cyril's birth to the minute (10:45 a.m.). Perhaps there is some symbolism, if not significance, in the fact that when their second son was born his parents forgot until several weeks later to register his birth—and then could not recall the day it occurred. Guy Fawkes Day was considered likely but unacceptable: 3 November was chosen.* Slowly and most likely unnoticeably, the ties that bound the Wilde family were beginning to loosen.

The boys were to remain happily unaware of this, however, until the scandal broke and they were, without explanation, whisked by a governess into Swiss "exile," as Vyvyan later chose to call it. He titled the first chapter of his autobiography "The Happy Years" and summarized that his "early childhood was as happy as that of most children of the period, considering the discomforts which they had to endure"—notably vile-tasting medicines and uncomfortable clothing. The mutual affection between the father and his sons that Oscar described from prison is veri-

---

* The baby did, however, come away with two more given names than Cyril: Vyvyan Oscar Beresford. Vyvyan later described his parents' choice of his name as a "fantasy," since it had no precedent in their families. He explained that he employed the same "fantasy" in arriving at the name for his own son: Merlin.

fied by Vyvyan: "Most small boys adore their fathers, and we adored ours; and as all good fathers are, he was a hero to us both."

Most of Vyvyan's specific recollections seem to justify Anne Clark Amor's assertion in *Mrs Oscar Wilde* that "as a parent Oscar was absolutely marvelous." But these recollections quickly make it clear that Amor's phrasing was not quite accurate: Oscar seems to have made an absolutely marvelous *playmate*. Vyvyan perceived that his father was not like other adults and reveled in the difference: "Grown-up people of that generation were apt to take themselves too seriously. There were exceptions, of course, notable among them being my father." The devil-may-care self-indulgence that was to lead Oscar astray in other departments of life made him a particularly charming and successful presence with children, as at least two eyewitnesses observed. Mrs J. Comyns Carr reminisced: "With children he was very popular, and in their company he lost much of his poseur manner; his smile became infectious in its gaiety, and his small eyes twinkled with merriment." With her five- and seven-year-old brothers, Helena Sickert said, "Oscar made himself a delightful playmate, talking poetical nonsense of exactly the right blend and carrying on mock-serious conversations, decorated with waves of open-mouthed laughter. I have never known any grown person who laughed more whole-heartedly and who made such mellow music of it."

Vyvyan's testimony supports these accounts—and Oscar's own assertion from prison—of his paternal skills. In an age when considerable parenting by the proxy of servants was usual, he appears to have been quite attentive: "He was a real companion to us, and we always looked forward eagerly to his frequent visits to our nursery." Decades later, Vyvyan attempted to explain such parental success: "Most parents in those days were far too solemn and pompous with their children, insisting on a vast amount of usually undeserved respect. My own father was quite different; he had so much of the child in his own nature that he delighted in playing our games. He would go down on all fours on the nursery floor, being in turn a lion, a wolf, a horse, caring nothing for his usually immaculate appearance."

It seems likely that Oscar often amused himself—and his friends—by turning the mundane events of parenthood into drollery. A charming example of this is a note thanking Ross for the gift of a pet for Cyril and Vyvyan: "The kitten is quite lovely—it does not *look* white, indeed it looks a sort of tortoise-shell colour ... but as you said it was white I have given orders that it is always to be spoken of as the 'white kitten'—the children are enchanted with it, and sit, one on each side of its basket, worshipping. It seems pensive—perhaps it is thinking of some dim rose-garden in Persia, and wondering why it is kept in this chill England."

There was much play outside in the Royal Hospital gardens nearby and at holiday sites like Lady Mount-Temple's grand, eccentric Babbacombe Cliff house (designed by Ruskin). But Vyvyan thought his father was "at his best" at the seaside. While he was a strong swimmer and also delighted to boat and fish with the boys, the special highlight was his building of sandcastles. This was "an art in which he excelled; long, rambling castles they were, with moats and tunnels and towers and battlements, and when they were finished he would usually pull a few lead soldiers out of his pocket to man the castle walls." The vignette is charming ... but profound and even troubling, too. For it highlights a distinctive characteristic Oscar shared with many another fate-beset hero: a disinclination to reside in the "real" world. Vyvyan in fact described this characteristic just a page before mentioning his papa's sandcastles: "My father lived in a world of his own; an artificial world, perhaps, but a world in which the only things that really mattered were art and beauty in all their forms."

Among Papa's beautiful artifices was a "never-ending supply" of fairy and adventure tales: "He told us all his own written fairy stories suitably adapted for our young minds." One day he read "The Selfish Giant" to them, and Cyril noticed him crying and inquired why. "He replied that really beautiful things always made him cry." Successful tale-telling requires finesse, as William Butler Yeats learned on a visit to Tite Street. He recalled in his autobiography the mortifying experience of offering to tell Vyvyan a tale and beginning, "Once upon a time there was a terrible giant"—at which the boy ran screaming out of the room. "Wilde looked grave and I was plunged into the shame of clumsiness." Oscar's awareness of the difficulty of telling tales, and the likelihood that many were extemporized in Tite Street, are demonstrated in an amusing conversation reported by Richard Le Gallienne. "It is the duty of every father to write fairy tales for his children," Oscar told him very seriously one day, "but the mind of a child is a great mystery. It is incalculable, and who shall divine it, or bring it its own peculiar delights? You humbly spread before it the treasures of your imagination, and they are as dross."

Then Oscar told Le Gallienne of Cyril's coming up one day and asking,

"Father, do you ever dream?" "Why of course, my darling. It is the first duty of a gentleman to dream." "And what do you dream of?" asked Cyril, with a child's disgusting appetite for facts. Then I, believing, of course, that something picturesque would be expected of me, spoke of magnificent things: "What do I dream of? Oh, I dream of dragons with gold and silver scales, and scarlet flames coming out of their mouths, of eagles with eyes made of diamonds that can see over the whole world at once, of lions with yellow manes, and voices like thunder, of elephants with little houses on their backs, and tigers and zebras with barred and spotted coats. . . ." So I laboured on with my fancy, till, observing that Cyril was entirely unimpressed, and indeed quite undisguisedly bored, I came to a humiliating stop, and, turning to my son there, I said: "But tell me, what do you dream of, Cyril?" His answer was like a divine revelation: "I dream of *pigs*," he said.

This is another delightful vignette that turns bittersweet on contemplation: for it glances at the more mundane and unpoetical aspects of parenting (perhaps glances, too, at Oscar's growing frustration with his unpoetical, practical-minded wife). That Oscar was not cut out for domesticity's "dreams of pigs" and took increasingly little notice of household affairs is made quite clear in a short 1894 note to Bosie canceling an invitation to stay *chez* Wilde at the seaside:

> A horrid, ugly Swiss governess has, I find, been looking after Cyril and Vyvyan for a year. She is quite impossible.
>   Also, children at meals are tedious.
>   Also, you, the gilt and graceful boy, would be bored. Don't come here. I will come to you. Ever yours
>
>   OSCAR

Oscar had as nearly a constitutional antipathy to governesses as to governors and governments. His usual careless glee was bound not to be to their liking. This bias shines forth in Vyvyan's description of the day Oscar came home with a splendid toy milk cart with many removable pieces. As soon as the indulgent father noticed its churns could be filled, he fetched a jug of milk from the kitchen. "We then all tore around the nursery room table, slopping milk all over the place." That is, until an unamused nurse put an end to the merriment. There is no need to labor the ominous portent of the spilt milk, except to say that this vignette is one of many in Oscar's life that reminds one of Falstaff: specifically, the moment when the sheriff's loud knock curtails the rumbustious "play extempore" at the Boar's Head tavern.

☆   ☆   ☆

THE GESTATION AND BIRTH of Vyvyan, we have seen, apparently marked the end of the romantic, passionate side of the marriage. At about this time the emergence of Oscar's homosexual identity and behavior must have commenced in earnest. (His famed pun-word presents itself for use irksomely often in his life.) One sad result of this coincidence was that the avocation of youth-chasing on one hand and the vocation of fatherhood on the other began to produce unattractive, sometimes poignant coincidences. For example, just months after a kind of estrangement had set into the marriage Oscar wrote a burst of aggressively cordial and artful letters to a young fellow named H. C. Marillier, in one of which he asked "Harry" what he was doing: "Is the world a dust-heap or a flower-garden . . . ? Poisonous, or perfect, or both?" Apt phrasing: since for the next several years Oscar himself succeeded in leading a double life of seemingly "perfect" urban respectability while pursuing (as he later put it) poisonous "modes of erotomania." In the year of Vyvyan's birth he was described by the magazine *Bat* as appearing "subdued, meditative, married" when seen at the performance of a play starring Lillie Langtry, but this was also the year he met Robert Ross. The next year, in 1887, Oscar put the *Pall Mall Gazette* in mind of Shakespeare's famously beyoked wit-cracker in *Much Ado About Nothing*: "Oscar's star has been low in the horizon since he cut his hair and became 'Benedick the married man.' " But, in private, his activities were becoming distinctly more Bohemian: soon to come were the flaring passion for John Gray and the gestation of the decidedly "poisonous" novel Gray was to give his name to.

About this time Oscar's solo visits to Paris began to last longer. In March 1891 he wrote from the Hôtel de l'Athénée describing Mallarmé's gift of his translation of Poe:

> My dearest Cyril, I send you a letter to tell you I am much better. I go every day and drive in a beautiful forest called the Bois de Boulogne, and in the evening I dine with my friend, and sit out afterwards at little tables and see the carriages drive by. Tonight I go to visit a great poet, who has given me a wonderful book about a Raven. I will bring you and Vyvyan back some chocolates when I return.

I hope you are taking great care of dear Mamma. Give her my love and kisses, and also love and kisses to Vyvyan and yourself. Your loving Papa

OSCAR WILDE

A lovely paternal performance ... but this is, alas, the sole known surviving letter from Oscar to his children. And even it, though surely a delight to its recipient, might have raised questions in Mamma's mind. Who was "my friend," for instance? And we might well wonder what else Oscar might have watched passing by from his café table ... and whether his evenings and nights were as subdued as he reported.

A few months later Oscar met Bosie for the first time, and early in 1892 he began to occupy separate rooms in Piccadilly. His main reason, or excuse, was usually the need for a quiet place to work, but on at least one occasion it was because "the drains at Tite Street have gone wrong." He also took up with Edward Shelley, his publisher's office boy, about this time. Clearly, with his increasingly busy shadow life and his ascent on the London literary and theatrical scenes, Oscar's attentions to his sons became ever more fitful. It is telling that the one extended Continental family vacation—a fortnight at Dinard in August 1893—occurred because, exhausted by twelve tense weeks alone with Bosie and the blowup over Bosie's unsatisfactory English translation of *Salome*, Oscar simply needed an escape. "I required rest and freedom from the terrible strain of your companionship," he recalled in prison; "it was necessary for me to be a little by myself." Melancholy and suggestive, that last phrase, as his description of a family outing.

Another curious family vacation had taken place several months earlier, in February 1893. This was the one at Babbacombe, and the "family" consisted of Oscar, Bosie, and the boys, along with a tutor hired by Bosie's mother (he proved a hopelessly pliable "governess"). But no Constance: as we noted, she was traveling in Italy at the time. The tutor's rather comic letter (see page 6) on his week at Babbacombe reports little work being accomplished and much playing "with pigeons and children." The boys must have had a grand time. But one can easily imagine the "beautiful and fascinating, but quite wicked" Bosie making many a sly quip about his eagerness for Cyril and Vyvyan to reach puberty. One suspects humor of this sort was what led the poor dazed tutor to confess he was leaving behind at Babbacombe "all that remains of my religion and my morals."

Occasionally, no doubt, Oscar must have been brought up short by his children—who are no fools in observing such things—for shirking his domestic duties. He himself confided one such occasion to Nellie Melba. One night he warned Cyril and Vyvyan about little boys who are naughty and make their mothers cry and what dreadful things would happen if they did not behave better. "And do you know what one of them answered?" Oscar asked Melba. "He asked me what punishment could be reserved for naughty papas who did not come home till the early morning and made mother cry far more?"

Others were becoming concerned, too: in May of 1893 his French friend Pierre Louÿs reproached Oscar for his treatment of his wife and family . . . indeed, broke off their friendship on this account. A few months later Beerbohm first met Oscar—in the company of Ross, Bosie, and Aubrey Beardsley—and was "quite repelled" by the flamboyant coterie behavior he saw. The Wilde family spent August and September of 1894 at the seaside in Worthing, but there are few reminders of Oscar the father in his letters from this time. One is a request that his publisher send Cyril a translation of the *Odyssey*: "I am very anxious he should read the best book for boys, and those who keep the wonder and joy of boyhood, ever written." But Bosie was also a visitor at Worthing, and this was also when Oscar became friendly with an eighteen-year-old named Conway who was a newspaper boy on the pier at Brighton. (When opposing counsel brought Conway's occupation up in court, Oscar parried, "It is the first I have heard of his connexion with literature.") The boy became part of the family circle, a playmate, in effect, to both Oscar and his sons. But, as the Queensberry Plea of Justification stated, "The said Oscar Fingal O'Flahertie Wills Wilde upon several occasions in the months of August and September in the year of our Lord One thousand eight hundred and ninety-four . . . at the Albion Hotel Brighton in the same County did solicit and incite one Alfonso Harold Conway to commit sodomy and other acts of gross indecency and immorality with him." The end was very near.

☆   ☆   ☆

THE AFTERMATH OF THE arrest was terrible and brought countless miserable moments. One was the older boy's seeing a telltale advertising placard in Baker Street and begging to be told what it meant. The answer he received was evasive, but soon after, while staying with relatives in Ireland, he learned the truth from newspapers left lying about. He carefully protected Vyvyan from similar knowledge for some time thereafter, though Vyvyan did recall seeing Constance in tears over a pile of press cuttings with his father's name glaring in large headlines. A few months later, in Switzerland, their uncle Otho informed them that their last name would henceforth be Holland, then sat them down to practice writing the new name. For further disguise Vyvyan became Vivian, and his second given name of Oscar was deleted. The next year, established at an English school in Heidelberg, Vyvyan recalled being devastated one day to come upon Cyril tearing out old name tags sewn into his cricket flannels, which had been overlooked during the renaming process: "I can see my brother now, in the comparative seclusion of the washing place, frantically hacking away at the tapes with his pocket knife."

Once in prison, Oscar began to think of his children and the future. "With regard to my children, I feel that for their own sake as well as for mine they should not be bred up to look on me with either hatred or contempt: a guardian amongst my wife's relations would be for this reason impossible." In the event, he was obliged to sign over the custody of the boys to Constance and her cousin Adrian Hope, who had for years been critical of Oscar. Oscar's fears of ostracism were in the end quite justified. Constance her-

self in the postprison years proved rather changeable in her attitude toward him (depending mostly on her perceptions of threat to
her financial position), but with her death he lost all serious hope
of contact with Cyril and Vyvyan. The conspiracy of her family to
excise Oscar from the lives of the two Holland boys, wrote Vyvyan,
"was very efficient." He did not learn of the specific nature of his
father's crime until 1904, when he was eighteen.

Just after his release, Constance was in touch with Oscar, but
not satisfyingly: "She sends me photographs of the boys—such
lovely little fellows in Eton collars—but makes no promise to allow me to see them: she says *she* will see me, twice a year, but I
want my boys. It is a terrible punishment, dear Robbie, and oh!
how well I deserve it." Three months later he wrote to Carlos
Blacker, who was something of a go-between, "I am greatly disappointed that Constance has not asked me to come and see the
children. I don't suppose now I shall ever see them." A few weeks
later he raised the stakes, suggesting that a reestablished connection with his sons might make the crucial difference in his recovery: "I must remake my maimed life on my own lines. If
Constance allowed me to see my boys, my life, I think, would
have been quite different. But this she would not do. I don't in
any way venture to blame her for her action, but every action has
its consequence." After Constance's death, Adrian Hope was implacable in his resistance to relations between father and sons,
even mere letters. Indeed, when Oscar asked whether he might
write letters for them to read on reaching their majority, he was
told they would be destroyed if sent.

The pathos of the boys' enforced separation from their father
during the last three years of his life was enormous, especially
when, as it seems likely, a reunion would have proved therapeutic
on both sides. One remarkable anecdote can suffice to give a flavor of these years for Oscar. Shortly after Vyvyan published *Son
of Oscar Wilde* in 1954, a letter came to him from Issy-les-
Moulineaux in France. It seems the now elderly writer had been
taken regularly by his mother, as a boy of about Vyvyan's and
Cyril's age, to dine at a restaurant where a "Monsieur Sébastian"

was also a steady customer, always dining with his back to a far wall, alone and silent. This boy's mother held this English gentleman up to him as a model of deportment, elegance, and good breeding, but he remembered his mother's concern at the diner's obvious unhappiness. The writer of the letter also recalled an "expression of great kindness, but of infinite weariness" in his face. One autumn evening, he continued,

> while putting on my overcoat after finishing my meal, I clumsily upset something, perhaps a salt-cellar, on Monsieur Sébastian's table. He said nothing, but my mother scolded me and told me to apologise, which I did, distressed by my clumsiness. But Monsieur Sébastian turned to my mother and said: "Be patient with your little boy. One must always be patient with them. If, one day, you should find yourself separated from them ..." I did not give him time to finish his sentence, but asked him: "Have you got a little boy?" "I've got two," he said. "Why don't you bring them here with you?" My mother interrupted, saying: "You mustn't ask questions, Lucien!" "It doesn't matter: it doesn't matter at all," he said with a sad smile. "They don't come here with me because they are too far away...." Then he took my hand, drew me to him and kissed me on both cheeks. I bade him farewell, and then I saw that he was crying. And we left.
>
> While kissing me, he had said a few words which I did not understand. But on the following day we arrived before him and a Bank employé who used to sit at the table on the other side of us asked us: "Did you understand what Monsieur Sébastian said last evening?" "No," we replied. "He said, in English: 'Oh, my poor dear boys!' "

THE TWO BOYS RESPONDED to the traumatic disjunctions in their lives differently. Cyril, aware of the nature of his father's ignominy at an earlier age, seems for the most part to have internalized his grief and sense of betrayal. Vyvyan wrote that, from the day Cyril saw the placard in Baker Street, "the hackneyed expression 'he never smiled again' was for him almost true." He added that Cyril's "self-enforced reticence turned him, while yet a child, into a taciturn pessimist." Cyril seems also to have accepted, in a way that would have mortified and saddened his father, society's premise that the only proper way for a man to behave is in the stereotypical "manly" way. He became a fine athlete, stroking the eight for Radley ("a school well known for athletes"), and at the Royal Military Academy, Woolwich, he was a successful one- and two-miler. On leave from the army in 1913, he trekked on a shooting trip across "the terrible plateau of Tibet" and into China. And in June 1914, at the age of twenty-nine, he wrote a revealing letter to Vyvyan from India discussing their childhood years and expounding the deplorable credo that he took away from the scandal of 1895. The more he thought about it, Cyril said, "the more convinced I became that, first and foremost, I must be a *man*. There was to be no cry of decadent artist, of effeminate aesthete, of weak-kneed degenerate." How this letter would have pained Oscar! It ended with a terrible announcement of how thoroughly Cyril felt he had distanced himself from the opprobrious image of his father: "I am no wild, passionate, irresponsible hero. I live by thought, not by emotion."

The unintentional pun on "Wilde" adds to the grim humor of these utterly un-Oscarian sentiments. Cyril added one last hope: "I ask nothing better than to end in honourable battle for my King and Country." He got his wish and became a martyr to the manly on 9 May 1915, when he was shot in what Vyvyan described as a duel with a German sniper in France.

Vyvyan lived a much longer and happier life, dying in 1967. As brothers he and Cyril, it seems, were as vastly different as Oscar and Willie. Cyril had always been the favorite of both parents, as Vyvyan himself acknowledged. His explanation: "My

141

arrival was a disappointment to my father, who wanted a daughter to remind him of his sister Isola" (she died, age ten, in 1867). Anne Clark Amor's assertion that Oscar "never mentions Vyvyan by name" is not quite accurate, but it is true that Cyril is the only son named in his agonized letters from prison. It is tempting to see other reasons for the preference in their different personalities. A letter from Constance to her friend Emily Thursfield during her first month alone with the boys in Switzerland described Cyril as a boy who is "good-natured to a fault" and who "cannot give pain to anyone or say no to anyone." Vyvyan was sketched as "much sharper and quicker than Cyril, very affectionate and tremendously self-willed, an exceedingly clever boy." Which is to say, Cyril was rather more like the kinds of young men Oscar instinctively gravitated toward in his liaisons: not competitive with him on his own ground, not "literary" (Vyvyan made a point of noting that Cyril could not spell), but seeming sensitive and amiable. Vyvyan, on the other hand, was obviously a chip off the old block. Perhaps the father recognized enough of his own willful, contrarian, and precocious self in Vyvyan to be just a little put off by him.

Thus, Vyvyan had at least two extremely good reasons to be resentful of his father: preference for his sibling and the great betrayal of his filial trust. One problem, however, was that it was a very long time before he could, so to speak, acquaint himself with his father. By age eleven he was aware that his father had done something wrong, but it was only when Adrian Hope's death in 1904 effectively lifted the Holland/Lloyd family embargo on Oscar's memory that Vyvyan began to learn the truth. His father's books were banned, and it was only by picking up a secondhand copy of *Dorian Gray* while at Cambridge ("certainly the best preparatory school for Oxford that I know," Oscar once said) that he was able to begin experiencing his writings.

One thinks of Vyvyan at this juncture and is reminded of a speech that occurs in *A Woman of No Importance*. Speeches, rather, for the words are spoken first by Lord Illingworth in the second act, then again, verbatim, by Mrs Arbuthnot in Act Four:

"Children begin by loving their parents. After a time they judge them. Rarely, if ever, do they forgive them." Is it possible that, sitting in Reading Prison and reviewing his life and works, Oscar recalled those terrible lines and wondered whether his mordant conclusion about children would prove correct in his case?

The single most moving experience in my researches, I confess, was discovering in Vyvyan's autobiography that Lord Illingworth's withering observation was one of several Oscarian truisms that are, in fact, not always true. For Vyvyan's closing pages show a remarkable equanimity and generosity of spirit—a truly Oscarian gentleness and unwillingness to visit rage or vindictive retribution, even for quite real and painful suffering endured. Vyvyan proved to be one child who judged and, in the end, forgave: "Time . . . has convinced me that my father was more the victim of circumstances than his own frailty. . . . He was the kindest and gentlest of men, and he hated to see anyone suffer." Vyvyan also had choice words for those who harried his father in his last miserable years (words not without pertinence today for Protestant fundamentalists and Catholic prelates): "Many deeply religious people are naturally cruel and consider that their religious beliefs and practices absolve them from the necessity of possessing any other virtues, particularly charity."

Even more affecting, though, is Vyvyan's description, as he put it, of the harassment he suffered from those who "base their religion on the Old Testament pronouncement that 'the sins of the fathers shall be visited upon the children.' . . . It [was] constantly dinned into me that I was different from other boys; that I was a pariah who could not take his place within the framework of the world." The lesson he took way from this ghastly experience was quite different from that of his brother. This lesson proved, finally and courageously, that he was truly his father's son: "I have learnt that it is impossible to hide one's head and to be happy at the same time, that it is better to sail under one's true colours and to face all comers bravely and resolutely."

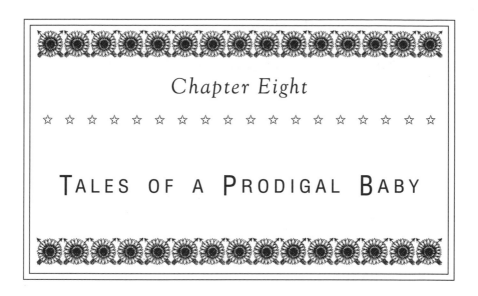

Chapter Eight

TALES OF A PRODIGAL BABY

In a real man a child is hidden—and wants to play.

—NIETZSCHE

It will be a marvellous thing—the true personality of man—when we see it. . . . It will be as wonderful as the personality of a child.

—"THE SOUL OF MAN UNDER SOCIALISM"

HIS SON VYVYAN WAS by no means the only one who noticed Oscar's essentially childish spirit. His closest friends became quite inured to it. Robbie Ross, telling of the unexpectedly emotional impact of the Paris deathbed scene on him, confessed that his old friend had become "a sort of adopted prodigal baby. I began to love the very faults which I would never have forgiven in anyone else." An interviewer for *Echo de Paris* quoted Oscar's statement at the age of thirty-seven, "I give myself absolutely to the present"; and many comments by Oscar's intimates suggest that he raised this childish delight in the present to a kind of life's philosophy, the practice of which began early. A Magdalen College classmate recalled, "The whim of the moment he openly acknowledged as his dictator." Ada Leverson perhaps caught best the essence of Oscar the playful philosopher in her observation that he "had a superb vitality, a short-sighted joy in living for the moment. All genius has its naif side, and he, a spectacular genius . . . had this naiveté in excess." She spoke also of a "*euphoria* that was characteristic of him"—just as Augustus John called him "an easy-going sort of genius, with an enormous sense of fun." It is thus no surprise to find Oscar described as "haunting the nursery" of his two boys in Tite Street.

This infantine quality (to use Henry James's tetchy epithet for Oscar's dramatic style) also suffused his physical presence throughout his life. Max Beerbohm described Oscar as "fat—fat not after the manner of ordinary men, but rather as some huge overgrown schoolboy" (in unpublished jottings Beerbohm also noted his resemblance to an "enormous dowager or schoolboy"). Le Gallienne said "he made one think of an enormous doll, a preposterous, exaggerated puppet such as smile foolishly from floats at the Nice carnival." And a reporter for the *Times-Picayune* of New Orleans made a most perceptive stab at explaining the colorful lecturer's remarkable charisma, observing that his "face has an air of youthful, almost infantile sweetness, which perhaps is the real secret of Mr Wilde's power over the people who admire him." Walt Whitman, we have seen, chimed in with his impression of "a great big, splendid boy."

Oscar was aware of this element in his nature, too. He once described Ross as "fond of children, and of people, like myself, who have childlike simple natures." That this childlike aspect of his personality is one of the principal secrets of his style and his success is doubtless. "He was like that *enfant terrible* in Andersen's fairy tale who called out, 'Why the king has nothing on,'" said Richard Le Gallienne; "and while his audience laughed, it awakened, and the truth beneath the phrases went home." Even in demise, Oscar evoked a fairy-tale association—with that most famous of all tumbles. In a letter reacting to pressures upon her to accept Oscar back after prison, Constance wrote her brother

Otho, "The Ranee [Lady Brooke] thinks that he has fallen and cannot rise. That is rather like Humpty Dumpty, but then I think his fate is rather like Humpty Dumpty's, quite as tragic and quite as impossible to put right."

Oscar, having written some of the most famous fairy tales in the language, was also likened, by the *Athenaeum*, to Hans Christian Andersen himself. Though his two volumes of children's tales, *The Happy Prince and Other Tales* (1888) and *A House of Pomegranates* (1891), do not loom large now in discussions of their author, they were very successful and have over the years been "dramatized endlessly" and adapted to every possible medium (including a Bing Crosby recording and, now, a Sir John Gielgud compact disc). Some of Oscar's contemporaries gave them a very high place among his works. O'Sullivan preferred them above all the others, and Pater's most lavish praise was elicited by the tales: "The whole, too brief, book abounds with delicate touches and pure English," he wrote, singling out "The Remarkable Rocket" for its "wise wit." Despite Oscar's jest that "the gods bestowed on Max the gift of perpetual old age," even Beerbohm was greatly taken by the children's tales. In the course of a 1904 revival of *Lady Windermere's Fan*, he bravely ventured that Oscar's "elaborately fantastic spirit" allowed him to achieve "his finest mastery in the forms of the fairy story and of the philosophic essay in dialogue."

The main reason for Oscar's success with the fairy tale—the main reason, surely, for almost every success in this literary form—was the remarkable and long-sustained interpenetration of the child and the adult in his personality. This combined potently with a strong vein of the fantasist and dreamer in him: "It is the first duty of a gentleman to dream," he told his boy Cyril. It is thus no surprise that the nine tales are fine specimens of their kind; only occasionally do they go "dangerously near the region of sham sentiment," as the *Saturday Review* said in its notice on *The Happy Prince*.

But there is something odd about them, given the almost universal acknowledgment of Oscar's boyish exuberance and

147

blithe spirit. Ellmann remarked on this oddity, namely, "a sadness unusual in fairy tales." He also observed, justly, that the tales seem to be presented "like sacraments of a lost faith." There is something peculiarly chastening, wistful, sometimes disconcertingly mordant in these tales, almost as if they were the product of a collaboration between Falstaff and Hamlet. Why might one end a tale with such a final paragraph as this: "Yet ruled he not long, so great had been his suffering, and so bitter the fire of his testing, for after the space of three years he died. And he who came after him ruled evilly." Why the aftertaste of melancholy that this and several of the other tales' denouements leave behind? Was some deep tragic and prophetic instinct urging Oscar to anticipate the mere three years he himself was to live after his "bitter" testing in prison?

To the last question, at least, Oscar once gave the explicit answer "yes"—though many years after the tales were actually written. Indeed, the answer came almost in the form of a fairy-tale parable. In *De profundis*, he told of saying to a friend while "strolling round Magdalen's narrow bird-haunted walks" one June morning that he wished "to eat of the fruit of all the trees in the garden of the world." And "so, indeed, I went out, and so I lived." But he confessed that his mistake was only to sample "the sun-gilt side of the garden" and shun "the other side for its shadow and its gloom." "I went down the primrose path to the sound of flutes. I lived on honeycomb. But to have continued the same life would have been wrong . . . I had to pass on. The other half of the garden had its secrets for me." Oscar then made the remarkable point that he had been divulging the secrets of the other half of the garden, with its "sorrow, despair, suffering, tears," in his works for years: "Of course all this is foreshadowed and prefigured in my art. Some of it is in 'The Happy Prince'; some of it in 'The Young King,' notably in the passage where the Bishop says to the kneeling boy, 'Is not He who made misery wiser than thou art?' a phrase which when I wrote it seemed to me little more than a phrase." After pointing out a similar "note of Doom" in *Dorian Gray*, *Salome*, and his essays, he added: "At every single moment of one's life one is what one is going to become." This expression of Oscar's awareness of a fearful prescience in his writings makes the tales particularly worth pausing over.

Delving behind and between the lines of fairy tales, however, is risky: one can so easily begin to look solemn or ungallant, and one can reemerge only with a flawless grasp of the obvious. Isobel Murray, a recent editor of the tales, has set up two radically opposed ways of approaching them. The simpler way, she has suggested, is to accept them without excessive critical exertion, as Ellen Terry did: "They are quite beautiful, dear Oscar, and I thank you for them from the best bit of my heart. . . . I should like to read one of them some day to NICE people—or even NOT nice people, and MAKE 'em nice." Murray thinks this latter approach may be the "more sane and more realistic." However, Oscar was no friend of sanity and despised realism in all its artistic forms, especially painting. "Modern realistic art," he caustically observed, "has not yet produced a Hamlet, but at least it may claim to have studied Rosencrantz and Guildenstern very closely." Oscar thought all true art was "really a form of exaggeration." The very year a not notably sane Van Gogh was painting his flamboyant *Starry Sky and Cypresses* and *Ravine at St.-Rémy*, Oscar declared that most modern realist painters "are doomed to absolute oblivion. They never paint what they see. They paint what the public sees, and the public never sees anything." He would have reveled in Van Gogh.

The second approach, favored by modern critics, Murray has suggested, is to search out "dark psychological motives" and find, for example, that they were fashioned by "the Wilde who had succumbed to the homosexual impulse." For those with a taste for this approach, Oscar himself had a word of warning: "All art is at once surface and symbol. Those who go beneath the surface do so at their peril." He was not forbidding this critical procedure, I think, but simply suggesting that the discoveries one makes beneath the surface may make one tremble, blanch, and . . . begin to think.

In the end, I think Oscar would have opted for the latter approach . . . with those tempted to explore the world of concealed "motives" and dangerous "impulses" and, thus, willing to risk some speculative peril. On the back cover of *The Chameleon*—the scandalous Oxford undergraduate magazine that was to play its part in the trials—appears a phrase from Robert Louis Stevenson: "A Bazaar of Dangerous and Smiling Chances." To be in such an exciting, dubious place was always Oscar's pleasure: it is the perfect point of embarkation for the risky expeditions he undertook both in life and art. His children's tales are thus far from peripheral *jeux*; indeed, they may be our passport to the center of the man. There are numerous indications in them and in Oscar's letters that children's tales are in fact no different from any other form of literary art: at their best they are probing, subversive, and (like his paradoxes) "dangerous."

My guess that Oscar would prefer the "delving" approach is made largely on account of the brief tale he called "The Devoted Friend." Here a Linnet tells a Water-rat (i.e., a muskrat) the story of a Miller who, by sheer force of rhetoric, manages to disguise total selfishness as altruism and generosity—a characteristic Oscarian stab at philanthropists. The Water-rat, who says he doesn't care about love but exalts friendship, consents to hear the story on one condition: "Is the story about me? . . . If so, I will listen to it, for I am extremely fond of fiction." The story *is* about him; he even identifies with the flatulent, hypocritical Miller. However, in the end—being a perfect specimen of the English public, which (Oscar wrote elsewhere) "likes things to be explained to them in a tedious way"—the Water-rat doesn't grasp its meaning. Indeed, he is quite furious to learn after the fact that the tale has had a moral:

"I am afraid you don't quite see the moral of the story," remarked the Linnet.
   "The what?" screamed the Water-rat.
   "The moral."
   "Do you mean to say that the story has a moral?"
   "Certainly," said the Linnet.

"Well, really," said the Water-rat, in a very angry manner, "I think you should have told me that before you began. If you had done so, I certainly would not have listened to you."

The Water-rat, a wicked send-up of the "solid stolid British intellect," utters a disgusted "Pooh" and scampers down his hole. This brusque dismissal eerily anticipates how the public and press treated Oscar himself when the trials rendered clear the "moral" of his fairy-tale London celebrity.

At the tale's end a duck paddles up to the Linnet, and they discuss the Water-rat briefly:

"I am rather afraid that I have annoyed him," answered the Linnet. "The fact is, that I told him a story with a moral."

"Ah! that is always a very dangerous thing to do," said the Duck.

And I quite agree with her.

Small wonder that the authorial voice pipes up in the story's last sentence to agree on the point. For the Linnet has merely done in this tale what Oscar did in virtually every literary genre he touched: insinuated "morals" (which is merely to say "ideas") that expressed his disgust at the old morality he saw entrenched all around him. And it was "a very dangerous thing to do" when one lived in a society constituted mainly of complacent, selfish, and self-righteous Water-rats.

Tales without subtexts or agendas are unworthy of the name, and there are several remarks in the letters that invite us to delve into their psychological motives—which, by the way, needn't be "dark" as Murray has suggested, but rather "light" and enlightening. Several times Oscar made the point that these tales, like most that prove durable, allow access to all ages. To one correspondent he wrote, just after *The Happy Prince* appeared, that the tales are "meant partly for children, and partly for those who have kept the childlike faculties of wonder and joy, and who find in simplicity a subtle strangeness." To Leonard Smithers, later one of his publishers, he described "the best" story in his first collection, "The Happy Prince," as "an attempt to treat a tragic modern problem in a form that aims at delicacy and imaginative treatment: it is a reaction against the purely imitative character of modern art—and now that literature has taken to blowing loud trumpets I cannot but be pleased that some ear has cared to listen to the low music of a little reed." There is a little false humility here: loudness can be deafening—Oscar said of one writer, "He is so loud that one cannot hear what he says"—and low music on the flute can be most affecting, as he was to discover a few years later in Algiers.

In a letter accompanying a gift of *The Happy Prince* a year later, in 1889, Oscar reiterated the humble pose but at the same time insisted on the earnest, "adult" agenda of his stories. They were, he said, "an attempt to mirror modern life in a form remote from reality—to deal with modern problems in a mode that is ideal and not imitative . . . they are, of course, slight and fanciful, and written, not for children, but for childlike people from eighteen to eighty!" But perhaps the essence of Oscar's fairy tales is fixed by a passing remark thrown off in a much later letter of 1898: "Ordinary critics always think that children are sentimental about literature: they are not: they have humour instead. Later on in life, humour goes." This lack of ordinary sentimentality—as distinct from several moments of remarkable pathos of a kind rarely encountered in fairy tales—gives them their sad penumbra, their "subtle strangeness."

THE SENSE OF ESTRANGEMENT felt by a late-Victorian homosexual, I think, helps to explain the subtle strangeness in several of the most moving tales. The validation of this identity is at least one of their subtexts, though it is subsumed in a more general process common to most fairy tales, namely, the process of self-discovery.

For Oscar, self-discovery was the purpose of all Life and Art, and it must be the supreme concern of the storyteller. His remark to Le Gallienne about fairy tales makes clear his awareness of this: "The mind of a child is a great mystery . . . who shall divine it, or bring it its own peculiar delights?" The thrust of Oscar's writings is always toward *self*-expression, and I suspect that what he meant by "childlike persons from eighteen to eighty" was simply his ideal audience: one that would come, as children are most likely to do before they lose their humor, without preconceptions and prejudices . . . or at least with the willingness to relinquish them in the process of self-discovery. Ellmann noticed that most characters in the tales "are brought to a recognition of themselves"; indeed, he elsewhere generalized that nearly all of Oscar's main fictional characters finally discover a hitherto-veiled true identity. This *sine qua non* for the completely fulfilling life lies at the heart of most of the tales. To be sure, self-discovery does not guarantee greater happiness, especially for the concealed homosexual, but simply a richer, more intense and unbrokered experience of the world.

Oscar would never have been so foolish or artlessly forthright as to compose his tales in such a way as to make them specifically "about" the oppression or repression of homosexual identity. They are masterpieces of open access: open not merely to those aged eighteen (and surely much younger) to eighty, but also to those whose "peculiar delights" would certainly have shocked the solid, stolid moralists of his day. In *The Happy Prince*, Oscar had written a thoroughly "safe" little volume that he could (and did) send to the likes of Ruskin and Gladstone . . . and even to his first female love interest, Florence Balcombe. One guesses that these recipients, like the Water-rat, did not discern all the morals the volume contained. Homosexual readers, however, may have perceived quite different morals and applauded the tales for different reasons. Indeed, I suspect Oscar sprinkled just enough subtly strange hints throughout the stories to let the homosexual cognoscenti know of his fellow-feeling.

It is therefore also easy to imagine him giving copies away to members of his rapidly growing gay circle as his small contribution to a slowly progressing cause. Was Clyde Fitch, an American eleven years younger than Oscar, one such recipient? There are several effusive letters from Fitch to Oscar in the Clark Library, and from Oscar to Fitch have survived one brief telegram—

> What a charming day it has been.
>
> OSCAR

—and one letter:

> Dear Clyde, Just a line to tell you how sorry I am that you have left town, and how I shall miss you.
>
> When you return we must make merry over a flagon of purple wine and invent new tales with which to charm the world.   O.W.

Oscar inscribed a copy of *The Happy Prince* for Fitch. Oscar's wording perhaps carries a suggestion of special fraternity: "Clyde Fitch from his friend Oscar Wilde. Faery-stories for one who lives in Faery-Land. Sept. '90." (Back in America, Fitch published his own volume of fairy tales in 1891; the last one—"The King's Throne," dated "Bushey, Herts. September 1889"—is dedicated "To Oscar Wilde.")

How might *The Happy Prince*—and *A House of Pomegranates*, had he received it as well—have struck Clyde Fitch at the time? What dangerous but exhilarating morals (in both senses of the word) might he have discovered ciphered in the tales? Let us imagine for the moment that my speculation about the younger man's sexuality is correct, put ourselves in Fitch's place, and read some of them through with his eyes.

The Prince of the title story is a statue poised on a column high above a city—London, of course—that encompasses great human misery. Telltale hints explain why. The Town Councillors are a bit dense as to Art; one of them thinks the statue lovely, "only not quite so useful" as a weathercock might be. And a

Mathematical Master disapproves of children dreaming. Fitch might well have guessed that the Prince was Oscar, for he "lived in the Palace of Sans-Souci" and has Oscar's own "low musical voice." And Oscar certainly was "high above the city" in his tastes and in the views he broadcast with such brilliant *hauteur*.

But there is also something of Oscar in a "little Swallow" who falls in love with a Reed growing nearby. It is difficult to read of this romance without thinking of Constance. The Swallow's brethren depart for Egypt, and, after a summer's courtship, he begins to feel "lonely" and "tire of his lady-love." "She has no conversation," says the Swallow; "she is domestic, but I love traveling." When she proves unalterably "attached to her home," he flies away, just as Oscar, at the time of writing the story, began flying away from Tite Street to the West End and Paris . . . though never so far as Egypt.

The Swallow happens to alight on the statue's column and is charmed into a fatal attraction for the Prince: he sacrifices the pleasure of traveling for the happiness of complete devotion to him. The Prince sends him out on reconnaissance, and the sights he reports are Dickensian: "the rich making merry in their beautiful houses, while the beggars were sitting at the gates . . . the white faces of starving children looking out listlessly at the black streets." (Directly behind the Wilde house was one such black street, Paradise Walk: Vyvyan recalled being absolutely terrified by what he saw of it from his nursery window.) The Prince compassionately begs the Swallow to delay his journey and carry jewels from the statue to various needy townspeople, just as a freezing winter begins to encroach.

Thus, the Swallow saves a boy who is "tossing feverishly on his bed," then a young writer in a garret with hair "brown and crisp," lips "red as a pomegranate," and "large dreamy eyes." On his third and final mission of mercy, the Swallow spies "under the archway of a bridge two little boys" who are "lying in one another's arms to try and keep themselves warm. 'How hungry we are!' they said. 'You must not lie here,' shouted the watchman, and they wandered out into the rain." By the time the Swallow has taken them some of the statue's gold leaf, he is near death: "but he would not leave the Prince, he loved him so well." The Prince, unaware of the bird's extremity, says: "I am glad that you are going to Egypt at last . . . you have stayed too long here; but you must kiss me on the lips, for I love you." In a kind of miniature *Liebestod*, the kiss transpires, and the Swallow falls dead at the foot of the statue.

Oscar's ending is poignant. The statue, now beggarly-looking, is declared "no longer useful" (the Councillors had thought it advertised their artistic taste) and is thrown into a furnace. But its broken lead heart refuses to melt. God sends one of his angels to fetch the "two most precious things in the city," and the angel returns with the lump of lead and the Swallow's corpse: " 'You have rightly chosen,' said God, 'for in my garden of Paradise this little bird shall sing for evermore, and in my city of gold the Happy Prince shall praise me.' "

On its face a potent, Christian story of *agape*. Oscar thought it the best in the collection. But it is also tempting to read it as a miniature, and moving, celebration of a tragedy of the Love that dare not speak its name, indeed a foreshadowing of Oscar's own reluctance to flee at the height of his freezing winter seven years later. It is easy to imagine Fitch reading the story as a *conte à clef*, a melancholy evocation of gay experience in a frosty, inclement, threatening society whose watchmen were always disturbing boys—and men—in each other's arms and shouting the equivalent of "You must not lie here." The subtle concealment of this "allegory" may explain why the well-closeted Pater singled out "The Happy Prince" for its "beauty and tenderness." When homosexuality reared its head more obviously in Oscar's later works, Pater shrank back in disgust, rather as the Town Councillors do at the sight of the poor-looking statue. Here is the first of several premonitions, in these tales, of Oscar's own downfall, when the formerly delightful celebrity was suddenly and peremptorily pulled down and discarded.

"The Remarkable Rocket" is less about the Cause than about Oscar the causeur. This story is a delicious assault on social snobbery and focuses on the pontifications that a very proud rocket makes to all the other fireworks assembled in the storeroom of a kingdom's Royal Pyrotechnist. The charm of the story (and, given the brief moment of any firework's glory, its irony) is that there is much of Oscar in the Rocket. This is no surprise, for many friends and acquaintances, like Beerbohm and Shaw, noticed a strong streak of Irish social snobbery in his makeup. He could, and often did, boast in so many words, "I am a very remarkable Rocket, and come of remarkable parents." The Rocket has Oscar's delightful penchant for paradox—"It is a very dangerous thing to know one's friends"—and his preference for fantasy over sanity: "Why anybody can have common sense, provided that they have no imagination." And the Rocket employs his imagination as Oscar did: "I never think of things as they really are; I always think of them as being quite different." The Rocket infuriates the solid, stolid Roman Candle and Bengal Light, the latter being especially disgusted by him, in the best *Punch* manner. "You are the most affected person I ever met," says he. As with Oscar, the Rocket's affectation is born of magnificent egotism: "I hate people who talk about themselves . . . when one wants to talk about oneself, as I do." In this, the Rocket verifies Oscar's observation, published the next year in "The Critic as Artist," on the "attractions" of egotism: "When people talk to us about others they are usually dull. When they talk to us about themselves they are nearly always interesting."

Alas, like Oscar, he proves at the crucial moment utterly self-destructive. He is warned not to cry, but willfully insists, "I shall weep if I choose." He does, and is the one dud at the King's midnight fireworks display. He suddenly becomes a Bad Rocket and is thrown over the palace wall and into a ditch. He is found by two little boys and put under a cooking-kettle. His pride miraculously still intact, the Rocket pictures his imminent glory in words that, yet again, glance ahead to 1895: " 'Now I am going to explode,' he cried. 'I shall set the whole world on fire, and make such a noise, that nobody will talk about anything else for a whole year.' And he certainly did explode." But alas his explosion is "silent." Everyone within earshot happens to be sound asleep.

☆   ☆   ☆

JUST AFTER THE JUDICIAL fireworks of 1895, one staunch defender asserted that tales like "The Happy Prince" and "The Selfish Giant" were "too obviously free from anything shocking." But now this view seems naive. For with "The Selfish Giant" we encounter another embedded homosexual allegory: a wish-fulfillment fantasy, one might say, of gay liberation. The story begins in a paradisal garden "with soft green grass . . . beautiful flowers like stars" and sweetly singing birds; here all the children are wont to play after school, and they all agree, "How happy we are to live here!" Unfortunately, the garden belongs to a Giant, who has been away visiting a Cornish ogre for seven years: "After the seven years were over he had said all that he had to say, for his conversation was limited, and he determined to return to his own castle." Aghast at seeing his property overrun, he expels the children, builds a high wall around the garden, and places a sign on it that would have been especially repugnant to the tale's author, had he encountered one on his walks along Lake Geneva:

TRESPASSERS
WILL BE
PROSECUTED

"He was a very selfish Giant."

The Giant embodies, among other things, Victorian propriety and the spirit of the ostraciser. Lady Bracknell, a not-distant relation of the Giant, was to perform exactly the same function in *Earnest*. He is the essence of that spirit Oscar vilified in "The Soul of Man Under Socialism" as the enemy of Individualism: "Selfishness always aims at creating around it an absolute uniformity of type. Unselfishness recognises infinite variety of type as a delightful thing, accepts it, acquiesces in it, enjoys it. . . . It is grossly selfish to require of one's neighbour that he should think in the same way." The paradise Oscar envisioned in his essay, it could be said, is one of Individual Play, and this required the charming and neutralizing of the Giants and Lady Bracknells of his day. All the obstructions to self-fulfilling play for all the "infinite variety" of human types had to be demolished.

The way Oscar worked out his story suggests that he was implicitly including homosexuals among the world's "infinite variety" of types to be embraced. As in "The Happy Prince," winter makes its appearance; indeed, it becomes permanent in the Giant's garden. "The only people who were pleased were the Snow and the Frost." Many months pass, and the Giant awakens one morning to the long-unheard sound of birdsong, and he discovers children again in his garden, who have sneaked in through a hole in the wall. They are all playing in the garden's twelve peach trees, except for one little boy in a far corner, too short to reach the lowest branches. The Giant steals up to him, takes him "gently in his hand," and lifts him into the tree. What then happens is curiously reminiscent of the spectacular moment in Wagner's *Die Walküre*, when a huge door suddenly opens on a glorious spring evening for the (incestuous) lovers Sieglinde and Siegmund: "The tree broke at once into blossom, and the birds came and sang on it, and the little boy stretched out his two arms and flung them about the Giant's neck, and kissed him."

The Giant becomes a perfect playmate for the children, but the little boy vanishes from their number. The Giant begins to pine: "The Giant loved him the best because he had kissed him." He remains very kind to all the children, "yet he longed for his first little friend, and often spoke of him. 'How I would like to see him!' he used to say." Years pass, the Giant becomes old and feeble, and then, one day in the dead of winter, he sees the boy out under a tree decorated brilliantly with white blossoms and golden fruit. He rushes out, finds the boy's hands and feet transfixed by nails, and rages at the evildoers. "Nay!" answers the child, "these are the wounds of Love." He reminds the Giant of the day he let the boy play in his garden: "to-day you shall come with me to my garden, which is Paradise." The next day the Giant is found under the tree, dead and covered with white blossoms.

There is nothing overtly homoerotic about the story, yet the beautifully liberating kiss is telling . . . as is the longing of the Giant for the boy (recall that Oscar was six feet, three inches tall). As we shall see in the next chapter, this was a familiar position for Oscar throughout his active homosexual career. But the ultimate and grander point of "The Selfish Giant"—applicable to all the sexualities—is that, following Christ, the Giant finally allows all the children to play in his garden. No wonder, then, that Oscar, in his essay on socialism, would praise the perceptiveness of Renaissance painters who posed "Christ as a little boy playing with another boy in a palace or a garden."

Oscar was here invoking his own perception of Jesus' imperative, which he laid out in "The Soul of Man Under Socialism," that "he who would lead a Christlike life is he who is perfectly and absolutely himself." The story presents an image of liberation, of true unselfishness, which is simply allowing others to live as they wish to live. As the boy charms the Giant or as Jack tries to charm Lady Bracknell, Oscar in some deep way hoped to charm the middle classes and the Law of Victorian society into acceptance of this image of liberation. The magical embrace in the story that occurs between two males may be innocent of innuendo. And yet, one wonders. We have already learned that he could not hold back the tears when he read the story to his boys. Perhaps he did so not only because, as he told Cyril, it was "beautiful," but also because, for a gay man, it was very sad.

There is a letter to Oscar from Fitch (about whom much more in the next chapter) at about the time Oscar signed a copy of *The Happy Prince* for him. It begins, "Perfect . . . *Perfect* . . . PERFECT! . . . It is the most delicate, the most exquisite, the most complete idyll I have ever read." One would like to think he was referring to "The Selfish Giant."

☆　☆　☆

"THE YOUNG KING," WHICH appeared three years later in *A House of Pomegranates*, displays signs of a distinctly more transgressive, though still by no means obtrusive, assertion of homosexual themes. This story tells of a monarch whose dreams show him the miseries of the world and transform him at the end into a figure of Christian *caritas*, appearing for his coronation in a goatherd's rags. This hero, however, has reached puberty and seems initially a distinctly "different" child of Sybaris. After his Professors of Etiquette depart, he flings himself on a lavish embroidered couch and lies there "wild-eyed and open-mouthed, like a brown woodland Faun, or some young animal of the forest newly snared by the hunters." (The image reminds one of Oscar's report from Morocco of all the attractive boys he encounters: "The mountains of Kabylia [are] full of villages peopled by fauns. . . . We were followed by lovely brown things from forest to forest.")

The young King has "a strange passion for beauty," and one manifestation of this strangeness is "the slim, fair-haired Court pages, with their floating mantles, and gay fluttering ribands" who sometimes accompany him. Redolent of some of the steamier, monstrous-orchid pages of *Dorian Gray* (or Huysmans's quintessential gay-decadent novel *À Rebours*) is the discovery of the King, after being missing for several hours, "in a little chamber in one of the northern turrets of the palace gazing, as one in a trance, at a Greek gem carved with the figure of Adonis." On another occasion he is seen "pressing his warm lips to the marble brow of an antique statue . . . inscribed with the name of the Bithynian slave of Hadrian." Unsuspecting readers might think nothing of this curious detail; but a gay reader would certainly recognize this reference to Antinous, a classical type of the pederastic love object. (Much later, amid his postprison sexual promiscuity, Oscar sullenly expressed to Ross his annoyance at so-called friends who would grudge him his "nights with Antinous.")

"The Star-Child" also bears some connection with *Dorian Gray*. It likewise is about a figure whose beauty—skin "white and delicate as sawn ivory," hair "like the rings of the daffodil"— makes him a cynosure. His beauty, however, like Dorian's, begins to "work him evil" and he grows "proud, and cruel, and selfish." Rather as Oscar mocked the ugliness of one of his young acquaintances, Walter Grainger, during his trial, the self-enamored Star-Child "would mock at the weakly and ill-favoured, and make jest of them." The tale can easily be read as a cautionary one aimed at the male Narcissus or, rather, the type of the young homosexual Adonis who is quite aware of his attraction and cynically exploits his charisma. Such persons become, like the Star-Child, "hard of heart." Indeed, the Star-Child's behavior before he is bitterly tested by a sudden transformation into "loathsome" ugliness is rather reminiscent of descriptions of the furious egotism of Lord Alfred Douglas.

More generally, the Star-Child epitomizes the vanity of all human pride. In this respect he learns the terrible lesson that Oscar was to learn during and after his imprisonment. The Star-Child's dark journey is uncannily like the one that lay in store for Oscar. He finds himself at one point in a dungeon, served only moldy bread and brackish water; he is also forced to wander "for the space of three years . . . over the world." In this world "there was neither love nor loving-kindness nor charity for him, but it was even such a world as he had made for himself in the days of his great pride."

The most ambitious, longest, and—from the standpoint of a homosexual subtext—perhaps most fascinating of all the tales is "The Fisherman and His Soul." Before looking into this subtext, though, this tale's several moments of striking autobiographical resonance deserve notice. At the end of his life Oscar confessed to having fed "endless hunger for pleasures that wreck the body and imprison the soul," and the same temptation to lose one's soul in pursuit of the heart's desire is experienced by the Fisherman. For he falls in love with a Mermaid, whose song causes him to sit "idle in his boat" and lose all "care of his craft." She asks for his soul in exchange for her love. This love which draws him away from his "useful" profession produces a wishful fantasy of secret and illicit consummation; the Fisherman tells the Mermaid: "I will send my soul away . . . and you shall be my bride . . . in the depth of the sea we will dwell together." He asks how to divest himself of his soul, and the Mermaid says she doesn't know, for "the Sea-folk have no souls."

It is not stretching credulity, I think, to imagine the story's Sea-folk as representative of homosexuals. Consider, for example, that the Priest consulted by the Fisherman is enraged at the notion of giving up one's soul. The soul, he says, is "given to us by God that we should nobly use it. . . . As for the Sea-folk, they are lost, and they who would traffic with them are lost also. They are as the beasts of the field that know not good from evil, and for them the Lord has not died." The Fisherman weeps at these "bitter words," but stands firm and demands to know what his soul profits him "if it stand between me and the thing that I love." The Priest erupts yet again, in precisely the verbiage Victorians employed to condemn homosexuality: " 'The love of the body is vile,' cried the Priest, knitting his brows, 'and vile and evil are the pagan things God suffers to wander through His world. Accursed be the Fauns of the woodlands . . . and their perilous joys.' " Yet again, one is reminded of Oscar's tempting fauns of Kabylia.

Perseverant, the Fisherman consults a Witch, who whisks him away to a midnight dance that is interrupted by a brilliant evocation of the homosexual gaze, when eyes meet and demonic fires are kindled. A man dressed in a suit of black velvet appears:

His face was strangely pale, but his lips were like a proud red flower. He seemed weary, and was leaning back toying in a listless manner with the pommel of his dagger. . . . A short cloak lined with sables hung from his shoulder, and his delicate white hands were gemmed with rings. Heavy eyelids [like Oscar's] drooped over his eyes.

The young Fisherman watched him, as one snared in a spell. At last their eyes met, and wherever he danced it seemed to him that the eyes of the man were upon him. . . .

Suddenly a dog bayed in the wood, and the dancers stopped, and going up two by two, knelt down, and kissed the man's hands. As they did so, a little smile touched his proud lips, as a bird's wing touches the water and makes it laugh. But there was disdain in it. He kept looking at the young fisherman.

Oscar, we have seen, experienced a very similar moment himself, while awaiting his wife one day outside Swan and Edgar's.

Finally, having separated himself from his Soul, the Fisherman leaps into the sea—that is, into the Other World of forbidden pleasure—and embraces the Mermaid, very much as the boy embraces the Giant in "The Selfish Giant": "The Tritons blew their horns, and the little Mermaid rose up to meet him, and put her arms around his neck and kissed him on the mouth." His Soul begs him to reconsider, but the Fisherman—like Oscar in his own life in the year of 1891—retorts that "Love is better than Wisdom." "Nothing is better than Wisdom," says the Soul, but the Fisherman insists that Love is better and plunges like Oscar "into the deep."

This Soul, of course, is an instrument of tyranny, an incarcerating myth, and the prime weapon of Society and the Law in imposing their morality upon the young Fisherman. His resistance, when he comes to recognize that "it was an evil Soul," is heroic. He vows to return to the sea, whence the Mermaid has vanished. His Soul tempts him, Satan-like, not to do so: "And ever did his Soul tempt him by the way, but he made it no answer, nor would do any of the wickedness that it sought to make him do, so great was the power of the love that was in him." Finally, amid "black waves" that come "hurrying to the shore," he is reunited with his love: "Dead at his feet it was lying." As the tide rushes in, the Fisherman refuses his tyrannous Soul's last entreaties to renounce his love for the Mermaid. The waves begin to roll over him as he kisses the dead Mermaid and—yet another *Liebestod*—soon he, too, expires. At the same moment the Fisherman's soul returns and is "one with him even as before."

What is the "gay moral" of the story? The same, I think, as the moral Oscar's son Vyvyan took away from his own life's experience, namely, that one must sail under one's true colors: to follow one's true love, notwithstanding empty, bigoted threats that this thing called a soul will be lost thereby. The Priest discovers the couple *in flagrante delicto*, albeit posthumously. Oscar arranges for his reaction to appear especially repugnant:

> When the Priest reached the shore he saw the young Fisherman lying drowned in the surf, and clasped in his arms was the body of the little Mermaid. And he drew back frowning, and having made the sign of the cross, he cried aloud and said, "I will not bless the sea nor anything that is in it. Accursed be the Sea-folk, and accursed be all they who traffic with them. And as for him who for love's sake forsook God, and so lieth here with his leman slain by God's judgment, take up his body and the body of his leman, and bury them in the corner of the Field of the Fullers. . . . Accursed were they in their lives, and accursed shall they be in their deaths also."

The pair is buried in this field, "where no sweet herbs grow."

The tale ends, yet again, with a poignantly orchestrated fantasy, one is tempted to say, of homosexual empowerment. Three years pass and the Priest, on approaching his altar, is surprised to find it covered with "strange flowers that he had never seen before." Their beauty troubles him, and their odor is "sweet in his nostrils. And he felt glad, and understood not why he was glad." Perhaps they were Oscar's favorite lilies of the valley . . . or green carnations. It turns out that they come from Fullers' Field. A refulgent transformation takes place, and the Priest, as it were, sees the light . . . just as the Selfish Giant reforms and Lady Bracknell relents. Yet another exalted embrace of the "infinite variety" of human types is performed: even the hitherto outcast Sea-folk and Fauns are sanctified. The Priest "came to the shore of the sea, and blessed the sea, and all the wild things [magnificent pun, even if unintended] that are in it. The Fauns also he blessed, and the little things that dance in the woodland, and the bright-eyed things that peer through the leaves. All the things in God's world he blessed, and the people were filled with joy and wonder."

But here, too, Oscar did not forbear a melancholy valedictory gesture: "Yet never again in the corner of the Fullers' Field grew flowers of any kind, but the field remained barren even as before. Nor came the Sea-folk into the bay as they had been wont to do, for they went to another part of the sea." A powerful image, one would like to think, of the scar and the cost of the repression of identity, sexual or otherwise.

☆   ☆   ☆

W. H. AUDEN OBSERVED about Oscar that "in few cases is the emotional root of thinking so obvious as it is in his." To the extraordinary degree that they reflect upon his own homosexuality and society's attitudes toward it, Oscar's stories encourage one to agree with Auden. They are also by no means tangential to his oeuvre, but rather utterly characteristic of it. One can underscore this by noting that his guiding devotion to the principle of imaginative personal self-definition figures powerfully in the two instances in which he chose to respond to criticism of his fairy tales.

When an anonymous reviewer for the *Saturday Review* made bold to suggest that, in "The Nightingale and the Rose," Oscar "stumbled a little along with his natural history," he responded with unusual heat,

> No doubt there will always be critics who, like a certain
> writer in the *Saturday Review*, will gravely censure the

teller of fairy tales for his defective knowledge of natural history, who will measure imaginative work by their own lack of any imaginative faculty, and will hold up their inkstained hands in horror if some honest gentleman, who has never been farther than the yew-trees of his own garden, pens a fascinating book of travels like Sir John Mandeville, or, like great Raleigh, writes a whole history of the world, without knowing anything whatsoever about the past.

The *Saturday Review* writer also asserted that the proper audience for *The Happy Prince* would "assuredly not be composed of children." "Children do not care for satire," opined the reviewer. When *A House of Pomegranates* appeared and the *Pall Mall Gazette* made a similar charge, Oscar responded with justified fury in a letter to the editor. It is a mark of the importance of the tales in Oscar's oeuvre that this criticism evoked one of the finest expressions of his credo as a writer. The letter is also perfect Oscar—defiant, caustic, Olympian:

> The writer of this review . . . starts by asking an extremely silly question, and that is, whether or not I have written this book for the purpose of giving pleasure to the British child. Having expressed grave doubts on this subject, a subject on which I cannot conceive any fairly-educated person having any doubts at all, he proceeds, apparently quite seriously, to make the extremely limited vocabulary at the disposal of the British child the standard by which the prose of an artist is to be judged! Now in building this *House of Pomegranates* I had about as much intention of pleasing the British child as I had of pleasing the British public. Mamilius [the boy-prince in *The Winter's Tale*] is as entirely delightful as Caliban is entirely detestable, but neither the standard of Mamilius nor the standard of Caliban is my standard. No artist recognises any standard of beauty

but that which is suggested by his own temperament. The artist seeks to realise in a certain material his immaterial idea of beauty, and thus to transform an idea into an ideal. That is why an artist makes things. The artist has no other object in making things.

The real point here, however, as in so many of the tales themselves, is that one must play—in both the ludic and the thespian sense—*oneself*.

The *Saturday Review* notice opened with the assertion, "One of the chief functions of the true fairy story is to excite sympathy." Oscar chose not to disagree with this in his outraged rebuttal, though he might well have done so. For most of his finest works, including the tales, display a clear preference for exciting thought rather than mere "sympathy." On the other hand, maybe he chose not to debate the point on this occasion because in these stories he was, in fact, very subtly urging sympathy of the most remarkable and liberating kind.

Chapter Nine

ASS-THETE: LOVER OF YOUTH

I have never learned anything except from people younger than myself and you are infinitely young.

—LETTER TO H. C. MARILLIER, 1885

Failure is to form habits.

—WALTER PATER, QUOTED IN *DE PROFUNDIS,* 1897

FOR CONFIRMED STRAIGHT MEN—mulierasts, as Robbie Ross liked to call them—the mammae are the iconic site of fixation par excellence. The equivalent, and similarly shaped, site for gay men is the glutei. For them the ideal object of desire is very likely to evoke gratifying posterior analysis. The Greeks, needless to say, had the word for a person with impressive buttocks, *kallipygos*. It is a shame that the lively and useful derivative English adjective *callipygian* has pretty much passed out of use, except among more erudite aficionados. "Tits" and "ass" seem to satisfy the lexical needs of much sexual discourse today.

Pensées derrières—pensée, delightful to note, is also the

Wild "Oscar;"
Or, Balaam, the Ass-thete,
A TAIL OF A COAT,
By the author of Mudges on the Lake Front.

'Also other new and amusing COAT
TAILS at Willoughby, Hill & Co.'s, corner Madison and Clark sts.

JUST MADE UP:
26 new patterns of Spring Overcoats,
price $7.50 to $18; modest, neat
nice-fitting, and very reasonable in
price.
1,200 new early Spring Suits, just what
is needed now, and the prices are $10,
$12, $14, $16, $18, $20.

PANTS
DOWN AGAIN!
Willoughby, Hill & Co., 1,000 pairs,
'tis a mark down of 50 cts.' to $2 each
pair,
Don't buy "npthing" without 1st £-ing
our new goods and low prices.

Open till Nine at night.

French for pansy—have probably always produced ribald humor and wordplay. There is some in Joyce's typically virtuosic pun-word in *Finnegans Wake*, "ersewild," as there was in the suggestion by a friend of Adrian Hall that he call his early-1970s theater piece about Oscar *The Bugger's Opera*. A similar urge has led me to commandeer the pun of a resourceful menswear firm in Chicago that, capitalizing on the publicity attending Oscar's visit to the city in 1882, sought to catch the eye with an advertisement featuring "Wild 'Oscar;' Or, Balaam, the Ass-thete." (In later years, Oscar would probably have had a witty remark for the highlighted phrase farther down: "PANTS / DOWN AGAIN!")

The pun of Messrs. Willoughby and Hill refers of course not to an anatomical part but to a four-footed beast and was no doubt intended in good Midwestern humor. Squelching such proposed fashions as tailcoats and knee-breeches also made good business sense for a firm eager to sell "modest, neat, nice-fitting" overcoats and 1,200 sensible spring suits. But as with much American humor at Oscar's expense—especially from the commercial patriarchy—there are a distinct edge and innuendo in the conceit, just as there are in the accompanying figure's limp hands, effeminate contrapposto, and turned-out feet. The biblical reference is to the children of Israel who had the habit of riding on "ass colts" and who "did evil . . . in the sight of the Lord, and served Baalim" (Judges 10:4–6). Oscar, the advertisement suggests, was devoted to entirely inappropriate aesthetic and sartorial gods. If there was a sexual aspersion—

and doubtless none was intended—it was of the most general kind, accusing Oscar of having a mollifying or mollycoddling effect on men . . . and a further debilitating effect on women. (When he visited San Francisco, Gertrude Atherton's husband forbade her to attend his lecture, being convinced that a "man who walked about with a sunflower in his hand and called himself an aesthete must be too improper for a decent woman to look at.")

Turning the wordplay of Willoughby and Hill into something more outrageous—making it a lisping pun on "athlete" rather than "aesthete"—is apt, I think, for our look now into Oscar's sexual life several years after he gave up his full-time apostleship on behalf of Aestheticism. My conceit also solves—with the kind of glee that brightens many of his letters to members of his gay circle—the problem of *what* to call Oscar the sexual being. In Victorian society nearly everyone knew the behavior and the behavers to exist, but to utter a name for it or even spell it was really too much. Queensberry tried and got it famously wrong on the insulting calling card he left for Oscar at the Albemarle Club: "For Oscar Wilde, posing as a somdomite." Even friends kindly disposed toward Oscar fell back upon what now seem like pejorative euphemisms: "wretched illness," "perversion," or "this physical and psychical disease."

Weirdly, one of the most impressive castigations of homosexuality in characteristic Victorian terms was composed by Oscar himself. It is contained in two of the most appalling and pathetic letters he ever wrote, petitions to the Home Secretary for early release from Reading Prison. He was manifestly desperate when he wrote them; the man who had perhaps kissed ass in the literal sense was now obliged to do so in the modern slang sense. This led him, in his attempt to ingratiate himself with the Secretary, to denounce his homosexuality in the most abject terms. He described his behavior in precisely the vilifying terms that Victorian prigs and puritans so often used to condemn it, referring to his "loathsome modes of erotomania," to those like himself who suffer from "sensual monomanias" and are prey to "morbid passions, and obscene fancies . . . that defile, desecrate and destroy." His vices, he said of himself in the third person, are "embedded in his flesh: spread over him like leprosy: they feed on him like a strange disease." Four months later, having received no response, he petitioned again, this time pretending to flagellate himself for this "insanity of perverted sensual instinct" that "clings like a malaria to soul and body alike." His exertions were of no avail: he served out his full two-year sentence.

Among the Victorian public, then, homosexuality was, as Edward Carpenter observed in 1894, simply "dismissed with opprobrious epithets well suited to give an easy victory to prejudice and ignorance"—opprobrious epithets like the ones Oscar heaped upon himself to the Home Secretary. Scientists and gay apologists were by this time, however, beginning to seek more neutral names for same-sex relations. Krafft-Ebing contributed "Contrary Sexuality" and called the individual an "Urning" (from the love born of Uranos, mentioned in Plato's *Symposium*). "Uranian" was a term used on occasion by Oscar himself. Whitman favored the concepts of "Comradeship" and "Adhesive Love." Carpenter was not pleased with the "bastard" word "homosexual," just then coming into use, because it combined a Greek prefix and Latin root. He preferred "homogenic" but also referred to the "Intermediate Sex."

BUT THESE ARE ALL such polite terms, and it does not seem worthwhile or indeed possible to acquaint ourselves politely with Oscar the sexual animal. Besides, the ribald pun has about it a flavor of the undergraduate bad-boyishness that Oscar cultivated among his gay circles until the end of his life. Indeed, the history of Oscar's ass-theticism begins in his days as an undergraduate at Magdalen College. Though most who have speculated on the matter have guessed that Oscar's active adult homosexual life began in 1886 or so, it seems clear from early letters to his classmates that such Love was at this time often spoken of, gossiped about, and made distinctly "insider's" humor of. In a letter to William

"Bouncer" Ward in July 1876 boasting of receiving a First in Classical Mods, Oscar told of reading Catullus, that raciest of Romans (along with Martial), mentioned haling Walt Whitman into his interrogation on Aeschylus, and joked about being awakened by the Clerk of the Schools "while lying in bed on Tuesday morning with Swinburne (a copy of)."

A month later he wrote Ward again, from Dublin, where he was visiting his mother on summer holiday. This letter broached a delicate matter that clearly shows Oscar attuned to the famed "unethical" substratum of English university life:

Oscar Wilde with two Oxford classmates, Reginald "Kitten" Harding and William "Bouncer" Ward; this photograph was taken 12 March 1876. From the Clark Library, Los Angeles.

I want to ask your opinion on this psychological question. In our friend *Todd*'s ethical barometer, at what height is his moral quicksilver? Last night I strolled into the theatre about ten o'clock and to my surprise saw Todd and young Ward the quire boy in a private box together, Todd very much in the background. . . . I wonder what young Ward is doing with him. Myself I believe Todd is extremely moral and only mentally spoons the boy, but I think he is foolish to go about with one, if he *is* bringing this boy about with him.

You are the only one I would tell about it, as you

173

have a philosophical mind, *but don't tell anyone about it like a good boy—it would do neither us nor Todd any good.*

He (Todd) looked awfully nervous and uncomfortable. I thought of Mark.

Who was Mark? Perhaps another member of a gay circle who took dangerous risks in pursuit of illicit pleasures. The next year Oscar happened to mention him again in a letter to Bouncer: "Did I tell you that in consequence of Mark's late hours the Dean refused to let him take his degree?"

The ironies of Oscar's observations about Todd, who went on to serve as chaplain in the Royal Navy for thirty years, are enormous. Within several years Oscar would himself cease mere mental "spooning" of the young men he fancied. And in the end he did not scruple at bringing boys about with him, escorting them into theaters full of people, and decidedly refusing to stay "in the background." The quicksilver in his ethical barometer fairly exploded. Another irony is the likelihood that Oscar, too, was insufficiently discreet during his Oxford years. This is certainly suggested by the uproar that attended the arrival of his 1881 *Poems* at the Oxford Union.

Although the Union's secretary had requested a copy, a rancorous debate arose as to whether it should be accepted. In the end—and apparently for the first and last time in the Union's history—it was voted to return the presentation copy. While vague charges of thinness and plagiarism were lodged and "immorality" was suggested, it seems the put-down had more to do with vindictive retaliation by his puritan contemporaries for the bohemian life he had led in Oxford. Such is the thrust of an editorial in the *Oxford and Cambridge Undergraduate Journal* a year later, just after a motion to acquire the *Poems* for the Coffee and Smoking Room was also defeated: "If a man leads an evil life in the University, even though he may not suffer for his acts at the time, yet his character will not have escaped the notice of all his colleagues, who afterwards will always have it in their power to call his remembrance to the past." The "members of this old University" were thus urged not "to act in such a way as to trail her honour in the dust" . . . and therefore to spurn Oscar's volume.

Some readers of Oscar's poems, notably one called "Charmides," did succeed in finding "evil life" in them. One such was Canon Miles, the father of Oscar's first London roommate, Frank Miles, who was gay. Concerned for his son's "good name," Canon Miles insisted in a letter to Oscar on "separation for a time" and reproached him for not seeing the risk of publishing a poem that "makes all who read it say to themselves . . . 'it is licentious and may do great harm to any soul that reads it.' "

This was in the summer of 1881. The next busy year was given to the American lecture tour, and the year following was filled by lectures around the British Isles and also Oscar's courtship of and engagement to Constance Lloyd. Marriage in 1884 ushered in two vigorous years of settling into "the house beautiful" in Tite Street and bringing two boys into the world. These half-dozen years were apparently a genuine interregnum separating his *perhaps* virginal homoerotic frisking at the "old University" and the day sometime in 1886 when he first met Robbie Ross. Ross, one of the more competent, upright, and trustworthy witnesses to Oscar's life, later told Frank Harris that he was "the first boy Oscar ever had."

That Oscar was poised in 1886 for flight with sweet birds of youth is strongly suggested in a letter he wrote early that year to H. C. Marillier, whom he had first met in 1881 when he was living in the Strand . . . and when Marillier was sixteen. The letter was written from "the region of horrible snow and horrible notepaper" (he was in Glasgow to lecture), but it is full of exotic warmth and intimacy:

> Your letter has reached me, like a strain of music windblown from a far land. You too have the love of things impossible—"ερως τῶν 'αδϑνάτων—l'amour de l'impossible (how do men name it?). Sometime you will find, even as I have found, that there is no such thing as a romantic experience; there are romantic memories, and

there is the desire of romance—that is all. Our most fiery moments of ecstasy are merely shadows of what somewhere else we have felt, or of what we long some day to feel. . . .

Much of this I fancy you yourself have felt: much remains for you to feel. There is an unknown land full of strange flowers and subtle perfumes, a land of which it is joy of all joys to dream, a land where all things are perfect and poisonous. . . .

Write to me at Tite Street, and let me know where you will be. Ever yours O.W.

Oscar did not know it, but he was here already beginning to write *The Picture of Dorian Gray.*

Time was fleeting: he was thirty-two in 1886. Ross, on the other hand, turned seventeen on that 25 May. The difference in their ages made a fitting inauguration to Oscar's homosexual career, if indeed (as one is tempted to doubt) Ross truly was the first male of his sexual acquaintance. For Oscar cultivated from his earliest middle age a devotion both to Youth and to youths. On this theme he spun some of his wittiest variations. "Frequenting the society of the aged and the well-informed," says Vivian in "The Decay of Lying," is "fatal" to the imagination. Lord Henry Wotton praises Dorian Gray, saying he has the "most marvellous youth, and youth is the one thing worth having." And in the notorious Oxford student magazine *The Chameleon* appeared this fine specimen of Oscar's aphoristic nonchalance: "The old believe everything; the middle-aged suspect everything: the young know everything." A few years before, in 1892, on the occasion of his first London premiere, for *Lady Windermere's Fan,* he struck the gong for Youth again in a remarkable letter to the editor of the *St. James's Gazette* that hinted rather boldly at the youthful coterie he had begun to gather about himself. He alluded first to the "delightful and immortal" curtain speech he delivered after the performance, then described "the pleasure of entertaining at supper a small number of personal friends." As "none of them was older than myself I, naturally, listened to their artistic views with attention and pleasure. The opinions of the old on matters of Art are, of course, of no value whatsoever." Edward Shelley, with whom Oscar was sequestering himself at the Albemarle Hotel during this time, must have been one of this party.

Oscar was always urging those about him (but especially his younger friends)—to adapt a phrase from *Dorian Gray*—to gather their harvest while it was yet spring. This was surely part of his flattering seducer's patter. On the glory of youth he frequently opined in private. In 1885, when he was thirty-one, he closed a letter to Marillier, whom he had met five years before: "Is it five years ago really? Then I might almost sign myself an old friend, but the word old is full of terror." Four years later Richard Le Gallienne divulged his age to Oscar, who replied, "Twenty-three! . . . It is a kind of genius to be twenty-three!" And as Oscar grew even older, his taste remained fixed upon males who were teenagers or a bit older . . . and who were clean-shaven.*

In the early 1890s Oscar's cult of Youth became increasingly populous. As Croft-Cooke has summarized this period, his "velocity with young men increased." He fancied himself, doubtless, acting in part the role of a wise (but not quite so elderly) Socrates . . . or perhaps acting the role of the older lover among Spartan homosexual couples, the *Eispnêlos* or "inspirer," to the younger *Aïtes* or "hearer" he was seducing into his charming company . . . and perhaps into his bed. But he was in fact becoming more and more notorious as (to borrow Nietzsche's wry description of Socrates) a "mocking and enamored monster and pied piper" of London.

---

*Oscar did not like facial hair. He harried at least two acquaintances, George Ives and André Gide, into shaving their mustaches. Just out of prison, he described to Reggie Turner a "pal" he had made on the inside. Oscar said he had a heart of gold but then explained why the friendship was not sexual: "He is not a 'beautiful boy.' He is twenty-nine years of age, but looks a little older, as he inherits hair that catches silver lines early: he has also a slight, but still *real* moustache. I am thankful and happy to be able to say that I have no feeling for him."

The Stranger Wilde

A GOOD EXAMPLE OF one of this amorous pied piper's conquests appears to have been Clyde Fitch, the young American (eleven years Oscar's junior) who associated with him in 1889–91 and went on to become his generation's most successful playwright.

Ellmann did not mention Fitch at all, and Hart-Davis referred merely to several "emotionally hero-worshipping" letters from him to Oscar preserved in the Clark Library. But these letters, on inspection, vividly suggest that far more than intellectual sparks flew between this particular *Eispnêlos* and *Aïtes*. Having read "The Portrait of Mr. W.H." with its shocking premise of Shakespeare's love for the boy actor Willie Hughes, Fitch addressed Oscar in his salutation as "You precious maddening man," then called the story *"great—and fine."* "I believe in Willie Hughes," he assured Oscar, ending this letter (with a pun in the salutation?),

> Invent me a language of love. *You* could do it.
> Bewilderdly,
> All yours   Clyde

Another letter suggests infatuation that goes beyond mere hero-worship: "Oh! you adorable creature! You *are* a great genius. And oh! such a sweet one. Never was a genius so sweet so adorable. . . . And I—wee I—i am allowed to loose the latchet of yr shoe. Am bidden tie it up—and I do, in a *lover's knot!* . . . You are my sight, and sound, and touch. Yr love is the fragrance of a rose—the sky of a summer—the wing of an angel—the cymbal of a cherubim." Fitch closes the letter, "All, always, in every weather, gloriously, absorbingly Yours Clyde."

Yet another letter is redolent of sexual exhilaration. "*Nobody* loves you as *I* do. When you are here I dream. When you are away I awake. . . . you great, *great* man. Make me what you will but only keep me yours forever. Clyde." On another occasion Fitch began his letter (with one exception there is no name in the salutation to cause scandal), "It is 3. And you are not coming. I've looked out of the window many many times. . . . You

Clyde Fitch, left, as Lydia Languish and Tod Galloway as Mrs Malaprop in an
Amherst College production of Sheridan's *The Rivals* (1885). Reproduced by
permission of the Trustees of Amherst College.

were right. Away with knowledge . . . I will only wonder & love." Oscar appears to have given Fitch a pet name, for the letter's closing is

> Passionately yrs am I,
> > His Brown-eyed
> > Fawn

Oscar was given to calling "fauns" those boys he found appealing (Fitch appears to have assumed the homonym "fawn"). And Fitch's eyes, as a portrait now at Amherst College shows, were indeed brown.

In what appears to be the last surviving letter, Fitch expressed gratitude for an invitation to Tite Street on his last night in London, making clear, I think, the sexual nature of the pet name:

> You have been the sun that has glorified my horizon, and if night came on, and the sun set in a sad splendor, the morning came with its own golden halo and shone sweetly into the thicket where the brown-eyed Fawn lay on his grass green bed, with a strangely shaped wound— like this—♥—in his side. A hunter in snaring his shadow had wounded his heart.
>
> But the Brown-eyed Fawn was happy. "He has my heart," he sang, "but the *wound*, the wound is mine— and no one can take it from me!" Clyde

A postscript adds an invitation to abandon Tite Street afterward for a presumably gay gathering: "George Power wishes me to ask you to come to a *quiet little* party at his rooms tonight. I have promised to go for a little when I leave Tite Street &

G.P. wishes you to come—if you will—I fancy there is to be some music . . ."*

By 1893 Oscar must have added many a Clyde Fitch to his roster, for that year he desired to order *forty* tickets for friends to attend the premiere of *A Woman of No Importance*. How the homosexuals in this phalanx must have chuckled among themselves at such lines as Lord Illingworth's observations, "Women kneel so gracefully; men don't," and "The future belongs to the dandy. It is the exquisites who are going to rule."

In his petition to the Home Secretary, Oscar confessed he had been "prey to [the] absolute madness" of homosexual desire for "two years preceding" his ruin. This may seem like fudging it by a few years, but is perhaps accurate insofar as the years of 1893 and 1894 did find Oscar becoming more reckless, allowing his liaisons to become highly visible to the public in various ways. His madness did then become "absolute" at this time. His predations also became more and more focused upon what Croft-Cooke called "cheeky little street rats." If Oscar had kept to his own class with lovers like Ross and Turner, Maureen Borland has suggested, "then Victorian society would have turned a blind eye." But the dozen or so sexual episodes listed in Queensberry's detailed Plea of Justification for his accusation of sodomy show that Oscar most certainly did not keep to his class.

Rather, he consorted with valets, grooms, billiard markers, newspaper and telegraph boys, and several boys with no visible or honorable means of support. Some were brought into the house at Tite Street; others were present at the family vacation cottage at Worthing. Most were entertained in one or another of his rented

---

*Fitch and Wilde seem to have remained on friendly terms. For just as scandal was breaking in 1895 Beerbohm wrote to Ada Leverson from New York, in his witty vein, of meeting "a rather nice man here, an American interested in Georgian things [Fitch's most famous play was *Beau Brummell*], a playwright, named Clyde Fitch. He was at one time a friend of Oscar. Ask Oscar what he thinks of him. I think they must have quarreled, as Clyde Fitch always speaks very charitably of Oscar." Could *Beau Brummell* (1890) have been inspired, in some part, by Oscar? Gide, after all, had described him at this time as "the most lord, the most Brummell, the most Byronian." Fitch, in 1897, gave Oscar advice on the American publication of *The Ballad of Reading Gaol*. Before he died in 1909, Fitch had written several dozen original and adapted plays. (See note on pages 441–43 for more on Fitch.)

rooms or hotels in the West End. Money was lavishly spent. Alfred Taylor, Oscar's occasional procurer, told William Parker, after Oscar "chose" his brother Charlie, "Your brother is lucky! Oscar does not care what he pays if he fancies a chap." "New" boys were almost invariably favored with dinner at Kettner's restaurant, and fancy cigarette cases were usually forthcoming. Questioned about this in court by Charles Gill, who had a reputation as a ladies' man, Oscar said, to great amusement among the lawyers in court:

> "I have a weakness for presenting my acquaintances with cigarette cases." "Rather an expensive habit, if in-dulged in indiscriminately, isn't it?" "Less extravagant than giving jewelled garters to ladies!"

Freddie Atkins was taken by Oscar to Paris and got his hair done by Pascal at the Grand Hotel; he was also present, surely as Oscar's guest, at the February 1895 premiere of *Earnest*. A Savoy Hotel page named Tankard was shipped over to Calais. Conway, the Brighton newsboy, received, as Oscar admitted in court, a walking stick, a suit of clothes, and a hat with a bright ribbon. But Oscar was quick to assure the court, "I was not responsible for the ribbon!"

Oscar was losing control. His Lord Henry says in *Dorian Gray* that a cigarette is the "perfect type of a perfect pleasure. It is exquis-ite, and it leaves one unsatisfied." So too, apparently, was the plea-sure afforded by young male sex partners; the inevitable shortfall in satisfaction must have quickened his promiscuities. He descended, one might say, from noble Greco-Socratic ideals into a thoroughly Roman decadence. Edward Carpenter, in his 1895 sketch of homo-sexuality in the ancient world, disparaged "the Roman age, whose materialistic spirit could only with difficulty seize the finer inspira-tion of the homogenic love, and which in such writers as Catullus and Martial could only for the most part give expression to its grosser side." And Martial and Catullus—whom Oscar had read so avidly at Oxford—were just the poets to capture the decidedly *Satyricon*-flavored last years of Oscar's freedom of London. I am thinking of the Catullus of

Just now I found a young boy
     stuffing his girl,
I rose, naturally, and
     (with a nod to Venus)
fell and transfixed him there
with a good stiff prick, like his own.

Or the Martial of

When you say, "Quick, I'm going to come,"
Hedylus, I go limp and numb.
But ask me to hold back my fire,
And the brake accelerates desire.
Dear boy, if you're in such a hurry,
Tell me to slow up, not to worry.

or

If from the baths you hear a round of applause,
Maron's great prick is bound to be the cause.

or

Natta calls "small" (beneath his lover's tunic)
A prick that makes Priapus seem a eunuch.

Oscar's "grosser side" truly did predominate. So it is scarcely a
wonder that several who described him at this time were reminded of rulers prominent in the Roman empire's famous decline and fall. After leaving Oscar in Morocco, Gide wrote to his
mother that Oscar "was born to be a Roman emperor—Heliogabalus or some other one." And Robert Sherard came to dinner in
Tite Street a month before and recalled him looking like a "Roman emperor of the decadence, Vitellius, indeed, rather than
Heliogabalus."

Oscar's final gust of ass-theticism before his fall was the astonishing trip to Morocco with Bosie in January of 1895, just when rehearsals for the premiere of *Earnest* were beginning ... and when Bosie's father was becoming increasingly incensed by their liaison. Oscar had ten years before written of Morocco as a land "of Moors, mosques and mirages." His purpose now, though still alliterative, was quite different: "boys as beautiful as bronze statues," he demanded from a local pimp. Oscar reported to Ross, "There is a great deal of beauty here. The Kabyle boys are quite lovely. . . . Bosie and I have taken to haschish: it is quite exquisite: three puffs of smoke, and then peace and love." They traveled outside Algiers, and Oscar told of exotic "villages peopled by fauns. Several shepherds fluted on reeds for us" (code, one suspects, for succulent pleasures). Bosie soon ran off to Biskra for some bronze boy or other, and Oscar was left on his own to entertain himself as a procurer for the young Gide.

OSCAR HAD WRITTEN SEVERAL years before, in a kind of apologia for the artist/murderer Wainewright, "To those who are preoccupied with beauty of form nothing else seems of much importance." When confronted with the murder of a young woman, Oscar noted, Wainewright responded by way of explanation, "It was a dreadful thing to do, but she had very thick ankles." The same combination of obsessiveness and callousness was much on display as Oscar himself, in his preoccupation with young male beauties, courted disaster ever more carelessly. He predicted as much in the new play that ushered in the fateful year on 3 January: "Men always look so silly when they are caught," says Mrs Cheveley in *An Ideal Husband*, "and they are always being caught."

On 14 February London audiences were to learn for the first time from Miss Prism that "good looks are a snare," and mere weeks later numerous such snares were indeed sprung on Oscar by Queensberry, his private investigators, the police, and several "unsexed blackguards" and "male strumpets" (as *Reynolds's News-*

paper called them) who were prepared to give evidence against Oscar in court.* He tried his best to defend himself in the vein of his many former eulogies of Youth, even after Queensberry's lawyer, Edward Carson, caught him at the outset in a lie about his age (Oscar called himself thirty-nine instead of forty). Many of his brilliant ripostes in the Old Bailey, in fact, were attempts to evade the sexual realities behind his devotion to Youth. When Carson asked whether he had ever "adored a young man madly," Oscar responded haughtily and most untruthfully, "I have never given adoration to anybody except myself." When asked how he could possibly stoop to entertaining grooms and valets, he replied: "The pleasure to me was being with those who are young, bright, happy, careless, and free. I do not like the sensible and I do not like the old."

Carson also read out in court a March 1893 letter Oscar had written to Bosie, in which he spoke of Bosie's "red rose-leaf lips" and said, "You are the divine thing I want." "Is that an ordinary letter?" Carson then asked. Oscar's answer suggests the very high road he attempted to take in most of the interrogation: "Everything I write is extraordinary." The prosecutor in the next trial also asked about the letter, "Do you think an ordinarily constituted being would address such expressions to a younger man?" The response was pure Oscar: "I am not, happily I think, an ordinarily constituted being." The prosecutor then essayed another attack on the same point . . . and again lost the volley amid loud laughter from the audience:

"Why did you take up with these youths?"
"I am a lover of youth!"
"You exalt youth as a sort of god?"
"I like to study the young in everything. There is something fascinating in youthfulness."

*It is important to emphasize that three separate trials took place: the first, Oscar's prosecution of Queensberry for libel, which collapsed and was withdrawn when it became clear that justification was provable; the second (twenty-five counts), against both Taylor and Wilde, at which the jury could not agree on a verdict; and the third (eight counts), when Oscar was tried separately and convicted.

ALFRED TAYLOR

SHELLEY

ATKINS

"So you would prefer puppies to dogs and kittens to cats?"

"I think so. . . . I should enjoy, for instance, the society of a beardless, briefless barrister quite as much as the most accomplished Q.C."

But slowly and relentlessly—and amid many a *mot juste*—were revealed in lavish fullness the damning details of what Oscar, in one of his last letters before the trials, confessed was a life "marred and maimed by extravagance": his regular attendance at "social" gatherings in the heavily perfumed rooms of his codefendant Alfred Taylor ("Rather a rough neighborhood, isn't it?" "That I don't know. I know it is near the Houses of Parliament"); his preference for "boys much beneath you in social station" ("I make no social distinctions"); his habit of taking boys to the Savoy and the sanitary consequences noticed by a hotel maid ("You deny that the bed linen was marked in the way described?" "I do not examine bed linen when I arise. I am not a housemaid").

Oscar's visual tastes are also given more particularly. Alfred Taylor told young Sidney Mavor that Oscar liked "young men when they're modest and nice in appearance" and expressed approval when Mavor arrived later for an intimate dinner at Kettner's: "I'm glad you made yourself pretty. Mr Wilde likes nice clean boys!" Indeed, the fact that Oscar could draw the line at a certain level of adolescent homeliness led to the one great *faux pas* in his testimony. This was when Carson suddenly asked him whether he had ever kissed one Walter Grainger, a boy he had employed as an "under-butler" when the Wildes vacationed at Goring in 1893. In "a moment of fatal folly," as H. Montgomery Hyde concluded, Oscar replied, "Oh, dear no! He was a peculiarly plain boy. He was, unfortunately, extremely ugly. I pitied him for it." Carson, of course, went for the jugular at this blurted admission and turned the tide of the trial.

Carson's task had been to convince the jury that the events asserted in his client's Plea of Justification were true. This remarkable 1,500-word document, in which all five names of the accused are repeated like a tocsin thirty-five times, listed at its end Oscar's heinous literary crimes. *Dorian Gray* was "calculated to subvert morality and to encourage unnatural vice," and Oscar participated in *The Chameleon*, which contained "divers obscene matters . . . relating to the practices and passions of persons of sodomitical and unnatural habits." But the plea's main gist was to lay out the dozen or so circumstances of assignations with young men, ranging from October

ALFRED WOOD

CHARLES PARKER

WILLIAM PARKER

1892 to September 1894. Typical of its style was this allegation for 1892: "The said Oscar Fingal O'Flahertie Wills Wilde on the twenty-second day of November . . . at a house situate at 29 Boulevard des Capucines in Paris in the Republic of France did solicit and incite one Frederick Atkins to commit sodomy and other acts of gross indecency and immorality with him." Two days later, at the same site, Oscar had his way with Maurice Shwabe. In January 1893 he took Alfred Wood home to Tite Street, and a few months later retired to the Savoy Hotel with a "certain boy" whose name was unknown to Queensberry. With Charlie Parker Oscar was itinerant, sojourning with him at the Savoy, at No. 7 Camera Square, No. 50 Park Walk, and No. 10 St. James's Place.

Hyde pieced together this summary of how Oscar's "peculiar inverted instincts" found satisfaction:

> His conduct . . . usually began with close physical contact and fondling. This would be followed by some form of mutual masturbation or intercrural intercourse. (Amongst the articles of clothing found in Taylor's rooms were several pairs of trousers with slits or vents in place of pockets, a feature plainly designed to facilitate masturbation.) Finally *fellatio* (oral copulation) would be practised with Wilde as the active agent, though this role was occasionally reversed. There seems to have been no question of *pedicatio* (anal penetration). It was suggested by only one of the witnesses who gave evidence at his trials that Wilde had committed sodomy. . . . Nor indeed was Wilde ever charged with this graver offence, which still [i.e., in 1948] carries the maximum penalty of life imprisonment.

That is, there was no *legal* question of anal penetration. Whether that occurred is open to speculation, for a legal system quite prepared to allow Oscar to escape to the Continent and avoid a trial was presumably also capable of pursuing him on the less unsavory

Lord Alfred Douglas, left, with Maurice Schwabe, who was one of those alleged in Queensberry's Plea of Justification to have associated indecently with Oscar. Photograph from the Clark Library, Los Angeles.

charge and turning a blind eye on the other, which in any case was much harder to prove in court.

The transcripts of the three trials offer several colorful vignettes of Oscar's behavior with his various tricks. Carson asked

Oscar, for instance, about his outlays for young Conway during the family holiday at Worthing. Did Oscar dress him up to "look more like an equal?" "Oh no! . . . I promised him that before I left Worthing I would take him somewhere, to some place to which he wished to go, as a reward for his being a pleasant companion to myself and my children." Where did he end up taking Conway?—to a hotel in Brighton for the night. Queensberry's counsel also expressed astonishment that Oscar would entertain apparent riffraff so lavishly and asked sneeringly about the Parker brothers, "Did you know that one . . . was a gentleman's valet, and the other a groom?" Oscar replied, "If I had I should not have cared. I didn't care tuppence what they were. I liked them. I have a passion to civilize the community." What form did this civilizing take? Charlie Parker described the bibulous evenings at Kettner's, with Oscar talking of "poetry and art during dinner, and of the old Roman days." This paints a droll picture. Oscar's habit of plying his boys with liquor had led earlier to this cheeky exchange, which drew another burst of laughter in court:

> "Did any of these men who visited you at the Savoy have whiskeys and sodas and iced champagne?"
> "I can't say what they had."
> "Do you drink champagne yourself?"
> "Yes; iced champagne is a favourite drink of mine— strongly against my doctor's orders."
> "Never mind your doctor's orders, sir!"
> "I never do."

Other information, distinctly less appealing and more melancholy, came to light during the exposition of all the counts that were lodged against Wilde and Taylor. For instance, Oscar's being turned out of the Albemarle Hotel in the middle of the night with a boy in tow; the issuance of writs by various firms for cigarette cases, jewelry, and other gifts he had lavished on Bosie and others; Oscar's taking Charlie Parker back to his Tite Street house for an assignation (at least the house was empty); the matinees he had at a house in Osnaburgh Street with Freddie Atkins, which left, according to a housekeeper, sheets "stained in a peculiar way"; the frequent "tea parties" at Taylor's, populated by numerous men sixteen to thirty years old; the chambermaid at the Savoy who opened an unlocked bedroom door and discovered a "boy of sixteen, with close-cropped hair and a sallow complexion" in Oscar's bed.

The cumulative effect of all the testimony was devastating. The public reveled both in the details of the scandal and in righteous indignation. W. E. Henley, the friend Oscar had once commiserated with over the fatal illness of his mother, caught the general flavor: "Oscar at bay was on the whole a pleasing sight. . . . Holloway and Bow Street have taken his hair out of curl in more senses than one. And I am pretty sure that he is having a damn bad time."

Those in Oscar's circle of friends, relatives, and sympathetic acquaintances may have been unaware of many of the sordid details, but they could not have been surprised at the general picture. After all, he had for years pontificated on the glories of self-indulgence: in "The Critic as Artist" he had announced, "Sin is an essential element of progress" and "saves us from the monotony of type." Oscar's intimates could not have failed to see how elaborately he had been seeking to avoid the monotony of heterosexual type. Nor, one imagines, could they have failed to appreciate and be saddened by the irony (and dead earnestness) of his telling the world, "Self-denial is simply a method by which man arrests his progress." Oscar's grand progress through the gay demimonde of London, however, was arrested in the end precisely because the ass-thete finally lost all power of self-denial.

Lord Henry lights a cigarette and informs Dorian Gray toward the end of the novel, "The basis of every scandal is an immoral certainty." This was true of Oscar's scandal, though the immorality behind it was not the one proved beyond doubt in the Old Bailey. The real immoral certainty lay in Oscar's appalling disregard of innocent bystanders who stood to be devastated by his pursuit of physical pleasures that, he later admitted, "wreck the soul": his wife and two boys, of course; his mother; his close friends; the poor family butler; and many a young man, one imagines, whom he amused himself with and then carelessly discarded. His ass-theticism was criminal more in the figurative than the literal sense.

When addressing the Home Secretary from prison, Oscar blamed the "malaria" of homosexual lust for his actions, but after his release he dropped that tactic as the mere pretense it was. Instead, he uttered many a confession of complete moral responsibility for what he had done. The "immoral certainty" at issue here was perhaps not more coolly and more devastatingly expressed than by a friend who much admired him, Sidney Low:

> I knew Oscar well. . . . He was one of the most gifted of mortals . . . and the wittiest conversationalist I ever met. His crime was the result I think of a physical and psychical disease. So Sir George Birdwood holds, and he is an author on this unsavoury subject. He maintains that many men are born with a tendency that way. Call it insanity if you like; but Oscar wasn't insane, and he could have held that tendency in check if he had not softened his will-power by a deliberate cultivation of self-indulgence.

THE SUBJECT OF SELF-INDULGENCE leads us, aptly enough, to a brief consideration of the most notorious and fateful of Oscar's juvenile attractions, Lord Alfred Douglas. Many words have been written about Bosie (a great many of them, pettish and self-serving, by Bosie himself). The highlights of his infamous role in Oscar's downfall are well known and require no rehearsal here. But something deserves to be said about the homosexual dynamic of his affair with Oscar.

Bosie has, of course, been cordially reviled by almost everyone who has written about their liaison. (Though one has to admire the air of equanimity Croft-Cooke managed to sustain in his lengthy biography of him.) Bosie was sixteen years younger than Oscar—twenty-one when they first met in 1891—but was far more advanced in the ignoble art of self-indulgence than his supposed mentor. In Bosie the Oscarian notion of liberating one's true personality through self-assertion was transformed, as Oscar himself put it, by "the terrible alchemy of egotism" into a fearsome blend of narcissism, petulant selfishness, and intemperate willfulness. He was, as Oscar also said, the kind of person who is always demanding "without grace" and receiving "without thanks." Max Beerbohm's initial reaction to Bosie was two-edged: "rather charming—a very pretty reflection of Oscar" and "obviously mad (like all his family I believe)." George Ives, one of Oscar's gay circle, met him and within forty-eight hours entered this perfect summation in his diary: "a difficult character, swayed by passion, shaken by impulse." Bosie's reckless homosexual adventuring doubtless encouraged Oscar in his own. Robert Sherard told of meeting Bosie for the first time "burning candles at the Brompton Oratory for a purpose which had better be left unrecorded," and Ives said he had "warned Lord A. more than once that he was indulging in homosexuality to a reckless and highly dangerous degree" (this was in the fall of 1893).

The essence of the Oscar-Bosie relationship is something of a gay cliché (a straight one, too). It is, I think, more than merely hinted at in the relationship between Lord Illingworth and Gerald in the play Oscar was writing when he and Bosie, Bosie's tutor, and the two boys were cavorting at Torquay while Constance was off in Italy. Surely studies from real life, the elder Illingworth is "lolling on a sofa" and the younger Gerald is confessing to being "fearfully idle" at school and "ignorant of the world" as the third act of A Woman of No Importance opens. Illingworth, assuming Oscar's beloved pontificator's pose, lectures him insouciantly on the grand old theme:

> Don't be afraid, Gerald. Remember that you've got on your side the most wonderful thing in the world—

youth! There is nothing like youth. The middle-aged
are mortgaged to Life. The old are in Life's lumber-
room. But youth is the Lord of Life. Youth has a
kingdom waiting for it. . . . To win back my youth,
Gerald, there is nothing I wouldn't do—except take exercise, get up early, or be a useful member of the
community.

Winning back one's youth being impossible, Oscar, like many a
deeply age-conscious queen since, sought to retain his youth vi-
cariously, by association. Bosie, too, behaved in commonplace
fashion as the idolized youth, becoming a virtuoso manipulator,
demander, and thrower of tantrums. It is an old, sad love story.

Gide, who was with them several times, most notably during
the Moroccan trip, was particularly devastating in his observations on the sort of "couple" they made. He recalled Bosie's "hissing, withering, savage voice" when aroused, which was apparently
often. Oscar told Gide the following, likely typical anecdote. Oscar, now a celebrity because of his plays, wished to dine quietly at
the Savoy Hotel with Bosie and chose an out-of-the-way table
near a small side entrance to the dining room:

> When he saw me come in by this little door, Bosy
> [Gide's spelling], who was waiting for me, made a scene.
> Oh! a terrible, frightful scene! "I won't have you come
> in by the side door," he said; "I won't tolerate it. I insist
> on your coming in by the main entrance with me; I
> want everyone in the restaurant to see us; I want every-
> one to say, "There goes Oscar Wilde and his minion!"

Gide was disgusted that, even as he told this anecdote, Oscar displayed "his admiration for Douglas and a kind of lover's pleasure
at being mastered." Not one of Oscar's straight friends
or acquaintances—even such tart-tongued gents as Frank Harris or Bernard Shaw—could have sketched this very odd couple
more wickedly than Gide: "Bosy interested me extremely; but

'terrible' he certainly was. . . . Wilde beside him seemed gentle, wavering, and weak-willed. Douglas was possessed by a perverse instinct that drives a child to break his finest toy; nothing ever satisfied him; he always wanted to go one better." (Gide also told of Bosie describing Cyril as very beautiful and then whispering "with a self-satisfied smile, 'He will be for me.'")

And waver Oscar most certainly did. All of Oscar's friends—and certainly his wife—must have been stupefied at how this brilliant scourge of hypocrisy and cant, this trenchant social critic, could so lose his own critical faculties and waste so much of his social reputation and money under Bosie's incomprehensible influence. (In prison, Oscar guessed he had lavished £5,000 on Bosie from late 1892 until his arrest.) Oscar was far from industrious to begin with, but under Bosie's malign star his habits worsened drastically. Here Oscar grimly describes a typical day in late 1893, when he kept rooms in St. James's Place:

At twelve o'clock you drove up, and stayed smoking cigarettes and chattering till 1.30, when I had to take you out to luncheon at the Café Royal or the Berkeley. Luncheon with its *liqueurs* lasted usually till 3.30. For an hour you retired to White's. At tea-time you appeared again, and stayed till it was time to dress for dinner. You dined with me either at the Savoy or at Tite Street. We did not separate as a rule till after midnight, as supper at Willis's had to wind up the entrancing day. This was my life for those three months, every single day, except during the four days when you went abroad.

With regularity (every three months, he said) Oscar tried to extricate himself from the relationship and its constant scenes and traumas. But always he was drawn back. From prison he wrote to Ross, "Time after time I tried, during those two wasted weary years, to escape, but he always brought me back."

The Stranger Wilde

In the jeremiad addressed to his onetime "red rose-leaf"–lipped lover in *De profundis*, Oscar cursed both loudly and deeply. Sometimes he sounds for all the world like Antony condemning Cleopatra:

> My heart was to thy rudder tied by th' strings,
> And thou shouldst tow me after. O'er my spirit
> Thy full supremacy thou knew'st.

But he also turned a merciless eye upon himself. And the criticism, one is inclined to say, is both harsh and just. In a particularly devastating passage he laid bare the nature of his own fault. "The basis of character is will-power," he told Bosie, "and my will-power became absolutely subject to yours." He wrote of the "ethical degradation I allowed you to bring on me" and of "my fatal yielding to you in your daily increasing demands. . . . My judgment forsook me. . . . Blindly I staggered as an ox into the shambles." His "gigantic psychological error," he believed, was to assume that his will was truly free. But the habit of giving in to Bosie "in everything had become insensibly a real part of my nature. Without knowing it, it had stereotyped my temperament to one permanent and fatal mood." Oscar remembered bitterly Pater's admonition not to "form habits" and confronted in these pages the fact that his habit, in this ghastly instance, had "proved to be not Failure merely but Ruin." This is Oscar's real confession. The *mea maxima culpa* he had addressed to the Home Secretary was merely rhetorical, extorted by the sufferings of his incarceration.

One might assume that *De profundis* would serve as an epitaph upon Oscar's love for boys, but in fact the lover of youth did rise from the ashes of abject mortification after his release. Bosie returned to Oscar's affections, if only fitfully and most unsatisfactorily, during the last three years. Lord Henry says that "all ways" end at the same point, "disillusion." The way of the ageing assthete certainly did. Just months before he died, Oscar wrote to Ross about Bosie, "Boys, brandy, and betting monopolise his soul.

He is really a miser: but his method of hoarding is spending: a new type." This turned out to be Oscar's very last extant remark about the lover whom he had once apostrophized,

> O sweetest of all boys, most loved of all loves, my soul clings to your soul, my life to your life, and in all the worlds of pain and pleasure you are my ideal of admiration and joy.

Chapter Ten

☆ ☆ ☆ ☆ ☆ ☆ ☆ ☆ ☆ ☆ ☆ ☆ ☆ ☆ ☆ ☆

PUNCH V. OSCAR II

With your perky paradoxes, and your talk of "crinkled ox-eyes,"
 and books of "Nile-green skin,"
That show forth unholy histories, and display the "deeper mysteries"
 of strange and subtle Sin,
You can squirm, and glose, and hiss on, and awake that nouveau frisson
 which is Art's best gift to life.

"DEVELOPMENT," *PUNCH,* SEPTEMBER 1890

BY THE END OF 1883, we have seen, Mr Punch was able to report with some glee that Oscar's fame was finally beginning to wane: a piece of mail addressed "Oscar Wilde, Poet. London." could be returned marked "Not Known."

But, after the passage of a half-dozen years, Oscar achieved the remarkable feat of rising from the ashes of oblivion for a second—and even more spectacular—flowering of celebrity. To be sure, this was a celebrity with a difference: Oscar steadily became less "our own cherished Oscar" and more the butt of ill-tempered, occasionally vituperative satire. The complacent, avuncular tone of condescension (as to a high-spirited child) displayed by most journalists toward Oscar in earlier years suffered a sea change during his period of retirement from the limelight. Most notably, one senses the steady infusion of bile and gall in the way he was treated in the press. An air of caustic, Juvenalian indignation became ever more noticeable. Beatrice's tart comment on Benedick in *Much Ado About Nothing* precisely captures the conflicted reaction to this Oscar redivivus: "He both pleases men and angers them, and then they laugh at him and beat him."

As Oscar returned to the public eye in 1889, he again became "Known" in the pages of *Punch*. References to him were scattered at first. On 5 January, the "Our Booking-office" column called attention to "a rather De Quincey-ish article in the *Fortnightly* by Oscar Wilde on Wainewright, the penman, pencilman, and poisoner." The reviewer was not pleased: "It reminds me of that *bizarre* 'Essay on Murder considered as one of the Fine Arts,' which . . . I wish the Opium-eater had never written." Several months later a dyspeptic swipe was taken at "that artistically got-up Magazine" *Woman's World*, which Oscar had been editing for two years: "In the October number . . . there is an article with the heading 'Spoons.' Out of four pictures of 'Spoons' here given, three are single. In the fourth plate—which is a large one, holding five spoons—there are two pairs, and one odd spoon out. The history, so far, of 'Spoons' is most interesting. What will be the next subject? Mashers?"

With the appearance of *The Picture of Dorian Gray* in 1890, however, the tone *Punch* took toward Oscar became decidedly more acerbic, even vindictive. This was probably not only because his manifold trespasses on Victorian mores and mediocrities were causing Mr Punch some genuine discomfort, but also because, as Ada Leverson was to observe, "People as a rule do not object to a man deserving success, only to his getting it." The vulgar, self-advertising Aesthete whom the magazine may have thought it had exterminated many years before was now resurrecting himself in even more spectacularly charismatic fashion. And he was also showing himself willing to leave the relatively harmless art connoisseur's lectern and deploy his now highly skilled pen in several literary media.

On rare occasions in the old days, Oscar had caused Mr Punch to turn solemn, remove his cap and bells, and put on boxing gloves. It happened, for instance, in 1882 in a brief essay aptly (and prophetically) titled "In Earnest." Here—after so many skits and caricatures of Aestheticism—we learn what Mr Punch really thought its definition was, in unminced, dead-serious terms: "an effeminate, invertebrate, sensuous, sentimentally-Christian, but thoroughly Pagan taste in literature and art, which delights in the idea of the resuscitation of the Great God Pan, in Swinburnian songs at their highest fever pitch, in the mystic ravings of Blake, the affectation of a Rossetti, the *Charmides* and revoltingly pantheistic *Rosa Mystica* of Oscar Wilde and other similar mock-hysterical imitations." A distinct vein of urgent, not-at-all mock hysteria such as this underlies many of *Punch's* attempts to reap laughter from Oscar in the 1890s.

A similar, if somewhat milder destructive gusto, for instance, pervades the review of *Dorian Gray* by "The Baron de Book-Worms" in the 19 July 1890 issue (the novel had appeared in *Lippincott's Magazine* the previous month). The novel was called "Oscar Wilde's Wildest and Oscarest work . . . a weird sensational romance." Its aphorisms "are Wilde, yet forced." The author's " 'decoration' (upon which he plumes himself) is indeed 'laid on with a trowel.' " Oscar's remark that the story was poisonous but perfect was modified: "There is indeed more of 'poison' than of 'perfection' in *Dorian Gray*." A homosexual element was pointedly alluded to in the description of Dorian as "beautiful" and "Ganymede-like," which probably accounted for the "unsavoury suggestiveness" that was found to "lurk" in the novel. The good Baron felt a "loathly 'leperous distillment' taints and spoils" the novel, and he ended his review by saying, "I have read it, and, except for the ingenious idea, I wish to forget it." The Dickensian E. T. Reed caricature that accompanied the review reflected his revulsion.

PARALLEL.

Joe, the Fat Boy in Pickwick, startles the Old Lady; Oscar, the Fad Boy in Lippincott's, startles Mrs. Grundy.

Oscar, the Fad Boy. "I want to make your flesh creep!"

Another remarkably caustic performance appeared two months later, in September 1890, after Oscar's essay "The Critic as Artist" appeared. This was a poem called "Development (*With acknowledgments to the Author of* Patience)"—a five-stanza take-off on the "fleshly" poet Bunthorne's delightful patter song that begins, "If you're anxious for to shine in the high aesthetic line . . ." Here Oscar was accused of paralyzing "every motor that's not vile," of having "swamped morality in 'intensified personality,' " of seeking excitement "with a flavour of the flesh," and of developing "like some cancer" in the "Art-sphere." Such imprecations are perhaps vague enough, but it is hard to avoid seeing in the following lines an allusion to the Love that dare not speak its name:

> If you aim to be a Shocker, carnal theories to cocker is the
>   best way to begin.
>   And every one will say,
>   As you worm your wicked way,
> "If that's allowable for him which were criminal in me,
> What a very emancipated kind of youth this kind of youth
>   must be."

As for the "developed" young man urged by Oscar in his essay, the poem's last line runs: "What a morbidly muckily emotional young man the 'developed' young man must be."

The following May, a "Booking-office" paragraph was devoted to the appearance of Oscar's volume of essays called *Intentions*, which included "The Decay of Lying." Baron de Book-Worms administered another slap: "No; let [Oscar] remain the head professor of the gay science of mendacity in the Cretan College." The Baron, of course, was using "gay" in the older sense, but by this time—as "Development" especially suggests—*Punch* was obviously in some sort aware that Oscar was professing the gay science in the post-Stonewall sense.

In March 1892, Punch honored Wilde with a second "Fancy Portrait" (see p. 11 above), due acknowledgment of the great success of his first London play, *Lady Windermere's Fan* . . . and the consummately scandalous publicity stunt of addressing his audience after the curtain while smoking a cigarette. A few months later, when Oscar's plans for a production of his French-language

A WILDE IDEA.
OR, MORE INJUSTICE TO IRELAND!

play *Salome* starring Sarah Bernhardt were quashed by the censor, he furiously threatened to emigrate to France. *Punch* leaped on this morsel with the drawing "A Wilde Idea" and this caption:

> The license for . . . *Salome* . . . having been refused by the Saxon Licenser of Plays, The O'Scar dreams of be-

coming a French Citizen, but doesn't quite 'see himself,' at the beginning of his career, as a conscript in the French Army, and so, to adapt the Gilbertian lines, probably—

> "In spite of great temptation
> To French na-tu-ra-li-sa-tion,
> He'll remain an Irishman!"

Mr Punch attended Oscar's plays and was amused, but he refused to admit this in the reviews they provoked. After *A Woman of No Importance* opened in April 1893, he repined at its "wearisome tirades, tawdry, cheap, and conventional" and its "old-fashioned theatrical melodrama," yet was obliged to say it was splendidly acted and even a "success"—though only because of its "Christy-Minstrel epigrammatic dialogue." Then he extrapolated Oscar's recipe for playwriting: "First catch your epigrams: preserve them for use: serve with *sauce piquante un peu risqué* distributed impartially among a variety of non-essential *dramatis personae* invented for the purpose." The responses to the two last plays— "Overheard Fragment of a Dialogue" for *An Ideal Husband* in January 1895 and "The Advisability of not Being Brought up in

| Massa Beerbones | Massa Johnson | Dr. Proudie Kemble | Lady Nickleby |
| Lord Shillingworth. | O'Wilde. | of Barchester. | Leclercq. |

CHRISTY MINSTRELS OF NO IMPORTANCE.

a Handbag" for *Earnest* in March 1895—were both uncharacteristically gentle and witty. But, then, they were written by Oscar's "Sphinx," Ada Leverson.

☆ ☆ ☆

INNUENDOS TOUCHING ON SEXUALITY, which had been largely visual during the "Aesthetic period" of Oscar's *Punch* career, became more verbal in its final stage. A clever piece called "New Year's Eve at Latterday Hall," which appeared at the end of 1893, offers an example. The fête it describes is visited by "a party of Ghosts" from the past, including Mr Pickwick and Madame Bovary. Dorian Gray attends and escorts Shakespeare's Juliet to dinner. Soon he finds he is "not getting on with her very well" and so strikes up a conversation with a "Young Subaltern" home on leave:

YOUNG SUBALTERN: How well you're looking! Younger than ever, by Jove! Which is curious. But why that absurd buttonhole?

DORIAN (*hurt*): You never like anything I wear. You Anglo-Indians are corrupt without being charming. This is a fault.

Dorian Gray taking Juliet in to dinner.

A stage direction then has Dorian arrange "his fringe

205

in an old Dutch-silver mirror on the opposite mantlepiece, framed in curiously-carved ivory Cupids." Later Dorian "takes out his little vinaigrette box exquisitely set with turquoises, cymophanes, amethysts, and tourmalines, and offers it to the Subaltern, who, evidently unaware of its use, pockets it." He then says to Dorian, "You got that out of a cracker, didn't you? I'll take it Home. For the kids." Clearly, a straight squelch of a gay overture.

When a notorious novel with clear gay overtones called *The Green Carnation* was published anonymously in September 1894—the author was Robert Hichens—people in many quarters assumed it had been written by Oscar. He was finally obliged to write the editor of the *Pall Mall Gazette* and announce, "I invented that magnificent flower. But with the middle-class and mediocre book that usurps its strangely beautiful name I have, I need hardly say, nothing whatsoever to do." Nevertheless, *Punch* went ahead a few weeks later with a sketch called "The Blue Gardenia" that clearly assumes Oscar was the author.

The next month, on 10 November, *Punch* followed up with a few extraordinary Oscarian pages that are filled with remembrances of satires past and premonitions of the final debacle that was just around the corner: a prose piece titled "Two Decadent Guys" (subtitle: "A Colour Study in Green Carnation"). Indeed, it is at once the wittiest and saddest piece that *Punch* ever devoted to Oscar.

Two characters in *The Green Carnation* were modeled on Oscar and Bosie: Amarinth and Lord Reggie, respectively. The *Punch* sketch's two "guys" are obviously modeled upon them, too: Sir Fustian Flitters and Lord Raggie Tattersall. In one of *Punch's* most inspired bits of Oscar-inspired comedy, the two are presented, as the accompanying drawing shows, as "guys"—the ragged, grotesque effigies of Guy Fawkes that were traditionally paraded and burned on Guy Fawkes Day (5 November). The figures are clearly those of Bosie (who sported a straw hat) and Oscar. The descriptions are eerily accurate and show that—as London became more and more aware of the couple as an "item"—*Punch* was becoming fearless in its allusions to their flagrant openness. Raggie: "the white weariness of his smooth face . . . the vacant fretfulness of his hollow eyes." Flitters: "He was taller, bulgier, and bulkier than his friend, and allowed his heavy chin to droop languidly forward." Both wear magenta cauliflowers in their buttonholes. Oscar's doting and Bosie's narcissism are wickedly captured. Flitters: "You are

"My dear Raggie, you are looking very well this afternoon."

wonderfully complete as you are!" Raggie: "That is so true! . . . I am very beautiful."

The gay coterie that surrounded Oscar and Bosie also feels *Punch*'s sting. Raggie says, "I feel in the mood to sally forth and paint the night with strange scarlet, slashed with silver and gold, while our young votaries—beautiful pink boys in paper hats—let off marvellous pale epigrammatic crackers and purple paradoxical squibs in our honour." Flitters interrupts, "See, Raggie, here come our youthful disciples! Do they not look deliciously innocent and enthusiastic? I wish, though, we could contrive to imbue them with something of our own lovely limpness. . . ." "Beautiful rose-coloured children," Lord Raggie murmurs, "how sad to think that they will all grow up and degenerate into pork-butchers, generals, and bishops."

Ominously (considering what was to occur five months later), Raggie soon sees "one of those unconsciously absurd persons they call policemen" coming toward them: "How stiffly he holds himself." Here *Punch* reverts one last time to its old theme of "manly" versus "un-." Raggie continues, "Why is there something irresistibly ludicrous about every creature that possesses a spine? Perhaps because to be vertebrate is to be normal, and the normal is necessarily such a hideous monstrosity. I love what are called warped or distorted figures." As the "crude copper" comes up to confiscate them, Raggie asks Flitters a question the irony of which takes the breath away: "Can we be going to become notorious—*really* notorious—at last?" This brilliant sketch makes it hard to imagine that the editors of *Punch* had not guessed what many of Oscar's friends had feared: that his recklessness would soon lead to ruin.

The end was indeed near. *The Yellow Book* had appeared on the scene, to Mr Punch's thorough disgust: its presiding genius *Punch* referred to as Daubaway Weirdsley. On 6 April, the very day after Oscar's libel suit against Queensberry collapsed and he was arrested, *Punch* published a skit called "April Foolosophy. (By One of Them)." The speaker proudly announces, "We are the real and only . . . Sexomaniacs." Among his aphorisms is this one: "The fool at forty is a fool indeed." He explains,

> It is only at the age of two-score that we attain to years of full indiscretion. We develop later than the rest of humanity; we undergo a severe probation before our claim to the title of complete nincompoop is recognised. Before forty there is yet a chance that the budding ninny may desert, and degenerate into a prig, a Philistine, or a physician. After that age he is safe, and can be depended on for unwisdom.

The writer of these lines must surely have known that Oscar Wilde was then forty years old . . . and that his years of "full indiscretion" truly had arrived. The speaker's last bit of "foolosophy" is "Fools stand in slippery places." How true that was to prove in Oscar's case, when he entered the Old Bailey a few weeks later.

☆ ☆ ☆

MR PUNCH BEHAVED BADLY in the aftermath. On 13 April he exulted nastily in a little poem titled "The Long and Short of It":

> Ars longa est! *All know what once that meant;*
> *But cranks corrupt so sickeningly have shindied*
> About *their* Art *of late, 'tis evident*
> *The rendering now must be, "Art is long-winded!"*
> For Vita Brevis,—*all true men must hope,*
> *Brief life for such base* Art—*and a short rope!*

In the very same issue, he permitted himself another poem, "Concerning a Misused Term," in which Art like Oscar's is blasted for its "effete / Unvirile . . . debased Petronian ways," the "worse than pornographic stain" of its "unsexed Poetry," and the "garbage-epigrams and pois'nous hints." It is an ineffably sad denouement to Oscar's *Punch* career. In the end, the magazine was faithful not to him but to its readership. The poem's final stanza captures quite accurately the ecstasy of revulsion that swept England at the time of the trials:

> *If such be "Artists," then may* Philistines
> *Arise, plain sturdy Britons as of yore,*
> *And sweep them off and purge away the signs*
> *That England e'er such noxious offspring bore!*

Two weeks later, in a sonnet "By an Angry Old Buffer" called "Sexomania," Mr Punch expressed all too candidly his—and the Victorian age's—panicky response to the confusions of gender that came most obviously with assertions of the women's movement but also, rather more *sub rosa*, with the striking emergency of gay culture in the early 1890s:

> *When Adam delved and Eve span,*
> *No one need ask which was the man.*
> *Bicycling, footballing, scarce human,*
> *All wonder now "Which is the woman?"*

But a new fear my bosom vexes;
To-morrow there may be no sexes!
Unless, as end to all the pother,
Each one in fact becomes the other.

The emphatic final curtain, though, came a few weeks later, while Oscar was out on bail awaiting the trial that would convict him. It is a poem with the too too perfect title "A Philistine Paean; Or, The Triumph of the Timid One." It begins with relief, apparently, at no longer having to assume effeminate attitudes:

At last! I see signs of a turn in the tide,
  And O, I perceive it with infinite gratitude.
No more need I go with a crick in my side
  In attempts to preserve a non-natural attitude.
Something has changed in the season, somewhere;
I'm sure I can feel a cool whiff of fresh air!

The "somewhere" was, obviously, the Central Criminal Court. The timid one rejoices in his "chance to be decent again" and his escape from "Mental malaria" (recall that Oscar, in prison, would refer to homosexual desire as "a malaria that clings to soul and body"). One may even "relish Dickens, yet not seem insane!" The poem ends with the couplet, "I know I'm relieved from one horrible bore,— / I need not admire what I hate any more."

Oscar had many years before quoted with approval Ouida's epigram, "When society is aware that you think it a flock of geese, it revenges itself by hissing loudly behind your back." The "Philistine Paean" spoke for the English public, which, liberated from good manners by a conviction for "gross indecency," was now perfectly willing to hiss the charismatic jester to his face.

In the end, one is bound to wonder how his British audience could for so long have remained blind to—or simply have chosen to ignore—Oscar's shocking real identity. At least one observer was able to answer this question with convincing shrewdness. This was Percival Almy, who interviewed Oscar for the March

1894 issue of a London magazine, *The Theatre*. At the end of his article, Almy added several paragraphs assessing what one would now call "the Wilde phenomenon." These constitute the most incisive contemporary explanation we have for Oscar's extraordinarily long "life" in the pages of *Punch*. Particularly acute, and an apt conclusion, is Almy's final observation, which doubtless applied to the vast majority of *Punch's* readership:

> His admirers are divided into two classes: first, those who do not believe a word he says—who call him Humourist; and secondly, those who are perfectly satisfied with the truthfulness of his statements as applied to their neighbours—who call him Satirist; and as these two classes constitute a very large proportion of Society, the secret of Mr Wilde's popularity as a writer is at once proclaimed.

Chapter Eleven

☆ ☆ ☆ ☆ ☆ ☆ ☆ ☆ ☆ ☆ ☆ ☆ ☆ ☆ ☆

THE MAN WILDE: HIS CRIME

Blackstone described "the infamous crime against nature" as an offense of "deeper malignity" than rape, a heinous act "the very mention of which is a disgrace to human nature.". . . To hold that the act of homosexual sodomy is somehow protected as a fundamental right would be to cast aside millennia of moral teaching.

—CHIEF JUSTICE WARREN BURGER, 1986

THOUGH THE CHURCH IN early-Renaissance England made homosexual intercourse a crime, sodomy was clearly a part of the scene and seems not to have been very strenuously prosecuted in ecclesiastical courts. It was a commonplace aspect of monastic life, and it may be that Henry VIII's suppression of the monasteries led him and his advisers, a few years later, to decide the time had come for the first civil injunction against sodomy in English law. In 1533, therefore, a statute declaring sodomy a felony was promulgated. The proclamation was phrased with some style, albeit Draconian:

> For as much as there is not yet sufficient and condign
> punishment appointed . . . for the detestable and abom-
> inable vice of buggery committed with mankind and
> beast . . . it may therefore please the King's highness,
> with the assent of his lords spiritual and temporal, and
> the commons of this present parliament assembled . . .
> that the same offence be from henceforth judged felony
> . . . And that the offenders being hereof convict . . .
> shall suffer such pains of death, and losses, and penalties
> of their goods, chattels, debts, lands, tenements, and
> hereditaments, as felons be accustomed to do.

Repealed twice—when Edward VI (1547) and Mary (1553) came
to the throne—this statute was finally re-enacted and declared
"perpetual" in the fifth year of Elizabeth's reign (1562).

In 1828, at the instigation of the Home Secretary, Sir Robert
Peel, many hanging crimes were abolished. Sodomy was not
among them. Only with the Offences Against Persons Act of
1861 did it cease to be punishable by death; Scotland lagged another twenty-eight years before following suit. Indeed, until 1967
the penalty for buggery, which required proof of anal penetration,
was ten years to life. For all homosexual acts short of buggery the
maximum penalty remained two years. Elsewhere in the world the
crime had long since vanished; in 1791 France decriminalized
same-sex relations entirely. No execution for the crime is recorded on the Continent after that date, but in the first three decades of the nineteenth century sixty English hangings for the
offense took place. In 1846 there were more hangings for sodomy
than for homicide.

Over the centuries English judges and legal scholars regularly
assumed theatrical poses of disgust when dealing with sodomy and
sodomites. The seventeenth-century English jurist Sir Edward
Coke, for instance, asserted, "Sodomites came to this abomina-
tion by four means, viz. by pride, excess of diet, idleness, and contempt for the poor." The venerable Blackstone, in his 1769
Commentaries on the Laws of England, could not even bear to let

the crime sully his inkwell: "I will not act so disagreeable a part, to my readers as well as myself, as to dwell any longer upon [the] subject." He then added, "It will be more eligible to imitate in this respect the delicacy of our English law, which treats it, in its very indictments, as a crime not fit to be named: '*peccatum illud horribile, inter christianos non nominandum.*'" The Law, it appears, as well as those who practiced such a *peccatum*, dared not speak its name. Blackstone went on to assert, "The voice of nature and of reason, and the express law of God" insist upon death for such miscreants, and noted, without any show of disapproval, that "among the antient Goths" such persons were "buried alive."

There is, however, something quite surprising about this brief synopsis of antihomosexual legislative history: it has nothing to do with Oscar's conviction and imprisonment. During the preceding three and a half centuries, the criminal law tended to be employed only against those who corrupted young persons or committed acts in public, outraging decency. Prosecutors were mainly of Mrs Patrick Campbell's mind, when she famously scoffed, "It doesn't matter what you do in the bedroom as long as you don't do it in the street and frighten the horses." Consensual sex between adults *in private*, in other words, was beyond the statute's concern. The legislative innovation that brought private consensual acts under sanction and caught Oscar in its net was, in fact, a mere ten years old.

The man responsible for the new law, in yet another quirk of fate, had been much admired by Oscar in his early London days. He was Henry Labouchere, a man wealthy from banking and formerly a diplomat posted in Washington (he was a Virginia landowner). He possessed a fine estate at Twickenham and was for many years editor of the magazine *Truth*, which he founded in 1876. He was a "witty and cultured writer and speaker, an aristocrat of French ancestry" and seems to have made quite an impression on Oscar. Somewhat bored with the conversation among some brokers and grain men of St. Louis during his lecture tour of 1882, Oscar asked whether anyone present read *Truth*. "Labouchere is the best writer in Europe," he told his hosts, "a most remarkable gentleman." A few weeks later he wrote from Sioux City, Iowa, to a London friend, "Weary of being asked by gloomy reporters 'which was the most beautiful colour' and what is the meaning of the word 'aesthetic,' on my last Chicago interview I turned the conversation on three of my heroes, Whistler, Labouchere, and [the actor Henry] Irving." A few years later Oscar's hero would turn into the author of his legal destiny.

For Labouchere espoused extreme political views and served as a Radical Member of Parliament for Northampton from 1880 to 1905. It was he who—after the first reading of a bill "for the Protection of Women and Girls, the suppression of brothels, and other purposes"—moved, in something of a surprise maneuver, that a new clause be added to it. This clause became Section 11 of the Criminal Law Amendment Act of 1885, which took effect on 1 January 1886. Section 11 ended up falling between a section allowing searches on suspicion that a woman or girl might be unlawfully detained for prostitution and a section concerning custody of girls under sixteen. It read, in full:

Henry Labouchere, from Max Beerbohm's *Caricatures of Twenty-five Gentlemen* (1896).

216

Any male person who, in public or private, commits, or is a party to the commission of, or procures or attempts to procure the commission by any male person of, any act of gross indecency with another male person, shall be guilty of a misdemeanor, and being convicted thereof shall be liable at the discretion of the court to be imprisoned for any term not exceeding two years, with or without hard labour.

The phrase "act of gross indecency" is so vague that Section 11 has recently been described as the "first legal classification of a sexual relation (as opposed to a sexual act) between men." In his brief description of how the bill was passed, Sir Travers Humphreys, one of Oscar's lawyers, thrice emphasized how little discussion the proposed addition evoked in Parliament. One member merely wondered at its inclusion in a bill dealing with other matters entirely. There was one amendment, agreed to without discussion: the maximum penalty was raised from one to two years.

After royal assent was given and the law was published, some controversy arose in the press and on speakers' platforms. Some labeled it The Blackmailer's Charter, and it certainly became that, many times over, in Oscar's case. Humphreys, in his memoirs, agreed that it was an invitation to extortion: "No one having experience in such matters would deny that the words 'in private' have materially assisted the blackmailer in his loathsome trade." Of course the section, embedded in an act addressing adolescent female prostitution, was difficult to isolate for attack. Indeed, the Home Secretary curiously anticipated the way antihomosexual views have today become part of a "family values" agenda when he defended Section 11 in Parliament by insisting, "The purity of the households of this country shall be maintained." After a few weeks, expressions of concern about the potentially disagreeable effects of Section 11 faded away.

The Stranger Wilde

☆　☆　☆

SECTION 11 ITSELF FADED away, as most laws of its kind do. It was forced out of *de facto* abeyance only in cases where reckless or notably scandalous activities made it impossible for the English public and its prosecutors to successfully avert their eyes. Cases, for instance, like the police raid in August 1889 on a brothel at 19 Cleveland Street manned by several "telegraph boys." A few aristocrats were on the premises. The proprietor was prosecuted, but obviously not for the purpose of discouraging such behavior at large: the trial was held in virtual secrecy and was abetted by complete silence in the press. Until, that is, Labouchere's *Truth* let the cathouse out of the bag in disgust at the usual English preference for ignoring disagreeable sexual matters. Another case like this erupted five years later at one of the regular Sunday-evening drag parties held by one John Preston in Fitzroy Street. The police attended on 12 August 1894 and arrested eighteen men, among them one Arthur Marling, who was dressed "in a fantastic female garb of black and gold." Alfred Taylor, who would later stand trial with Oscar, was also arrested during this raid.

Laws that are rarely enforced decay as inevitably as unembalmed corpses. By the time Section 11 was resurrected for its most famous deployment in history, it had lost its moral force. Bosie pointed this out acidly and accurately in his autobiography: "The prosecution of Oscar Wilde never had any moral force behind it, and as a result produced nothing but a crop of evil and calamity. It was dictated by Vengeance and Hypocrisy, unaccompanied by any genuine moral purpose." The Vengeance, of course, derived from the middle class's gleeful retaliation for all the subversive satire and derision Oscar had visited upon it for years. The Hypocrisy, on the other hand, derived from an obvious and long-standing willingness throughout English society to let homosexuals go about their business if they simply had the good manners to be discreet about it. Edward Carpenter made this point

218

admirably in his groundbreaking essay "Homogenic Love" of 1895:

> The homogenic passion ramifies widely through all modern society. . . . Among the masses of the people as among the classes, below the stolid surface and reserve of English manners, letters pass and enduring attachments are formed, differing in no very obvious respect from those correspondences which persons of opposite sexes knit with each other under similar circumstances; but . . . hitherto while this passion has occasionally come into public notice from the police reports, etc., in its grosser and cruder forms, its more sane and spiritual manifestations—though really a moving force in the body politic—have remained unrecognized.

This is a fine expression, from the dawn of gay liberation history, of what activists are to this day often obliged to remind the public at large: "We are everywhere." Bosie, in high dudgeon in Paris a few months later, knew homosexuals were everywhere, and he was prepared to announce the fact in an article he composed for publication in *Le Mercure de France*: "I know *for an absolute fact that the* London police has on its books the names of *more than 4000 persons* known as habitual pederasts, and yet none of them are prosecuted, and many of them occupy the highest and most respected positions in politics, art and society." Bosie's figure doubtless underplays the city's homosexual population. Given greater London's population at the time (six and a half million), there must have been many homosexuals whose names were *not* on the police list.

There are other suggestions that *laissez-faire* had mainly been the watchword before Oscar. A passage from the *Westminster Review* of 27 May 1895 implies that the Queensberry publicity jolted the police out of their customary torpor in enforcing Section 11: "The police appear to have been on the track of the scandals now disclosed for some time; but it was Lord Queensberry . . . to whom the actual exposure is due." The editorialist went on to attack the *laissez-faire* attitude toward homosexuality, expressing the rabidly moralistic, clean-the-Augean-stables sentiment that was then sweeping England: "There are those who believe that the proper way to meet evils of this kind and to save society from corruption is to pretend that the evils do not exist, and to hush them up. We do not share this view. Exposure and publicity are great cleansers of the social system." *Reynolds's Newspaper,* on 26 May, expressed even more disgust at the long history of looking the other way: "Many of our readers may not remember the Bolton and Parke scandal, but all are familiar with the Cornwall and French case in Dublin, the Cleveland Street atrocities, the conviction of De Cobain. These came to the surface, but the police were perfectly aware of their existence long previously, and of the existence of many similar cases." Names of several implicated "men of social position" are retailed by *Reynolds's,* with the barbed observation that, "curiously enough, all these men were Tories."

Laissez-faire had certainly predominated in Oscar's personal case; this was one reason he had been lulled into recklessness. Frank Harris, who said he learned Oscar was gay only with the Queensberry trial imminent, must have been the last person in London—or in London society, at any rate—to have the scales fall from his eyes. Oscar once told an interviewer for the *Echo de Paris* that Paris pleased him very much: "While in London one hides everything, in Paris one reveals everything." But the comparison was merely relative. Oscar worked less and less assiduously at concealing his sexual preferences *everywhere;* as his friend Vincent O'Sullivan observed, "If Oscar . . . made little concealment in London, he made none at all in Paris." Several of his friends came to Humphreys in his chambers before the Queensberry trial and told him that Oscar had "always" had his "tendencies." When young André Gide saw the fateful name on the board in the lobby of his Algiers hotel in early 1895, he almost fled. He described Oscar and his reputation at the time to his mother in a letter. He surely exaggerated for her sake, but what he said was true in essence: "That terrifying man, the most dangerous product of modern civilization—still, as in Florence, escorted by young Lord Douglas, both of them on the London and Paris blacklists, and, if one weren't far away, the most compromising people in the world." In London Oscar and Bosie were beginning to be refused service in restaurants, and more circumspect gay friends, like George Ives, were wearying of telling them to be more discreet. The inclination of Oscar and Bosie to act both "up" and "out" heightened the risk of a collision with Section 11. Even so, the elaborately repugnant efforts of "a funny little man," as Bosie called his father, were required to bring the collision off.

RARELY INVOKED, SECTION 11 for several years drew little attention, let alone attack (attackers, of course, were bound to be accused of a personal interest). But at least one brilliant and devastating assault on Section 11 was written before it felled Oscar. Its author lived in Fitzroy Square, just a stone's throw from the sites of the Cleveland Street and Fitzroy Street scandals. Perhaps this Bloomsbury neighborhood was bathed in lavender even then. The author of this attack, it happens, did not have a personal interest to declare, except, as was usual for him, an interest in sane, humane resolution of social follies. The man was Bernard Shaw.

The background for Shaw's assault on Section 11 can be briefly summarized. When Labouchere broke the Cleveland Street scandal in *Truth*, another editor, Ernest Parke, followed suit in the weekly *North London Press*. Parke was threatened with a libel suit by one of the young aristocrats mentioned as habitués of the brothel. This infuriated Shaw, a friend of Parke's, and he composed for publication the following letter, dated 26 November 1889, full of vintage Shavian outrage, wit, good sense, and gusto:

> Sir, I am sorry to have to ask you to allow me to mention what everybody declares unmentionable; but as a majority of the population habitually flavor their con-

versation with it to the extent of mentioning it at every sixth word or so, I shall not make matters worse by a serious utterance on the subject. My justification shall be that we may presently be saddled with the moral responsibility for monstrously severe punishments inflicted not only on persons who have corrupted children, but on others whose conduct, however nasty and ridiculous, has been perfectly within their admitted rights as individuals.

To a fully occupied person in normal health, with due opportunities for healthy social enjoyment, the mere idea of the subject of the threatened prosecutions is so expressively disagreeable as to appear unnatural. But everybody does not find it so. There are among us highly respected citizens who have been expelled from public schools for giving effect to the contrary opinion; there are hundreds of others who might have been expelled on the same ground had they been found out. Greek philosophers, otherwise of unquestioned virtue, have differed with us on the point. So have soldiers, sailors, convicts, and in fact members of all communities deprived of intercourse with women. A whole series of Balzac's novels turns upon attachments which are represented as redeeming them from utter savagery. Women, from Sappho downwards, have shewn that this abnormal appetite is not confined to one sex. Now I do not believe myself to be the only man in England acquainted with these facts. And I strongly protest against any journalist writing, as nine out of ten are at this moment dipping their pens to write, as if he had never heard of such things except as vague and sinister rumorus concerning the most corrupt phases in the decadence of Babylon, Greece, and Rome. All men of the world know they are constantly carried on by a small minority of people. . . .

I appeal now to the champions of individual rights

... to join me in a protest against a law by which two adult men can be sentenced to twenty years penal servitude for a private act, freely consented to and desired by both, which concerns themselves alone. There is absolutely no justification for the law except the old theological one of making the secular arm the instrument of God's vengeance. It is a survival from that discarded system with its stonings and burnings; and it survives because it is so unpleasant that men are loth to meddle with it even with the object of getting rid of it, lest they should be suspected of acting in their own personal interest. . . . You, Mr Editor, or I, or any man who knows London life, could without a moment's hesitation, point out at least one gentleman and one lady as to whose character in this respect there is no . . . doubt . . . but we do not find that their social acceptance is much, if at all, less than that of their untainted peers.

We are now free to face the evil of our relic of Inquisition law, and of the moral cowardice which prevents our getting rid of it. When the corruption of children (which is quite on a different footing, and is a legitimate subject for resolute repression) made it necessary the other day to expose a den of debauchees [in Cleveland Street], the Press was paralyzed with superstitious terror; and not a word was said until you, fortified by your parliamentary position, let the cat out of the bag. My friend Mr Parke, promptly following it up, is menaced with proceedings. . . . One result of this is that the scandals can no longer be ignored by the general Press. The only question now is, shall they be discussed with sane straightforwardness and without affectation; or are they to be darkly hinted at and gloated over as filthy, unmentionable, abominable, and every other adjective and innuendo that can make them prurient and mischievous? . . . I protest against the principle of the law under which the warrants have been issued; and I

hope that no attempt will be made to enforce its outrageous penalties in the case of adult men.

yrs, &c
G. Bernard Shaw

Shaw's rhetorical concessions to his audience were shrewdly
judged: allowing for some to think the conduct in question "nasty
and ridiculous," for example, and insisting on the protection of
children from "debauchees." Otherwise, the letter is wholly admirable. Jeremy Bentham had decades earlier thought in private of
sodomy as an "imaginary offense," and Shaw was here vigorously
pursuing that view. The "you, Mr Editor" addressed by Shaw, alas,
was Henry Labouchere himself. The venerable editor of *Truth* apparently did not care for the truth expressed in Shaw's letter and
refused to print it. Parke was convicted of libel and sentenced to
a year in prison.

Section 11 was also subjected to attack, as it were, from the
other side. Edward Carpenter chose to end "Homogenic Love"
with his thoughts on this law. These produce the essay's moving
and eloquent peroration:

> It has to be remarked that the present state of the Law
> ... is really quite impracticable and unjustifiable, and
> will no doubt have to be altered.
>
> The Law, of course, can only deal, and can only be
> expected to deal, with the outward and visible. It can-
> not control feeling; but it tries—in those cases where it
> is concerned—to control the expression of feeling. It
> has been insisted on in this essay that the Homogenic
> Love is a valuable social force, and, in cases, an indis-
> pensable factor of the noblest human character; also
> that it has a necessary root in the physical and sexual
> organism. This last is the point where the Law steps in.
> "We know nothing"—it says—"of what may be valu-
> able social forces or factors of character, or of what may
> be the relation of physical things to things spiritual; but

when you speak of a sexual element being present in this kind of love, we can quite understand that; and that is just what we mean to suppress. That sexual element is nothing but gross indecency, *any form of which by our Act of 1885 we make criminal.*"

Whatever substantial ground the Law may have had for previous statutes on the subject—dealing with a specific act (sodomy)—it has surely quite lost it in passing so wide-sweeping a condemnation on all relations between male persons. [Carpenter here inserts a footnote: "Though, inconsistently enough, making no mention of females."] It has undertaken a censorship over private morals ... which is beyond its province, and which—even if it were its province—it could not possibly fulfill; it has opened wider than ever before the door to a real social evil and crime—that of blackmailing; and it has thrown a shadow over even the simplest and most natural expressions of an attachment which may, as we have seen, be of the greatest value in national life.

That the homosexual passion may be improperly indulged in, that it may lead, like the heterosexual, to public abuses of liberty and decency we of course do not deny; but as, in the case of persons of opposite sex, the law limits itself on the whole to the maintenance of public order, the protection of the weak from violence and insult [another tart footnote: "Though it is doubtful whether the marriage-laws even do this!"] and of the young from their inexperience: so should it be here. Whatever teaching may be thought desirable on the general principles of morality concerned must be given—as it can only be given—by the spread of proper education and ideas, and not by the clumsy bludgeon of the statute-book.

Such eloquence tempts one to place Carpenter's essay in the company of Sir Philip Sidney's *Defence of Poesy*, Milton's *Areopagitica*, or Tom Paine's *Rights of Man*. In the final sentence of his final paragraph, Carpenter reiterated the folly of attempting to legislate private, consensual homosexual pleasure out of existence: "If the dedication of love were a matter of mere choice or whim, it still would not be the business of the State to compel that choice; but since no amount of compulsion can ever change the homogenic instinct in a person, where it is innate, the State in trying to effect such a change is only kicking at the pricks of its own advantage—and trying, in view perhaps of the conduct of a licentious few, to cripple and damage a respectable and valuable class of its own citizens."

CARPENTER'S GRAND SENTENCES WOULD be an unmitigated pleasure, but for one very depressing fact: the views he expressed were almost exactly in accord with the impassioned *minority* opinion of Harry Blackmun in the 1986 United States Supreme Court case *Bowers v. Hardwick*. In this case, the Court, by a five-to-four majority, upheld a Georgia state law that, like the 1885 Act, forbids homosexual acts by consenting adults in private. (It is some small comfort that one member of the majority, Justice Lewis Powell, later acknowledged his vote as a mistake.)

Coming ninety-one years after the conviction of Wilde, *Bowers v. Hardwick* proves a shocking reminder that the legislative rationale so acutely lambasted by Shaw and Carpenter has been with us for a very long time. All of the thirteen original states had sodomy laws when they ratified the Bill of Rights. When the Fourteenth Amendment was ratified in 1868, such laws were on the books of thirty-two of the thirty-seven states. And all fifty states had sodomy statutes until, in 1961, Illinois adopted the American Law Institute's Model Penal Code, which decriminalized private, consensual, adult sexual conduct.

There is more than a little of Shaw's sarcastic ridicule in Justice Blackmun's dissent. Particularly apt, for an attack on a legal concept hatched in the reign of Henry VIII, was his quotation from Oliver Wendell Holmes's great dissent in *Lochner v. New York*: "It is revolting to have no better reason for a rule of law than that so it was laid down in the time of Henry IV. It is still more revolting if the grounds upon which it was laid down have vanished long since, and the rule simply persists from blind imitation of the past." Blackmun (like Carpenter) also made clear that this matter was about (in the words of another famous dissent, that of Brandeis in *Olmstead v. United States*) "the most comprehensive of rights and the right most valued by civilized men . . . the right to be left alone."

Blackmun also derided with vigor the Georgia law's definition of sodomy ("any act involving the sex organs of one person and the mouth or anus of another") and the State's "apparent willingness to enforce against homosexuals a law it seems not to have any desire to enforce against heterosexuals." (The Georgia Supreme Court, in 1939, had even specifically held that the law did not prohibit lesbian activity.) Blackmun's subsequent assertions uncannily echoed the premises of Shaw and Carpenter, as, for example, when he cited a 1972 Supreme Court majority opin· ion: "A way of life that is odd or even erratic but interferes with no rights or interest of others is not to be condemned because it is different." Blackmun followed this up with a more fundamental point also made above by Carpenter: "What the Court really has refused to recognize is the fundamental interest all individuals have in controlling the nature of their intimate associations with others."

After making a strong case for the application of the Fourth Amendment to the case ("the right of the people to be secure in their . . . houses"), Blackmun turned to Georgia's explanations of the purpose of the law. He gave the judicial equivalent of a Bronx cheer to the notion that the Georgia law protected the state from the spread of communicable diseases. "The record before us is barren of any evidence to support" this claim, he concluded. Georgia's Attorney General, Michael Bowers, also asserted his state's right "to maintain a decent society" (echoing the Home

Secretary's "purity"-minded defense of Section 11 in the 1880s). But Blackmun refused to accept the notion that, merely because acts of sodomy "for hundreds of years, if not thousands, have been uniformly condemned as immoral," this was sufficient to permit them to be banned. "Traditional Judeo-Christian values" are not constitutional values: "That certain, but by no means all, religious groups condemn the behavior at issue gives the State no license to impose their judgments on the entire citizenry." He then cited a 1975 ruling to the effect that "mere public intolerance or animosity cannot constitutionally justify the deprivation of a person's physical liberty."

The *Bowers v. Hardwick* ruling—being so sympathetic to a law like Section 11—was disheartening. Fortunately, even though there were, according to the FBI, 107,600 arrests for sodomy in the nation in 1990, the tide has turned in Justice Blackmun's direction. Since 1960 the number of states banning sodomy has fallen from fifty to twenty-four, plus that singularly chaste District, Columbia. As recently as 1992, the Kentucky Supreme Court, in a four-to-three ruling, struck down its homosexual sodomy law.

Behind all the close argument and numerous citations of precedent, the essential principle of Blackmun's opinion—in which Justices Brennan, Marshall, and Stevens joined—was simply: live and let live. The view, as it happens, was also eloquently expressed by Oscar's contemporary, Carpenter, in the following words. Blackmun did not cite them, but he might happily have done so.

> Summarizing then some of our conclusions on this rather difficult question we may say that the homogenic love, as a distinct variety of the sex-passion, is in the main subject to the same laws as the ordinary love; that it probably demands and requires some amount of physical intimacy; that a wise humanity will quite recognize this; but that the degree of intimacy . . . is a matter

which can only be left to the good sense and feeling of those concerned.

It is sad to think these words were written just when Oscar, in his last year of "senseless pleasure and hard materialism," was inventing his exuberantly careless *Earnest* and consorting rashly with Bosie in Paris, London, Florence, Worthing, and Brighton.

The acts that led Oscar into the shadow of Section 11 had terrible consequences not merely for himself. Nietzsche, defining his conception of genius, wrote, "Great men . . . are explosives in which a tremendous force is stored up; their precondition is always . . . that for a long time much has been gathered, stored up, saved up, and conserved for them—that there has been no explosion for a long time." By the mid-1890s Oscar had situated himself perfectly to be such an explosive genius, shaking the Victorian epoch with laughter but at the same shaking its foundations and clearing the path for a new dispensation. However, his "explosion," like that of the remarkable Rocket in his fairy tale, went off all wrong and laid waste to the just-coalescing homosexualist movement. Sane thinkers, rather than being liberated to speak their minds, were driven further underground, where they and their successors remained for several more decades.

The "Oscar Wilde troubles" proved notably disastrous to Carpenter, as he recalled twenty years after: "Wilde was arrested in April 1895 and from that moment a sheer panic prevailed over *all* questions of sex, and especially of course questions of the Intermediate Sex." When Carpenter's publisher, Fisher Unwin, got wind of the mere existence of "Homogenic Sex" (it had been discreetly printed by the tiny Manchester Labour Press), it canceled a contract with Carpenter for a book on the heterosexual subject of *Love's Coming-of-Age* and dropped his already published *Towards Democracy* from its list.

One book in particular—the most famous and bloody-minded of all the assaults on "Oscarism"—gives a telling flavor of the oppressive energies unleashed by his conviction. This is *De-*

generation, by Max Nordau, first published in German in 1893 under the title *Entartung*. This moralizing jeremiad was probably the most elaborate and widely disseminated of all attacks on what Nordau called the "egomaniacs" of the *fin de siècle*, its Aesthetes, Decadents, and Diabolists. Sounding very much like the satirists of *Punch*, but with no sense of humor whatsoever, Nordau assailed the Aesthetes ("the chief of whom is Oscar Wilde") for their "exaggeration of the importance of art" and "love of the artificial." He attacked Oscar's predilection for "strange costume," his "tortuously disdainful prattling," and his "purely anti-socialistic, egomaniacal recklessness." To which, had Oscar been able to read German, he would have replied: "Perfectly true!" Indeed, in 1894 Oscar was asked by the editor of the *National Review* to contribute a slashing attack on the *"fin de siècle"* phenomenon in the Nordau style. He replied brusquely,

> Dear Sir, I never write 'slashing' articles: slash does not seem to me to be a quality of good prose. Still less would I feel inclined to write an article attacking all that is known by the term *'fin de siècle.'*
>
> All that is known by that term I particularly admire and love. It is the fine flower of our civilisation: the only thing that keeps the world from the commonplace, the coarse, the barbarous.

Unfortunately, Nordau's feast of rant appeared in its first English translation with cruelly perfect timing, in February 1895. Nordau's assertion that Wilde "apparently admires immorality, sin and crime" was perfect grist for scandal mills during the trials. *Degeneration* became enormously popular and required seven more printings in 1895 alone.

Nordau presciently epitomized the tone of English morality in the period After Oscar. His conviction turned the relatively benign and at least mannerly middle classes from a Dr Jekyll into something like an enraged Mr Hyde. Or to put it another way: like the smile in Dorian's picture, the smile of the English public, which had laughed so cheerfully at Oscar for years in the pages of *Punch*, turned cruel and vindictive.

The sad effect of Oscar's fall upon the increasingly vigorous homosexual rights movement of the early 1890s is captured in a poignant letter that John Addington Symonds wrote to Carpenter two years before the trials. In this letter he urged the publication of scientifically sound books "upon the homosexual passion." Such books would "force people to see that the passions in question have their justification in nature." He ended with the hope that "a new chivalry" might emerge that would allow homosexuals to live openly and comfortably in society. The trials of Wilde brutally crushed this hope and played some part in delaying the arrival of this new chivalry, which even now seems but imperfectly realized.

Chapter Twelve

☆ ☆ ☆ ☆ ☆ ☆ ☆ ☆ ☆ ☆ ☆ ☆ ☆ ☆ ☆ ☆ ☆

WHY HE STAYED

A man of genius has been seldom ruined but by himself.
—SAMUEL JOHNSON

Nothing should be able to harm a man except himself.
—"THE SOUL OF MAN UNDER SOCIALISM"

THERE IS A STRANGE and amusing scene in *The Importance of Being Earnest* that for decades was lost to the world, the so-called Gribsby scene. It seems that as rehearsals progressed it became clear to the producer, George Alexander, that the play was too long. He succeeded in convincing Oscar to crush his four acts into three, largely by means of excising a scene in which a lawyer named Gribsby arrives at the Manor House, Woolton, to arrest Algy for a debt of £762.14.2. This he has incurred at the Savoy Hotel under the name of Ernest Worthing. Though the scene did find its way into a 1903 German edition of the play titled *Ernst sein!*, it vanished until the original manuscript came to light in 1950 in a trunk belonging to the widow of one of Oscar's friends.

How sarcastically the gods must have laughed as Oscar composed this scene, considering what they had in store for him. For his subsequent life was to imitate the art of this scene in several grotesquely ironic details. Miss Prism's astonishment—"seven hundred sixty-two pounds for eating! How grossly materialistic!"—was to be echoed by Oscar himself, in a letter to the governor of Reading Prison just before his release: "I am not a scrap ashamed of having been in prison. I am horribly ashamed of the materialism of the life that brought me there." In prison he would also recall that disaster came as a result of an unpaid hotel bill, though not from the Savoy. Exactly two weeks after *Earnest* opened, on what Oscar called "that fatal Friday" (1 March), he was in his lawyer's office, Bosie at his side urging him to sue his father: "Instead of being in Humphreys' office weakly consenting to my own ruin, I would have been happy and free in France . . . if I had been able to leave the Avondale Hotel. But . . . the proprietor said he could not allow my luggage to be removed from the hotel till I had paid the account [£140] in full. That is what kept me in London."

Surely the most poignant premonition of disaster in the Gribsby scene, though, is the discussion of Algy's proposed place of incarceration:

> GRIBSBY: We have to be at Holloway not later than four
> o'clock; otherwise it is difficult to obtain admis-
> sion. The rules are very strict.
> ALGERNON: Holloway!
> GRIBSBY: It is at Holloway that detentions of this char-
> acter take place always.
> ALGERNON: Well, I really am not going to be imprisoned
> in the suburbs for having dined in the West End.

The lawyer coolly seeks to put a good face on Algy's destination: "The surroundings, I admit, are middle-class; but the gaol itself is

fashionable and well-aired." His remark that "there are ample opportunities of taking exercise" causes Algy to explode: "Exercise!
Good God! No gentleman ever takes exercise." This exchange
looks ahead to Oscar's being questioned by the prosecutor in his
first trial about an alleged site for a sexual encounter that was
"ten minutes' walk" from Tite Street. He answered, "I don't
know, I never walk."

But Oscar was soon to test the accuracy of his Gribsby's sanguine description of Holloway. On Friday morning, 5 April, his libel case collapsed, and Queensberry was judged not guilty on the
grounds of "justification" for his accusation that Oscar "posed" as
a sodomite. Oscar was charged all costs in the case, and he left
the court a marked man under Section 11 of the Criminal Law
Amendment Act. He dawdled in London all afternoon, mostly
listening to his friends urging him to flee to France. Finally he
was arrested at 6 p.m., processed at Bow Street Station, then
transferred to Holloway. He was to remain there until 7 May,
when he was finally granted bail pending his retrial after the hung
jury at his first trial. His letters to various friends written during
this month contrast harrowingly with the haughty badinage of
the Gribsby scene: "I have no books, nothing to smoke, and sleep
very badly. . . . I am ill—apathetic. Slowly life creeps out of
me. . . . I sicken in inanition." Fashionable and well aired, indeed.

Max Beerbohm, in America on tour as Beerbohm Tree's secretary, heard the awful news and wrote to Ada Leverson from the
Waldorf Hotel, "Poor Oscar! Why did he not go away while he
could?" This question is perhaps the most momentous and fascinating posed by Oscar Wilde's life. It was obviously on everyone's
lips at the time, and the enormous surprise and mystification over
his failure to take his chance and run show just how commonplace that course of action was then considered to be. Frank Harris captured the general view at the time when he observed,
"Knowing English custom and the desire of Englishmen to pass in
silence over all unpleasant sexual matters, I thought he would be
given the hint to go abroad and allowed to escape. That is the
ordinary, the usual English procedure."

235

This "procedure" appears to have been in place. Clarke, Oscar's brilliant leading counsel, recalled in his unpublished memoirs of the trial, "I hoped and expected that he would take the opportunity of escaping from the country, and I believe he would have found no difficulty in doing so." Early on the morning of 5 April, according to Harris, one of Oscar's assisting counsel came and said, "If you wish it, Clarke and I will keep the case going and give you time to get to Calais." The last surviving lawyer in the case remembered in 1948, "Wilde was given every opportunity to leave the country. . . . The authorities would, I believe, have been quite willing that he should go abroad." It was even thought in some quarters that the police waited until the last boat-train left for Dover at 4 p.m. before moving in on the Cadogan Hotel in Sloane Square, where Oscar sat drinking heavily and agonizing. Even Queensberry, his adrenaline flowing after his vindication in court, sent Oscar a characteristically bellicose message that presumed Continental exile to be likely: "If the country allows you to leave, all the better for the country! But, if you take my son with you, I will follow you wherever you go and shoot you!"

Why did Oscar not join the more than five hundred jittery gentlemen who were alleged, doubtless with some exaggeration, to have crossed the Channel the evening of 5 April? Why did he not think happily of leaving the bloody sceptered isle, whose inhabitants he had so often scorned? Why, indeed, did he not submit happily to exile, just as his ageing Lord Augustus does in *Lady Windermere's Fan,* when wise and witty Mrs Erlynne demands emigration in exchange for her hand in marriage: "All the conditions she makes are that we live entirely out of England. A very good thing too. Demmed clubs, demmed climate, demmed cooks, demmed everything. Sick of it all!" Why, finally, did Oscar not listen to the chorus of friends, relations, and lawyers who—with two notable exceptions—were unanimously urging him to vanish . . . and who would have sung a rousing hallelujah if he had done so?

Oscar supplied numerous answers to the great question.

Some ring true; others evoke suspicion because they seem either convenient, self-deluding, prevaricating, or merely would-be witty. Members of his social circle offered their speculations, both at the time and in volumes of memoirs and retrospects that appeared regularly during the next several decades. Subsequent biographers and scholars have had their say, too. All of the proposed answers to the question—there are more than a dozen—bear weighing, even some of the manifestly light ones. That any one of them offers the whole truth pure and simple seems most unlikely, not least because, as Algy tells Jack in *Earnest*, "the truth is rarely pure and never simple." However, this scarcely makes a census of the explanations for Oscar's fateful inertia any less intriguing.

ONLY ONE OF OSCAR'S expressed reasons for holding course toward his judicial Armageddon was in his famed nose-in-the-air vein. Backstage at the St. James's Theatre during a performance of *Earnest* just two days before Queensberry was committed for his libel trial, Alexander chided Oscar for appearing in public with Bosie and Constance, then asked, "Why don't you withdraw from this case and go abroad?" With his patented bravado, Oscar replied: "I have just been abroad, and now I have come home again. One can't keep on going abroad, unless one is a missionary, or, what comes to the same thing, a commercial traveler." Though the jest contained some truth (he had just returned from his trip to Algiers), Oscar transformed it into an outrageous piece of hypocrisy a few days later by slipping away again, to Monte Carlo with Bosie.

A more ominous consideration was the stance of Oscar's two surviving family members, Lady Wilde and his brother, Willie, who lived together in a small, dingy flat in Oakley Street, Chelsea. Here Oscar stayed for a few ghastly days after he was released on bail to await the final trial. Willie performed idiotically as usual in his role as dipsomaniacal sibling rival, proclaiming to Oscar and every visitor (among them a sympathetic William Butler

Yeats), "Oscar is an Irish gentleman: he will stay to face the music." Oscar even told Harris that if he were to leave Oakley Street Willie had threatened to tell the police. He also hinted darkly that Willie had urged his solicitors to "buy letters of mine; he has blackmailed me."

Willie, virtually everyone agreed, was a fool, and Oscar seems never to have paid him much heed, but Speranza was obviously another matter. An ageing Irish firebrand of the mid-century and the heroine of two notorious Dublin trials of her own, she was precisely the wrong mother for a man in Oscar's position to have. She had once written a volatile article for a revolutionary Irish weekly. When its editor was put on trial in 1848 for printing it (anonymously), according to one of her obituaries, "the intrepid young woman stood up in the Criminal Court in Dublin while the literary incitement to treason was being read aloud, and proclaimed herself the author of the article and invited the officers of the Crown to put her on her trial." The memories of such Hibernian heroics—which in the event proved successful—must have addled her brain. She thus fell naturally into the role of an Irish Volumnia to her son's Coriolanus and announced to him, "If you stay, even if you go to prison, you will always be my son; it will make no difference to my affection; but if you go I will never speak to you again." It is impossible now to weigh the impact of this ultimatum on Oscar's decision. If it was significant, Oscar might well have exited Oakley Street for the Central Criminal Court with a speech of Shakespeare's Coriolanus, with but one hypermetrical word change:

> *O my mother, mother! O!*
> *You have won a happy victory to Ireland;*
> *But, for your son, believe it—O, believe it—*
> *Most dangerously you have with him prevail'd,*
> *If not most mortal to him.*

But there is at least one hint in Oscar's work that he might have been conscious of the self-aggrandizement lurking in his mother's ultimatum. It comes in the comments of Lord Illingworth, the Oscarian character in A *Woman of No Importance*. He observes, "A mother's love is very touching, of course, but is often curiously selfish. I mean, there is a good deal of selfishness in it." On the other hand, Oscar appears to have employed the excuse of his mother's ultimatum seldom in the frantic conversations of the time and never to his chief harrier, Harris. Nor did he seem to hold the courtroom debacle she insisted upon against her afterward. In prison, after she died in 1896, he eulogized, "I have never known anyone with such perfect faith as my mother. She was one of the great figures of the world."

Oscar also refused to budge in respect of the two courageous sureties for his £5,000 bail, Reverend Stewart Headlam and Percy Douglas. To the former Oscar had said more than once, "I have given my word to you and to my mother, and that is enough," and to Harris he said, "I couldn't leave them to suffer; they would lose their thousands." But this may have been a conveniently "noble" tactic, for it was made very clear to Oscar that he should not let this scruple stand in his way. Douglas said emphatically that he would not take his losses amiss (even offered to make good on Headlam's portion), and Humphreys later stated, "Wilde was told, so I was afterwards informed, that his sureties would not suffer if he absconded." Harris responded to this excuse by offering to shoulder some of the financial burden himself and pragmatically suggested to Oscar, "You can pay the other thousand or so within a very short time by writing a couple of plays. American papers would be only too glad to pay you for an interview. The story of your escape would be worth a thousand pounds." This did not change Oscar's mind.

To Robert Sherard, who visited him at his mother's house, Oscar declared he was "too ill to go anywhere." Sherard did observe that he was "in a fever all the time" and had an "unquenchable thirst" which kept his friends "running out all day to fetch soda-water and lemonade." Nothing more grievous was noticed at the time by others in Oscar's circle, though, and the services of a physician appear not to have been required during this period. Oscar also appeared to hold up under the stresses of the courtroom with some show of poise. Beerbohm was present and reported him "thinner and consequently fine to look at." The excuse of ill health thus is not very convincing.

Occult powers appear to have played a part in Oscar's thinking. He and his wife had several times consulted fortune-tellers. In the summer of 1894, one of them predicted a trip with Bosie in January, and Oscar wrote to tell him: "The only thing that consoles me is what the Sibyl of Mortimer Street (whom mortals term Mrs Robinson) said to me. If I could disbelieve her I would, but I can't, and I know that early in January you and I will go away together for a long voyage." The prescient sibyl's success at foretelling the Algerian trip perhaps encouraged Oscar to believe another of her predictions. She made it just a few days before Queensberry offered his Plea of Justification, naming ten young men with whom Oscar had been involved. Elated over her cheerful prophecy, Oscar hastened a telegram to Ada Leverson with the news: "We have been to the Sibyl Robinson. She prophesied complete triumph and was most wonderful." Just two weeks later he would be writing to Leverson again . . . from Holloway: "With what a crash this fell! Why did the Sibyl say such fair things?" His faith in the fortune-teller apparently revived, however. Leverson described him during his secret stay in her house as being "extremely optimistic, firmly believing in a palmist's prophecy of triumph."

This hopeful Oscar was apparently forgetting an earlier prophesy of Mrs Robinson's. He once told Vincent O'Sullivan that she had said to him, "I see a very brilliant life for you up to a certain point. Then I see a wall. Beyond that wall I see nothing." The wall surrounding Reading Prison? or what Frank Harris called "the impenetrable blank wall of English philistinism and contempt"? or the imprisoning wall of self-delusion? In any event, the Sibyl of Mortimer Street had scored a bull's-eye with her prediction.

Oscar also appears to have harbored optimistic notions about

his chances after the first jury failed to reach a verdict. Bosie recalled that he "thought he had a 'good chance of being acquit-
ted.'" One report had suggested that only a single juror had refused to convict, while Beerbohm said he had learned that "nine
out of the twelve jurors were for him." Even in the event of a
conviction, Oscar hoped for leniency. As he awaited the final
trial, he asked Harris, "A year, Frank, they may give me a year?
half the possible sentence: the middle course that English judges
always take: the sort of compromise they think safe?" Harris
hadn't the heart to discourage him but privately "felt no such
confidence in English judges; their compromises are usually
bargainings; when they get hold of an artist they give rein to their
intuitive fear and hate." In due course Harris's cynicism was re-
warded: when Justice Wills pronounced sentence he called such
people as Oscar "dead to all sense of shame," branded his as "the
worst case I have ever tried," and gave him the maximum sentence of two years at hard labor.

WHEN PRESENTED WITH DETAILED plans for escape, Oscar dragged
his heels in more mundane fashion. Harris, for instance, learned
that a Jew of his acquaintance owned a steam yacht moored
downriver on the Thames at Erith and asked whether he could
charter it for a few days. When he explained that his purpose was
to spirit Oscar to Dieppe, the boat was put at his disposal for
nothing. The lengthy narrative of Harris's futile attempt, during a
late-evening walk around Kensington, to cajole Oscar into em-
barking on the yacht verges on the comic: the vigorous, can-do
optimist colliding with the anchorite pessimist: "Oh, Frank, I'd
love to . . . but I can't. I dare not. I'm caught, Frank, in a trap;
I can only wait for the end." Harris tried everything: "There's a
little library on board of French books and English; I've ordered
supper in the cabin—lobster à l'Americaine and a bottle of
Pommery." An enclosed carriage "with a pair of fast horses" was

Frank Harris, from Max Beerbohm's *Caricatures of Twenty-five Gentlemen* (1896).

at the ready. He pictured their dining "comfortably at the Sables d'Olonne . . . where sunshine reigns even in May from morning till night." Harris's blood rose each time Oscar responded, "It's impossible! . . . I should be seized by the police. You don't know the police." Harris replied, "Nonsense, the police can't stop you and not a man of them will see you from start to finish. . . . On board the yacht no one will touch you." (At this point he might have quoted from *Dorian Gray*: "On a yacht one is safe.") Oscar hardened his stance: "I could not go about in France feeling that the policeman's hand might fall on my shoulder at any moment. I could not live a life of fear and doubt; it would kill me in a month." To which Harris sensibly countered, "They won't get you at all; they don't want you. You're making mountains out of molehills with nervous fancies." By the time he left Oscar off at his mother's, Harris admitted that he was beside himself: "I was consumed with rage and contemptuous impatience." As to the great question, he was at a total loss: "I had done the best I knew and I had failed. Why? I had no idea. I have never known why he refused to come. I don't think he knew himself."

Harris, of course, was stupendously different from Oscar; he was a short, boisterous terrier with a bass voice like "a beaten Eastern gong." "One does not meet with Frank Harris: one collides with him," said one acquaintance, and Shaw wrote to Harris himself, "You were more pugnacious than six Queensberrys rolled into one." Oscar had always found Harris dear but terribly wearing. He reported in typical fashion, for instance, on a visit with Harris after release from prison: "Frank Harris is of course exhausting. After our literary talk in the evening I stagger to my room, bathed in perspiration. I believe he talks the Rugby game."

One is tempted to speculate that Oscar was simply too polite to respond in the negative when Harris pleaded, "Surely it is better to spend a week with me than in that dismal house in Oakley Street, where the very door gives one the creeps." Perhaps the offer of a yacht from one of his circle of gay chums—similarly provisioned, but with the addition of a fetching cabin boy or two—would have proved much more successful. Shaw, as usual, made trenchant comedy of the whole notion: "To be called on to gallop *ventre à terre* to Erith . . . and hoist the Jolly Roger on board your lugger, was like casting a light comedian and first lover for *Richard III*. Oscar could not see himself in the part." Oscar had in fact praised pirates just the year before, calling them "very fine fellows," but cabin boys, not pirate kings, were Oscar's true delight.

Which brings us to his chief cabin boy, Lord Alfred Douglas. He was a villain many times (and many ways) over in Oscar's life, even a villain in our search for an answer to the present question. For he spoke of a letter he received from Oscar that might have held it—"a very touching letter giving his reasons for not going. It made me weep at the time, and even now I don't like to think about it. . . . Oscar said in his letter that he could not 'run away' and 'hide' and 'let down' his bails." Alas, the letter was among the 150 or so from Oscar that Bosie destroyed in the process of leaving his pagan days behind him.

Would the letter have revealed the truth? We have seen that Oscar's grasp on his emotions and on the realities in his life often failed under Bosie's spell. The terrain of the relationship was Alpine in its peaks of giddy elation and its abysmal crevasses of vituperation. Oscar's view of Bosie depended utterly on his "elevation" at any given moment. Fortunately, the contents of a few of Oscar's letters to Bosie from April and May of 1895 are known. They show quite clearly that Oscar, in desperation, turned the crisis into a Matterhorn of loving-kindness for Bosie by an impressive effort of romantic idealization. Of course, his friends would have called it all a pitiful and mawkish exercise in self-delusion, but Oscar could well have responded with Mrs Arbuthnot's pronouncement in A *Woman of No Importance:* "Only love can keep any one alive."

Given the stinging excoriation Oscar was to address to Bosie in *De profundis,* the aromatic verbal garlands of adoration in his letters from prison and from the Leverson house make appalling reading. To Ada and Ernest he confided after a few days in Holloway, "A slim thing, gold-haired like an angel, always stands at my side.... He moves in the gloom like a white flower." To Sherard he wrote, "Nothing but Alfred Douglas's daily visits quicken me into life." To Bosie himself, the color purple is pervasive, as in this letter written just before the last trial began: "From your silken hair to your delicate feet you are perfection to me.... O my love, you whom I cherish above all things.... O sweetest of all boys, most loved of all loves, my soul clings to your soul, my life to your life." Alone in his cell or in the Leversons' attic nursery in Courtfield Gardens, Oscar fairly shouted the Love that dare not speak its name. "My sweet rose, my delicate flower, my lily of lilies," he wrote, "it is perhaps in prison that I am going to test the power of love." Such ebullitions of chivalry make it clear that he was casting the two lovers in the grand tradition of Damon and Pythias, Achilles and Patroclus, David and Jonathan.

Oscar's related inclination was to cast himself as achieving a noble self-sacrifice by submitting to the legal process. "Every great love has its tragedy, and now ours has too, but ... to have had you for a part of my life, the only part I now consider beautiful, is enough for me." In this, Oscar was perhaps unconsciously assuming the heroic courtroom posture of his mother, when she stood by her philandering husband at a famed Dublin paternity trial. Oscar recalled the event for Harris:

> She stood up in court and bore witness for him with perfect serenity, with perfect trust and without a shadow of common womanly jealousy. She could not believe that the man she loved could be unworthy, and her conviction was so complete that it communicated itself to the jury. Her trust was so noble that they became infected by it, and brought him in guiltless. . . . It is only noble souls who have that assurance and serenity.

William Wilde, like Bosie, was no saint: he had sired three illegitimate children before marrying Speranza. Oscar would probably not have cared for the analogy of that Dublin trial with his, since, for the moment, Bosie could do no evil. He was in Oscar's mind a paragon who would see him through the imminent judicial gantlet.

Still, great love can be visited upon despicable lovers, and Oscar's utterances to Bosie, though fulsome, seem genuine. It is hard to read them without concluding that his love and the declarations it evoked strengthened Oscar's resolve to face up to English justice and to irradiate the Old Bailey with serene assurance as Speranza had done in a Dublin court many years before.

Chivalric romanticism having nothing to do with love may also have encouraged Oscar to stay and fight. Queensberry and his lawyers had attacked not only his sexual behavior but his writings. An author as proud as Oscar and accustomed to giving his critics as good as he got in letters to the editor was bound to feel some urge to vindicate his Art in a hugely theatrical venue like the Old Bailey. He envisioned the trial as a scene of Aesthetic vindication and perhaps imagined deploying to devastating effect the serene, aloof pose of *noblesse oblige* he had been practicing for years. This notion was folly: his alleged Aesthetic misdemeanors were the merest window-dressing in the case; the blood sport was bound to be the running to ground of a violator of Section 11.

This fact was made clear when Harris, Bernard Shaw, Oscar, and Bosie met at the Café Royal to strategize before the libel trial began. Oscar asked Harris whether he would testify in court that *Dorian Gray* was not corrupt but in fact a highly moral book. Shaw recalled Harris's response: "For God's sake, man, put everything on that plane out of your head. . . . It is not going to be a matter of clever talk about your books. They are going to bring up a string of witnesses that will put art and literature out of the question. Clarke will throw up his brief. He will carry the case to a certain point; and then, when he sees the avalanche coming, he will back out." Which was *exactly* what happened. But Oscar disdained the advice, and a furious Bosie said, "Your telling him to run away shows that you are no friend of Oscar's." Shaw wittily recalled Oscar exiting with a grand air and Bosie following him, "absurdly smaller, and imitating his walk, like a curate following an archbishop."

In the scandalous first number of the Oxford undergraduate magazine that contained Bosie's soon-to-be-infamous "Love that dare not speak its name" sonnet, Oscar contributed a clutch of aphorisms. One of them had it that "in examinations the foolish ask questions that the wise cannot answer." Oscar appears to have left the Café Royal thinking he could take this Olympian approach to the interrogations he would be subjected to in court. This, too, was a miscalculation. Harris had warned him before he first went on trial, "Don't be witty next time in court. The jury hate it. They regard it as intellectual superiority and impudence." Many witty or droll ripostes in the transcripts suggest that this good advice Oscar also chose to pass on rather than take himself. The postmortem that appeared in *Reynolds's Newspaper* proved Harris right: "His ornate and gushing language, his bastard affectation of literary culture, did him as much harm as anything else with the jury."

Related to Oscar's misapprehension about the purpose of the trial—and also encouraging hope for a positive outcome—was what some friends thought was his naive underestimation of the eagerness among Englishmen to visit comeuppance upon the prince of the Aesthetes. When he was told the middle class (the jury class) was dead against him, he jested: "Have no fear, the working classes are with me—to the boy." Many years later Ford Madox Ford sketched Oscar's social set with some accuracy: "This little earnest or posing world considered itself as a hierarchy, as an aristocracy entirely aloof from the common sort." Oscar seems not to have had a sense of the vindictive glee, the great gust of *Schadenfreude*, that was unleashed by his fall. Shaw concluded that Oscar had foolishly underestimated "the force of the social vengeance he was unloosing on himself" and overestimated the social scope of his charisma: "The vulgar hated him for snubbing them; and the valiant men damned his impudence and cut him. Thus he was left with a band of devoted satellites on the one hand, and a dining-out connection on the other, with here and there a man of talent and personality enough to command his respect." Oscar might have taken a hint of the narrow class appeal of the Wilde phenomenon from the box-office receipts for *Earnest*: the stalls and boxes were full but, according to the *Illustrated Sporting and Dramatic News* of 9 March 1895, the "pit and gallery were the reverse of crowded." Even the one weekly paper that treated Oscar with some humanity, *Reynolds's*, was willing to make the Wilde case a matter of class: "The public are now familiar with the fact that sexual offenses between males is a common practice among our leisured and cultured classes."

And so the literary and social lion assumed that he was entering the arena with Queensberry in something like full mane. He soon learned otherwise. At lunch in a private room of a Great Portland Street restaurant after the second trial, Oscar struck Harris as "mentally stunned by the sudden fall, by the discovery of how violently men can hate. He had never seen the wolf in man before; the vile brute instinct that preys upon the fallen. He had not believed that such exultant savagery existed . . . now it appalled him."

☆ ☆ ☆

The Stranger Wilde

OSCAR WAS A LION of many prides. All were crushed at once, and the inertia induced by this shock must have been a great thing in itself. When Harris visited Holloway, he asked Oscar once again why he had not fled: "I couldn't think at first . . . I couldn't think at all. I was numbed." Beerbohm saw him afterward in Courtfield Gardens and also thought him traumatized: "The scene that evening at the Leversons' was quite absurd," he reported, with Oscar seeming "to have lost his nerve."

Terrible though the shock must have been, one cannot help thinking that certain salient aspects of Oscar's personality may help us to a more convincing explanation for his inertia. There are certainly hints enough in his former writings that he might resist taking the easy and obvious way out. The imp of the perverse that leads Dorian Gray to chide Basil Hallward because "He says things that annoy me. He gives me good advice" had long been resident in Oscar's psyche. He had also written once, "Nothing is so fatal to personality as deliberation." Was he acting upon "personality" in those flustered hours of 5 April? Or was he acting upon the principle announced by Gilbert in that most Oscarian essay, "The Critic as Artist": "It is to do nothing that the elect exist. Action is limited and relative."

Or was Oscar, during his two weeks free on bail, repeating in real life his habitual artistic difficulties with plot, with *moving* his characters? In 1890 Oscar admitted in a letter about *Dorian Gray*, "I am afraid it is rather like my own life—all conversation and no action. I can't describe action: my people sit in chairs and chatter." Three years later *Punch*, apropos of the premiere of *A Woman of No Importance*, reported little progress: "Mr Wilde's *dramatis personae* are all gathered together, with nothing to do and plenty to say." Of *Earnest*, mere weeks before the fall, the *Times* critic opined, "Plot continues to be Mr Oscar Wilde's most vulnerable point." Did a "trivial comedy" à la Wilde require a plot? asked *Punch* in its issue of 23 February. The answer: "Nothing to speak of." That, in a phrase, describes the plot of the decidedly untrivial tragicomedy that was soon to unfold: again, much talk and no action. When the ghastly plot demanded it, Oscar seemed unable to move his own character.

All these droll premonitions emphasize the facetiousness of fate and Oscar's role as its hapless victim. Oscar, a "born actor" in Constance's view, must have been tempted in several ways to play this role. He was doing so when he moaned to Harris, "I'm caught . . . in a trap; I can only wait for the end." But it would be a mistake to accept entirely the timid, quavery Oscar sketched out by Harris, as Shaw perceptively pointed out to Harris himself: "You reveal Wilde as a weaker man than I thought him. I still believe that his fierce Irish pride had something to do with his refusal to run away from the trial." Such pride may have been the real reason behind Oscar's saying to a friend, "I can't see myself slinking about the Continent a fugitive from justice," and to Bosie, "A false name, a disguise, a hunted life, all that is not for me." Pride could well have caused him to revolt at the notion of flight, and it is ironic that Ross was later to describe Oscar's pride as a main goad during his nomadic existence on the Continent under the false name of Sebastian Melmoth: "Many people were kind to him, but he was too proud, or too vain, to be forgiven by those whom he regarded as social and intellectual inferiors. It galled him to have to appear grateful to those whom he did not or would not have regarded, before the downfall."

But *was* it merely a matter of Irish pride? Other "romantic" or "heroic" motivations, which may have looked to a skeptical Shaw like pride, floated in Oscar's mind at the time. One of these has already been mentioned: his idealized self-sacrifice on the altar of love for Bosie. There are others, and they are more fascinating, profound, and moving. We see hints of their existence in observations at the time that counter the picture of a wishy-washy Oscar. Beerbohm Tree said he played the "grand seigneur to the last." Ada Leverson recalled a "look of immovable obstinacy" coming over his face when anyone mentioned flight. She told of her own sole effort to beg him to leave, a little note she wrote and sent upstairs to him: "When he came down to dinner, he gave me back my note, saying 'That is not like you, Sphinx.' "

And then he talked of books, making at this time his witty remark about Dickens: "One must have a heart of stone to read the death of Little Nell without laughing." On his last night before the final trial, Sherard described Oscar in a manner worthy of Socrates with the cup of hemlock: "There was an extraordinary calm and dignity about him ... he seemed to me to anticipate what did happen ... and acted like a man who is taking a last farewell of life." Even Harris spoke of the "imperious mask, which he had lately accustomed himself to wear."

Oscar had often extolled "the truth of masks." Several heroic masks may have tempted him in his predicament, and perhaps they do tell some truth about his behavior. One mask was that of the abused artist-genius, which he had certainly worn often in his life. Donning it enabled him to strike the defiant pose of Rodin's Balzac (a sculpture Oscar admired greatly). Lord Chiltern is told by Mrs Cheveley, "You have a splendid position, but it is your splendid position that makes you so vulnerable," and Oscar had thrived for years upon the attacks to which his haughty eminence had made him vulnerable. In 1891 he had written, "On the whole, an artist in England gains something by being attacked. His individuality is intensified. He becomes more completely himself." The trial, he perhaps hoped, would lay bare English philistinism once and for all ... and spectacularly complete his identity as an artist in the process. The trial might also "elevate" the artistic quality of what had become in fact a private feast of low-life vulgarity. In *Dorian Gray* he had written with breathtaking prescience, "It often happens that the real tragedies of life occur in such an inartistic manner that they hurt us by their crude violence, their absolute incoherence, their absurd want of meaning, their entire lack of style." No wonder he wanted to bring *Dorian Gray*—and Art—into the dock with him.

Another mask, the one that appealed to his mother, was that of St. Oscar, who would slay the dragon of Victorian complacency, mediocrity, and hypocrisy, though not with a lance or lancet but with charm. His lawyer Humphreys believed he "had a pathetic belief in his own power to influence others," and this

might have encouraged Oscar to look upon the trial as the ultimate test of that charismatic power which had made him emperor
of London dinner parties. Mary McCarthy shrewdly observed that
redoubtable Lady Bracknell in *Earnest* is really Britannia, the
moral dragon whose capitulation to the hero's vice-ridden charms
is the supreme victory. Oscar may have daydreamed that the Law
would likewise capitulate to his charm in the Old Bailey. If so, he
was still under the mistaken impression that his life was destined
to be a brilliant comedy.

Another mask that Oscar seems to have fancied was that of
a modern-day Socrates. Nietzsche called Socrates a "mocking and
enamored monster and pied piper of Athens," and for years Oscar
had played precisely this role in London. He led the Decadents in
their effort, as *Punch* hysterically phrased it,

> to asphyxiate
> With upas[i.e., poison]-perfume sons of English race,
> With manhood-blighting cant-of-art to prate,
> The jargon of an epicene disgrace.

Indeed, a full two years before the trials Beerbohm had prophesied about Oscar even more accurately than Mrs Robinson: "If he
had lived in the days of Socrates, he would surely have been im-
peached on a charge not only 'of making the worse cause appear
the better' . . . but also of 'corrupting the youth.'" Having spent
his career in England, like Socrates, corrupting the minds of the
young and believing in gods of his own invention, Oscar was
bound to find the Socratic posture before his own lawgivers appealing. Sherard observed his pleasure in the role on his visits to
Oakley Street, and Oscar was explicit to Harris about the "larger"
ramifications of his dilemma. Speaking with "a certain grave conviction," Harris reported, Oscar said (quoting Shelley's elegy for
Keats): "Socrates would not escape death, though Crito opened
the prison door for him. I could not avoid prison, though you
showed me the way to safety. Some of us are fated to suffer, don't
you think? as an example to humanity—'an echo and a light unto

eternity.' " Oscar, as Ellmann observed, obliged a hypocritical society to take him as he was, and here was his chance to reduce the morality of the Victorian epoch to absurdity by forcing it to perform the ostracism of its onetime darling with elaborate formality.

But the tragedy of Socrates is a political one. Oscar also fancied himself wearing the mask of the tragic pessimist in the ancient Greek fashion: the hero doomed by his own hubris. More will be said in the following chapter of Oscar's (and many others') invocation of tragedy in his life, but it should be noted here that he must have thought of the Old Bailey as an ideal place for a first-rate tragic denouement. At some level he must have felt, as Miss Prism deeply intones in the Gribsby scene, "As a man sows, so let him reap." (Mrs Cheveley had made the point a few weeks earlier at the premiere of *An Ideal Husband:* "Sooner or later we all have to pay for what we do.")

In *De profundis,* Oscar would later speak candidly of that fatal flaw, indifference, which afflicts all tragic heroes: "At the great moment my will-power completely failed me. . . . My habit—due to indifference chiefly at first—of giving up to you [Bosie] in everything had become insensibly a real part of my nature. Without my knowing it, it had stereotyped my temperament to one permanent and fatal mood." The fatal mood was apparently much on Oscar's mind on the trip to Algiers with Bosie, for Gide recalled Oscar as being sunk in a mood of tragic apprehension. "I have been as far as possible along my own road," Oscar told him, "I can't go any farther. *Something* must happen now." And it did. Just three weeks later Queensberry created the *peripeteia,* or turning point, of the tragedy by leaving his insulting card at Oscar's club. To avoid the consequences of his hubris awaiting him in the Central Criminal Court would have been not merely inartistic, but craven and futile. Perhaps, when he thought about leaving for France, he feared the Furies more than the police.

One other romantic mask that might have tempted Oscar deserves mention: the mask of the hero stepping finally and completely out of the closet and into the judicial limelight on behalf of what some then called the Intermediate Sex. Of course, there is no hint of this mask in any reports of Oscar's conversations during the crisis. Perhaps wearing this mask was broached during the several private visits he had from friends in his gay circle. But with the Leversons, Beerbohm, his brother, and any contemporaries who were to write about these days later, the subject was clearly out of bounds. Even so staunch a supporter as Harris would have been stupefied at the notion of taking a stand in the name of what was to became gay liberation. Harris, who professed not to have been aware of Oscar's homosexuality until the trials, assured Oscar he would stand by him. But he added: "The thing has always seemed fantastic and incredible to me and now you make it exist for me."

The trials made "the thing" exist for the Victorian age in brilliant fashion. They were, as many have suggested, a defining event in the "coming out" of the homosexualist movement. Could it have been somewhere in Oscar's mind, now that he was caught in the judicial vise, to create a *cause célèbre*? Did he, perhaps, recall a speech he had written three years earlier for the Oscarian character in *Lady Windermere's Fan*: "There are moments when one has to choose between living one's own life, fully, entirely, completely—or dragging out some false, shallow, degrading existence that the world in its hypocrisy demands." Did he, one might even wonder, begin rolling over in his mind the splendid speech about the Love that dare not speak its name he was to deliver at his first trial:

> It is that deep, spiritual affection that is as pure as it is perfect. It dictates and pervades great works of art like those of Shakespeare and Michelangelo. . . . It is in this century misunderstood, so much misunderstood that it may be described as the 'Love that dare not speak its name,' and on account of it I am placed where I am now. It is beautiful, it is fine, it is the noblest form of affection. There is nothing unnatural about it. It is intellectual, and it repeatedly exists between an elder and

a younger man, when the elder has intellect, and the younger man has all the joy, hope, and glamour of life before him. That it should be so, the world does not understand. The world mocks at it and sometimes puts one in the pillory for it.

Beerbohm was present and reported that the speech was "simply wonderful—and carried the whole court right away—quite a tremendous burst of applause." This rousing response must have surprised Oscar, but surely he knew that reports of this speech in the papers would be read with delight and exultation by countless anxious English homosexuals. One such fervent but discreetly closeted homosexual was George Ives, and he transcribed Oscar's speech from his copy of the *Daily Telegraph* into his diary in full and hailed him as one of "the great of the earth." Many other gay men and lesbians must have applauded silently in this vein.

As the third trial was to make clear, the idea that such eloquent conviction would carry the day was only an illusion—one that would have disastrous consequences for a gay movement in its chrysalis stage. Yet again something Oscar had written in the past would return to haunt him: "Whenever a man does a thoroughly stupid thing, it is always with the noblest motives."

Chapter Thirteen

TRAGEDIAN: *AMOR FATI*

Most men and women are forced to perform parts for which they have no qualifications. Our Guildensterns play Hamlet for us, and our Hamlets have to jest like Prince Hal. The world is a stage, but the play is badly cast.

—"LORD ARTHUR SAVILE'S CRIME"

My formula for greatness for a human being is amor fati.

—NIETZSCHE

IN PARIS, AFTER HIS release from prison, Oscar entertained the Frenchmen Gustave Le Rouge and Ernest La Jeunesse in conversation one evening, sipping occasionally from a straw one of his favorite beverages, a cocktail of whiskey and champagne. Le Rouge was particularly struck by Oscar's ability to talk about his misfortunes "without a trace of bitterness and with such an air of indifference that he might have been referring to some other person." During the conversation, Le Rouge recalled, Oscar told the following story, presumably by way of suggesting how the force of destiny had ruled his life:

There was a time in my life when I had really nothing more to wish for. I was rich, held in great affection, famous, and in perfect health. At the time I was resting at Sorrento in a delightful villa whose garden was filled with orange trees. The sea lapped at the base of the terrace. From it my eye could follow the delightful, undulating curves of a countryside as sensuous as the body of a young girl.

On this terrace I was absentmindedly contemplating the white sails which studded the sea at its horizon. Suddenly I began to reflect, with a secret feeling of terror, that in reality I was too happy, that such improbable bliss could only be a trap set by my evil genius. For a long time this idea haunted me.

In the end I recalled the adventure of that tyrant of antiquity—Polycrates I think was his name—who had thrown a highly esteemed precious ring into the sea to ward off misfortune.

I resolved to imitate Polycrates. It's true that his sacrifice had proved vain, but perhaps I would prove more fortunate. As far out into the sea as I could I flung a ring set with a huge diamond that I kept in memory of a very dear friend. I thought I had appeased the hostile gods with this sacrifice and I regained my composure.

At this point La Jeunesse interrupted in his high-pitched falsetto to say, "Is there any need to add that the ring was brought back to you, like Polycrates's, discovered by a fisherman in the belly of an eel?" At this, Oscar broke into "a strange smile," obviously because he had the perfect capper to La Jeunesse's attempt to steal the story's punch line. "You won't believe it," said Oscar, but "it was a little fisherman, far too handsome a fellow, who brought it back to me."

Whether the story was true or not hardly matters. It was certainly in keeping with Oscar's constitutional eagerness to turn his life into Art. It was also true to the genre which always fascinated him, the genre with which he identified most deeply: Tragedy, with its enticing Harbingers, inexorable Furies, and tocsins of Doom. He was a lover of exquisite things, and "behind every exquisite thing that existed," he wrote in *Dorian Gray*, is "something tragic." During his reckless trip to Algiers in 1895 he told Gide, "You must always aim at the most tragic." Tragedy was, for him, "the exaggeration of the individual," and he had from his college days preached—and lived—the philosophy of individualism. Tragedy seems, in retrospect, to have been inevitable for Oscar.

Tragedy was, indeed, almost an *idée fixe* for him. Vincent O'Sullivan has told us that he was devoted to the Romantic notion that a true poet is "vowed to disaster" and that, in his last years, "the two figures he was readiest to talk about, whom it seemed he could not help talking about, were Napoleon and Jesus Christ." About the latter Oscar asked in *De profundis*, "Is there anything that for sheer simplicity of pathos wedded and made one with sublimity of tragic effect can be said or approach even the last act of Christ's Passion?" Of the former, he said, "St. Helena was necessary as the crown of his life. On a rock, chained, must the hero die." Though he once said that he had always thought his life would be a brilliant comedy, tragedy turned out to be his true *métier*. The melancholy, mendicant wanderings of Monsieur Sebastian, the dismal little Hôtel d'Alsace, the string of scruffy prostitutes he employed in his last years—they were all the necessary crown of his life. If only figuratively, chained upon a rock he died . . . or so, at least, he was eager to have it appear.

The moral of the Polycrates story is thus also pure Oscar: it is futile to attempt to evade destiny . . . or heredity or the truth of one's personality and sexuality. Rather, one must embrace one's destiny and love it: *amor fati*.

☆ ☆ ☆

The Stranger Wilde

WE KNOW OSCAR BELIEVED that life is terribly deficient in form. Ernest asks in "The Critic as Artist" if "Life then is a failure?" Gilbert (that is, Oscar) replies: "From the artistic point of view, certainly." He was right: most parts in the world's play are badly cast, catastrophes are often exceedingly ill prepared, and many a denouement lasts much too long. Plots creak; clichés abound; suspense dissipates fecklessly; characters flatten or thin into transparency. This is the fate of the human "drama" for the vast majority of ordinary people.

Oscar Wilde, however, was not an ordinary person. Asked at the Old Bailey whether a letter he had written to Bosie was "ordinary," he responded haughtily but accurately, "I do not pose as being ordinary, great heavens!" Though in prison, in his most depressed mood, he could feel that his was a "revolting and repellent tragedy," it has been accounted one of the most extraordinarily well-composed, well-played, and memorable of the so-called tragedies of real life in history. Max Beerbohm said it was "one of the tragedies that will live always in romantic history," and George Ives called it, simply, "the greatest tragedy of the whole nineteenth century." For Hugo von Hofmannsthal, Oscar brought Sophocles to mind: "He walked towards his catastrophe with the same steps as Oedipus, the seeing-blind one." Gide, after being with Oscar and Bosie in Algiers, confided to his mother before the catastrophe, "You see types like that in Shakespeare's historical tragedies. And Wilde! Wilde! what life is more tragic than his!—if he paid more attention, were he capable of attention, he would be a genius, a great genius."

How perceptive Gide was. But as Shakespeare's protagonists show us, tragedy and "paying attention" are mutually exclusive: the tragic hero must, in some profound way, fail to pay attention to the wisdom of the world—the tedious, earth-treading wisdom of Polonius. The tragic hero's attention must be distracted by something undreamt of by the world; he must, finally, be distracted by his own self. Coriolanus speaks for this tragic race when he insists,

TRAGEDIAN: *AMOR FATI*

I'll never
Be such a gosling to obey instinct, but stand
As if a man were author of himself,
And knew no other kin.

Oscar likewise asserted his freedom to inscribe his own personality, and this opened up for him the possibilities of a brilliant tragic performance. "A spirit who has *become free*," wrote Nietzsche of the world's rare genuine self-creators, "stands amid the cosmos with a joyous and trusting fatalism," and it was precisely Oscar's assertion of his freedom to be author of himself that made him such a quintessentially Nietzschean spirit, especially in the intoxicating cocktail of joyousness and fatalism that his character imbibed. Only such a cocktail can produce a memorable tragic action.

But Oscar's "tragedy" was made memorable not merely by the Tragic Flaw, the Fall from a Great Height, the years-long Arch of Suspense, and the shrieking laughter of Ironic Gods that were so prominent in its unfolding. A plethora of fine little touches, pregnant details, and seemingly peripheral stylishness also helped to raise this tragedy to the level of artistic sublimity. It was, of course, no small advantage that so many large and small supporting roles in Oscar's *dramatis personae* were marvelously acted. Frank Harris's foghorn bass made a perfect foil for Oscar's languid low mezzo. Bosie was an exquisitely waspish ingenue/villain, his father the quintessential blithering British stage idiot. Cyril and Vyvyan made excellent Mamilliuses to their father's fixated Leontes (though fixated not by jealousy but by adulterous sexual desire), while Speranza played a charmingly mad combination of Volumnia and Mistress Quickly to his Coriolanus/Falstaff. Robbie Ross, of course, was Oscar's devoted and honorable Horatio, present at the end to hear the noble heart crack and sing him to his rest. Several other colorful comprimarios we have yet to meet, among them the heavyset Lady of Wimbledon and the sterling-hearted Dancing Parson of the West End. There is also a goodly number of diminutive, peripheral villains—the revolting

Osrics and Oswalds, Rosencrantzes and Guildensterns—like W. E. Henley, Charles Brookfield, and George Alexander (who will shortly make their entrance). Finally, though many felt that Constance was seriously overparted in the pathetic role of the queenly Oscar's consort, she in fact played it with remarkable poise and patience.

And could any catastrophe possibly have been ushered in, over a period of more than a dozen years, by so many pregnant foreshadowings and ominous coincidences? Lord Henry tells Dorian, "There is no such thing as an omen. Destiny does not send us heralds." But in regard to Oscar's life this is utterly wrong, as Ellmann made clear in his remark that this "life is as full of tragic prolepses as an Ibsen play." In prison, Oscar wrote that "the note of Doom" in his life ran "like a purple thread . . . through the gold cloth of *Dorian Gray*," but in fact the purple thread of Doom ran through virtually his entire adult life. There is, thus, no surprise in Auden's finding in the large 1962 edition of Oscar's letters "an excitement similar to watching a Greek tragedy in which the audience knows what is going to happen while the hero does not."

Many of these premonitions of disaster we have already noticed, and others are to come; but a few of the choicer ones can be sampled here. There is, for example, the anecdote describing Oscar walking with a lady friend across the Front Square of Trinity College in Dublin and seeing his friend and classmate Edward Carson in the distance. "There goes a man destined to reach the very top of affairs," Oscar said; to which his companion replied, "And one who will not hesitate to trample on his friends in getting there." She was right. Carson, in the fullness of time, became Queensberry's lawyer at the libel trial and by his skillful interrogations brought Oscar's world crashing down.*

Another charming-but-portentous anecdote from his college

---

*Like many an Oscar story, this one cannot be verified. But Oscar—who said, "Nothing that actually occurs is of the smallest importance"—would hardly have let this prevent him from introducing it, so long as it carried "artistic" point. In telling the story, he might also have neglected to say that Carson disliked the idea of opposing a former classmate and at first declined Queensberry's brief.

days is a Magdalen classmate's recollection of Oscar's answer to a question about his ambitions in life: "Somehow or other I'll be famous, and if not famous, I'll be notorious." Even a Latin examination that Oscar wrote while at Oxford contains an uncanny premonition of his future life. One of the three set passages he was asked to translate describes the brilliant but unsavory orator, M. Aemilius Scaurus, who eventually committed suicide while under judicial condemnation. It is tempting to think that Oscar's examiner, John Percival (later Bishop of Hereford), chose this passage with his already "notorious" Magdalen College student in mind. For we learn from Oscar's translation that Scaurus was "a man full of wit and most ready in repartee," but that he could never shake himself from an "inveterate laziness," that his speeches were poorly prepared but full of "fiery eloquence," and that some were so scandalous as to be "publicly burnt by order of the House." Was Percival having satiric fun or perhaps not so subtly warning Oscar of the dangers that his nonchalant collegiate lifestyle was courting?

Ellmann's remark about the plethora of prolepses was occasioned by a poem by Rennell Rodd, an Oxford classmate, inscribed "to Oscar, July 1880" with a quatrain in Italian. It accurately prophesies, fifteen years before the fact, the scene of 1895 and runs, in translation: "At your martyrdom this greedy and ferocious mob to whom you speak will gather; all will come to see you on the cross, and none will sympathize with you." Much later, in 1891 after *Dorian Gray* appeared, Oscar defended his novel in a conversation with Samuel Jeyes, who had written a vicious attack on it for the *St. James's Gazette*, by saying he meant every word in it. To which Jeyes is said to have replied presciently, "If you do mean them you are very likely to find yourself at Bow Street one of these days."

But it is surely the foreshadowings that Oscar scattered throughout his own works that evoke the pleasurable and eerie frissons that always attend a skillfully conceived tragic action. Never did he write more truly of himself than when he had Vivian say in "The Decay of Lying," "Literature always anticipates life. It does not copy it, but moulds it to its purpose." There is, for example, the splendid moment in "Lord Arthur Savile's Crime" when Lord Arthur recognizes that the dreadful prediction of the palmist Podgers will come true:

> Looking at him, one would have said that Nemesis had stolen the shield of Pallas, and shown him the Gorgon's head. He seemed turned to stone, and his face was like marble in its melancholy. He had lived the delicate and luxurious life of a young man of birth and fortune, a life exquisite in its freedom from sordid care, its beautiful boyish insouciance; and now for the first time he became conscious of the terrible mystery of Destiny, of the awful meaning of Doom.

The author of such a passage clearly had a taste for tragedy; as he wrote it, did he remember the terrible moment when he saw the harbinger/urchin outside Swan and Edgar's? (see page 107 above). And did he recall this petrifying moment in his story when his own chiromancer, Mrs Robinson, found in the lines of his palm a "blank wall" beyond which she could see nothing? At any rate, this passage is but one of many that explain why Oscar thought autobiography "irresistible": it exactly describes his life before the "nemesis of character" dragged him down.

Another resonantly self-referential passage occurs in his first extended essay, the study of Thomas Griffiths Wainewright. Oscar opens with a summary of the notorious artist turned murderer: "Of an extremely artistic temperament, [he] followed many masters other than art, being not merely a poet and a painter, an art-critic, an antiquarian, and a writer of prose, an amateur of beautiful things, and a dilettante of things delightful, but also a forger of no mean or ordinary capabilities, and as a subtle and secret poisoner almost without rival in this or any age." Oscar was all of the above (at least one painting survives), though his forgeries and poisonings were entirely figurative. The essay was as much about himself as Wainewright.

Dorian Gray, of course, is filled with tragic premonitions. We hear of Dorian's "mad hungers that grew more ravenous as he fed them" and of how "strange rumours about his mode of life crept through London." Basil warns him about "these hideous things that people are whispering," and then asks, "Why is your friendship so fatal to young men?" A litany of five of Dorian's victims follows:

> There was that wretched boy in the Guards who committed suicide. You were his great friend. There was Sir Henry Ashton, who had to leave England, with a tarnished name. You and he were inseparable. What about Adrian Singleton, and his dreadful end? What about Lord Kent's only son, and his career? . . . What about the young Duke of Perth? What sort of life has he got now? What gentleman would associate with him?

Oscar left something like the same kind of "demoralizing" wake in London, though his depredations were among distinctly lower classes. These classes, by the way, figure in another fatefully ironic coincidence of Oscar's life and art. One of his aphorisms for *The Chameleon* in December 1894 was "If the poor only had profiles there would be no difficulty in solving the problem of poverty." The next month, from Algiers, he would interrupt a promiscuous escapade to tell Ross, "The beggars here have profiles, so the problem of poverty is easily solved."

His dramas, too, play their part in the crescendo to the tragic catastrophe. Wickedly ironic, in retrospect, is Lord Illingworth's remark that one can "live down anything except a good reputation" and Mrs Allonby's belief that the Ideal Man should "persistently compromise us [women] in public, and treat us with absolute respect when we are alone." Oscar appears to have behaved in exactly this way toward poor Constance in the many months leading up to his arrest. Then there is Salome—in whose costume Oscar was once photographed—thirsting for the prisoner in the cistern: "Jokanaan, I am amorous of thy body! Thy body is white like the lilies of a field that the mower hath never mowed. . . . The roses in the garden of the Queen of Arabia are not so white as thy body." Two years later, from prison, he would write to Bosie in startlingly similar terms: "My sweet rose, my delicate flower, my lily of lilies. . . . white narcissus in an unmown field."

Such psychological adventure as Salome fatally indulges in is praised two years later in *An Ideal Husband*. Lord Chiltern says that all "psychological experiments" are "terribly dangerous," and Lord Goring (that is, Oscar) replies, "Everything is dangerous, my dear fellow. If it wasn't so, life wouldn't be worth living." A few minutes later Chiltern refines this dangerous credo, asserting: "To stake all one's life on a single moment, to risk everything on one throw, whether the stake be power or pleasure, I care not—there is no weakness in that. There is a horrible, a terrible courage." In January and February 1895, when this speech was uttered nightly on the stage of the Haymarket, Oscar staked all on two dangerous trips to Algiers and Monte Carlo. And it could only be called "terrible courage" that caused him to say yes to Bosie's incitements to legal action, to stake all on the one throw of a libel suit against Queensberry. Here, again, he was behaving like the artist-in-tragedy praised by Nietzsche: "The tragic artist is no pessimist: he is precisely the one who says Yes to everything questionable, even to the terrible." Four years later, in 1899, after making corrections for the first edition of *An Ideal Husband*, Oscar told Reggie Turner with good reason, "Some of its passages seem prophetic of tragedy to come."

The appalling anticipations of the Gribsby scene in *Earnest* could easily obscure some of the finer instances of Oscar's fencing with fate—as when he allowed Gwendolen to observe, "Once a man begins to neglect his domestic duties he becomes painfully effeminate," or when he named the play's magnificent dowager after the country seat of his boyfriend's disapproving mother, or when he gave Ernest Worthing's London address as "B.4, the Albany," Piccadilly, which was where George Ives in fact lived in a homosexual *ménage*. Even more daringly, an early scenario had the blithely dandiacal Algy character named Lord Alfred.

More and more, Oscar was tempting the gods into action. How fitting that the weather outside brilliantly foretold doom on the glittering evening of *Earnest*'s premiere (another perfect touch: it was Valentine's Day). "There was a snow-storm more severe than had been remembered in London for years," recalled Ada Leverson. "A black, bitter, threatening wind blew the drifting snow."

ALL THE AMAZING MINUTIAE of ironic coincidences and strange anticipations that the ever-witty Fates arranged for Oscar helped to raise his tragedy from the "vulgar and repellent" to the sublime. But it could not have achieved its grandeur on the strength of such exquisite detail alone. A Fall from a Great Height was, of course, a necessity, and the premiere of *Earnest* provided as cleverly stage-managed a precipice as could be desired, especially the way Ada Leverson fondly remembered it: the "distinguished audience such as is rarely seen nowadays," the crowd outside blocking Little King Street to catch a glimpse of all the celebrities, "the loudest cheers . . . for the author, who was as well-known as the Bank of England." Everyone, Leverson wrote, "was repeating his *mots*. . . . And every omnibus-conductor knew his latest jokes. . . . Society at the moment was enthusiastic," and there was a positive "craze" for "that rarest of human creatures, a celebrity with good manners." Oscar appears to have conquered Paris in similar fashion years earlier, for Gide wrote of Oscar's visit in late 1891 in the same roseate fashion: "His expression and his gestures were triumphant . . . his books surprised and charmed. . . . He was rich; he was tall; he was handsome; he was gorged with happiness and honors. Some compared him to an Asiatic Bacchus; others to a Roman emperor; still others to Apollo himself."

But the great description of the peak from which Oscar fell comes from himself, in his long letter to Bosie written in prison:

The Stranger Wilde

The gods had given me almost everything. I had genius,
a distinguished name, high social position, brilliancy,
intellectual daring: I made art a philosophy, and philosophy an art: I altered the minds of men and the colours
of things: there was nothing I said or did that did not
make people wonder. . . . I awoke the imagination of my
century so that it created myth and legend around me:
I summed up all systems in a phrase, and all existence
in an epigram.

Much of this is undeniably true. Even what is debatable is redolent of "that healthy natural vanity" which Oscar praised as "the
secret of existence." But it is also the vanity that, when one does
not pay attention, transforms into hubris and tempts the gods of
tragedy to their work of annihilation.

Then, too, superlative tragedy requires heroic impersonation.
"When people play a tragedy," Oscar said, "they should play it in
the 'grand style.' All smallness, pettiness, meagreness of mood or
gesture is out of place." Fueled by vanities both healthy and unhealthy, Oscar was able to rise to the occasion. He said he
thought Whistler spelled Art "with a capital 'I,'" and that, one
could say, is how Oscar spelled Life. The vast majority of people
spell it lowercase, become conventional, become comedians; the
chosen few—the self-chosen few, rather—who become tragedians
exert themselves to be unconventional, to isolate themselves from
their fellows. No tragic hero properly so called can lack the instinct for such separatist exertions. In one of his book reviews,
Oscar quoted with approval this aphorism of Mrs John Taylor:
"Vanity, like curiosity, is wanted as a stimulus to exertion; indolence would certainly get the better of us if it were not for these
two powerful principles." Both of these principles operated vigorously in Oscar's personality; combined with his "intellectual daring," they thrust him, strangely, into isolation. Strangely, that is,
for a man so brilliantly sociable as he. Oscar had a taste for sol-
itariness, and this was another prerequisite for a potent tragic per-

formance. When he wrote simply in *De profundis*, "I had things that were different," he was speaking for most tragic heroes.

Perhaps it was an awareness of these "things"—as well as his recognition that fine tragedy requires largeness of gesture—that made him refuse to slink off to the Continent. The choreographer Paul Taylor noticed in his autobiography that in Renaissance tragedies "subordinate characters were allowed to succumb to external forces, but tragic heroes died from within." Very true, but this "dying from within" must nevertheless be, somehow, made a spectacle of. Oscar's courtroom scenes did this wonderfully . . . and courageously. He continued to author himself to the very end. Indeed, it is much to be regretted, from the standpoint of tragic art, that the climactic scene at the Old Bailey was deprived of its crowning speech. For after Mr Justice Wills pronounced the, to him, "totally inadequate" sentence of two years at hard labor, Oscar asked amid murmurs of "Oh!" and "Shame!": "And I? May I say nothing, my lord?" The judge did not reply, simply motioned to the warders to remove the new convict.

Dying from within requires a Flaw. A few months after prison, Oscar wrote to a friend that it was useless to struggle in the net of Nemesis and asked, rhetorically, "Why is it that one runs to one's ruin? Why has destruction such a fascination? Why, when one stands on a pinnacle, must one throw oneself down?" His inclination on this occasion—"No one knows, but things are so"—was to throw up his hands in mystification.

But there are passages enough in his works from before the fall and in his letters written afterward to suggest that Oscar knew his tragedy was a profoundly self-conscious and self-wrought one—and that petty blaming of others for it would ruin the tone utterly. One thinks of the "terrible blindness that passion brings upon its servants" he speaks of in his 1889 tale "The Birthday of the Infanta," precisely the blindness which made possible Queensberry's lengthy, sodomy-filled Plea of Justification. Or one thinks of his frequent professions of devotion to flaws, as in his witty paradox about regretting "the loss even of one's worst habits. . . . They are such an essential part of one's personality" . . . or in Lady Hunstanton's admiring remark to Lord Illingworth about his always finding "that one's most glaring fault is one's most important virtue." Oscar paid the price for this courageous devotion to his own personality, flaws and all, which Richard Le Gallienne so much admired. His "affectations and eccentricities," said Le Gallienne, "came of his being himself as few have had the courage to be—'an art which nature makes.'"

Oscar had gone into the arena with his eyes open; he could hardly repine in the aftermath, as he had already made clear in *Dorian Gray*: "Each man lived his own life, and paid his own price for living it. The only pity was one had to pay so often for a single fault. One had to pay over and over again, indeed. In her dealings with man Destiny never closed her accounts." Oscar's recognition of the "justice" in the fatal consequences of his self-assertion made him attempt to suffer his eclipse without the smallness of gesture or meagerness of mood that, he said, would ruin the grand tragic style.

Rather, the mood struck in many of his letters of the last three years is one of "ripeness is all." He also turned a mercilessly clear eye on himself as he continued, in the aftermath, to cast himself as a tragic victim of hubris. "I let myself be lured into long spells of senseless and sensual ease," he wrote from prison, "I amused myself with being a *flâneur*, a dandy, a man of fashion. I surrounded myself with the smaller natures and the meaner minds. I became a spendthrift of my own genius. . . . Tired of being on the heights I deliberately went to the depths. . . . I grew careless." To Gedeon Spilett, he confessed, "It is the sin of pride which has always destroyed men. I had risen too high, and I fell sprawling in the mire." Indeed, the mire rather than the rock and chains was to be his tragic image of choice. To Carlos Blacker he wrote in the summer after his release, with a solemn air of all passion spent, "I fear we shall never see each other again. But all is right: the gods hold the world on their knees. I was made for destruction. My cradle was rocked by the Fates. Only in the mire can I know peace."

Smaller natures would have descended to deflecting recriminations, scapegoating, and self-serving exculpations (like Othello's fatuous notion that he loved "too well"). But, except for several imbroglios caused by panic over his precarious finances, Oscar brought off the anticlimax of his tragedy with considerable dignity. As Le Rouge, among many others, noticed, he managed an impressive, if melancholy-soaked, equanimity. Yeats wrote that though he was "an unfinished sketch of a great man," Oscar nevertheless "showed great courage & manhood amid the collapse of his fortunes." His "tragedy," said Le Gallienne, "he bore with remarkable fortitude." And, if Beerbohm's view is accurate, he bore it with remarkable self-conscious tragedic art. For Beerbohm said of Oscar's tragedy that "the protagonist had an artist's joy in it. Be sure that in the dock of the Old Bailey, in his cell at Reading, on the centre platform of Clapham Junction, where he stood 'in convict dress, and handcuffed, for the world to look at,' even while he suffered he was consoled by the realisation of his sufferings and of the magnitude of his tragedy."

Just before leaving prison Oscar confided to his warder, "I am no longer the Sirius of Comedy. I have sworn solemnly to dedicate my life to Tragedy. If I write any more books, it will be to form a library of lamentations." He was destined to write no more books, just a few brief "lamentations" over the English penal system. But he refused to desist from the tragedy of his real life—the "long and lovely suicide" he spoke of as far off in the past as 1886—which he had been performing for many years. Like Falstaff, when his extemporaneous merriment at the Boar's Head tavern is interrupted by the ominous knock of the sheriff, Oscar refused to relinquish the stage. Instead, he insisted, as Shakespeare's fat rogue does, "Play out the play!"

Chapter Fourteen

☆ ☆ ☆ ☆ ☆ ☆ ☆ ☆ ☆ ☆ ☆ ☆ ☆ ☆ ☆ ☆

FALLEN EAGLE:
DEVILS AND ANGELS

I suppose there has never been so great a scandal and sensation!
—MAX BEERBOHM

How fascinating all failures are!
—WILDE, ON VISITING JEFFERSON DAVIS

LORD HENRY SAYS IN *Dorian Gray,* "We can have in life but one great experience at best." Oscar had defied a shameful law shamelessly and thus brought about the great experience of his life: his arrest on 5 April and his conviction and sentencing on 25 May.

His friends, of course, agonized in private and communicated furtively with each other. Many a letter of the time must have ended as does one from Ada Leverson to a friend of Oscar's: "I need not ask you to burn my letter, as I am sure you will." A few more acquaintances who had fallen under his spell remained relatively calm. The old nurse in the Leverson household adored Oscar, and Leverson recalled her always saying, "I never believe

BITER BIT

The arrest of Oscar Wilde, a drawing that appeared in the *Illustrated Police Budget* with the caption: "Pet of London society, one of our most successful playwrights and poets, arrested on a horrible charge."

a word against Mr Wilde. He's a gentleman, if ever there was one." The box-office manager of the Haymarket Theatre ended his brief memoir, "Well, well; I know nothing of his sins, and am bound to say that he amused me, and I always liked him." Everywhere else hysteria and melodramatic hyperbole raged. Frank Harris described "the hatred of Wilde" as seeming to him "universal and extraordinarily malignant." Vincent O'Sullivan observed that if Oscar "had attempted to steal the Crown Jewels ... or blow up Queen Victoria and her Parliament assembled ... he could not have been more, or more publicly, vituperated." He added that the "most ignorant and brutal attacks on Wilde came from America." The young Willa Cather, for instance, predicted from Nebraska that Oscar's conviction would mean the end of "the most fatal and dangerous school of art that has ever voiced itself in the English tongue."

Bosie's summary of English hostility toward Oscar in his autobiography very aptly employed an image from pugilism: "At the noble game of hitting a man when he is down the English can give points to any other nation on earth." Oscar wore a green carnation in his buttonhole at the premiere of *Earnest*, and two months later *Punch* called this "vitriol-tinted flower" a symbol of Oscar's "noxious" and "worse than pornographic" cult of "pseud-

Hellenic decadence." Now the pages of newspapers themselves were tinted with vitriol. The *Westminster Review* announced that it would not do to pretend "evils of this kind" do not exist or to "hush them up." And it congratulated Queensberry for "throwing the search-light of justice upon that hideous circle of extensive corruption of which . . . Oscar Wilde had been the centre." *Lloyd's Weekly* harrumphed in its postmortem on "The Wilde Scandal" on 26 May, "Now that the hand of Justice has fallen heavily upon its meretricious leaders, we trust their pernicious cult may also be sternly rooted out in the youths of our own and future generations." W. E. Henley, the editor of the *National Observer*, hissed the villain mightily:

There is not a man or woman in the English-speaking world possessed of the treasure of a wholesome mind who is not under a deep debt of gratitude to the Marquess of Queensberry for destroying the High Priest of the Decadents. The obscene imposter, whose prominence has been a social outrage ever since he transferred from Trinity Dublin to Oxford his vices, his follies, and his vanities, has been exposed, and that thoroughly at last.

The only comedy in all this contumely was that its purveyors became oddly tongue-tied about naming the vice in question. The best that could be managed was "indecent practices," "gross scandals," "acts of indecency" of "a most hideous kind."

Contrary voices were not appreciated. "It was impossible to say one word in Wilde's defence or even in extenuation of his sin in any London print," Harris wrote. He was then principal owner and editor of the *Saturday Review,* and wrote for it a short plea to suspend judgment and defer insults until after the trial. His printers told him he would be ill advised to print this plea and refused to touch it. Later, Messrs Smith and Sons, "the great booksellers

... sent to say that they would not sell any paper that attempted to defend Oscar Wilde; it would be better even, they added, not to mention his name."

The fortunes of Oscar's very name were indeed appalling. Cecily says in *Earnest*, "A man who is much talked about is always very attractive." If so, Oscar became most attractive ... but his name was anathema. Ada Leverson's daughter has told us Oscar's "name was seldom pronounced ... initials alone would be used." George Alexander pasted over Oscar's name on the playbills and removed it from the programs for his lucrative run of *Earnest*. His wife's very proper Aunt Mary cut his name from the spine of all his books in her library. The three given names of his younger son, we have noted, were reduced by one, "Oscar," and in the fall of 1895 the wife and sons became Hollands rather than Wildes.

The name remained in eclipse a long time in some quarters. An obituary for Speranza more than a thousand words long appeared in the *Daily News* on 5 February 1896; it failed to mention her son once. His real name did not replace his prison number—C.3.3.—on the title page of *The Ballad of Reading Gaol* until the seventh edition in 1899. And in the same year his publisher brought out (at Oscar's own behest) the first edition of *Earnest* with a title page neatly solving the "name" difficulty:

THE

IMPORTANCE OF BEING EARNEST

A TRIVIAL COMEDY FOR

SERIOUS PEOPLE

BY

THE AUTHOR OF

LADY WINDERMERE'S FAN

The 18 March 1899 issue of *Outlook* carried a favorable review of the volume that, in the same spirit, also managed to avoid mentioning the author's name. Finally and incredibly, Oscar's courageous lawyer Sir Edward Clarke chose not even to mention the case—one of the most famous of the century—in the memoirs he published in 1918.

Though caricatures by courtroom sketch artists appeared in the papers, it might be said that even Oscar's face vanished. For the formal, full-length oil painting of him by Pennington had been bought by Ernest Leverson at the sheriff's sale and hung in the Leverson house during this time. However, it "was covered at the time of the trials." Later, Oscar was to recall with sarcasm how "dangerous" the portrait had become: it was a painting a man could "not have in his drawing-room as it was obviously, on account of its *subject*, demoralising to young men, and possibly to young women of advanced views . . . a portrait that was a social incubus."

Various events of April and May recorded in anecdotes show just how hemmed in with horrors Oscar was. Burne-Jones, his Aesthete idol and friend, assumed Oscar would commit suicide and was amazed when he didn't. It was certainly a way out: just six months before, on 18 November 1894, Queensberry's eldest son, Lord Drumlanrig, apparently shot himself because, it seems likely, a scandalous association with the Earl of Rosebery was coming to light. More to the point—and just three weeks after Drumlanrig's death—a Major Parkinson, arrested in Southwark on a "shameful charge," slit his throat with a broken glass while in Holloway Prison. The day after Oscar's arrest, his friend George Ives peered into the barrel of a pistol, then addressed the bullet in it in his diary: "It is thine to save me from the force of all the state." (Oscar later said this "escape" did not cross his mind. "I was never really tempted to kill myself," O'Sullivan reported him as saying.) Duels on the Continent incited by Oscar were reported. On 18 April, the *Daily News* ran a Reuters item:

A duel was fought in the neighbourhood of Paris this afternoon between MM. Jules Huret and Catulle Mendès, two well known literary men. The weapons used were swords, and the encounter resulted in M. Mendès receiving a slight wound. The duel arose out of some remarks which M. Huret made . . . in which he referred to the amicable relations subsisting between M. Catulle Mendès and Oscar Wilde, and to which M. Mendès took exception. It is believed that other duels arising out of the same motive are pending.

Oscar was of course subjected to "cuts" from his weaker and falser friends. O'Sullivan was especially disgusted by the hypocrisy of those who abandoned Oscar, even though they "knew perfectly well Wilde's reputation at the time they were eager to be seen in his company." More than three decades later, John Gray—Oscar's onetime lover and protégé, presumably haunted by just such behavior—penned a poetic *mea culpa*:

> *A night alarm; a weaponed crowd;*
> *one blow, and with the rest I ran;*
> *I warmed my hands, and said aloud:*
> *I never knew the man.*

Many who vanished in the hour of crisis could have admitted the same.

☆ ☆ ☆

IT WAS A TREMENDOUS plunge . . . and has evoked impressive imagery from those who either observed or have tried to imagine it. Horace Wyndham concluded, "Of Oscar Wilde it may be said that 'when he fell he fell like Lucifer.' " Indeed, Milton's famous lines on Satan's fall from grace are scarcely out of place when we think of Oscar sunk in misery that first month in Holloway Prison. Him the almighty English middle classes and their Law

> *Hurl'd headlong flaming from th'ethereal sky*
> *With hideous ruin and combustion down*
> *To bottomless perdition, there to dwell*
> *In adamantine chains and penal fire . . .*

A less imposing image from Shakespeare occurred to Frances Winwar: "It was a genuine Aristotelian tragedy—the fall of an eagle as against the fall of a sparrow."

And the plunge had ramifications. Ellmann stated flatly that the 1890s ended with Oscar's demise in 1895. Something like this view was expressed at the time when Edward Garnett ran into Ford Madox Ford on the steps of the British Museum just after the sentencing. Though Ford considered the event a "lamentable error in public policy," he did not like Wilde and found his works "derivative and of no importance, his humor thin and mechanical." When a stunned Garnett informed him that "this is the death-blow to English poetry," Ford was "so astonished" that he "laughed out loud." But much later, in 1911, Ford was to write in his memoirs, "Looking back, I recognize how true Dr Garnett's words were. For certainly at about that date English poetry died."

As for the homosexual movement, if it did not exactly die, it certainly became moribund for some time. The first tentative, still mostly behind-the-scenes publicists for the cause reacted like stunned snails and returned to their shells. In January of 1895 George Ives was already fretting about the risks to what he called "the great movement" courted by Oscar's flamboyant circle: "After going among that set it is hard to mix in ordinary society. . . . I wish they were less extravagant and more real. . . . I see the storms of battle coming." When the battle did come, Ives recognized, the notion of closing ranks with Oscar was out of the question: "The great movement will go on, though individuals fall: if it were a true case of the Faith we should stand side by side but this would be impolite and useless now."

The fall of a great celebrity is bound to bring out some of the worst in human nature. Fisher Unwin's deviltry toward Carpenter and his books in response to the "Oscar Wilde troubles" was nastily vindictive, but quite peripheral. Several other devils much closer to Oscar emerged from the wings to perform in various appalling ways. The virulence of W. E. Henley—a friend Oscar once consoled on the illness of his mother—we have already sampled. Then there was Henry Labouchere. Aside from being the legislative villain responsible for Section 11, Labouchere mercilessly harassed Wilde during the trials in his magazine *Truth*. He also complained bitterly after the sentencing that, during parliamentary deliberations, the penalty for the crime had been dropped from seven to two years. George Alexander, who had also been the producer of *Lady Windermere's Fan*, will go down in history not only as the manager who kept *Earnest* on the boards without the author's name, but also as the first to have the bright idea of selling rather than giving theater programs to patrons. He was to act in Oscar's plays (and own rights in them) for many years, yet Oscar told this awful anecdote of running into him on the French Riviera after his release: "Yesterday I was by the sea and suddenly George Alexander appeared on a bicycle. He gave me a crooked, sickly smile, and hurried on without stopping. How absurd and mean of him!"

Another devil was Charles Brookfield. He had collaborated on a musical parody of *Lady Windermere's Fan* in 1892 (it included a character who dressed like Oscar and imitated his voice). Oscar's irritation over it did not prevent him from offering—or Brookfield from accepting—the part of Phipps, servant to the "Oscar" character Lord Goring, in *An Ideal Husband*. When the Queensberry matter ignited, Brookfield informed on Oscar and, according to Harris, "constituted himself private prosecutor in this case and raked Piccadilly to find witnesses against Oscar." It is ironic that Brookfield was eventually to become that government officer Oscar had reviled most of all: Censor of Plays.

One devil came from Oscar's own family. "Demmed nuisance, relations!" says Lord Augustus in *Lady Windermere's Fan*; how often Oscar must have thought this in the company of his brother, Willie. One inch taller than Oscar at six feet, four inches, Willie was an infinitely smaller personage in whom fecklessness and dysfunctionality vied for supremacy. Beerbohm skewered him neatly: "Quel monstre! Dark, oily, suspect yet awfully like Oscar: he has Oscar's coy, carnal smile & fatuous giggle & not a little of Oscar's esprit. But he is awful—a veritable tragedy of family-likeness." Lillie Langtry pronounced Willie "thoroughly uninteresting." Among his accomplishments were "improved" endings for Chopin's preludes and an unkind review of his brother's first London play.

At the time of the trials Willie was living with Speranza in Oakley Street, and he succeeded in making a perfectly obnoxious sibling rival of himself, the sort of person Dickens had in mind when he wrote of "a blood relation (in the murderous sense)." His letters to Oscar during his first month in prison were upsetting: "Willie has been writing me the most monstrous letters. I have had to beg him to stop." Harris was disgusted by Willie's "theatrical insincerity," and Sherard was appalled by his "almost melodramatic protestations that a Wilde would not flee." Shaw recalled Willie saying, with what Shaw called "maudlin pathos and an inconceivable want of tact," that Oscar "was NOT a man of bad character: you could have trusted him with a woman anywhere." Willie's pompous efforts on his brother's behalf thoroughly exasperated Oscar, who finally exploded, "My poor brother writes to me that he is defending me all over London; my poor, dear brother, he could compromise a steam-engine." Beerbohm even reported that Willie "has been extracting fivers" from one of Oscar's lawyers. No wonder Oscar hastily accepted an offer of escape from Oakley Street made to him a few days later. Like Oscar, Willie died (in 1899) at age forty-six. Oscar ended a letter thanking Ross for wiring the news: "Between him and me there had been, as you know, wide chasms for many years. *Requiescat in Pace.*"

The chief and most colorful devil, of course, was John Sholto Douglas, eighth in what Oscar called "the mad, bad line" of Marquesses of Queensberry. Lord Henry boasts in *Dorian Gray*, "I choose my friends for their good looks, my acquaintances for their good characters, and my enemies for their good intellects." But in Queensberry, Oscar could not have chosen one of more thuggish and repellent intellect as his enemy. The Marquess was a perfect type of the modern homophobic zealot, except that he was not a Christian fundamentalist but a rabid atheist. He presented an almost seriocomic picture of debased humanity, a personality reminiscent of Shakespeare's "thing most brutish" in *The Tempest* to both his son and Oscar: the former spoke of his father's "fit of canting hypocrisy and Caliban fury"; the latter told Bosie, "My business as an artist was with Ariel. You set me to wrestle with Caliban." Even the cool memoir of one of Oscar's lawyers written more than *fifty* years later turns livid on the subject of Queensberry and casts him as a perfect Caliban: "He was a coarse-minded and violent-tempered individual, filled with envy, hatred, malice, and all uncharitableness towards the members of his family."

Queensberry had honed not only the rules of boxing, but also the rules, in Joyce's phrase, of the "noble art of self-pretence." Bosie's mother had divorced him on the grounds of adultery in 1887, yet he had the nerve to lecture in Prince's Hall, Piccadilly, in 1893 on "Marriage and the Relations of the Sexes: An Address to Women." In this amazing performance Queensberry argued for "some variation from the rigid monogamic order" and asserted, too, "There is no law of nature, human or divine, in man's present state, which confines him to one woman as his only wife." Deliciously, later in 1893 his second wife left him almost immediately after their marriage and sued successfully for an annulment.

He was also a terrible father. In an 1881 lecture on "The Religion of Secularism and the Perfectibility of Man," the Marquess had occasion to assert, "We produce our posterity, not only in body, but in the soul." If so, the notion applied damningly to himself: his eldest son probably homosexual and likely a suicide, his son Sholto arrested in Bakersfield, California, on an insanity charge a few days before Oscar was first put on trial, and then Bosie—filled with hatred and malice like his father. Only Percy—who according to Hyde had a "somewhat chequered career, which ended in penury in South Africa"—seemed to approach normality.

How Bosie hated his father! In his autobiography, he tartly observed, "My intense admiration of my father was doubtless not at all impaired, but on the contrary greatly increased, by the fact that I hardly ever saw him." Then the pot accurately describes the kettle: "My father was entirely self-centered—nay, more, he was utterly selfish." Bosie visited Oscar every day at his rooms in St. James's Place when *An Ideal Husband* was being written, and the play surely alludes to the abysmal gulf between Bosie and the Marquess. Lady Markby observes, for instance, "There are so many sons who won't have anything to do with their fathers, and so many fathers who won't speak to their sons." When the father and son did talk, it must have sounded pretty much like the dialogue Oscar gives to the ageing Earl of Caversham and his son, Lord Goring:

> LORD CAVERSHAM: Can't make out how you stand London Society. The thing has gone to the dogs, a lot of damned nobodies talking about nothing.
>
> LORD GORING: I love talking about nothing, father. It is the only thing I know anything about.
>
> LORD CAVERSHAM: You seem to me to be living entirely for pleasure.
>
> LORD GORING: What else is there to live for, father? Nothing ages like happiness.

Later in the play the Earl explodes at his son's Oscarian mode of expression—"That is a paradox, sir. I hate paradoxes"—and goes off grumbling to the smoking room.

Queensberry's antics leading up to the trial are famous: his barging into the Tite Street house to threaten Oscar; the bouquet of vegetables he left at the theater on *Earnest's* opening night (having been barred entry to the performance); the insulting card left at the Albemarle Club. During the trial he turned more hideous, especially to the accused: "I used to see your father bustling in and out in the hopes of attracting public attention, as if anyone could fail to note or remember the stableman's gait and dress, the bowed legs, the twitching hands, the hanging lower lip, the bestial and half-witted grin." When Oscar was bailed out, Queensberry's thugs harried him from one hotel to another, until

Queensberry assaulting his son, Lord Douglas. Drawing that appeared in *The Evening News*, 22 May 1895.

he was forced to fall on his mother's doorstep "like a wounded stag." Queensberry was of course outraged when Percy became a surety, and wrote insultingly to Percy's wife after Taylor was convicted: "Must congratulate on verdict. Cannot on Percy's appearance. Looked like a dug up corpse. Fear too much madness of kissing." This led in due course to fisticuffs between the two in Bond Street and the arrest of both parties for disorderly conduct. After the conviction and some noisy breast-beating, the Marquess calmed down. But his fatuousness did not subside: Bosie told of his father offering him money to "go to the South Sea Islands where, he said, 'you will find plenty of beautiful girls.'"

Queensberry's behavior was so erratic, incidentally, that some thought him mentally unbalanced. There is droll support for this theory, unwittingly provided by the mad Marquess himself in his "Perfectibility of Man" lecture. Pursuing his thesis that the soul is the "result . . . of bodily organization," he asserted that the soul vanishes during unconsciousness. He then adduced this stunning argument: "To those who have never themselves been unconscious through concussion of the brain, this argument will not appear of great weight; but to others who, like myself, have had a severe concussion . . . this argument will be proof positive." Like Oscar, he died in 1900.

☆ ☆ ☆

AFTER HIS FALL, OSCAR had to eat many words he had written in the past. Among them were these uttered by his raffish cynic Lord Darlington: "I am afraid that good people do a great deal of harm in this world." But many very good people—believing apparently in Mrs Erlynne's motto, "manners before morals!"—emerged during the scandal, as Oscar was soon to learn while sequestered in Holloway. Ten days after his arrest, he wrote, "I hear that wonderful things are being done for me—by people of noble beautiful souls and natures." They were proving that humanity produces angels as well as devils, though the former often seem distinctly in the minority.

Indeed, while he was in prison Oscar's often-trumpeted cynicism toward "good" people seems to have been replaced by humility and appreciation for those who came to his aid. Several letters written after his release speak of this change. On the same day, 3 June 1897, he wrote to one correspondent, "I have learnt in prison-cells to be grateful. That, *for me,* is a great discovery," and then to another, "I have learnt gratitude—a new lesson for me—and a certain amount of humility as regards myself."

Some of these angels ministered to Oscar in minor yet still courageous ways. Yeats visited Oakley Street with letters of support from Ireland; Ellen Terry sent a bouquet of violets; and Beerbohm reported that Oscar's painter friend Will Rothenstein was going around "the minor clubs insulting everyone who does not happen to be clamouring for Hoscar's instant release." Two lonely MP's protested in Parliament. One Sydney Grundy dared to write a letter to the *Daily Telegraph* protesting the removal of

Oscar's name from the premises of the St. James's where *Earnest* was playing. In the judicial arena angels were present as well: Clarke and his assistants, of course, who were serving *pro bono*, but also the judge for the trial in which the jury could not agree on a verdict. The *Evening News* described Justice Charles as "one of the mildest-looking of our justices," and he seems to have presided in a manner that consistently gave the defendant the benefit of the doubt. Two papers made bold to hint than the judge was responsible for the hung jury. The *Evening News* noticed, "Seldom has a calmer, more dispassionate, more absolutely colourless presentment of a case been heard, than the summing-up of Mr Justice Charles," and the *Westminster Review* went a bit further: "The severely colourless summing-up of Mr Justice Charles may have contributed somewhat to the abortive result." (The article, however, went on to ascribe the outcome "mainly" to the excellence of Clarke's advocacy.)

Also angelic in his way was little Sidney Mavor, one of the "male strumpets" assembled to give evidence against Oscar in court. At Bosie's urging, he somehow mustered the courage to recant an incriminating statement and insist that he had been frightened into making it by the police. Rather more impressive was the behavior of the codefendant, Alfred Taylor, whom the press vilified even more avidly than Oscar. "Of Taylor we do not need to speak," said *Reynolds's*, but then did speak: "He was a despicable creature at best. A poor, loathly sensualist, who added to his natural inclinations the horrid function of procurer." Much had been made of Taylor's exotic notions of interior decoration (heavily draped windows, perfume, artificial light), his lack of profession or even of a servant, and certain odd rituals. The appalled *Evening News* reported one boy saying, "Taylor told him all about his being married to a man, and being dressed as the bride, and how they had a wedding breakfast." The poor loathly sensualist, however, did summon the remarkable courage to refuse an offer of freedom if he would turn Queen's Evidence against Oscar. After serving his term, he emigrated to America and disappeared from history.

On the publicity front, some well-intended but abortive activity occurred. Bernard Shaw drafted a petition on Oscar's behalf, then happened upon Willie in St. Martin's Lane: "I spoke to him about the petition, asking him whether anything of the sort was being done, and warning him that though I and Stewart Headlam would sign it, that would be no use, as we were two notorious cranks, and our names would . . . do Oscar more harm than good." The petition was dropped. A few months later, in Paris, the expatriate American poet Stuart Merrill drew up a petition to Queen Victoria, but no leading French literary figures would sign it.

In the public press—hostile though the climate was—a few angelic voices resounded amid the uproar. On 26 May *Reynolds's Newspaper*, under the headline "Male Prostitution," did attempt to deflect the storm of disgust from "the unhappy man who has been convicted" and toward the "unsexed blackguards . . . notorious harlots and blackmailers . . . and half-baked riff-raff" who had testified against Oscar. In a splendid final paragraph the paper vigorously interrogated:

> Has the Crown bribed them to give evidence by the promise of a pardon? And is no notice to be taken of the Judge's remarks with reference to Lord Alfred Douglas? We strongly protest against any one or two men being made the scapegoats for a nest of ruffians. . . . We shall await the action of the Government. And, certainly if, at least, the beastly witnesses who trafficked illegally with their bodies are not brought to justice, there will be an uneasy and just suspicion in the public mind that the prosecution has resorted to methods to obtain a conviction in this case that do not square with an Englishman's notion of justice and fair play.

A few days later, *Reynolds's* published a letter dated 29 May by one C.S.M. that opens with the acidly phrased argument that a victimless crime was at issue:

The Stranger Wilde

Sir,

Mr Oscar Wilde has been sentenced to two years' imprisonment with hard labour. What for? For being immoral? No. A man may commit adultery with another man's wife or fornication with a painted harlot who plies her filthy trade in the public streets unmolested with impunity. It is because this man has dared to choose another form of satisfying his natural passions the law steps in. Yet he has not injured the State or anybody else against their will.

Why does not the Crown prosecute every boy at a public or private school or half the men in the Universities?

In the latter places 'poederism' is as common as fornication, and everybody knows it.

The writer was twenty-three-year-old Christopher Millard, who later, as Stuart Mason, published an important Wilde bibliography and who later was himself convicted under Section 11.

Also courageous was the composer and pianist Dalhousie Young, a twenty-nine-year-old stranger to Oscar, who published a pamphlet titled *Apologia pro Oscar Wilde* (it is dated 31 May). Young "questioned whether this [sexual] act should be forbidden by law at all" and boldly suggested that "the act we are considering is one done by mutual consent by two men, an act which does not in any way render them unable to fulfill the duties of citizenship, and which does not affect directly or indirectly, for good or for ill, any other person." Young (who was married) became acquainted with Oscar after his release, gave him an advance on a libretto based on *Daphnis and Chloe,* and even offered to buy him a house in France (the offer was declined). Oscar found Young "a dear simple nice fellow."

The defenses of Millard and Young are fine, but even more sarcastic and devastating to the rationale of Section 11 was an editorial that appeared in the issue dated 18 June of a periodical called *The Torch:*

A dozen fishmongers, margarine-merchants, clerks and corn dealers; otherwise, twelve independent citizens, have declared Oscar Wilde guilty of "acts of indecency"; and a judge has accordingly sentenced him to two years imprisonment with hard labor, a punishment, in that man's opinion, quite inadequate to the crimes committed. And the howling chorus of the press-jackals applauded this horrible thing.

Save a few honorable exceptions, not a word of commiseration has been written about this poor, crushed man, once the pet of London society, now abandoned by nearly all his friends and despised by every brute.

And why?

Moralists, judges, jurymen and pork-butchers tell us that the acts committed by Wilde are the most horrible, the most abominable, the most disgusting one can imagine, and that people who commit them lower themselves beneath the beasts. To which I reply that this being the alleged opinion of the said pork-butchers, jurymen, judges and moralists, they have purely and simply to abstain from committing them.

That's all! . . .

In Wilde's case . . . there is no question of violence done to anybody. There was neither violation nor even seduction. Subject to a passion, which it is not my place or anybody else's to judge of, Wilde sought to satisfy this passion, with the free consent of the creatures who so vilely turned round and gave evidence against him.

These individuals having all, long since, reached the age of discretion, and having all prostituted themselves before they made Wilde's acquaintance, I fail to see the harm done to society, and consequently the right of society to claim redress, *i.e.* to punish . . .

If there was any indecency at all in this case, then it was displayed by the prosecutors, by the evidence, by the repugnant behaviour of the Marquess of Queensbury

[sic], who with foul impudence and cruelty came day after day to the Old Bailey to grin in the face of his victim, this poor Wilde.

The indecency was in the attitude of the press-jackals, draining hard cash out of this case by means of artificially increased sale of their prostituted papers, rejoicing themselves in Wilde's pain and distress, and every day giving a detailed account of every new wrinkle on his face.

Here the writer paused to praise the Reverend Stewart Headlam (1874–1924), "that glorious Christian in the truest sense of the word," for bailing Oscar from prison. He then moved into a peroration at once affecting and withering:

As to Wilde, his attitude in the dock under the terrible circumstances was a very dignified one. He did not say one bitter word against the miserable wretches who gave evidence against him. He admitted all that he possibly could. At the end of the trial he gave his tormentors a last and striking lesson in decency. It was when the Solicitor General asked him whether he thought Taylor's conduct proper. Wilde's reply: "I have not to judge other people's actions" contained a lesson which unhappily jurymen and judges did not profit by.

Wilde's sentence was a monstrosity engendered by mere hypocrisy.

And now he's in prison, and the world, our highly moral and decent world, is safe.

Alfred Taylor, in his separate trial, had splendid moments, too. When the Solicitor General asked him, "You are an old Public School boy. Was it not repugnant to your Public School idea, this habit of sleeping with men?" Taylor replied with characteristic poise, "Not to me. Where there is no harm done I can see nothing repugnant in it."

FALLEN EAGLE: DEVILS AND ANGELS

☆ ☆ ☆

SEVERAL OTHER IMPORTANT ANGELS deserve our notice. Obviously of great heart and bravery were the two sureties who made up Oscar's £5,000 bail. Percy—whom Wilde was afterward to call "that *candidissima anima*" ("most resplendent soul")—suffered mainly from his father's fury. He never wavered, and at one point made it clear Oscar could skip bail without ruining him financially or losing his friendship. Headlam proved a fascinating and apparently wholly admirable angel. A Cambridge man of very broad artistic tastes, he was at ease among theatrical people from time spent in a Drury Lane parish: he possessed Rossetti and Burne-Jones pictures, used Morris wallpaper; he was responsible for the introduction of pianos into London schools; and the idea of Shakespeare matinees for children was his. He was devoted to classical ballet, and was in fact nicknamed "the dancing parson" by the press. Shaw described him as one of the new clergymen "who demand the right to go to the theater and say 'd—m.' . . . He left none of his views unspoken. Naturally he was always in hot water with stupid people." (Ellen Terry said he "had a narrow escape of a lisp.")

Headlam had met Oscar only twice in passing before deciding to stand his bail, He said he did so because Wilde "had shown him beauty on a high hill." The gesture was not without its perils. He lost friends and a housemaid, "who fled at once." He was also threatened with stoning outside his Upper Bedford Place house (the house, incidentally, where Oscar was first taken after release from prison). This did not bother him: "I knew quite well that this action of mine would with many people damage my already damaged reputation . . . but if my reputation suffered, my character did not." Sometime later at a School Board meeting, a spectator rose and asked, "Isn't this the man that went bail for the notorious convict, Wilde?" To which Headlam replied: "Yes, I am the man, and by the laws of England every one is reckoned innocent until he is proved guilty. And I would do it again tomorrow."

An equally admirable angel in her own way was a young

woman by the name of Adela Schuster. The daughter of a Frankfurt banker, she lived in a villa called Cannizaro in Wimbledon and apparently first met Oscar in late 1892. In February 1893 he wrote "in despair" at having to cancel a visit to her, and in a letter to him the next November she said, after reading *Lady Windermere's Fan*, "It so enchanted and electrified me . . . it is admirable, it is perfect." She was apparently a very large woman, and Oscar gave her the nickname "Miss Tiny"—though he also often referred to her in correspondence as "the Lady of Wimbledon." It seems clear that Schuster became what we would now call a fag hag in Oscar's circle. He visited Cannizaro several times, apparently always delighting her completely.

Oscar told Harris what happened when Schuster heard about his dire judicial straits: "A very noble and cultured woman, a friend of both of us, Miss S——, a Jewess by race tho' not by religion, had written him asking if she could help him financially." When Oscar admitted he was "in uttermost distress," Schuster "sent him a cheque for £1,000, assuring him that it cost her little even in self-sacrifice and declaring that it was only inadequate recognition of the pleasure she had had through his delightful talks." Harris then added a thought that in fact applies to the actions of all those who came to Oscar's assistance: "Such actions are beyond praise; it is the perfume of such sweet and noble human sympathy that makes this wild beasts' cage of a world habitable for men." Oscar himself was moved to similar eloquence in prison; he ended a letter to Ross with the request to send "whatever of remembrance and reverence she will accept, to the Lady of Wimbledon, whose soul is a sanctuary for those who are wounded, and a house of refuge for those in pain."

Schuster did not let things rest with a £1,000 check. More than two dozen letters from her to Oscar's chief London go-between while in prison, More Adey, exist. They record very affectingly her great empathy and generosity of spirit. On 2 December 1895 she offered more money to secure Oscar's tangled family finances: "I would not hesitate to promise any moderate sum if I could feel quite certain that I were doing no injustice to Mrs

Wilde." On 11 January 1896 she was eager to see that Oscar be allowed to get more books: "Surely they [the prison officials] must recognize that exercise is as necessary for his *brain* as it is for the bodies of other" prisoners. In February she offered to meet Constance as a go-between; in March she admitted to Adey that he had guessed correctly about the source of the anonymous gift:

> You are right in your guess about the £1000, but kindly say nothing about it to anyone. I have not mentioned it to anyone, mainly because I promised Mr Wilde not to do so. And this I did of my own free will—he *asked* for no secrecy, but thought he would be less loth to accept it if he knew it would not be talked about. I had heard his mother was ill and in need, and I knew he was penniless.

In June she asked for a list of "very very reputable people, *who would not mind* their names being mentioned to the Home Secretary as being anxious for Oscar's release." Adey regularly copied out letters he received from Oscar for her, and often wrote himself to keep her up to date. Typically, he wrote on 16 March 1897, "His Dante was the greatest consolation that he had. This was one of the books which you sent him." Her concern persisted after Oscar's release, and we have Ross's vivid description of his final days because he described them in a long letter to her on 23 December 1900; there is something particularly touching in his assuring Schuster, "As long as he was allowed champagne, he had it *throughout* his illness." Even more touching, though, is a letter Frank Harris wrote to Ross two decades later, in November 1916, just after Harris's Wilde biography had appeared. Miss Tiny, ever loyal, did not like what she read and let Harris know it: "Miss Schuster objects, and rightly, to my saying that Oscar was very cold and hard and incapable of friendship."

Oscar's two staunchest and (because they were practical-minded) most helpful friends in all this were Robbie Ross and More Adey. Ross—whom Oscar had canonized "St Robert of Phillimore" (he lived in Phillimore Gardens)—was doubtless Oscar's most devoted friend, and Oscar often acknowledged his friendship in later years. On 11 December 1897 he wrote to his publisher of Ross, "Of all my old friends he is the one who has the most beautiful nature . . . natures like his are not found twice in a lifetime." Ross handled much of Oscar's finances in the last years, became his literary executor (eventually bringing his estate into the black), and became friendly with the two sons. (Vyvyan recalled being embarrassed by Ross's emotional reaction at their first meeting years after Oscar's death.) When Ross died in 1918, his request that his ashes repose in Oscar's Père-Lachaise monument was honored. More Adey (1858–1942) was the only close gay friend who stayed in England throughout the tensest months (Ross gave in to his mother's pleas that he flee for a time), and he served in various practical and diplomatic capacities, including negotiations with Constance's lawyers and family. He also succeeded Ross as Oscar's literary executor.

One other remarkable angel remains to be mentioned: Oscar's "dear Sphinx," Ada Leverson. She was an elegant, spirited, and witty woman of a type often attracted to—and found very attractive by—circles of gay men. In her mid-thirties, she had been married fourteen years to a decent but stolid City of London man twelve years her senior . . . named, it happens, Ernest. The marriage was not happy (an affair with the fourth Earl of Desart was to come), and she was eagerly disposed to become a fixture in Oscar's entourage over the three years preceding the trials. She managed, indeed, to shock the other women in her family by entertaining at her salon so many men who were able to visit in the daytime. Bosie remembered her as "a brilliant and witty writer." By 1895 she was contributing to *Punch*: on 12 January a short parody of *An Ideal Husband* appeared; on 2 March came her little skit on *Earnest*, "The Advisability of Not Being Brought Up in a Handbag." They delighted Oscar. Her first story appeared in that cruel month of April, and she went on to become a notable minor novelist after the turn of the century.

She was clearly comfortable in the company of gay men—a handsome *bon vivant* fag hag in contrast to the retiring, cultured Adela Schuster. Ross apparently joked once that she was almost ravishing enough to turn him straight, for Beerbohm wrote him,

"Mrs Leverson is delighted at your saying that she almost persuadeth you to be a 'mulierast.'" But then, such men were bound to like a woman who, when a guest excused himself by saying, "I go to bed early to keep my youth," could respond, "I didn't know you were keeping a youth." Ada also did not object, apparently, to entertaining Oscar when he chose to escort young male friends rather than his wife. Several weeks before the arrest, she asked him to bring whom he wished to a dinner party, and he wrote to accept: "I have selected a young man, tall as a young palm tree." His name was Tom, "a very rare name in an age of Algies and Berties." Tom lived at Oxford, "in the hopes of escaping the taint of modern education. I met him on Tuesday, so he is quite an old friend."

Some of the Leversons' kindnesses during the trials were small. Encouraging messages to Oscar in Holloway arrived immediately; Ernest's copy of Shakespeare was also sent. Once at his mother's on bail, flowers for his buttonhole arrived daily, and Ernest secretly assumed control of the money Oscar had received from Miss Tiny. The great and socially daring kindness came when the Leversons recognized how miserable Oscar was in such proximity to his mother and brother: they invited him to stay secretly in their house in Courtfield Gardens. Ada wrote to More Adey, "Oscar is coming *today*. I am going to fetch him at 12 so if you would like to see him do come any time." Here was truly noble hospitality as Nietzsche once defined it: "To keep open house with one's heart—that is liberal, but that is merely liberal. One recognizes those hearts which are capable of *noble* hospitality by the many draped windows and closed shutters . . . Why? Because they expect guests with whom one does not 'put up.'"

The events of these emotion-charged days are movingly recalled in Ada's memoir, *Letters to the Sphinx*. The father who was never to see his sons again was domiciled—more of the gods' savage irony!—in a child's nursery, where "the most serious and tragic matters were discussed." Beerbohm, Harris, and some gay friends visited him. So did Constance, with a message from her lawyer urging Oscar to flee. "I loved her very much, and was grieved to see her leave in tears," Ada remembered. Even his loyal old hairdresser came daily to shave him and wave his hair. Oscar made certain rules: he refused to come downstairs before six to avoid embarrassing encounters, and he refused to discuss his situation in Ada's presence. "When we were alone he would walk up and down, always smoking a cigarette, talking in the most enchanting way about everything except the trouble."

With Oscar pure tragedy was impossible, of course; comedy insinuated itself inevitably. He asked for writing things one day to record one of his improvisations; when Ada could not find any, he said: "You have all the equipment of a writer, my dear Sphinx, except pens, ink, and paper." Harris cornered Ada at one point and asked her, "Can you row?" Oscar told Ada many amusing stories. She remembered one about drinking absinthe in Paris:

> After the first glass, you see things as you wish they were. After the second, you see things as they are not. Finally you see things as they really are, and that is the most horrible thing in the world. . . . Three nights I sat up all night drinking absinthe, and thinking that I was singularly clearheaded and sane. The waiter came in and began watering the sawdust. The most wonderful flowers, tulips, lilies, and roses sprang up and made a garden of the cafe. "Don't you see them?" I said to him. *"Mais non, monsieur, il n'y a rien."*

A bittersweet story, coming from a man who drank often and too well, who practically founded his career upon "wonderful flowers" . . . and whose illusions were in the process of destruction.

One evening guests and spirits were mustered for a dinner party. Sherard remembered that Oscar "was bright" once during this week: it must have been on this occasion. For Beerbohm was also present: "All his life Max was to remember Oscar coming down depressed, and then reviving under the impulse of wine and friendship to sparkle and rhapsodize in his old best form." How many present that evening—including Oscar—dared to think this was to be the last dinner-party triumph of his life?

Chapter Fifteen

CLOSET PHILOSOPHER

To speak the truth is a painful thing. To be forced to tell lies is much worse.
—*DE PROFUNDIS,* 1897

Permanence of temperament, the indomitable assertion of the soul (and by soul I mean the unity of mind and body), such are the things of value in anyone.
—LETTER TO FRANK HARRIS, 1899

FOR CENTURIES, SEXUAL EXTROVERTS have made satiric fun of the minor hypocrisies and concealments of their more timid brethren. A droll example of this vein of humor occurs in this epigram by Martial dating from about A.D. 85. Not the least of its charms is that Oscar, too, would have derided the sartorial conservatism of the closeted one:

> He favours drab, dark cloaks, he has a passion
> For wearing Baetic wool and grey; the fashion
> For scarlet he calls 'degenerate,' 'un-Roman,'

And, as for mauve, that's 'only fit for women.'
He's all for 'Nature'; yet, though no one's duller
In dress, his morals sport a different colour.
He may demand the grounds of my suspicion.
We bathe together, and his line of vision
Keeps below waist-level; he devours
Ocularly the boys under the showers,
And his lips twitch at the sight of a luscious member.
Did you ask his name? How odd, I can't remember.

It is inconceivable that Oscar and his gay friends did not make similarly ribald private jests—involving stable hands, collegiate choristers, or telegraph boys—about "Closet cases" of their acquaintance. Such persons provide a fertile field for humor . . . bittersweet humor of course, since closeted homosexuals are among the more melancholy comedians who, as Oscar observed, behave conventionally in order to gain Society's good regard. In fact, at the end of this chapter we shall make the acquaintance of two denizens of the Closet who caused Oscar, late in his life, much rather seriocomic frustration.

For all the inside humor incipient in the Closet and the Closeted, however, they also evoked from Oscar the most emphatic and oft-reiterated "philosophy" he ever promulgated. Indeed, if any theme can be said to unify this philosophy, it is surely this *idée fixe* of his social and political thought: a concerted and devastating attack on the Closet. And the "genius" of this philosophy he put equally into his life and art.

Before exploring how this philosophy emerged throughout Oscar's life, certain obstacles to calling him a philosopher at all must be confronted. Some of these obstacles were thrown up by Oscar himself. He was, of course, always instinctively eager to ridicule solemn systematizers who are tempted to extrapolate neat "rules" for coping with what he termed "practical and external life." Thus, for example, he wrote approvingly to Frank Harris of the trend away from philosophy in the Shakespeare criticism of his day: "It is a great era . . . the first time that one has looked in the plays, not for philosophy, for there is none, but for the wonder of a great personality—something far better, and far more mysterious, than any philosophy." To anyone looking for a philosophy in Oscar's writings, these are obviously intimidating words. All the more so since Oscar's own "great personality" was architected with such wonderful whimsy and romance: rose windows, outrageous gargoyles, secret passageways, and crenelated turrets everywhere. He would at least have *professed* dismay to think that his personality might have been upstaged by a mere philosophy.

Oscar's comfort in the presence of Shakespeare's mysterious personality points to another obstacle, namely, his intimate familiarity with the Closet from the inside and his obvious recognition that an attack upon it and the social repression that made it necessary could not be made directly or artlessly. Some disguise was necessary. Not being able or willing to declare his interest, Oscar made a lavish show of insisting that the artist and his art must be kept quite distinct and of deploring the public's prying interest in the artist at the expense of the work he produces. His classic statement on this subject comes, not surprisingly, in his response to ill-meant insinuations that his own life was reflected in *Dorian Gray*: "A critic should be taught to criticise a work of art without making any reference to the personality of the author. This, in fact, is the beginning of criticism."

This line of defense was spectacularly disingenuous. It was simply a species of the time-honored distancing gambit often employed by messengers bearing scandalous or subversive messages. "*Mores non habet hic meos libellus,*" said Martial of himself: "His book no way reflects his morals." The fact, however, was that *Dorian Gray* and so many of Oscar's fictions and feuilletons are astonishingly autobiographical, sometimes even boldly confessional. He never opined more truly about himself than when, in "The Critic as Artist," he asserted, "Autobiography is irresistible. . . . When people talk to us about others they are usually dull. When they talk to us about themselves they are nearly always interesting." It is impossible to read any of Oscar's important works apart from the realities of his personal life; often their connectedness with real-life experiences is precisely what makes them "interesting." That the duller reaches of his Victorian audience regularly failed to catch on to all his blatant subterfuges—regularly failed to accept his dare to confront their truth—must have been part of Oscar's continuing pleasure. This obtuseness of his audience must also have encouraged him to skate on ever thinner ice in his personal life. He was, in doing so, testing just how far he could take perhaps the most self-revealing of all his aphorisms: "If one tells the truth, one is sure, sooner or later, to be found out."

Autobiography is rarely absent in his writings, from the most profound revelations to the most innocuous, but allusive, nomenclature: Lord Henry Wotton is a bow to the notorious exile Lord Henry Somerset; the servant Lane in *Earnest* a tweaking of Oscar's publisher, John Lane; Dorian an homage to the beautiful John Gray. How Oscar's autobiographical subtexts were perceived at the time depended upon the reader. For those disinclined to poke beneath the surface of things, *Dorian Gray* was cheeky badinage; for the more shrewd and suspicious, the novel was "grubbing in muck heaps" and written "for none but outlawed noblemen [Lord Somerset again] and perverted telegraph boys." The *Christian Leader* fumed that it "portrays the gilded paganism which has been staining these latter years of the Victorian epoch with horrors that carry us back to the worst incidents in the history of ancient Rome."

George Ives finally read *Dorian Gray* in 1892 and shuddered at the blatancy of Oscar's self-exposure. He confided to his diary, in poignant words, that he did not have Oscar's sally-forth spirit and so was bound to remain lonely and closeted: "It seems very brilliant . . . but though admiring the acting and the cold cutting cynicism I am not of it. Under control, patient, immovable, crushing down good and evil under the ice mantle of suppression—with the few exceptions, neither loving nor loved—yet I have a Cause . . . ah, the world is a terrible school." Clyde Fitch, whose heart throbbed briefly over Oscar in the early 1890s, appears to have taken the same sad closeted path in his later life.

For after he died, enormously wealthy, in 1909 at the age of forty-four, a good friend wrote, "He lived alone and was lonely."

The Cause to which Ives referred was gay liberation, though if asked to name it he would likely have consulted *Dorian Gray* and called it the New Hedonism. Solemn, secretive, conservative (the illegitimate son of aristocratic parents), Ives was made very nervous by Oscar's penchant for "acting up" and took an entirely different course in service of the Cause. More pragmatically and safely, he founded in 1893 a secret homosexual society called the Order of Chaeronea. There is no indication Oscar took part in this group, and this is no surprise: bashful fraternities were decidedly not his style. His indulgence in Freemasonry was inevitably quite short-lived.

One can whimsically imagine Oscar declining an invitation into the Order of Chaeronea just as he wittily declined an invitation to dine with the Thirteen Club, an antisuperstition society, on 13 January 1894:

> The aim of your society seems to be dreadful. Leave us some unreality. Don't make us too offensively sane.
>
> I love dining out; but with a society with so wicked an object as yours I cannot dine. I regret it. I am sure you will all be charming; but I could not come, though thirteen is a lucky number.
>
> OSCAR WILDE

Secrecy and concealment were part of Oscar's personality, but it is quite difficult to imagine him happily taking part in any organized underground political organization. That would have been too offensively sane: more stimulating was a life before the public, couching truth-freighted "insanity" in the form of beguiling paradoxes. What Oscar clearly preferred to an audience of converts was a potentially hostile audience that required to be charmed, manipulated, and finally subjugated by his power.

And make no mistake, Oscar thirsted for power. He always sought to do to his British public what Lord Henry seeks to do with Dorian: "He would seek to dominate him." Dominating the members of the Order of Chaeronea would have been a paltry victory; dominating not only London's choicest dinner-party tables but Victorian society was a more challenging and heroic enterprise. His chief method in this was simply to stimulate thought, as he cheerfully granted during the Queensberry trial. His adversary Edward Carson read out one of his clever paradoxes—"Wickedness is a myth invented by good people to account for the curious attractiveness of others"—and asked whether this was "a safe axiom to put forward for the philosophy of the young." To which Oscar replied, "Most stimulating." Carson read out another seditious maxim and again asked, "Is it good for the young?" "Anything is good that stimulates thought at whatever age." Stimulating thought was a *public* activity, and Oscar's personality and abilities were bound to make him prefer a celebrity's mode of attack over the clandestine lucubrations of a Society of Chaeronea.

This incendiary method fretted George Ives severely, with good reason as it turned out. But Ives—like many a complacent and unsuspecting Victorian—was curiously dense about Oscar's intentions in his public intellectual extravagances. This difficulty in deciphering Oscar's agenda Ives mulled over in his diary in October 1893:

> A teacher, he either cannot or will not give the key to his philosophy, and till I get it I can't understand him. He seems to have no purpose, I am all purpose. Apparently of an elegant refined nature and talented as few men are, brilliant as a shining jewel, yet he teaches many things which cannot be held and which are so false as not even to be dangerous.

Poor Ives. John Stokes, who sifted through his gargantuan diary of nearly 125 volumes and more than three million words, summarized him as "a man who always missed the joke," and here he comes *so close* to grasping the key to Oscar's philosophy and its mode of delivery . . . then lets it slip. For Oscar *did* possess a purpose, one he would have been mortified to divulge forthrightly as a political activist might. And he was also a master at asserting ideas "which cannot be held." Even in his Magdalen College days, his pal "Dunskie" Hunter-Blair recalled, he was noted for always uttering "untenable propositions" and "preposterous theories." The joke, which Ives missed so utterly, was that these "things which could not be held" were not false but so blindingly true and so ruinous to certain tenets of Victorian morality that they simply could not be taken seriously. The saving assumption was that Oscar could not possibly have meant what he said. He seems to have been pleased to let this assumption flourish among the ignoscenti for a very long time.

Certain observers like Max Beerbohm and Ford Madox Ford, we have seen, perceived what Ives could not: that there indeed was "purpose" behind Oscar's apparent frivolity. Ives was one among many who have been lulled into blithe acceptance of the buoyant, "trivial" Oscar as the real one, often by his own virtuoso invitations to do so. This pied-piper concealment of serious intention Oscar employed with perfect aptness in his first hints to friends about *The Importance of Being Earnest*. To one he said of his work in progress, "It is quite nonsensical and has no serious interest, will I hope bring me in a lot of red gold." To another, along with tickets to the premiere, he sent a note saying his comedy was "written by a butterfly for butterflies." And the play was, in general, received as a delightful, perfectly harmless bouquet of bad-boyish witticisms from the day's premier social butterfly. Audiences and reviewers enjoyed *Earnest* in the vein of the first half of its generic subtitle: "A Trivial Comedy for Serious People." Even today, it is hard, amid so much spirited blitheness, to take this play not only as a serious discourse about cucumber sandwiches but also as a play that is, deep down, about the "Neronian hours" Oscar spent with beautiful boys in various West End hotels while his wife and children slept snugly, if not peacefully, in Tite Street. Jack Worthing's "Bunburying" is a theatrical simile for, among other things, the prevarications and protections of the

Closet. The plot of *Earnest*, it could be said, takes its genesis from the kind of note Oscar sent to Ives a year or two before writing his famous farce: "I am off to the country till Monday: I have said I am going to Cambridge to see you—but I am really going to see the young Domitian [Bosie?], who has taken to poetry."

Others far more shrewd than Ives have committed this mistake of naiveté in embracing Oscar and his work as a whole. W. H. Auden certainly did. He took the Cucumber Sandwich view when he summarized that Oscar's "philosophy of individualism" simply "boils down to 'let's have fun'" and when he dismissed much of this philosophy as "one kind of seducer's patter." Auden, in fact, uttered perhaps the most grievous of all the countless backhanded compliments that Oscar has evoked over the past century when he concluded, "Surely, the really nice thing about Wilde is that his life is so much more honest than his writings." Auden also underplayed the serious and emphasized the trivial, in all too typical fashion, by asserting that Oscar "was a phoney prophet but a serious playboy." Though Auden did not specify what exactly Oscar was a prophet of, his charge of hypocrisy is a serious one. After all, a phoney prophet is unlikely to make a very satisfactory philosopher. The accusation deserves some effort at rebuttal.

The weakness in Auden's view lies in his phrase "let's have fun." Perhaps he was seduced into it by Lord Henry's patter about a "new hedonism" and about pleasure being "the only thing worth having a theory about." Oscar, of course, bowed to no man in his devotion to the *gaudeamus igitur* spirit, but behind this pose lay an unshakable conviction that the only true rejoicing must come from the untrammeled exploration and definition and self-fulfillment of one's own personality. Having made light of this credo, Auden was bound to make light of all the rest of Oscar. One is rarely disposed to congratulate Lord Alfred Douglas on his insight, but at least on this one point, I think, he was as brilliantly right as Auden was wrong. For Bosie concluded, many years later, that his old friend was by no means a phoney prophet: "Long after Wilde was dead, and after I was married and had utterly got away from the Wilde cult and tradition, I went on sub-consciously believing ... that his views about morals, whether one liked them or not, were based on abstract truth and were un-answerable and irrefutable." (Bosie, ever fickle, said later on the same page that he afterward lapsed into the conviction that Oscar was "really a very wicked man"—which Oscar would probably have quipped is the same thing as being a purveyor of abstract moral truths.)

Our eminent trespasser knew that the severe mien of a moral philosopher might be unpleasant to look upon, and so he worked hard to disguise this facet of his identity. But there is at least one character in his plays in whom, I think, Oscar quite candidly re-vealed his main method of disguise. He is, indeed, one of the many Oscarian characters who are always tempting us into Auden's comfortable but mistaken assumption that his chief pur-pose was to "have fun." This is Lord Goring, the "flawless dandy" who trod the stage of the Theatre Royal for the first time on 3 January 1895, when Oscar's own dandyism had him teetering at the abyss. Goring is thirty-four but (like Oscar) "says he is youn-ger." He is "fond of being misunderstood." He is dressed to kill. But, astonishingly, Oscar also gives him a useful profession: he is a philosopher—"the first well-dressed philosopher in the history of thought."

Lord Goring is as Oscarian a character in spirit as Oscar ever invented. The dandy, of course, he played in real life with ease and flair. And, like his character, Oscar proved himself a brilliant subverter of what Goring says is "called nowadays a high moral tone." However, late in the play a stage direction describes Gor-ing as "pulling himself together for a great effort, and showing the philosopher that underlies the dandy." Rarely did Oscar himself vouchsafe his audience a view of this side of his character. He knew it could easily ruin his public image. Nor was the pose in character for one who had raised seeming indolence to a high art. "Showing the philosopher" does require "great effort," and Oscar disliked being seen to expend effort of any kind, except, as he said, in conversation. And yet ... a philosopher does underlie the dandy. So cleverly was he disguised from Oscar's audiences, inside the theater and out, that it comes as a bracing shock, I hope, to be asked now to look at him as an eager, earnest, if unprecedentedly well-dressed philosopher.

☆ ☆ ☆

THE PRINCIPAL TENET OF Oscar's philosophy perhaps holds the explanation for the most momentous event of his life: his emergence—with many a preliminary feint and under various disguises—from the Closet. Though, in the end, considerable emotional duress (applied by Bosie) caused him to risk the final, awful self-outing, his self-exposure had been a work in progress, almost a vocation, for several years.

Though Lord Illingworth, Lord Goring's virtual stage twin, jests about the dangers of entertaining convictions and "taking sides," Oscar did indeed take a side in his philosophy: the side of the Individual or Self as against Society or the Public. On this point he became, for once in his life, like the Catharine Wheel in his tale "The Remarkable Rocket": "She was one of those people who think that, if you say the same thing over and over a great many times, it becomes true in the end." The following brief survey of his expressions of this view may, in consequence, risk a certain tedium, but it is worth presenting not merely because Oscar's theme and variations on the priority of the Self are so imaginatively sustained, but also because they constitute, quite simply, his golden rule.

The first appearance of Oscar's *philosophia contra cubiculum* that I can discover came very early . . . from his days as a prize Greek and Latin scholar at Oxford. Indeed, this debate comes quite literally *in* philosophy. In his student copy of Aristotle's *Nicomathean Ethics,* inscribed "1877 Magdalen College," Oscar entered on a blank page this note on the subject of the "end, or object, or the good of Human Life": "Man makes his end for himself out of himself: no end is imposed by external considerations, he must realize his true nature; must be what *nature* orders, so must discover what his nature is." Here—though he did not consciously intend it as such—is as satisfying a renunciation of the Closet as one could wish. Like the appearance of the great theme in the last movement of Beethoven's Ninth Symphony, this marginal *obiter dictum* serves as the basis for many subsequent paraphrases, extensions, and reprises. These eloquent reiterations, also like Beethoven's, produce the cumulative effect of something approaching grandeur.

The crescendo does not really begin, though, until the end of the 1880s, after he had left behind the apostleship of things beautiful, the lecture platform, and the preoccupations of family life. Once he joined in systematic satiric battle with his age in the late 1880s, the great theme began to resound regularly. Perhaps remembering the athletic exertions of most of his Oxford classmates, Oscar paraphrased his observation in Aristotle in "The Decay of Lying" (1889) by having Vivian assert, "Egotism itself, which is so necessary to a proper sense of human dignity, is entirely the result of indoor life." In the same essay, he initiated the corollary theme of Art—like the ideally self-asserting person—being beholden to nothing "external": "Art never expresses anything but itself. It has an independent life, just as Thought has, and develops purely on its own lines." Art, he added, is thus bound to be contrarian: "So far from being the creation of its time, [Art] is usually in direct opposition to it." Two years later, in a letter to the editor of the *Pall Mall Gazette*, he would make the same point again: "No artist recognises any standard of beauty but that which is suggested by his own temperament."

The year 1890 proved a kind of *annus mirabilis* for declarations of the primacy of self-definition. In that February Oscar found his individualist ethic ratified when he chanced to review a translation of the writings of the Chinese sage Chuang-tzu, who lived in a happy time when "every man kept his virtues to himself, nobody meddled in other people's business." The review makes clear that Chuang's "perfect man" was also Oscar's: "He lets externals take care of themselves. Nothing material injures him. . . . His mental equilibrium gives him the empire of the world. He is never the slave of objective existences." Chuang's ideals of "self-culture and self-development" were praised, and (in a sly thrust at the Victorian moral majority) Oscar allowed that these ideals are "somewhat needed by an age like ours, in which most people are so anxious to educate their neighbours that they have actually no time left in which to educate themselves." In the first part of "The Critic as Artist," which appeared a few months later, Oscar declared the egotistic charms of autobiography happily irresistible and also asserted, "The longer one studies life and literature, the more strongly one feels that behind everything that is wonderful stands the individual." Art, he concluded, "springs from personality."

Then, in June of 1890, came *The Picture of Dorian Gray*. Lord Henry, who clearly has dipped into the *Nicomathean Ethics* and perhaps even into Chuang-tzu, tells Dorian, "The aim of life is self-development. To realize one's nature perfectly—that is what each of us is here for. People are afraid of themselves, nowadays." How, given all the novel's other coded and not-so-coded allusions to homosexuality, could such a statement have been read by gay readers of the time without an enormous sense of challenge and liberation? But the *locus classicus* for this preeminent Oscarian theme comes later, when the three main characters gather to discuss, as Aristotle does, the "good" in life. The "correct" answer is given by Oscar to Lord Henry: "To be good is to be in harmony with one's self. . . . Discord is to be forced to be in harmony with others. One's own life—that is the important thing." Basil Hallward's response to this speech, given what history had in store for Oscar, is heavy with irony: "But, surely, if one lives merely for one's self, Harry, one pays a terrible price for doing so?" To which Lord Henry blithely replies, "Yes, we are overcharged for everything nowadays."

If *Dorian Gray* was Oscar's most (in)famous and lyric attack on the dark tower of Society's oppression of homosexuality, "The Soul of Man Under Socialism," which appeared the next year, is his most vigorous discursive assault, though the object of attack is never made explicit. In this essay we find perhaps the first and

classic definition of all so-called "victimless" crimes such as homosexuals are regularly prosecuted for committing: "Man has
sought to live intensely, fully, perfectly. When he can do so without exercising restraint on others, or suffering it ever, and his activities are all pleasurable to him, he will be saner, healthier, more
civilised, more himself." Oscar identified certain great men of his
century as precisely those who had the courage to isolate themselves, to keep themselves "out of reach of the clamorous claims
of others," and thus to "realise the perfection of what was in"
them—the "great man of science," Darwin, the "great poet"
Keats, the "supreme artist" Flaubert. The point was rephrased
more starkly a few pages on: "What a man really has, is what is
in him. What is outside of him should be a matter of no importance."

This was followed by Oscar's lengthy incorporation of
Christ's message into his agenda: "He said to man, 'You have a
wonderful personality. Develop it. Be yourself. . . . He who would
lead a Christ-like life is he who is perfectly and absolutely himself." In this essay Oscar pursued his attack upon his main enemies, the Public and its Opinion, by insisting, "The things people
say of a man do not alter a man. He is what he is. Public opinion
is of no value whatsoever." He added, for good measure, that a
man "may commit a sin against society, and yet realize through
that sin his true perfection." (No wonder that Oscar, in a letter
at this time, would say that the word "vice" is "tainted in its signification with moral censure.")

The courage of such assertions, manifestly applicable to the
situation of the Victorian homosexual, is impressive. One wonders how they could possibly have been taken as anything less
than a call for liberation of "the contrary sex." Near the end of
the essay, indeed, Oscar pronounced—in emphatic italics—his
ban on all attempts by Society to legislatively forbid the harmless
behavior of others. Sexual preference is not mentioned, but it is
hard to imagine that it played no part in the sentiment: "*Selfishness is not living as one wishes to live, it is asking others to live as one
wishes to live.*"

In 1892, with the beginning of his theatrical successes, the *sub rosa* assault on the Closet continued under the cover of comedic insouciance. Cecil Graham, in *Lady Windermere's Fan*, hews to the theme of courageous selfhood when he declares, "Whenever people agree with me, I always feel I must be wrong." (A variation, two years later: "A truth ceases to be true when more than one person believes in it.") Still, there is at least one speech in the play—uttered by one of the several "Lords" Oscar invented to speak on his behalf—that is impossible to read now without a sense of its autobiographical veracity:

> There are moments when one has to choose between living one's own life, fully, entirely, completely—or dragging out some false, shallow, degrading existence that the world in its hypocrisy demands.

Many of Oscar's friends (and Constance herself) believed that 1892, when Lord Darlington first spoke these words to Lady Windermere, was indeed the time he finally made precisely such a fateful choice.

During this period Oscar fashioned many a *bon mot* from the notion that to be misunderstood is a badge of merit. Lord Goring delights in being misunderstood since, in a hypocritical world, it is bound to be the consequence of talking honestly: "I usually say what I really think. A great mistake nowadays. It makes one so liable to be misunderstood." His is the Oscarian voice of one who is "out"; Chiltern's, on the other hand, is the voice from the Closet. He is the character who cherishes a ghastly secret (his corrupt behavior as a government official) and who must treat the truth quite gingerly. One way to interpret him is as a terrible object lesson in the costs of the closeted life. His *cri de coeur* in the second act (like many a line from the plays) leaps out especially vividly when this subtext is kept well in mind: "I would to God that I had been able to tell the truth . . . to live the truth. Ah! that is the great thing in life, to live the truth. (*Sighs . . .*)"

Trial, conviction, and imprisonment served only to steel Oscar's convictions. One passage from *De profundis*, in fact, paraphrases with curious, almost eerie, exactness the sentiment he had inscribed in his Aristotle twenty years before: "I am not alluding to any external sanction or command. I admit none. I am far more of an individualist than I ever was. Nothing seems to me of the smallest value except what one gets out of oneself." And toward the end of his prison term he confided to Ross this wistful statement of his "religion": "Still I believe that at the beginning God made a world for each separate man, and in that world which is within us one should seek to live." A sentence or two later he reminded Ross of his moody state of mind and of "how fluid a thing thought is with me."

But one thought in his life always remained solid: his conviction that one must define one's own self . . . and one's own fate. Even after his fame, family, fortune, and his once handsome features had deliquesced, this conviction remained unaltered, even if it was now expressed in more melancholy ways. To Smithers he wrote in late 1897, "Vanity, that great impulse, still drives me to think of a possible future of self-assertion." The next year an old acquaintance wrote him and referred to his former life as unnatural and insane. He replied, politely but firmly, "When you allude to my life being in some respects 'unnatural and insane' you are judging of the life of another by an alien standard." He then added his by 1898 old refrain: "For myself, of course, the aim of life is to realise one's *own* personality—one's *own* nature."

Oscar's very last utterance on his life's great theme—which always puts me in mind of the pose of Rodin's defiant Balzac—I have chosen as the second epigraph for this chapter.

☆ ☆ ☆

THE "FLAWLESS DANDY" WAS also a philosopher. To italicize this part of his identity, I would like to pause for a few pages over one of the most remarkable and curious coincidences in the history of moral philosophy and of the gay liberation movement. This is Oscar's extraordinary affinity with the first great contrarian philosopher of the modern period, Friedrich Nietzsche.*

Just as Jeremy Bentham was the first legal philosopher to theorize systematically against the oppression of sexual minorities (his writings piled up in a closet and were never published), Nietzsche was the first moral philosopher to make a concerted, indeed witheringly trenchant, attack on the majoritarian tyranny of the Public, its Opinion, Morality, and Law. Though neither Oscar nor Nietzsche explicitly attacks the Closet, their premises and argumentation lead inexorably to the conclusion that it could be counted among the social constructs they scorned. As has been observed, Max Nordau knew enough of English culture to sense the "deviant" affinities between Nietzsche and Wilde and expressed great disgust at them in *Degeneration*. Since the 1890s, many have drawn more favoring attention to their fraternity. Shaw referred to the "Nietzschean son" of Sir William Wilde, and Gide said that knowing Oscar prepared him well to appreciate Nietzsche. Much later, Ellmann made the felicitous comparison, even broadened it, by way of giving color to the somber side of Oscar's mind: "Wilde was a moralist, in a school where Blake, Nietzsche, and even Freud were his fellows."

What is doubtless most remarkable about the philosophical affinities between Oscar and Nietzsche is that the two men appear to have known nothing of each other. There is no mention of Nietzsche in Oscar's works or correspondence, and he knew no German. (His vow to study the language in prison was never acted upon.) Vincent O'Sullivan recalled, simply, that he "did not care about Germany."† Lord Goring hints at the truth in this remark, "It is love, and not German philosophy, that is the true explanation of this world."

---

*Nietzsche was born ten years before Oscar, but both men died in 1900. The year I have suggested for the beginning of Oscar's concerted moral philosophizing, 1889, was, in another extraordinary coincidence, also the year insanity struck Nietzsche, ending his mere dozen years of flourishing activity.

†But Germany later cared much about Oscar. In 1908 his literary executor, Ross, credited Germany for repaying the debts of his estate: "The bulk of them was paid by the receipts of the German performances of his plays, chiefly *Salome* long before, let me add, Dr Strauss had set music to the words."

There is much irony in the fact that this sentiment was first uttered in 1895. For in that year, with "The Case of Wagner," Nietzsche began to appear in London in English translation. *Zarathustra* appeared in 1896 when Oscar was in prison, and it would certainly have been denied him if he had requested it. Most of Nietzsche's publications did not appear in English until well after Oscar died. Had Oscar been familiar with some of these works, I doubt he would have given Lord Goring his line: for here was one German philosopher who had much to say about love—and sexuality—as part of "the true explanation" of the world. Indeed, as we have seen, Nietzsche asserted that "the degree and kind of a person's sexuality reach up into the ultimate pinnacle of his spirit."

A more emphatically odd couple can scarcely be imagined. The German's eyes always gave the impression of staring, while Oscar's heavy eyelids exuded blasé indolence. Oscar was tall and tended to sprawl; Nietzsche, a compact five feet, eight inches, gave the impression of rigidity. Utterly unlike Oscar, Nietzsche showed a notorious shyness and lack of wit in company. Many observers noted Oscar's childlike presence, whereas Nietzsche was commonly called *altklug,* German for "old before one's time." Most of his early life he was perceived as "a rigidly earnest man" and was even nicknamed "the little pastor" (his father was a Lutheran one). Oscar reveled in an entourage; Nietzsche was wretched at making friends and once admitted that he found a soul mate in that "loneliest thinker," Spinoza.

How poorly a meeting between the perfect sybarite and the extreme ascetic would have proceeded! Nietzsche was an inveterate hiker—"Only thoughts reached by walking have value," he said—and might have dragged Oscar into the dread out-of-doors. On the other hand, Oscar would have been deeply distressed by the hospitality indoors, for, as Stefan Zweig recalled of Nietzsche, there was "No glass of wine, no glass of beer, no alcohol, no coffee at his place, no cigar and no cigarette after his meal, nothing that stimulates, refreshes, or rests him." Oscar would doubtless also have shuddered at the black suits Nietzsche always wore and the spartan rooms in nondescript boardinghouses he always rented.

Could they have gotten beyond these enormous superficial differences, though, and talked about ideas, they would have discovered much in common. Both were educated in their countries' most venerable schools (Nietzsche at Schulpforta) and achieved particularly high honors in Greek. Yet both became vocal critics of their nations' educational systems, and both firmly believed, as Nietzsche wrote, "The surest way to corrupt a youth is to instruct him to hold in higher esteem those who think alike than those who think differently." Both held very strong political views but also possessed thoroughly apolitical personalities. "Nietzsche is certainly not a political person," concluded one of his teachers. They shared a primarily aristocratic theory of culture, and, generally speaking, this culture was essentially male. A disconcerting vein of misogyny runs through the works of both, though Oscar never cast his views quite so brutishly as the German, who asserted, "Everything about woman has one solution: pregnancy," and "Woman is not yet capable of friendship: women are still cats and birds. Or at best, cows."

On several subjects their combative opinions were also in perfect accord. They shared, for instance, an extremely low view of journalism. Nietzsche considered journalism and the "newspaper-reading public" an affront to decency and would have relished Oscar's observation, "By giving us the opinions of the uneducated, it [journalism] keeps us in touch with the ignorance of the community." They would surely have charmed each other with their mutual suspicion of philanthropists; several times Oscar virtually paraphrased Nietzsche's aphorism "If all alms were given only from pity, all beggars would have starved long ago." And neither was in the least bit shy about criticizing his countrymen. The Oscarian verve of the assertion "The English public likes tediousness, and likes things to be explained to them in a tedious way," is perfectly matched by Nietzsche's remark, "Germans . . . know the secret of being boring with spirit, knowledge, and feeling and . . . have accustomed themselves to feel boredom as moral." They were cosmopolitans at heart, and were thus disgusted by narrow-minded patriotism and complacent nationalism. Nietzsche, by the way, knew enough about the typical Englishman to have an opinion of him as low as Oscar's. "Man does *not* strive for pleasure," he wickedly said; "only the Englishman does."

But all these are peripheral affinities. It is their unanimity on more fundamental matters that truly astonishes. Both were brilliant disconcerters, unmaskers, demolition experts. Nietzsche's motto—"to make the individual *uncomfortable,* that is my task"— was also Oscar's. Both relied, to brilliant effect, on feats of paradoxing to achieve their aims; both could boast, as Nietzsche did, "I have the gift of *reversing perspectives.*" The "gay kind of seriousness and . . . *wisdom full of pranks*" that Nietzsche found in Socrates he would surely have found abundantly in Oscar. Thus, Shaw's praise of the German applies just as well to his countryman: Nietzsche, said Shaw, had the "power of putting the merest platitudes of his position in rousing, startling paradoxes . . . of getting underneath moral precepts which are unquestionable to us and upsetting them with a scornful laugh."

In their eagerness to upset, both became virtuoso risk-takers and eulogists of The Other. Nietzsche said aphorisms should be "peaks" where the air is "thin and pure, danger near, and the spirit full of gay sarcasm," and so indeed are many of the best aphorisms he and Oscar invented. Oscar, praiser of pirates and poisoners and regular skater on thin ice, would surely have applauded the credo Nietzsche announced in 1882: "Believe me, the secret of the greatest fruitfulness and the greatest enjoyment of existence is: to *live dangerously!* Build your cities under Vesuvius! Send your ships into uncharted seas! Live at war with your peers and yourselves! Be robbers and conquerors . . . !" Shaw called Nietzsche "a Devil's Advocate of the modern type." So was Oscar.

What fueled all this detonating energy in both men, however, was a powerfully affirmative conviction about the necessity of liberating the self, the individual personality, from the bonds of oppression and self-repression. They shared Montaigne's amazement at that "malady peculiar to man, and not seen in any other creature, to hate and disdain himself," and they attempted in a variety of polemical ways to eradicate this tendency. They despised the moralist's purse-lipped frown. "We immoralists," boasted Nietzsche, have "made room in our hearts for every kind of understanding, comprehending, and *approving*. We do not easily negate; we make it a point of honor to be *affirmers*." This eagerness always to be "saying Yes to life even in its strangest and hardest problems" led Nietzsche to praise, in the birth of Greek tragedy, the "psychology of the orgiastic as an overflowing feeling of life and strength, where even pain still has the effect of a stimulus." He at the same time ridiculed those who would turn common sense and reason into tyrants and who would fear that "any concession to the instincts, to the unconscious, leads *downward*." (Thomas Mann made this fear and panic at concession to instinctive desire the crux of Aschenbach's growing attraction to the boy Tadzio in *Death in Venice*.)

Pursuing his immoralist "transvaluation of all values," Nietzsche became a partisan of the impulsive, instinctive Dionysian spirit as opposed to its rational, orderly, Apollonian counterpart. Carl Pletsch's convenient précis of the Dionysian spirit as Nietzsche conceived it, I think, also describes a mainspring of Oscar's philosophy of art and life:

> It contains the death wish and every other destructive instinct as well as the life instinct. It is the maelstrom of every impulse caught in the flux of time, the enemy of all that is fixed and ordered. Dionysian perception yields a terrifying understanding of existence that humankind does well to conceal from itself in everyday life ... the Dionysian is the more profound of the two modes of perception ... [and] can only be ignored at the price of cultural sterility.

The Dionysian embrace of personal desire, however terrifying and "morbid," lies at the heart of two of Oscar's most famous fictions,

The Picture of Dorian Gray and *Salome*. Many passages in *Dorian Gray* (like the following one) give expression to the terror of Nietzsche's Dionysian impulse: "There are moments, psychologists tells us, when the passion for sin, or for what the world calls sin, so dominates a nature, that every fibre of the body, as every cell of the brain, seems to be instinct with fearful impulses." That *Salome*, more than any of the other plays, so blatantly manifests Oscar's Dionysian instinct may explain Ada Leverson's remark that "in truth he cared little for any of his plays excepting only *Salome*." Culturally sterile late-Victorian England would certainly have found it abominable, had the Lord Chamberlain allowed it to be performed (the first English performance did not take place, in fact, until *1931*).

This opening up to dangerous, forbidden, but profoundly self-revealing experiences required an obvious corollary: an emphatic insistence by both men that such experiences must be evaluated aesthetically rather than morally. Nietzsche's assertion that "it is only as an *aesthetic phenomenon* that existence and the world are eternally *justified*" may seem to apply most clearly to Oscar's early Aesthetic apostleship, but it also underlies much that came after. Their enemies being eager to subjugate Art and the Artist to morality, the two men became proponents of *l'art pour l'art*. "The fight against purpose in art is always a fight against the moralizing tendency in art, against its subordination to morality," wrote Nietzsche candidly: *"L'art pour l'art* means 'The devil take morality!' " In just this spirit Oscar often sang the praises of any Art (or person or profession) that was "useless," proffered no "views"—simply was. He also expressed on numerous occasions the belief that as soon as the Artist submits to morality he ceases to be one. This was a basic Nietzschean principle, too: "Submission to morality can be slavish or vain or selfish or resigned or obtusely enthusiastic or thoughtless or an act of desperation, like submission to a prince: in itself it is nothing moral."

The Closet is a kind of "act of desperation." It is a defensive response to the quintessential admonition of all moralizers: "Change yourself!" This cry, of course, both men were very pleased to resist. Many an Oscarian witticism has as its germ the kind of truculent disgust for those inclined to visit their moral views on their fellow man that is apparent in this passage from Nietzsche's *The Twilight of the Idols*:

> How naive it is altogether to say: "Man *ought* to be such and such!" Reality shows us an enchanting wealth of types, the abundance of a lavish play and change of forms—and some wretched loafer of a moralist comments: "No! Man ought to be different." He even knows what man should be like, this wretched bigot and prig: he paints himself on the wall and comments, "*Ecce homo!*". . . The single human being is a piece of *fatum* . . . one law more, one necessity more for all that is yet to come and to be. To say to him, "Change yourself!" is to demand that everything be changed.

If Oscar had been so abrupt and mordant in public, he would have been expelled very quickly from London's fashionable drawing rooms and from his Victorian public's bemused affection. But (as his letters often show) he was perfectly capable of such Nietzschean sarcasm in private.

That Oscar shared Nietzsche's disgust at the moralist's impositions upon others is shown in a charming anecdote he told more than once about a common event in any household with small children. Cyril was in an obstreperous mood one evening, refusing to say his prayers and hitting his younger brother. When Oscar went upstairs and chided him, Cyril replied, "I was not naughty . . . it was Vyvyan; he was naughty." But soon he knelt and recited the Lord's Prayer, then said, "Now I'll pray to myself." Constance came in and asked whether the prayers had been said: "Yes, mother . . . I said I was sorry and asked God to make Vyvyan a good boy." This greatly amused Oscar, who told Harris,

"I had to leave the room, Frank, or he would have seen me smiling. Wasn't it delightful of him! We are all willing to ask God to make others good." A writer for the *London Sun* reported a more extended moral to the same anecdote: "Oscar . . . said it was human nature all over. We were all anxious to have other people made good, provided we were not troubled ourselves, only we had not the candour to say so; children were often the truest cynics."

That submission to morality—Prussian or Victorian—verges on obscenity was finally just a corollary for both men. Self-definition was the *primum mobile* of their philosophy: they both insisted that the easiest, most ignominious way of life is accommodation to the world and the hardest, most courageous way is complete self-inhabitation. Both were linked in their day with "decadence," "morbidity," and "degeneration," but for them true degeneration lay in the seeming "altruism" or "selflessness" of the moralists: "The best is lacking when self-interest is lacking," wrote Nietzsche; "instinctively to choose what is harmful to *oneself* . . . that is virtually the formula for decadence." Instead, Nietzsche urged, "Don't for anything in the world take one step toward accommodation! One can only have success if one remains true to oneself." Oscar—"whose egoism was superb" (said Ross)—founded his life on this Nietzschean theorem.

The classic Nietzschean statement of this view occurs in his last major work, *The Antichrist*, which first appeared in the fateful year 1895 (the title carries another irony, for in "The Soul of Man Under Socialism" Oscar had offered his own "anti" Christ):

> A virtue must be *our own* invention, *our* most necessary
> self-expression and self-defense: any other kind of virtue
> is merely a danger. . . . "Virtue," "duty," the "good in it-
> self," the good which is impersonal and universally valid
> [are] chimeras and expressions of decline, of the final
> exhaustion of life. . . . The fundamental laws of self-
> preservation and growth demand the opposite—that ev-

317

eryone invent *his own* virtue, *his own* categorical imperative.*

For both Oscar and Nietzsche, Goethe was the great nineteenth-century embodiment of this heroic choice of self-definition. Not surprisingly, their praise of him takes almost exactly the same form. Oscar: "Self-culture is the true ideal of man. Goethe saw it, and the immediate debt that we owe to Goethe is greater than the debt we owe to any man since Greek days." Nietzsche: "What he wanted was *totality;* he fought the mutual extraneousness of reason, senses, feelings, and will. . . . He disciplined himself to wholeness, he *created* himself." All of this, in a sense, is simply to propose a kind of *ars vivendi:* making art out of one's life. Oscar succeeded remarkably in doing something of the kind, as he suggested in his famous aside to Gide that he had put his genius into his life, only his talent into his writings.†

It is, for my purposes, a happy coincidence that this oft-

---

*Samuel Johnson, late in life, had occasion to utter a bluff "John Bull" version of this credo (complete with a fine, if unintentional pun): "You may be wise in your study in the morning, and gay in company at a tavern in the evening. Every man is to take care of his own wisdom and his own virtue, without minding too much what others think."

Walt Whitman's equivalent expression of Nietzsche's credo—in sweetly homespun phrasing—deserves notice, too. It occurs in a letter to one of the most important young men in his life, Harry Stafford, about a new edition of *Leaves of Grass:* "My own feeling abt my book is that it makes (tries to make) every fellow *see himself,* & see that *he has got to work out his salvation himself*—has got to pull the oars, & hold the plow, or swing the axe *himself*—& that the blessings of life are not the fictions generally supposed, but are real, & are mostly within reach of all—you chew on this."

More succinct was the formulation uttered by Martin Mull on the David Letterman show (18 December 1992): "Why be influenced by a person when you already are one?"

†A remarkable, more recent parallel to the philosophy of Nietzsche and Wilde is to be found in the later writings of Michel Foucault (1926–1984), as one might guess from the titles of the second and third volumes of his *History of Sexuality: The Use of Pleasure* and *The Care of the Self.* Foucault was profoundly influenced by Nietzsche and, like Oscar, too, was constantly testing the boundaries of "good" and "evil." A recent summary, by Alexander Nehamas, of Foucault's work late in life (before his death from AIDS after several years' immersion in gay sadomasochistic sexual practices) reminds one again and again of Oscar. Foucault is "a man who was willing to take serious risks with his thought as well as his life. . . . His sexual activities were fraught with danger. . . . [He] was a great Nietzschean hero. . . . [He] belonged to . . . the tradition of philosophy as a vocation, as an art of living. . . . He made himself into a model of autonomy, of a voice of one's own." Nehamas concluded: "In such cases as Socrates, Nietzsche, and Foucault [and he might well have added Wilde], the personal and the public, the aesthetic and the political, are as entangled with one another as the 'life' and the 'work.'"

quoted remark of Oscar's was also anticipated by Nietzsche. Had Oscar been able to read it when it appeared in 1880, just as he was settling down to make himself a London celebrity, he would have found his future—and his way out of the Closet—figured clearly forth. By a quirk in the history of words, the title of the work in which the passage appears—*The Gay Science*—is even more apt now than when Walter Kaufmann translated it, two decades before the Stonewall riot:

> *One thing is needful.* "Giving style" to one's character—a great and rare art! It is exercised by those who see all the strengths and weaknesses of their own natures and then comprehend them in an artistic plan until everything appears as art and reason and even weakness delights the eye. . . . It will be the strong and domineering natures who enjoy their finest gaiety in such compulsion, in such constraint and perfection under a law of their own. . . . For one thing is needful: that a human being attain his satisfaction with himself—whether it be by this or by that poetry and art; only then is a human being at all tolerable to behold. Whoever is dissatisfied with himself is always ready to revenge himself therefor; we others will be his victims, if only by always having to stand his ugly sight. For the sight of the ugly makes men bad and gloomy.

LET US DESCEND NOW from philosophy and consider some of Oscar's encounters with the closeted and their view of the world. Though he did not comment on the phenomenon in his extant letters written before prison, it is still possible to extrapolate from a few of his earlier remarks a distinct antipathy to the closeted life. Consider, for instance, Walter Pater, one of Oscar's early Aesthetic-period idols. Pater was utterly unlike Oscar and his flamboyant set; the *Dictionary of National Biography* tells of his "hatred of noise and extravagance of all kinds" and his "exceedingly quiet and even monotonous life" as an Oxford recluse who cohabited most of his adult life with his two sisters. Inevitably the idol/disciple phase ended, and Pater soon took, as O'Sullivan said, a "save me from my friends" attitude toward what he perceived as Oscar's flamboyant vulgarity. Though he expressed himself delighted with *Dorian Gray* some years later, he had urged that some obvious homosexual passages be deleted and refused to review it because it was "too dangerous." One can well imagine the stiff and proper Pater being nervous in the company of such a peacock as Oscar. O'Sullivan, in fact, recalled him once saying "something very severe about 'Mr Wilde,' as he called him, which I prefer to leave in darkness." When Oscar was told in 1894 that Pater had died, he said something that was also severe . . . perhaps his way of suggesting the considerable price of a life lived so resolutely in the Closet: "Was he ever alive?" Max Beerbohm made the same point, I suspect, when he remembered Pater as "a poor creature enough, from the standpoint of wholesome humanity" and as a man with a "timid and exacting soul."

Another infinitely more discreet homosexual, John Addington Symonds, reacted defensively to *Dorian Gray* when Oscar sent him a copy. Symonds wrote shortly after to a friend, "It is an odd and very audacious production, unwholesome in tone, but artistically and psychologically interesting. If the British public will stand this, they can stand anything. However, I resent the unhealthy, scented, mystic, congested touch which a man of this sort has on moral problems."

Henry James and Oscar—archetypes of the closeted and the queenly—also did not get on well, though Oscar did opine during his American tour that "no living English novelist" ranked with James and Howells. James came away from a Washington encounter convinced that " 'Hosscar' Wilde is a fatuous fool, tenth-rate cad . . . an unclean beast." To Boston's redoubtable Isabella Stewart Gardner James wrote dyspeptically of being present at a party with "the repulsive and fatuous Oscar" and being gratified that no one paid him any attention. Ten years later he was living in

Rye and vying with Oscar for fame as a London playwright; to his chagrin, his *Guy Domville* failed and was succeeded at the St. James's by *Earnest*. James continued to be dismissive of "the unspeakable one," as he called Oscar, and the "candid and primitive simplicity" of his plays. A perfect response to this swipe came some years later, when Oscar read *The Turn of the Screw*: "It is a most wonderful, lurid, poisonous little tale . . . I am greatly impressed by it. James is developing, but he will never arrive at passion, I fear." The discretion and passion, respectively, of the two personalities were of course bound to jar. Lord Illingworth's remark—"Nothing is serious except passion. The intellect is not a serious thing, and never has been"—is as damning a squelch of the fastidious Jamesian style (and of the Closet) as one could wish. James could hardly have enjoyed hearing Illingworth hold forth thus from his stalls seat at the Haymarket in 1893.

After his release from Reading Prison and exile to the Continent, where discretion was decidedly less necessary, Oscar's response to the timidities of the closeted changed from bemusement to annoyance. The presumption that evoked Oscar's impatience with the Closet—namely, that it invites one to renounce one's true identity—is notably evidenced in his response to the behavior of two acquaintances whose self-development was stymied by its narrow perimeters.

One was George Ives. It is a choice irony that Ives was the person who suggested that the circle of feisty homosexual Oxford undergraduates name their new magazine *The Chameleon*, for that animal could well be called the mascot of the Closet. Also ironic: Ives praising Oscar, in his deportment at his trials, as a man who "sticks to his colours." One of the very few times that Ives dared to display his own true colors in public occasioned a congratulation from Oscar himself. Ives, in 1894, had written to *The Humanitarian* attacking an essay by Grant Allen that argued for the free expression of sexuality, but only within the family. Ives asserted that the so-called New Hedonism must embrace all love and all pleasure, including, the implication was clear, homosexual pleasure. This view caused quite a stir. The *Review of Reviews* damned Ives's "dissertation in praise of unnatural vice" and suggested that "the New Morality" might have "gone elsewhere for its ideal than to Sodom and Gomorrah." This backlash discouraged Ives from any future gay polemics, but Oscar was quite delighted and cheered Ives on for igniting the *Review of Reviews* attack: "When the prurient and the impotent attack you, be sure you are right."

From this point on it was downhill for Oscar and Ives. When Ives finally learned how overtly gay the contents of *The Chameleon* were to be, he turned fearful . . . with good reason, as it happened. Oscar chided this craven retreat, reminding him of his stroke of valor in *The Humanitarian*: "You have thrown a bomb and [now] you object to a cracker. . . . It will do a great deal of harm—that is good." When Mr Justice Wills pronounced sentence on Oscar, Ives filled his diary with passionate outrage, but his public protest was perfect in its closeted obliqueness: he renounced operagoing while Oscar was in prison.

Though touched by Ives's failed effort to visit him in prison ("He is such a good fellow and so clever"), Oscar's meetings with Ives on the Continent in later years proved aggravating, mainly because of Ives's mania for discretion. For example, he sent Oscar a copy of a volume of poems called *Book of Chains*. One of them was a prose poem likening Oscar to a flower uprooted by a "common churl." Oscar might well have been pleased by the optimistic conclusion, which suggested that his martyrdom would in the end be a useful one:

> And the brute said, Now indeed this is stamped out, and this vile weed shall grow no more. But the fool had scattered the seed, and the wind took it up upon its wings and spread it over miles of land; and so that flower was multiplied.

But Oscar made it clear he was put off by the fact that Ives had published his book anonymously. He told Ross (note the acerbic "of course"), "George Ives has sent me his poems—of course without an inscription. His caution is amusing. He means well, which is the worst of it."

Late in 1899 Ives confessed in his diary that "we disagree in the philosophy of life." This would have been obvious to anyone who saw them together in the last Parisian months, Oscar taking whiskey and Ives milk. But what truly upset Oscar was Ives's inability to relax his Uranian soul in public. In February 1900, Ives wrote and asked to see Oscar, but not in so public a place as a café near the Hôtel d'Alsace. (Oscar was ashamed to receive visitors in his apartment there.) This ignited a burst of caustic fireworks; resentment had obviously been building for years. As one of Oscar's most vivid expressions of frustration over the pathologically closeted mentality, his deeply sarcastic letter to Ives deserves quotation at length:

My dear George . . .

Do, when again, if ever, you come to Paris let me know, and also let me know your address. Don't have with *me* the silly mania for secrecy that makes you miss the value of things: to you it is of more importance to conceal your address from a friend, than to see your friend.

You called on me twice, but would not leave either your name or address with the concierge: please don't do that again: I dislike to be told that a young man— you are still young of aspect [ouch! Ives was thirty-three]—called twice, and refused to give his name. It annoys me.

Also, when you send me a *petit bleu* to ask me to make an appointment with you, please put your address: otherwise I can't reply. I received your *dépêche* all right, but could not answer.

As regards seeing you in private in preference to seeing you in public, the matter is indifferent to me as far as the place is concerned. It is a pleasure to me to see you. . . . The ordinary meeting-places are clubs in

London and cafés in Paris. You must not imagine that people in cafés listen to the conversation of others; nobody bothers to do anything of the kind. People in life listen primarily to their own conversation, then to the conversation of the person or persons with whom they are, if the latter are interesting.

Your proposal that I should breakfast with you in a cabaret the other side of the Arc de Triomphe, frequented, you said, only by *cochers de fiacre* was too appalling. There are seemly inexpensive restaurants in proper quarters where two gentlemen can breakfast quietly, without the noisy and vulgar surroundings of your cabmen. . . .

I like to talk to you about literature, life, the progress of thought, its power to touch the world. . . . It is not necessary to go to a remote cabman's shelter for such discussions.

On the whole, George, you are a great baby. One can't help being angry with you. Ever yours

OSCAR

Ives apparently excused the lack of a return address and stood up for his cabmen's dive. Oscar fired off the following wicked squelch to his hopeless friend: "I know you *intended* to put your address in your telegram, but the habit, the bad habit, of secretiveness made you omit it. What a warning! . . . I have no doubt your little eating house, where the *cochers de fiacre* go, is delightful to you, but really George, it is hardly the place to invite others to. You should keep it as a private luxury, a cheap haven of unrest."

Oscar's last two notes to Ives were more sweet-tempered (in one he asked for £10) and tweaked Ives gently. "I will be charmed to see you in Paris, but you must come to proper, seemly restaurants," he wrote on 6 September. Two days later, on receipt of £5, he thanked his tedious friend and urged him, with a slight want of tact, to bring interesting company on his next visit:

"I hope you will come over soon, and not alone: but don't conceal your charming friends: you usually hide them from me."

The friendship with Ives, whom a student of his diaries called "a monumental bore," was not close. Nevertheless, contemplating this friendship leaves one in a bittersweet mood, simply because it stretched over several years. Oscar, after all, had aphorized once, "Friendship is far more tragic than love. It lasts longer." His friendship with another profoundly uneasy homosexual, however, was blessedly short. Oscar's letters chronicling the demise of this increasingly unhappy association move, hilariously, in the direction of high camp and display Oscar's best gallows humor. This friendship, to be sure, was one of convenience from the beginning. Oscar told Ross of the auspicious first meeting at Napoule in December of 1898: "A nice fellow called Harold Mellor, who is staying at Cannes, comes over constantly to see me. . . . He has a pretty Italian boy with him. They stayed last night at Napoule, and we had plum-pudding and Mellor ordered Pommery-Greno, so I kept Christmas pleasantly." Quite simply, Mellor was wealthy enough to afford champagne; Oscar wasn't.

A few weeks later, after making his remark about Henry James never arriving at passion, Oscar thought to mention being with Mellor for a few days. The implication is obvious: he was beginning to discover Mellor's identity as a Closet case in the Jamesian style. But, being poverty-stricken and eager to live cost-free for a time, Oscar nevertheless accepted Mellor's subsequent invitation to sojourn at his villa on Lake Geneva. So for the month of March 1899 he took what he would later call the "Mellor cure."

His droll correspondence from Gland makes the experience sound increasingly ghastly. By midmonth he sounded a bleak note to Ross, without explanation: "I don't like Mellor very much, and would like to get away, but, at present, it is impossible." In five days' time the horrible truth had dawned on him: he had accepted rustication with his utter opposite . . . a miser, a styleless bore, and a secretive homosexual. To Reggie Turner he vented his growing stir-craziness: "The villa is pretty and comfortable: but I

don't like Mellor: he is a silent, dull person, cautious, and economical: revolting Swiss wines appear at meals: he is complex
without being interesting: he has Greek loves, and is rather
ashamed of them: has heaps of money, and lives in terror of poverty." The same day, in a letter to a young man he had never met,
he sublimated his anger wittily: "I don't like Switzerland: it has
produced nothing but theologians and waiters." In another letter
written that day to his publisher, he reverted to bluntness:
"Mellor carries out the traditions of the ancient misers. If I ask
him to lend me five francs, he grows yellow and takes to his bed.
I discover some new fault in him daily."

Mellor's "most horrid Swiss *vin ordinaire*" sharpened Oscar's
tongue marvelously. On 21 March, perhaps having drunk several
glasses of the stuff, he wrote to Ross, "There is insanity in his
family. His mother is under restraint, and his brother went mad
and killed himself. His own insanity is misanthropy, and meanness. I am philosophic about it now; indeed we only meet at
meals. In the evening he reads *The Times*, or sleeps—both audi-
bly." By the twenty-seventh he divulged the ultimate insult to
hospitality: "Mellor keeps his own [cigarettes] carefully locked
up! All eccentricities are in some way or other interesting, except
meanness, and Mellor is too grotesque for words."

This harrowing, if inexpensive, month taught Oscar a painful truth, which he described to Ross on his last day *chez* Mellor:

> He really is too insane, and impossible. I never disliked
> anyone so thoroughly. My visit has taught me a curious
> and bitter lesson. I used to rely on my personality: now
> I know that my personality really rested on the fiction
> of *position*. Having lost position, I find my personality of
> no avail. Mellor has treated me as I would not have
> treated the most dull and unimportant of the lower
> middle-classes. I feel very humble, besides feeling very
> indignant: the former being my intellectual realisation
> of my position, the latter an emotion that is a 'survival'
> of old conditions.

The next morning an amicable and tearful parting was performed, and Oscar escaped with great relief to Genoa in search (he told Ross) of "a young lad, by name Edoardo Rolla, one of the sea-farers." And he added, "After the chill virginity of Swiss Alps and snow, I long for the red flowers of life that stain the feet of summer in Italy." It was also a gleeful escape from a claustrophobic month in the wrong country: the Closet. Oscar made this point in the last letter he posted from the villa; its salutation read:

> *Gland*
> *At the House of the Enemy*
> *Among the Cities of the Plain*

In the body of the letter Oscar invents this withering epitaph for his friendship with Mellor, referring to Molière's hypocrite and miser: "Tartuffe and Harpagon sum him up, though on too grand a scale."

Oscar's brief encounter with Mellor in Paris a year later made a perfect coda. Mellor, Oscar informed Ross, "is now in Paris with his slave Eolo, who like all slaves is most tyrannical. He and I are great friends. I think Harold is on the verge of acute melancholia. At present he has almost arrived at total abstinence—drinks and talks mineral waters. I like people who talk wine."

☆ ☆ ☆

OSCAR'S OBSERVATION OF "acute melancholia" in Mellor on seeing him for the last time is poignant. One cannot help feeling this was the same point Oscar had made, years earlier, when he told George Ives he was "morbid." It was, I think, his way of expressing his disapproval of those who become accomplices to the oppression of homosexuality. Typically, Oscar chose, in his remark to Ives, a word with two edges to it. For "morbid" and "morbidity" were at the time code words by which homosexuals were identified in Victorian England. It is "often charged" against homosexuality, wrote Edward Carpenter in 1894, that it is "essentially unnatural and *morbid* in character." Symonds, in 1890, had made the charge against *Dorian Gray*, criticizing its "morbid & perfumed manner of treating such psychological subjects."

Carpenter proceeded to demolish this stereotype in a remarkably modern-minded discussion in which he ridicules the temptation to label "anything a little exceptional" as "morbid" and pointing out that the most "purely scientific authorities" of the day (Moll, Krafft-Ebing) were the "least disposed to insist upon the theory of morbidity." As to the idea that homosexuality was caused by "nerve-degeneration" or "nervous troubles," he deftly suggested that "such troubles ought perhaps to be looked upon as the *results* rather than the causes of the inversion." He went on to describe the debilitating effects of the Closet in words not as eloquent, perhaps, as Oscar's on the Love that dare not speak its name in the Old Bailey but just as trenchant:

> It is difficult for outsiders not personally experienced in the matter to realize the great strain and tension of nerves under which those persons grow up from boyhood to manhood—or from girl to womanhood—who find their deepest and strongest instincts under the ban of the society around them; who before they clearly understand the drift of their own natures discover that they are somehow cut off from the sympathy and understanding of those nearest to them; and who know that they can never give expression to their tenderest yearnings of affection without exposing themselves to the possible charge of actions stigmatized as odious crimes. That such a strain . . . should cause nervous prostration or even mental disturbance is of course obvious.

Oscar, in his own way, was making precisely Carpenter's point. It was unlike him to tell others to change themselves, but neither was he inclined to suffer in silence when he found—as was the case with Ives and Mellor—that the closeted mentality and its at-tending morbidities affected his own comforts and pleasures.

It is worth noting that Oscar anticipated by a good four years Carpenter's attack on the code word "morbid." This was in "The Soul of Man Under Socialism." The essay came a year after all the innuendos of renegade sexuality spawned by *Dorian Gray*; it now seems impossible to read it as anything less than an attack on a culture that would make the Closet attractive to so many of Oscar's fellow Uranians. Again like Nietzsche, he reversed per-spectives wickedly, making the public and not the artist (i.e., the homosexual) the morbid party. The passage makes a most fitting finale simply because it finds Oscar emphasizing, once again, the fearless expression of the self, even in the face of a fully arrayed and hostile society:

> There is one other word that they [the public] use. That word is 'morbid.' . . . It is a ridiculous word to ap-ply to a work of art. For what is morbidity but a mood of emotion or a mode of thought that one cannot ex-press? The public are all morbid, because the public can never find expression for anything. *The artist is never morbid. He expresses everything.*

Chapter Sixteen

☆ ☆ ☆ ☆ ☆ ☆ ☆ ☆ ☆ ☆ ☆ ☆ ☆ ☆ ☆ ☆

PARIAH-DOG

I wish the world would let me alone.
—LETTER TO ERNEST DOWSON, 1897

I now live in echoes and have little music of my own.
—LETTER TO FRANCES FORBES-ROBERTSON, 1899

IN THE 1889 DIALOGUE "The Decay of Lying," Vivian declares, "Ours is certainly the dullest and most prosaic century possible. . . . The dreams of the great middle classes of this country . . . are the most depressing things that I have ever read. There is not even a fine nightmare among them." Once again, words from a former life to haunt Oscar Wilde. Far be it from him to do anything dull, prosaic, or—perish the thought—middle-class. His dream would prove a fine nightmare indeed: within a week of his arrest he would moan from Holloway Prison, "I am dazed with horror. Life has at last become to me as real as a dream."

The fine nightmare was interrupted for a moment in the

331

early morning of 19 May 1897, when Oscar was released by the authorities in London after an overnight stay in a nearby prison. More Adey and Stewart Headlam brought him to Headlam's house in Bloomsbury for breakfast. Oscar was delighted at his first taste of coffee in two years, and Headlam found him eager to talk about Dante and how best to study him. The Leversons came by, and Ada described the scene in her memoirs:

> We all felt intensely nervous and embarrassed. We had the English fear of showing our feelings, and at the same time the human fear of not showing our feelings. He came in, and at once he put us at our ease. He came in with the dignity of a king returning from exile. He came in talking, laughing, smoking a cigarette, with waved hair and a flower in his buttonhole, and he looked markedly better, slighter, and younger than he had two years previously. His first words were, "Sphinx, how marvellous of you to know exactly the right hat to wear at seven o'clock in the morning to meet a friend who has been away!"

In the evening he left England forever on a night boat bound for Dieppe. From there he wrote Ada the next day, "Dear Sphinx, I was so charmed with seeing you yesterday morning that I must write a line to tell you how sweet and good it was of you to be of the very first to greet me. When I think that Sphinxes are minions of the moon, and that you got up early before dawn, I am filled with wonder and joy."

And so, on this bittersweet note, began the period of three and a half years during which Oscar was to wander the Continent, like his mother in her last years a "leaning tower of courage." His new mood—and its attending melancholic humor—were perfectly reflected in the name he chose to travel under, Sebastian Melmoth: Sebastian from the saint of the persecuted, Melmoth from the itinerant romantic hero of Maturin's novel

Melmoth the Wanderer.
Those left in the world who cared about Oscar would have to accustom themselves to a new person. Jorge Luis Borges observed once that "the fundamental spirit of his work is joy," and this new person would often find himself obliged to explain—with varying degrees of sorrow and humor—"Neither to myself, nor others, am I any longer a joy."

Drawing by Walter Sickert of "Sebastian Melmoth" on his release from prison. From the collection of Mary Hyde, Viscountess Eccles.

These times were rife with pathos. After Oscar died, Ross made a shrewd précis of his last years for Adela Schuster: "Two things were absolutely necessary for him, contact with comely things, as Pater says, and social position. . . . Social position he realised after five months he could not have. . . . He chose therefore a Bohemian existence, entirely out of note with his genius and temperament." Oscar's own description of a typical Parisian day bears Ross out:

> I live a very ordinary life. I go to cafés like Pousset's where I meet artists and writers. I don't frequent places like the Café de la Paix. I dine in modest restaurants for two or three francs. My life is rather dull. I cannot flaunt or dash about: I have not got the money nor the clothes.

He was particularly eager to avoid embarrassing contact with the chic and haughty set he had once entertained. Thus, he explained to Reggie Turner his desire to avoid expensive trains on his release: "While I can sit at ease with the poor, I could not with the rich: for me to enter a first-class carriage containing other people would be dreadful: they would not like it, and I would know they would not. That would distress me." This reticence in the presence of his former "audience" was often remarked upon during this time. Adolphe Retté, for instance, described the last time he saw Oscar, in Paris: "His face had something humble and penitent about it which distressed me. He held his hand out timidly, as if he feared people would not take it. It was a painful sight."

The life of "the pariah-dog of the nineteenth century," as he called himself, was filled with vignettes of exquisite humiliation. The former Lord of Language wrote his publisher from Italy, "I have no note-paper, and no money to buy any, so I write to you on foolscap." Lodgings he could afford were dismal. He complained from Paris of being in "a poor little Bohemian hotel, only suited for those Sybarites who are exiled from Sybaris." He was speaking, it happens, of the Hôtel d'Alsace, in which he would die two years later. (Ironically, its kind, generous, sympathetic *propriétaire*, Edouard Dupoirier, was to become a chief angel during his guest's final decline.) Ross caught Oscar in a lie, and he replied, "My dear Robbie, I am so sorry about my excuse. I had forgotten I had used Nogent before. It shows the utter collapse of my imagination." Cigarettes he continued to smoke, but the taste of champagne haunted him. It is "now a strange luxury, occasionally . . . offered to me by devoted friends: if it is not, I always ask for it." Whenever Harold Mellor ordered a bottle of Pommery for him, Oscar wrote, "the exquisite taste of ancient life comes back to me."

In early 1899 he found himself at the Hôtel Terminus in Monte Carlo. Was this, one wonders, where he stayed with Bosie on that reckless trip in April 1895 . . . and did he recall, as he registered, Lady Bracknell's astonishment at "persons whose origin was a Terminus"? In any case, he reported to Harris, "The middle-class English who are at the hotel have objected to my presence, and this morning I was presented with my bill and requested to leave by twelve o'clock." He refused, partly out of pride but mainly because he hadn't the money (he pawned a ring for ten francs to raise the sum).

Oscar was writing to Harris to beg for money. The bankruptcy of his literary estate, his inability to earn money, and the small £3-a-week allowance from Constance (stopped for a time when she learned he was again in Bosie's company) all conspired to make Oscar at first, in Harris's words, "cunning in the art of getting money without asking for it" and later expert in frontal assaults. He who estimated he had spent £5,000 on Bosie in less than three years now had to become thoroughly attentive to the most minute sums. This did not suit him: "I never could understand mathematics, and life is now a mathematical problem. When it was a romantic one, I solved it—too well." The practical result in his daily life he related to a young friend from Paris: "I am always worried by that mosquito, money; bothered about little things, such as hotel-bills, and the lack of cigarettes and little silver *francs* . . . my soul is made mean by sordid anxieties. It is a poor ending, but I had been accustomed to purple and gold."

It had not been always thus. Ada Leverson called him "the most generous man I have ever met," and, in a curious way, two alms-giving episodes demonstrate the abyss that lay between Oscar "before" and Oscar "after." The first, recalled by Richard Le Gallienne, offers vintage Oscarian comedy. As the two strolled in the Haymarket a beggar asked for money, saying he had no work and no bread to eat.

"Work!" said Wilde. "Why should you want to work? And bread! Why should you eat bread?"

Then, after an elaborate pause, he continued, putting his hand good-naturedly on the tatterdemalion's shoulder:

"Now, if you had come to me and said that you had work to do, but you couldn't dream of working, and that you had bread to eat, but couldn't think of eating

335

bread—I would have given you half-a-crown."—
Another pause—"As it is, I give you two shillings."

So Wilde, with his accustomed generosity, made
the poor fellow happy and had his own little joke in the
bargain.

Oscar detested Rudyard Kipling, but Kipling had the perfect
phrase for such a performance: juice de spree.

Just how drastically pariahdom drained Oscar of such juice is
suggested in an anecdote recorded by Vincent O'Sullivan. As he
walked with him along the streets of Naples in December 1897,
"one of those tragic beggars of Naples arose in a doorway where
he had been crouching and held out his hand." But there was to
be no performance this evening: a stricken look came over his
face, he gave the man some money, and as they walked on Oscar
was heard to murmur in English, "You wretched man, why do you
beg when pity is dead?" "From that hour," O'Sullivan added, "I
felt that the inexorable curtain had begun to fall."

In the light of this Neapolitan encounter, the following passage from the memoirs of Nellie Melba, describing a chance
meeting with Oscar the next year, is filled with pathos:

> I was walking one morning along the streets of Paris,
> three years after the *débâcle,* when there lurched round
> the corner a tall shabby man, his collar turned up to his
> neck, a hunted look in his eyes. I was about to pass on,
> when he stopped.
>
> "Madame Melba—you don't know who I am? I'm Os-
> car Wilde," he said, "and I'm going to do a terrible
> thing. I'm going to ask you for money."
>
> I could hardly bear to look at him, not from hatred
> but from shame and pity. I took all I had from my
> purse—about ten louis—and he quickly took it—almost
> snatched it—muttered a word of thanks and was gone.
> I never saw him again.

☆ ☆ ☆

ALSO SHOCKING TO PRACTICALLY everyone but Oscar was the nearly total cessation of his writing. Just two days before his release, he wrote about several friends he had made in Reading prison: *"They take their punishment so well, so cheerfully: I go out with an adder in my heart, and an asp in my tongue."* This prediction is, in general, not borne out in his relations with his friends and by the tone of his post-prison letters. Ross's postmortem is more accurate: "Among his many fine qualities he showed in his later years was that he never blamed anyone but himself for his own disasters. He never bore any ill-will to anybody." And yet . . . the asp and the adder may have been present nevertheless. Their presence may explain why Oscar—whose works, the asp-stung *Ballad of Reading Gaol* aside, have so little of the adder in them—never touched his pen as an artist again. Except for the *Ballad*, published in 1898, his last five years brought just two "publications," letters to the editor of the *Daily Chronicle* on prison reform.

Well-meaning friends urged a lucrative return of "our Oscar," the comedian of old. They were unaware—or simply unwilling to admit—that, as Celia says in *As You Like It*, "was" is not "is." Oscar was repeatedly obliged to remind them of this fact in his letters. Free less than a month, he admitted, "I no longer make *roulades* of phrases about the deep things I feel . . . violin-variations don't interest me." A few months later he explained to Carlos Blacker that he had "been obliged to decline [actor-manager Charles] Wyndham's offer. I simply have no heart to write clever comedy." With Frank Harris the next year he tried bravado ("Why should I write any more? I have done enough for fame") and, when that did not work, terrible bleakness: "As regards a comedy, my dear Frank, I have lost the mainspring of life and art. . . . I am going under: the morgue yawns for me. I go and look at my zinc-bed there." The next month, to Blacker, he phrased the extinction of his pen in more purple fashion, referring to the *Ballad* as "my *chante de cygne*. . . . I am sorry to leave with a cry of pain—a song of Marsyas, not a song of Apollo; but Life, that I loved so much—too much—has torn me like a tiger, so when you come and see me, you will see the ruin and wreck of what was once wonderful and brilliant, and terribly improbable."

Amid the ruin and wreck, to be sure, shafts of Oscarian humor still emerged now and then, refracted though they always were through a dark glass. A few months after his release, he wrote, "Tragedy and comedy are so mixed in my life now that I lose the sense of difference," and this was to remain true until the day he died. A typical seriocomic story concerned his regaining his former excess weight. For long "a three-decanter man," he drank even more in these years. One Paris acquaintance recalled that "at the drinking suggestion of any stranger he would run and swallow eagerly a large glass of absinthe. . . . Absinthe was his one remaining emotion, and for absinthe he would have hobnobbed with a porter." Shaw, with his usual merciless candor, called him in his last years an "unproductive drunkard and swindler." This regimen, combined with so much time spent, as Oscar admitted, "earnestly idling," led him to regain his former excess weight. When Ross offered him a new suit from his old London tailor, Oscar wittily accepted: "People who repent in sackcloth are dreary, but those who repent in a suit by Doré, and intend the suit for another, are worthy of Paradise. . . . A rather painful fact, apparent to all, must now be disclosed. Pray mention it to no one but Doré, and break it to him gently. I am distinctly stouter than I was when the last suit was made." The professions felt, as usual, his dart. "I enclose what seems a legal document," he wrote to Ross, adding, "I judge solely from its want of style." As for doctors, a letter to Reggie a few days later suggests that his old knack for paradox was not utterly extinct: "I should go and see my doctor today, but I don't like to, as I am not feeling very well. I only care to see doctors when I am in perfect health; then they comfort one, but when one is ill they are most depressing."

As Oscar's various diseases progressed, Harris thought that

THIS

TO

THIS?

he kept "his joyous humor and charming gaiety" to the last. When psoriasis caused him to scratch constantly, he exclaimed to Ross, "Really, I am more like a great ape than ever; but I hope you'll give me lunch, Bobbie, and not a nut." (The joke might have reminded Oscar of the cartoon titled "Mr Wild of Borneo" the *Washington Post* published on 22 January 1882, with the caption: "We present in close juxtaposition the pictures of Mr Wilde of England and a citizen of Borneo, who, so far as we have any record of him, is also Wild, and judging from the resemblance in feature, pose and occupation, undoubtedly akin.") To one visitor he quipped, "My wallpaper and I are fighting a duel to the death. One or the other of us has to go." Late in February 1900, Ross was informed, "I am now *neurasthenic*. My doctor says I have all the symptoms. It is comforting to have them *all*, it makes one a perfect type."

On 1 November 1900, Oscar's doctor took Ross aside and warned him that the patient had at most five years to live if he did not completely alter his dissolute habits. Ross talked "straightly" with Oscar about this conversation the next day and recalled, "He of course laughed and said he could never outlive the century as the English people would not stand it, that he was already responsible for the failure of the [Parisian centennial]

Exhibition, as English people on seeing him there had gone away."

Humor even crept onto his deathbed in a macabre way, though Oscar must have been beyond appreciating it. Ross, a devout Catholic, took it upon himself to call a Passionist Father to the bedside for a conversion *in articulo mortis*. The patient's consciousness was necessary for administration of the last sacraments, but this lay in some doubt. To taste the drollery of what happened we must recall that Oscar was the nineteenth century's most famous and ardent smoker of cigarettes. Nellie Melba had once performed research and discovered *six* cigarette cases on his person. Well, the sanguine priest finally saw a happy sign that the dying sinner was mentally competent: "I was if anything more convinced as to his inward consciousness when, in my presence, one of the attendants offered him a cigarette which he took into his fingers and raised to his face, although, in the attempt to put it between his lips, he failed."

Oscar's pagan gods, with this last sarcastic fillip to add to his denouement, must have looked down and laughed at the good father leaning over the bed and thus taking heart.

☆ ☆ ☆

SOMETHING ELSE BESIDES OSCAR'S sense of humor failed to change in his last years: his youth was beyond recall, but he could still have his youths.

If there was some notion that penal servitude would encourage Oscar to reform his pederastic vice, it was a spectacular failure. As he had so often done, Oscar anticipated an important event in his life in something he had published: in 1890 he had said there was "no doubt that reformation is a much more painful process than punishment." About his reckless life *in general* Oscar was often eloquent in his self-reproaches, regretting "the endless hunger for pleasures that wreck the body and imprison the soul" and lashing his conscience for all the past "days of gilded infamy—my Neronian hours, rich, profligate, cynical, material-istic." But the *way* he was reckless he still considered to be nobody's business but his own.

On this he was adamant. Criticism from England of his re-newed association with Bosie drew this indignant response: "A patriot put in prison for loving his country loves his country, and a poet in prison for loving boys loves boys. To have altered my life would have been to have admitted that Uranian love is igno-ble. I hold it to be noble—more noble than other forms." He was disgusted at the implication that he would be welcomed back for his "airy mood and spirit," but only if a conversion of his sexual preference could be extorted from him. To Harris he wrote, "I be-lieve they would like me to edit prayers for those at sea, or to re-cant the gospel of the joy of life in a penny tract. They do not see that only the utterly worthless can be reformed." (This was merely a variation on Lord Darlington's remark seven years earlier: "Ah! you are beginning to reform me. It is a dangerous thing to reform any one, Lady Windermere.") Even when Ross, one of Oscar's oldest and most loyal gay friends, remonstrated with him over his recreations, he reacted in his usual blithe spirit: "It is quite true that when you talk morals to me, which you do quite beautifully, I always pipe on a reed and a faun comes run-ning out of the thicket. You at once say, 'What a lovely faun!' The rest is silence."

And many a faun came at his beck, though now francs or lire rather than charismatic celebrity were more likely to draw them from their thickets. Letters to his gay friends from this time are peppered with witty gossip about his adventures. "Do you re-member the young Corsican at the Restaurant Jouffroy? His posi-tion was menial, but eyes like the night and a scarlet flower of a mouth made one forget that: I am great friends with him. His name is Giorgio: he is a most passionate faun." Of another in-fatuation he wrote, "The curves of his mouth are a source of end-less wonder and admiration to me. Out of such a mouth I would drink Lethe in this world and in the next ambrosia." A few months later he reported from the Hôtel des Bains in Napoule,

"The inhabitants have beautiful eyes, crisp hair of a hyacinth colour, and no morals—an ideal race."

In March 1898, on his way to Harold Mellor's Swiss villa, he stopped in Genoa and spent three days with "a beautiful young actor" he picked up there. No wonder, beside himself from Mellor's tedious company ten days later, he was thinking of leaving expensive Paris to find a place "near Genoa, where I can live for ten francs a day (boy *compris*)." But a few weeks later, back in Paris, he told Ross of making friends with "a charming American youth, expelled from Harvard for immoral conduct! He is very amusing and good-looking." The Harvard boy had competition, though, as a nickname-filled missive the same month suggests: "Casquette is well, and has a blue suit. Edmond de Goncourt has returned from prison and shows himself on the Boulevard in a straw hat. I am still devoted to Le Premier Consul, but I also love a young Russian called Maltchek Perovinski, aged eighteen."

The Roman spring of Oscar's last year produced some particularly droll correspondence. The purpose of his visit was decidedly different from that of Tannhäuser, the famous Wagnerian penitent to whom Oscar had occasionally referred with tongue in cheek. He wrote to Ross, "I have given up Armando, a very smart elegant young Roman Sporus [a favorite of Nero]. He was beautiful, but his requests for raiment and neckties were incessant; he really bayed for boots, as a dog moonwards. I now like Arnaldo." Within days, however, Ross must have been amused to receive Oscar's report of a papal audience with Leo XIII: "I gave a ticket to a new friend, *Dario*. I like his name so much: it was the first time he had ever seen the Pope: and he transferred to me his adoration of the successor of Peter: would I fear have kissed me on leaving the Bronze Gateway had I not sternly repelled him. I have become very cruel to boys, and no longer let them kiss me in public." After visiting Naples and Switzerland, Oscar was by early September back in Paris and feeling nostalgic for cisalpine pleasure: "My dear Neapolitans have returned to Naples and I miss that brown faun with his deep woodland eyes and his sensuous grace of limb. A slim brown Egyptian, rather like a handsome bamboo walking-stick, occasionally serves me drinks at the Café d'Ègypte, but he does not console me for the loss of the wanton sylvan boy of Italy."

In 1893, two years before the troubles, Pierre Louÿs, his French friend and the dedicatee of the original French version of *Salome*, confronted Oscar over his relationship with Bosie, his flamboyant coterie, and his treatment of his family. Oscar refused to back down and ended up saying good-bye. "I wanted a friend; now I shall have nothing but lovers," he told Louÿs. That sad prophecy turned out to be accurate: by "friend" of course he meant a true lover, and by "lovers" he meant sexual partners. Before the fall his charming conceits, musical voice, and celebrity—if not his physical attractiveness—were able to secure his desires. In the years following his release, he was more often obliged to buy affection.

This *modus operandi* prevailed for the rest of his life. He said to Frank Harris in prison, "I shall be very lonely when I come out, and I can't stand loneliness and solitude; it is intolerable to me, hateful, I have had too much of it." A man so desperate for companionship was bound to let the cash nexus become ever more blatant as his physical, intellectual, and spiritual decline progressed—and as nubile young men became less eager to offer themselves *gratis* in exchange for his charming badinage. "My companions are such as I can get," he wrote from a tavern in the Boulevard des Italiens in May 1898, "and I of course have to pay for such friendships." As the end neared, he explained himself movingly, mournfully in a letter to Ross: "I have fallen in and out of love, and fluttered hawks and doves alike. How evil it is to buy Love, and how evil to sell it! And yet what purple hours one can snatch from that grey slowly-moving thing we call Time! My mouth is twisted with kissing, and I feed on fevers."

☆ ☆ ☆

THERE IS MUCH CANDOR, pain, and mortification in Oscar's letters from his last three years. With a little imagination, much more can be read between their lines. But what, finally, was his state of mind in these last years? As with practically every important question about Oscar's later life, the best answer lies in something he had written years before. Ten years earlier, in "The Critic as Artist," Gilbert—speaking in Oscar's inimitably seigneurial voice—pontificates on life:

> When one looks back upon the life that was so vivid in its emotional intensity, and filled with such fervent moments of ecstasy or of joy, it all seems to be a dream and an illusion. What are the unreal things, but the passions that once burned one like fire? What are the incredible things, but the things that one has faithfully believed? What are the improbable things? The things that one has done oneself . . . life cheats us with shadows, like a puppet-master. We ask it for pleasure. It gives it to us, with bitterness and disappointment in its train . . . we find ourselves looking with callous wonder, or dull heart of stone, at the tress of gold-flecked hair that we had once so wildly worshipped and so madly kissed.

The premonitions in that last sentence of Oscar's subsequent descriptions of Bosie are particularly haunting: his being "gold-haired, like an angel" and his lips being made for the "madness of kisses," and (in the most bizarre pun of his career) Oscar's worshipping "wildly" his "golden-haired boy with Christ's own heart." Surely the passage catches the essence of Oscar's pariah mood. It is a breathtakingly accurate, if unwitting, prophecy and would have left even the Sibyl of Mortimer Street awestruck.

Chapter Seventeen

☆ ☆ ☆ ☆ ☆ ☆ ☆ ☆ ☆ ☆ ☆ ☆ ☆ ☆ ☆ ☆

WILDESHAWSHOW

Your wildeshaweshowe moves swiftly sterneward!
—JAMES JOYCE, *FINNEGANS WAKE*

Great antipathy shews secret affinity.
—OSCAR WILDE

WILLIAM BUTLER YEATS THOUGHT that, if no catastrophe had occurred in 1895, Bernard Shaw and Oscar Wilde would have "long divided the stage between them." He added, however, that "they were most unlike—for Wilde believed himself to value nothing but words in their emotional associations, and he had turned his style to a parade as though it were his show, and he Lord Mayor." Shaw, to the contrary, valued words as weapons to be rigorously deployed in political trench warfare. They were for nothing so superfluous as a Lord Mayor's ceremonial procession, but rather for harangues from the speaker's platform, Fabian Society debates, or mercilessly clever letters to the editor. James Joyce also emphasized the radical dissimilarity of Shaw and Wilde by associating them with another literary odd couple: Laurence Sterne, the gentle, eccentric fantasist and philanderer who wrote *Tristram Shandy*, and Jonathan Swift, the ferocious ironist of *Gulliver's Travels*.

Yeats's remark sets the mind off in agreeable contemplation of the "what if" of a few decades' theatrical rivalry between the two inimitable Irishmen. What a lively show Wilde and Shaw would have produced, had they been able to joust in splendid, blandishing tandem for more than the mere two years together on the London theatrical scene that were allotted to them. Oscar boasted to Shaw that they constituted the "great Celtic School" of drama, declaring *Lady Windermere's Fan* Opus 1 and Shaw's *Widowers' Houses* Opus 2 (both opened in 1892). Had Queensberry not left his goading card at the Albemarle, perhaps Oscar's jest might have been turned into a reality. As it was, they reached only Opus 8 or so.

Their comedy team, like most others, would have thrived in part by the hilarious oddness of the couple they made. The briefest highlighting of their dominant traits suggests a kind of Alpha-and-Omega polarity in their personalities. Oscar, we know, detested good advice and people who dispense it; Shaw told all and sundry what was good for them with manic glee. This tendency toward an "infernal meddlesomeness" he cheerfully confessed: "What infuriates people is my incorrigible habit of constituting myself, uninvited, their solicitor, their doctor, and their spiritual director without the smallest delicacy. . . . I treat every one sympathetically as an invalid, injudicious in diet, politically foolish, probably intemperate, more or less mendacious and dishonest; and, however friendly my disposition and cheerful my way of putting it, they don't like it. I can't help it." (Shaw admitted this after asking an actor friend pointblank whether he was addicted to morphia!) Oscar was constitutionally languid; Shaw was possessed by "the mere habit of energy," which, he said, often turned him into nothing more than "a writing and talking machine." The self-appointed tempo of his frantic daily work routine was a vigorous *presto vivace* (his key D-flat major). Oscar's tempo was more on the order of a *lento molto;* he was a famous loller and admitted in a letter to Shaw himself, "I am lazy." Both men despised the Censorship, but their different responses to it were characteristic: when *Salome* was banned Oscar threatened airily to emigrate to France (but didn't budge) and scattered a few one-line barbs. Shaw, with far more deliberate energy, wrote more than fifty articles against censorship over his lifetime, along with an unremitting blizzard of speeches and letters to newspapers. (Shaw, by the way, wrote to Wilde after *Salome* was banned from the stage, "I have always said that the one way of abolishing the Censor is to abolish the Monarchy of which he is an appendage.")

Oscar on many occasions praised purposelessness and condemned "useful" professions. He was decidedly of Algy's view in *Earnest*: "I don't mind hard work where there is no definite object of any kind." Shaw was arguably the most relentlessly useful figure of this or the preceding century. Oscar asserted in the Old Bailey that no proper work of art has "views" to put forth: "Views belong to people who are not artists." But views "belonged" to Shaw in relentless abundance, artistry be damned if need be. He required views to express as most people require oxygen. "Every play, every preface I wrote conveys a message," he admitted; "I am the messenger boy of the new age." Though Oscar possessed a social conscience, he was seldom driven to parade it publicly. A notable exception were his letters to the editor of the *Daily Chronicle* on prison reform, written after his own release from Reading: they are his only writings that could be called Shavian. On the other hand, Shaw, who defined a social conscience as the "instinctive habit of never acting or even thinking without reference to the opinions and welfare of millions of other men," was a whirling dervish of earnest argumentation in the service of such a conscience. Oscar's notion that "it is only the intellectually lost who ever argue" Shaw laughed to scorn. In a self-interview that appeared in 1892, Shaw put a fine point on their different ways by observing that Wilde "wrote for the stage as an artist. I am simply a propagandist."

Aiming to capture the essence of Shavian earnestness, Max Beerbohm devised a fine simile that bears, as it happens, on Oscar, too. Of Shaw's early unsuccessful novel, *Cashel Byron's Profession*, Beerbohm wrote:

> All through the book we hear the loud, rhythmic machinery of his brain at work. The book vibrates to it as does a steamer to the screw; and we, the passengers, rejoice in the sound of it, for we know that tremendous speed is being made. As a passage by steam is to a voyage by sail, so is Mr Shaw's fiction to true fiction. A steamboat is nice because it takes us quickly to some destination; a sailing-yacht is nice in itself, nice for its own sake.

Shaw doubtless read these lines without a glimmer of repentance, for, as he later told Tolstoy, "I am not an 'Art for Art's sake' man, and would not lift my finger to produce a work of art if I thought there were nothing more than that in it." Beerbohm, in expressing the appeal of art that exists for art's sake, might well have invoked any of Oscar's numerous urgings of the priority of "being" over "doing" in art . . . of art that is "nice for its own sake." He might also have suggested that, perfect as the steamship image is for the carefully engineered, propulsive Shavian style, the slower, more serendipitously zigzag and graceful movement of a sailing ship aptly captures the Oscarian ethos. One thing is certain: Oscar would have expressed exactly Beerbohm's view of *Cashel Byron's Profession*, if it had appeared during his book-chat years at *Woman's World*. For in one of his columns (in 1889) he complained, "Many of our novelists are really pamphleteers, reformers masquerading as story-tellers, earnest sociologists seeking to mend as well as to mirror life." A perfect description of Shaw.

Another way to make something like Beerbohm's point from a different perspective is to notice how Shaw and Oscar, respectively, take after Don Juan and the Devil in Shaw's *Man and Superman*. Both characters are disgusted by the complacencies of

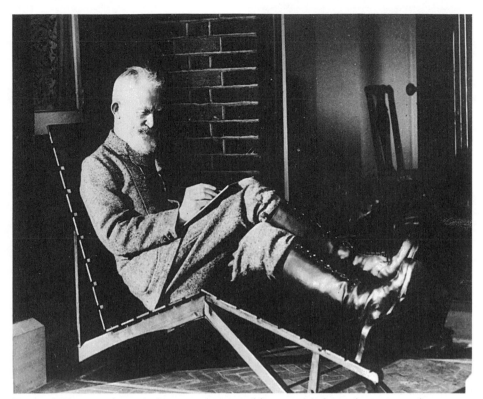

Bernard Shaw, in his usual attire on a suitably spartan chaise longue, at about the time he finally allowed publication of his first novel, *Immaturity*. Photograph from the Huntington Library, San Marino, California.

Victorian morality, but each responds differently. The Devil is described in terms oddly reminiscent of Oscar: "He does not inspire much confidence in his powers of hard work or endurance, and is, on the whole a disagreeably self-indulgent looking person." A true Oscarian and pessimist at heart, the Devil prefers to confront the appalling mores of the day with playful fantasy. Frank Harris, in his very plausible summary of Oscar's "attitude towards life," also suggested that he took the path of Shaw's Devil. After quoting Goethe's creed that "a man must resolve to live not only for the Good and Beautiful, but for the Common Weal," Harris said, "Oscar did not push his thought into such transcendental regions." Don Juan, on the other hand, is a true Shavian optimist and opts for the "work" of impelling humanity to evolve—"the work of helping Life in its struggle upward." It is precisely in this arena, as G. K. Chesterton believed, that Shaw was at his greatest and most wholly admirable: "Socialism . . . is the noblest thing for Bernard Shaw; and it is the noblest thing in him. . . . He cares more for the Public Thing than for any private thing."

These are all, of course, the grand diameter lines that measure the distance separating Bernard from Oscar. Other dissimilarities are more mundane, though often telling. Their very physiognomies must have made a match on a par with Laurel and Hardy: Oscar with his round, fleshy boyish head and Shaw with, as one woman described it, the "face of an outlaw . . . wild and determined, a very brigand of a face." Though at just under six feet Shaw was a few inches shorter than Oscar, his taut, slender body was in striking contrast with Oscar's girth (which a New York tailor measured, in 1882, at thirty-eight and a half inches at the waist, seventeen inches at the neck).

Vastly different diets accounted for much of the disparity. A vocal and notorious vegetarian and avoider of spirits, Shaw's "temperance-beverage face" so entranced and appalled Beerbohm that he drew more than forty caricatures of it. Oscar's face showed him very well known in Sybaris, and also proved for Beerbohm a caricaturist's delight. Also vastly different were their notions of exercise. When an interviewer ventured to observe, "Exercise is such a good thing," Oscar retorted, "Exercise! The only possible form of exercise is to talk." Shaw, however, swam a daily hundred laps or so at the Royal Automobile Club when he was in London and thought nothing of thirty-mile bicycle rides, long walks, and wood-sawing when in the country.

Clothing made them exquisitely different, too. Oscar's flamboyant finery—silk linings, ruffs, capes, low patent-leather shoes, and so on—could not have differed more from the ostentatiously "practical" ensembles in which Shaw usually paraded in public. Most famous was a woolen suit designed by the guru of sanitation Dr Gustave Jaeger, who condemned vegetable dyes and linen and silk while exalting flannel. This brown Jaeger suit, G. K. Chesterton observed, became indelibly part of Shaw's public image, "as if it were a sort of reddish brown fur . . . like the hair and eyebrows, a part of the animal." Shaw's "much ridiculed jaegerism" (as he called it) was as calculated in its way as Oscar's theory of dress. Michael Holroyd made this point when he said that the Jaeger uniform was "the Shavian equivalent to Oscar Wilde's aesthetic costumes." The Jaeger ensemble, by the way, did include the knee-breeches so favored by Oscar in his Aesthetic ensembles, and Shaw wore them well into his seventies. Though Shaw often appeared in expensive, well-tailored suits for social occasions, he worked hard to present a public posture of disdain for the frivolities of sartorial fashion. Oscar, of course, put these frivolities on a high altar. A disdain for sartorial preciosity helps to explain why Shaw admired William Morris as the most serious man among the leaders of the Aesthetic Movement, for he was quite the dowdiest of them. Oscar, predictably, chided Morris (from the safe distance of Salt Lake City) for proclaiming the doctrine of artistic dress but wearing "the very shabbiest and ugliest of nineteenth century clothes."

Oscar's tastes for luxury made him a highly delighted and delightful visitor to France, which Shaw said in 1922 he had written off as "a dud country years ago." Shaw's explanation for his failure as an author in France, I think, suggests why the Oscarian style fared so much better there: "I have given up all hope of getting into touch with France. . . . Every attempt I have made has been baffled on the ground that it would offend French susceptibilities; and as my journalistic tactics are nothing but attacks on susceptibilities—whether English, Irish, or American makes no difference—to insist on my respecting French susceptibilities is to silence me completely." Finding barley water preferable to champagne and having no use for the French literary scene (he said he avoided "literary and artistic society like the plague"), Shaw was bound to have little use for the City of Light. In March 1906 he wrote to his Austrian theatrical agent—his plays were highly successful in the German-speaking theater—"My wife insists on dragging me to Paris for twelve days at Easter so that Rodin may make a bust of me!!!!!"

Their respective samplings of the pleasures of Algeria were

also characteristic. Oscar, in 1895, reveled in all the indolent luxuries of hotel life, boys, and hashish. Shaw, on holiday in 1909 touring with his wife, Charlotte, in their car, drove furiously for hundreds of miles, found it "a demoralizing country," and exploded regularly over time lost from his writing: "I am shockingly off any work but driving."

GBS, then: open-faced, exasperating, admirably public-spirited, all his works leaving (said Borges) the flavor of "liberation." Oscar: disingenuous, charming, magnificently selfish, and his works leaving (also said Borges) the flavor of "joy." GBS the rostrum-thumping forensic pyrotechnician; Oscar, the sedentary café raconteur and causeur. GBS the incorrigibly déclassé ("I sing my own class: the Shabby Genteel, the Poor Relations"); Oscar the regular nibbler on the upper crust (Shaw thought him "a snob to the marrow of his bones"). GBS the famously emphatic (he once began a letter, "It is utterly totally completely entirely absolutely positively emphatically and finally stark staring smash bang impossible . . ."); Oscar the lounger, who practically never raised his voice in dudgeon. GBS, the rumbustious, unclubbable, self-styled crank, whose contempt for *belles lettres,* said Holroyd, "made him into a Man of Derision"; Oscar the eminently sociable virtuoso of the salon, light-penned belletrist, and Man of Delight. Could a drawing room—or London—possibly have contained both of them without spontaneous combustion?

THE ANSWER, SURPRISINGLY, is yes. This, it seems, was mainly because the two Irish peacocks had the good sense to leave each other largely to their own devices, though they might have met regularly as writers for some of the same periodicals, like *The Fortnightly* and the *Pall Mall Gazette.* Even though they barely knew each other personally, Shaw was nevertheless able to produce many years later one of the most vivid and provocative summations of Oscar's character ever composed. This essay began as a letter to Frank Harris, written just after Shaw had read the manuscript of Harris's book on Oscar. In due course the letter became an appendix in the book (with both Harris and Shaw trading pot-shots in footnotes).

In these "Memories of Oscar Wilde" Shaw said he doubted that they met more than a dozen times and could definitely rec-ollect only six of them. As sometimes happens when two vivid personalities cross paths, they both turned shy and awkward. Their first meeting, at one of Lady Wilde's salons ("desperate af-fairs," said Shaw), seems to have set the tone for their acquain-tance: "He came and spoke to me with an evident intention of being especially kind to me. We put each other out frightfully; and this odd difficulty persisted between us to the very last." That a certain element of jealousy on Shaw's part underlay the tension between them is likely. After all, Oscar had made his London ce-lebrity splash within a year or two of his arrival in late 1878 at age twenty-four. Shaw, two years Oscar's junior, had a much, much longer Unknown Period, having arrived in 1876 at age twenty. All his novels had sunk sternly and swiftly from sight, and for many years he was more notorious than famed as a ubiquitous platform speaker and rambunctious music critic. It was not until 1911, when he was fifty-five, that he had his first long-run theat-rical success, *Fanny's First Play*. Hesketh Pearson even remem-bered that Shaw "really disliked Wilde, of whom, I believe, he was also jealous, because the only time I noticed real hostility to-wards a fellow being in Shaw's manner and speech was when we were discussing his famous fellow-countryman."

A very early suggestion of this jealousy may be the character of the fashionable poet Patrick Hawkshaw in Shaw's first, and long-unpublished, novel, *Immaturity*. In a 1921 preface for its first publication, Shaw said that many of its characters "owed some-thing to persons I had met," but he added that only one, the pet-ulant artist Cyril Scott, was based on a figure known to the public (Cecil Lawson). Perhaps Shaw was here being strictly accurate: Oscar had been in London less than a year when the novel was completed on 28 September 1879 and was by then only a Chelsea-wide celebrity. Or perhaps, Shaw's jealousy long since annulled, he was in 1921 no longer of a mind to sully the memory of his long-gone compatriot. (Hawkshaw becomes a reprehensible bankrupt—prophetic touch!—toward the novel's end.)

But numerous details of Hawkshaw's characterization combine to give us, virtually to the life, the Oscar of his first London years. He is a "young man" but already a "celebrity"—known for sonnets inspired by "pagan deities." One bears the title "The New Endymion." A very proper character in the novel (doubtless a *Punch* reader) thinks him "a puppy" and finds "a good deal of blatherumskite" in his poems: the same judgments that were to greet Oscar's *Poems* in 1881. Hawkshaw is (unlike the novel's very shy central character—obviously Shaw himself) extravagantly idle and at ease in the late-afternoon salon. In one bit of dialogue full of portent, he is asked whether he is earnest: "I am always in earnest until three o'clock, when I assume my cap, bells and [calling-]card case." He moves with "languid grace" and exudes a "careless gaiety." Industry is not to his taste: the word "work" makes him shudder; he prefers writing sonnets to epics, and even does that (as Oscar did) in brief fits. He is perfectly happy to receive visitors before noon in bed.

Also pure Oscar-to-come is Hawkshaw's remark, "What an accursed thing it is to have relatives!" The poet pleasures himself in a "skill in composing pretty phrases," indulges social snobbery, and "studies to conciliate society" with extreme politeness— precisely as Oscar did. Shaw was in later years particularly aggravated by Oscar's dilettantism, and Hawkshaw is decidedly a dilettante, especially in musical matters, and expert at duping his public.

There is no record of Shaw's actually meeting Oscar before finishing *Immaturity,* and Hawkshaw's "slight" figure is most unlike Oscar's. But Shaw might well have been aware of Oscar's presence and even seen him from afar: Oscar's flamboyant Oxford reputation did precede him to London, and he was, as well, the son of a very famous Irishwoman (who moved to London shortly after Shaw began his novel). In any event, a few details tempt one to think that Hawkshaw displays elements of a specifically Oscarian caricature predating the colorful ministrations of *Punch* and Gilbert and Sullivan. In the novel a formal recitation of Hawkshaw's translation of an unidentified Greek play "with music by Mendelssohn" is featured. Oscar's distinction as a Greek scholar was well known, and there is a letter from Oscar to Macmillan's, dated 24 March 1879 (the very month Shaw commenced writing *Immaturity*), broaching the possibility of his translating two plays by Euripides. At this recitation the poet, "his manner more effusive than usual," sports Oscarian dove-colored trousers, primrose gloves (poetic license for lavender?) and "a bronze-hued scarf, fastened by a brooch representing a small green beetle with red eyes." It is very tempting to think of this as an allusion to the green scarab ring that became a hallmark for Oscar. But perhaps even more telling is what occurs when Shaw's alter ego in the novel has an interview with Hawkshaw, ensconced in his bed: "Both meditated on the power that each possessed in disconcerting the other." For this, as we have seen, was what Shaw recalled, forty years later, as the keynote for their infrequent social intercourse.

Though there is much brutal candor in Shaw's "Memories," it is, happily, hard to find evidence of the genuine "dislike" for Oscar that Pearson observed. The tone is rather one of frustrated bemusement, as in this mention of a happenstance meeting outside the stage door of the Haymarket: "Our queer shyness of one another made our resolutely cordial and appreciative conversation so difficult that our final laugh and shake-hands was almost a reciprocal confession." On one "really pleasant afternoon" they bumped into each other, incongruously enough, at some kind of naval commemoration on the Chelsea embankment. A full twenty-five years later, Shaw exulted in this one experience of the Famous Oscar: "The question what the devil we were doing in that galley tickled us both. It was my sole experience of Oscar's wonderful gift as a raconteur. I remember particularly an amazingly elaborate story which you have no doubt heard from him." Shaw recounted the entire story, about a young inventor with mad ideas for packing extra seats in theaters, then continued:

> Wilde and I got on extraordinarily well on this occasion. I had not to talk myself, but to listen to a man telling me stories better than I could have told them. . . . And he had an audience on whom not one of his subtlest effects was lost. And so for once our meeting was a success; and I understood why Morris, when he was dying slowly, enjoyed a visit from Wilde more than from anyone else.

Another meeting Shaw recalled makes for pleasing symmetry, as on this occasion it was Oscar who made the audience. Both attended a lecture "somewhere in Westminster" after which Shaw spoke at some length on socialism. "Robert Ross surprised me greatly," Shaw recalled, "by telling me, long after Oscar's death, that it was this address of mine that moved Oscar to try his hand at a similar feat by writing 'The Soul of Man Under Socialism.' "* The story is plausible, for Oscar's essay is certainly the closest he ever came to the rousing call-to-arms style of Shaw.

The last meeting Shaw could remember occurred at the Café Royal after the premiere of *Earnest* and as Queensberry stormclouds gathered. Frank Harris and that "horrid little brat" Lord Alfred Douglas made up the luncheon party. Shaw had

---

*A report describing this sole recorded dual public performance by Oscar and Shaw, from *The Star* of 7 July 1888, perhaps deserves notice (the occasion was a lecture by Walter Crane on "The Prospects of Art Under Socialism" in Willis's rooms): "Mr Oscar Wilde, whose fashionable coat differed widely from the picturesque bottle-green garb in which he appeared in earlier days, thought that the art of the future would clothe itself not in works of form and colour but in literature. . . . Mr Shaw agreed . . . [and] pronounced Bunyan the tinker [and author of *Pilgrim's Progress*] a supreme genius, and voted Beethoven rather vulgar, saying that if a middle-class audience were told 'Pop goes the Weasel' was a movement from Beethoven's Ninth Symphony they would go into ecstasies over it." Ernest Rhys recalled another meeting from about this time that is not mentioned by Shaw. The occasion was "the first glimpse I had had at close quarters of that incorrigible Fabian. Later that same evening Oscar Wilde came in, and he and Shaw had a characteristic passage of arms, both gay and bitter."

"turned traitor" over *Earnest,* thinking it Oscar's "first really heartless play." Being Shaw, he told its author this and even venture to speculate out loud that perhaps it was a work of Oscar's youth "furbished up for [the St. James Theatre manager] Alexander as a potboiler." Shaw recalled that Oscar "indignantly repudiated my guess, and said loftily (the only time he ever tried on me the attitude he took to John Gray and his more abject disciples) that he was disappointed in me. I suppose I said, 'Then what on earth has happened to you?' but I recollect nothing more on that subject except we did not quarrel over it."

The "Memories" are filled with such unminced-Shavian bluntness. He opened by likening Oscar to the "worthless rascal" hero Des Grieux in Prévost's novel *Manon Lescaut* (an "elaborately illustrated edition" of which is included in Lord Henry Wotton's library in *Dorian Gray*). He then suggested that Oscar, by his actions, told the world, in effect, "I will be utterly selfish; and I will be not merely a rascal but a monster; and you shall forgive me everything." He insisted that Oscar's "Irish charm, potent with Englishmen, did not exist" for him, and railed at length over Oscar's vulgar snobbery and dilettante pretentiousness, particularly as they were manifest in his apostleship of Art ... "in which capacity he was a humbug." He also deplored how social adulation went to Oscar's head and spoiled his sense of reality. Such merciless truth-telling must have been what led Oscar to utter his famous witticism about Shaw: "An excellent fellow: he has no enemies; and none of his friends like him." Shaw quoted this *mot* at his own expense in an 1896 letter to Ellen Terry, adding insouciantly, "and that's quite true."

Shaw, for all his vociferation, ended by granting that Oscar was surely too good company to have been excluded from heaven. Even so, he then administered a splash of cold water: "He can hardly have been greeted [in heaven] as 'Thou good and faithful servant.' The first thing we ask a servant for is a testimonial to honesty, sobriety and industry; for we soon find out that these are the scarce things, and that geniuses and clever people are as com-

mon as rats.* Well, Oscar was not sober, not honest, not industrious."

On the other hand, Shaw's professional view of Oscar was
unstinting. Of their days together writing anonymously for the
Pall Mall Gazette, he recalled in 1889, "All the long reviews of
distinctly Irish quality during the 1885–8 period may, I think, be
set down either to me or to Oscar Wilde, whose reviews were
sometimes credited to me. His work was exceptionally finished in
style and very amusing." When Lady Campbell uttered her famous insult about Oscar in 1893, Shaw chided her: "Wilde is
doing us good service in teaching the theatrical public that 'a
play' may be a playing with ideas instead of a feast of sham emotions. . . . No, let us be just to the great white caterpillar: he is no
blockhead and he finishes his work, which puts him high above
his rivals here in London." The next year, 1894, came this impressive admonition to a friend who also had harsh words for Oscar; it clearly shows that Shaw recognized and admired his
intellectual stature: "You must give up detesting everything per-
taining to Oscar Wilde or to anyone else. The critic's first duty is
to admit, with absolute respect, the right of every man to his own
style. Wilde's wit and his fine literary workmanship are points of
great value. There is always a vulgar cry both for and against every man or woman of any distinction . . . you have heard it about
Whistler . . . Ibsen, Wagner—everybody who has a touch of genius."

Mixed though Shaw's feelings were about Oscar and the occasions on which they rubbed elbows, his kindness and human
decency never failed him. After Oscar was arrested, Shaw attempted to circulate a petition on his behalf, and during the last
Parisian years Shaw said he "made a point of sending him inscribed copies of all my books as they came out; and he did the
same to me." In 1897 *The Academy* magazine published a list of

---

*Harris added his footnote to this assertion: "The English paste in Shaw; genius is about the rarest
thing on earth whereas the necessary quantum of 'honesty, sobriety and industry' is beaten by life into
nine humans out of ten.—F.H." To which was added: *"If so, it is the tenth who comes my way.—G.B.S."*

forty names for a proposed British Academy of Letters. Among the responses this list evoked was one from Shaw, urging the addition of Oscar's name: "The only dramatist, besides Mr Henry James, whose name could be justified is Mr Oscar Wilde."

Shaw's sole published article on Oscar appeared only in German, in Vienna's *Neue Freie Presse* in 1905, just after the first publication of *De profundis*. Naturally, it took the form of a "last word," and its tone is generally laudatory. Shaw castigated English society for behaving "so weakly, so narrowly, so unjustly toward the great man" and ended with this eloquent coda:

> Our present-day morality is a repugnant and, as Wilde would have said, "vulgar" error. It is not even ethical. And Wilde's claim to greatness rests on the fact that our morality could not fool him, and the moralists of his time could neither break nor dishonor him.
>
> He held fast to his pose to the very last, because it was an honest pose. For that very reason it has been unspeakably annoying to English morality which, too, is a pose, but without benefit of the excuse of being an honest one.

☆ ☆ ☆

SHAW'S CENSORIOUS "MEMORIES of Oscar Wilde" would seem to render all but certain the conclusion that the two men were utterly unlike each other. All the more astonishing, then, are the likenesses that begin to emerge as one considers the two men together. In some respects, indeed, they begin to assume the surreal likeness of identical twins, separated at birth by fate—perhaps by a forgetful nurse at some London railroad terminus or other. As this chapter's second epigraph suggests, these bases of likeness may even be more fascinating and illuminating than the well-known disparities in their characters.

The most profound similarity—from which most of the others flow—is what could be called their indomitable courage of personality. Sounding precisely the note of so many who met Oscar, the actress Lillah McCarthy recalled, "I never knew what a vivid personality meant until I knew Shaw. He, of all men, is most alive." This Oscarian vitality of presence was particularly noticeable when Shaw sat for his bust by Rodin. Rainer Maria Rilke, the sculptor's assistant at the time, was positively stunned by how Shaw kept "still with such energy" and how he compacted his whole being into his upper torso: "he can do this so powerfully that his entire being leaps into the bust from that spot, feature by feature, with astonishing intensity." Rilke explained this power as deriving from Shaw's knowing how to come to terms with life and put himself in harmony with it ("which is no small achievement"). Many observers said much the same thing about Oscar, among them A.J.A. Symons: "He seemed thoroughly in accord with himself." Obviously, Shaw was of Oscar's mind about the joy of life lying in the intensity of experience. Oscar would have applauded Shaw's insistence that "happiness is not the object of life; life has no object: it is an end in itself; and courage consists in the readiness to sacrifice happiness for an intenser quality of life."

Such deep self-satisfaction, of course, can be mistaken for (or collapse into) mere pride, and both men were often accused of this sin. Curiously, though, the aspersion often turns somehow into compliment. Beerbohm, for instance, said of Oscar, "Vanity is one of the most salient and not the least charming of his qualities." Another friend, Coulson Kernahan, also emphasized perceptively the positive side of Oscar's (and, I think, Shaw's) vanity when he noted, "There is this to be said of Wilde's vanity, that its very nakedness was its best excuse. A loin-cloth, a fig-leaf would have offended, but it was so artlessly naked that one merely smiled and passed on. Moreover, it was never a jealous or a malicious vanity . . . [but] was as entirely free from venom as was his wit." Always with comic intent, Shaw carried vain posturing to coloratura heights that even Oscar could not have matched. He was capable of ending a letter thus: "Meanwhile a serene friendliness, sustained at a high level by a magnificent consciousness of intellectual superiority, continues to animate my feelings towards both of you." On another occasion he sought to make one thing perfectly clear to his Viennese theatrical agent: "*I am never wrong*. Other people are sometimes—often—nearly always wrong, especially when they disagree with me; but I am omniscient and infallible." No wonder Holroyd has felt obliged to speak of Shaw's "Everest of vanity." But it was, as with Oscar, ultimately a self-fulfilling rather than a merely selfish vanity of a kind that both men would have recommended every person to indulge. Shaw wrote once that the music critic "who is modest is lost." So, he might have said, is any human being.

Another occupational hazard of those possessed of vivid and immodest personalities is a tendency to create their worlds from the inside rather than from external prescription. "Life is an adventure," Shaw in fact wrote, "not the compounding of a prescription," and among the "Maxims for Revolutionists" he appended to *Man and Superman* is the thoroughly Oscarian (and Nietzschean) idea, "The golden rule is that there are no golden rules." They insisted on full freedom for the play of personal creative fantasy, and this led some bystanders to accuse them of trying to live in an "unreal" world. Yeats, we have seen, felt Oscar "lived . . . an imaginary life," and William Archer perceived Shaw the same way: "He does not live in the real world, but in an *a priori* world of his own. . . . He sees things not as they are, but as it suits him to think they are."

People who create their own worlds can also look very much like children. Indeed, the joy that Borges found dominant in Oscar and the sense of liberation he found preeminent in Shaw may, in this sense, be much the same thing, namely, exuberant pleasure in the free *play* of personality. The ineffably childish spirit I have already remarked upon in Oscar is also very much in evidence in Shaw, who admitted at age thirty-one that he had "but imperfectly acquired" the "sense of being grown up." Rilke captured this playful spirit in his description of the third sitting, when Rodin placed Shaw "in a cunning little baby-chair (all of which afforded this satirist and really not uncongenial scoffer an exquisite pleasure)." When Rodin cut off the head of the clay bust with a wire, "Shaw . . . witnessed this decapitation with indescribable joy." This sort of glee surely helped H. G. Wells to his conclusion that Shaw was "an elderly adolescent still at play."

Shaw had very early identified Oscar as a man who played with everything, but so, too, was Shaw, as Margery Morgan suggested in an analysis of *Arms and the Man* in her book titled, aptly, *The Shavian Playground*. Every theatrical device in this "Christmas pantomime" of a play, she says, "suggests a puppet play for human actors, or a moving toy shop. . . . The ease with which Shaw regressed to childishness can be regarded as a sign of psychological weakness and emotional immaturity . . . [but] it is this childishness that constitutes Shaw's genius. He used it as a means of attacking insidiously and openly every form of humbug and pretentiousness, including the unnaturalness of moral virtue that children instinctively detect." Her perception applies as well to Oscarian dramaturgy, which was also regularly chided for mechanical contrivances and puppet-characters.

These two men shared another trait common to prodigious personalities: they did not mind in the least being "wrong." Indeed, because Shaw held Oscar's own expressed belief that "whatever is popular is wrong," he reveled in the sensation of being an "out of the way young man." Like Oscar, he did not find the eagerness of others to agree with him appealing. When *Pygmalion* opened with huge success in 1914, he was bemused: "There must be something radically wrong with the play if it pleases everybody, but at the moment I cannot find what it is." He was also just as eager as Oscar to annoy the tasteful, smug, and moral majority. He thirsted for the kind of review the *Daily Telegraph* gave to Oscar's first play: "It is a bad one, but it will succeed." And he, too, loved to razz sacred institutions, most notably Shakespeare. To one correspondent he wrote, in 1905, "I have striven hard to open English eyes to the emptiness of Shakespeare's philosophy, to the superficiality and second-handedness of his morality, to his weakness and incoherence as a thinker, to his snobbery, his vulgar prejudices, his ignorance, his disqualifications of all sorts for the philosophic eminence claimed for him." Of Gilbert and Sullivan's operettas only *Trial by Jury* and the rarely performed *Utopia Limited* pleased him. Even the most august preprandial British custom was not safe: he spoke once of "that most horrible form of dipsomania, the craving for afternoon tea." Particularly in his music criticism, Shaw delighted in upsetting the pious, the professorial, and the bourgeois, even if it meant playing ragtime on a harmonium: "Most people think that a harmonium is sacred ... and their notion of blasphemy is to play ragtime on a harmonium. I love playing ragtime on harmoniums, just to shew them that one can do it without being struck dead." "Bad taste," Shaw simply boasted, "is what I'm good at."

Oscar praising pirates in the *Pall Mall Gazette* and Shaw penning a "vindication of burglars" for the *Penny Illustrated Paper* is a minor example of their contrarian spirits united in action. But these *jeux d'esprit* also reflect their deep belief in the necessity of the heretical spirit. Shaw's assertions that "every genuine religious person is a heretic" and that disobedience is "the rarest and most courageous of the virtues" are pure Oscar. It is such sentiments, one assumes, that caused Yeats to assert, "When a man is so outrageously in the wrong as Shaw he is indispensable."

My favorite anecdote revealing Shaw's devotion to the contrary spirit occurred, Oscar-like, in a spark of curtain-speech wit after the premiere of *Arms and the Man*. When one solitary voice among the deliriously happy audience uttered a "Boo!" Shaw addressed him, "My dear fellow I quite agree with you, but what are we two against so many?" The capper, however, is that the man who booed was Reginald Golding Bright, who later became Shaw's London theatrical agent.

Inevitably, both Shaw and Oscar assumed the jester's motley. Some of their friends looked with distress upon this stooping to humor, as William Archer did in Shaw's case: "He loses influence by being such an incorrigible jester ... by wearing his cap and bells in and out of season." But Shaw, like Oscar, knew how charming the jester's role can be. Defending the outrageous style of his days as the pseudonymous music critic Corno di Bassetto,

Shaw confessed, "Bassetto was occasionally vulgar; but that does not matter if he makes you laugh. Vulgarity is a necessary part of a complete author's equipment; and the clown is sometimes the best part of the circus." And so it was that Shaw employed many of the patented Oscarian techniques of creating hilarity: inversions of popular conventions, hit-and-run aphorisms (Shaw's wife compiled an anthology of them just like Constance's *Oscariana*), and pontifications that were delectably idiosyncratic. Their weapons of choice, of course, were the paradox and the Irish bull. Chesterton defined the latter as "a paradox which people are too stupid to understand," and he observed, "Irishmen make Irish bulls for the same reason they accept Papal bulls. It is better to speak wisdom foolishly." And both men were master paradoxers. Shaw caught the style perfectly in the postcards he had printed up denying requests for his autograph: he often added his signature before mailing them.

The two men incited much mirth, but they were also both great laughers themselves. Of Shaw Helena Sickert vowed, "His laughter I shall hear till I die." The evening of his death his friend St. John Ervine reminisced for the BBC that when Shaw laughed "he laughed with his whole body. He threw his shoulders about while the laughter ran up his long legs and threatened to shake his head off."

As we have seen was the case with Oscar, beneath all this hilarity lay a bedrock of profound gravity. Shaw made it no secret that this was his fundamental *modus operandi*, too: "I found that I had only to say with perfect simplicity what I seriously meant just as it struck me, to make everybody laugh. My method is to take the utmost trouble to find the right thing to say, and then to say it with the utmost levity. And all the time the real joke is that I am in earnest." Each man cultivated with extraordinary inventiveness an utterly personal comic veneer—"without my veneer I am not Bernard Shaw," said he—from behind which they made their devastating attacks.

They were both, finally, deep and earnest observers of human folly. What William Archer said of Shaw—that he was something "much rarer" than a great dramatist, namely, "a philosophic humourist, with the art of expressing himself in dramatic form"—is likewise true of Oscar and the "drama" of his London celebrity. For all their blandishing charisma, the two men were stunningly clear-sighted debunkers. Oscar, in a letter accompanying a presentation copy of his *Salome*, congratulated Shaw on his attacks upon censorship, adding, "England is the land of intellectual fogs but you have done much to clear the air." As usual, there is a little self-congratulation in the praise, for Oscar was also a master dispeller of intellectual fogs. They differed only in their methods: Shaw, on the whole, dispelled the fogs with the sunlight of his relentless common sense, Oscar with the moonlight of fantasy, romance, and whimsy.

Many other odd coincidences tie the lives of Shaw and Oscar together. Their parents, it happens, were married in the same Dublin church. Both had disorderly fathers (Oscar's a philanderer, Shaw's "a miserable drunkard") and humorless mothers (Shaw's "had no comedic impulses, and never uttered an epigram in her life"). Both settled soon into sexless marriage arrangements, and both displayed a vein of misogynistic humor. Oscar would have been amused by Shaw's assertion, for instance, "Woman's greatest art is to lie low, and let the imagination of men endow her with depths."

Both had occasion to give Beerbohm Tree a hard time for his attempts to play Shakespeare. Shaw on his Falstaff: "Mr Tree might as well try to play Juliet"; Oscar on his Hamlet: "funny . . . without being vulgar!"* And both had the hardest time with conventional dramaturgy, somehow managing the miracle of eking out success in spite of an inability to invent plots, sustain action,

---

*Le Gallienne wittily rehearsed the circumstances of the remark, made backstage at the Haymarket after Tree's first performance of the role. Tree, "all excitement, perspiration, and grease paint," eagerly asked Oscar what he thought. "Wilde assumed his gravest, most pontifical air, spacing out his words with long pauses of even more than his usual deliberation." Tree hung "expectant on each slow-dropping word, nervous and keyed up . . . anxiously filling the pauses with 'Yes, yes, my dear Oscar . . .'" while Wilde continued to keep him on tenterhooks with further preliminary ejaculations. . . . At last, when he could hold the suspended compliment no longer, Wilde ended with: 'My dear Tree—I—think—your Hamlet . . . is . . . *funny without being vulgar!*' "

or create three-dimensional human characters. Of Shaw's serious characters, Beerbohm said they "are just so many skeletons, which do but dance and grin and rattle their bones."

ONE FINAL BASIS OF the "secret affinity" between Oscar and Shaw—perhaps the most important—remains to be explored: their shared Irish ancestry. Indeed, many years later Shaw wrote to Bosie and emphasized the significance of this fact: "You must always remember that we were Irishmen, resenting strongly the English practice of making pets of Irishmen. We understood one another on this point, and thereby made our relationship quite unintelligible in England."

In "The Critic as Artist," in the most haunting and imposing passage Oscar ever wrote, Gilbert discourses on "the scientific principle of Heredity" and how it impinges upon our free will and makes puppets of us all:

> It has shown us that we are never less free than when we try to act. It has hemmed us round with the nets of the hunter, and written upon the wall the prophecy of our doom. We may not watch it, for it is within us. We may not see it, save in a mirror that mirrors the soul. It is Nemesis without her mask. It is the last of the Fates, and the most terrible.

Thus, "in the sphere of practical and external life" Heredity—"what we are" physiologically and psychologically—robs us of freedom. In the "subjective sphere" its effects are more ominous, especially if one reads the following passage as being, finally, about the agonizing psychomachia of a man whose love dare not speak its name:

> In the subjective sphere, where the soul is at work, it comes to us, this terrible shadow, with many gifts of

strange temperaments and subtle susceptibilities, gifts of wild ardours and chill moods of indifference, complex multiform gifts of thoughts that are at variance with each other, and passions that war against themselves. And so, it is not our own life that we live, but the lives of the dead. . . . It is wiser than we are, and its wisdom is bitter. It fills us with impossible desires, and makes us follow what we know we cannot gain.

But one thing, Gilbert says, the soul can do under this terrible burden of Heredity: "It can lead us away from surroundings whose beauty is dimmed to us by the mist of familiarity, or whose ignoble ugliness and sordid claims are marring the perfecting of our development."

Such an instinct for spiritual travel led Oscar himself finally out of the Closet, but it also led him out of Ireland. In this, he behaved precisely as Shaw did. For both, the soul required more room to breathe than Ireland—and Dublin in particular—could afford them. Shaw was, as usual, blunt on the subject: "When I left Dublin I left (a few private friendships apart) no society that did not disgust me. To this day my sentimental regard for Ireland does not include the capital." For any man of genius, said Shaw, "emigration was practically compulsory," and his intentions as he trained his sights on London—"England had conquered Ireland; so there was nothing for it but to come over and conquer England"—were exactly those of Oscar as he moved down to the capital from his way station at Oxford. In 1896, in a letter to his future wife, Shaw turned the necessity for this exodus into one of his witty paradoxes: "As long as Ireland produces men who have the sense to leave her, she does not exist in vain."

Oscar and Shaw did conquer London, one sooner, the other later. These conquests were due in no small part to their ability to overcome the burdensome aspects of their Irish identity (Oscar quickly lost his Irish accent) and to deploy with devastating cleverness the gifts their Irishness conferred on them. Not the least gift was the one, as Shaw put it in *John Bull's Other Island*, for

"Irish exaggeration and talky-talk." (Mrs Cheveley says in *An Ideal Husband* that London society would be "quite civilized" if "one could only teach the English how to talk, and the Irish how to listen.") Indeed, the paradoxes that attend being Irish, the seemingly constant intertwining of the deplorable and the charming, are one of the best keys to the Shavian and Oscarian style. Each man proved himself a true Irishman by consistently evoking, in Gilbert's phrase in "The Critic as Artist," thoughts that are "at variance with each other." Shaw captured the effect perfectly when he boasted, "I am an Irishman—intensely proud of being Irish (quite unreasonably)." He also displayed his mixed feelings about the Irish by refusing to return to his native land for the last twenty-seven years of his life ... yet leaving a third of his estate to the National Gallery of Ireland.

Like Shaw, Oscar became splendidly *sui generis*. They were both, as Archer said of Shaw, full of "irrepressible idiosyncrasy" and came to occupy their own inimitable Isles of Man somewhere between Englishness and Irishness. Following out the threads of their Irish identity—given their gift for paradox, tall tales, and obnubilating Hibernian talky-talk—would be an enormous task. A more suggestive and economical approach, I think, is to pause briefly over Shaw's great play on the subject of the Irish and the English, *John Bull's Other Island*, which he completed four years after Oscar's death. It is the most resonantly autobiographical of Shaw's plays—Chesterton judged it the "most real" of them all— and it boasts a character who, I would like to suggest, is Shaw's unconscious homage to Oscar ... a wonderful act of penance for the caricature in Patrick Hawkshaw.

This character, however, does not show us Oscar in his *bon vivant* guise, but rather the Oscar of the passage on Heredity: Oscar the melancholy, philosophic humorist. This character is Peter Keegan, a defrocked priest whose former parish of Rosscullen is invaded by Tom Broadbent, a successful English land developer, and his partner, Larry Doyle (the play's Shaw character). Doyle is an Irishman who has emigrated to London—"the very center of the world"—to make his way. "I had only two ideas at the time," says Doyle of his flight from Ireland, "first, to learn to do something; and then to get out of Ireland and have a chance of doing it." Broadbent is blunt and garrulous and—if he weren't so full of "eupeptic jollity"—might remind one of all the bluff English philistine traits of a Queensberry. For him there is no "subjective sphere." He sees "only two qualities in the world: efficiency and inefficiency." As with many of Oscar's own stage Englishmen, cleverness doesn't agree with him. "Don't be paradoxical," he tells Doyle. "It gives me a pain in the stomach." Complacently happy in his rapacity, Broadbent also has a clear view of "the thorough Irishman" that is not entirely inaccurate. Curiously, it could serve as a sketch of Oscar himself: "rash and improvident but brave and goodnatured; not likely to succeed in business . . . but eloquent, humorous, a lover of freedom."

In an odd way, Broadbent's utter lack of access to the deeper poetry (and melancholy) of the Irish personality manages to convey something of the rather cheerful but dense way England embraced Oscar during most of his long reign as a London celebrity. What the English never really glimpsed was the Peter Keegan in him. For Keegan is, like Oscar, a dreamer and a figure of ostracism. Oscar's observation, "Society often forgives the criminal; it never forgives the dreamer," is, quite simply, the premise for the character of Shaw's erstwhile St. Francis. Shaw was adamant that Keegan be played by "a poetic actor . . . a masterly speaker"— another bit of Oscarian typecasting, one might think. Rather like Oscar after his fall, we first meet Keegan posed in a melancholy trance, bearing (though nearing the age of fifty) the face "of a young saint" and an intense gaze that might "pierce the glories of the sunset."

And what could be more fitting for a figure of Oscarian imaginative fantasy than Keegan's first conversation? It is with a "true Irish grasshopper," whose view of the sunset, Keegan guesses, helps it to "face out the misery and poverty and the torment" of Irish life. Doyle says "an Irishman's heart is nothing but his imagination," and this play-opening little *coup de théâtre* emphasizes Keegan's embodiment of the Irish heart and soul. The

369

touch is Oscarian, not only in its fairy-tale whimsy, but also because for him the imagination was the great weapon for jousting both with Heredity and "practical and external life."

Keegan is a figure of the isolated philosopher, the aloof artist, the seer of truth in a land "of intellectual fogs" and superstition and greed. He alone seems to have, as he says, "eyes in his soul as well as his head"—precisely where Gilbert argues they must be in the passage on heredity. His favorite haunt is a ruined round tower in a desolate nearby valley. Part of his sadness lies in his sense of how utterly the wisdom he has attained has been neutralized: as he was defrocked, so Oscar was imprisoned. Now he admits he is "only a poor madman, unfit and unworthy to take charge of the souls of people." Keegan's Nietzschean preference for a more solitary self-wisdom comes out when Broadbent asks whether he feels "at home in the world." Keegan replies ("from the very depths of his nature," according to the stage direction), "No." To which Broadbent responds solicitously, "Try phosphorus pills. I always take them when my brain is overworked."

Keegan's one set-to with Broadbent is a perfect image of Oscar's constant satiric confrontations with English society. Many of Keegan's digs—delivered in a "peculiar vein of humour"—seem but Oscar paraphrased. When he tells Broadbent, "There was a time, in my ignorant youth, when I should have called you a hypocrite," one is particularly reminded of Oscar's remark about England as a "land of hypocrites." Broadbent insists on taking all of Keegan's irony-laden aspersions in jolly humor because he is "only a whimsical Irishman."

In the last act, Shaw gives to Keegan a great withering aria in Oscar's most mordant style—one that is aimed at many of the objects of Oscar's own scorn:

> This world, sir, is very clearly a place of torment and penance, a place where the fool flourishes and the good and wise are hated and persecuted, a place where men and women torture one another in the name of love;

where children are scourged and enslaved in the name of parental duty and education; where the weak in body are poisoned and mutilated in the name of healing, and the weak in character are put to the horrible torture of imprisonment, not for hours but for years, in the name of justice. It is a place . . . where charity and good works are done only for hire to ransom the souls of the spoiler and the sybarite. Now, sir, there is only one place of horror and torment known to my religion; and that place is hell. Therefore it is plain to me that this earth of ours must be hell.

Broadbent, like Oscar's English public, prefers the wit rather than the devastating sense of the speech: "Your idea is a very clever one, Mr Keegan: really most brilliant." Utterly unfazed, Broadbent adds, "I find the world quite good enough for me: rather a jolly place, in fact." Broadbent's vision of earthly delight, not surprisingly, is one that Oscar spent considerable effort to avoid: "a solid four-square home: man and wife: comfort and common sense." His panacea for the economic and spiritual malaise of Rosscullen is likewise prosaic: a hotel and golf course. Keegan challenges Broadbent's fatuous venture capitalism ironically and obliquely at first, then, when that fails, more acidly and bluntly. Shaw and Oscar were of the same ilk. Chesterton wrote of Shaw, "He always challenges," and then made the comparison: "An even stronger instance of this national trait can be found in another eminent Irishman, Oscar Wilde."

Keegan's clear vision of the "dead heart and blinded soul" of Ireland; the fact that his "way of joking is to tell the truth"; his way (as Broadbent says) of "extracting" poetry from everything; his outcast status: all these would have made Keegan, I think, the character in *John Bull's Other Island* most fascinating to Oscar. Indeed, a character with these traits—as well as Keegan's mystical communion with nature—had once before riveted Oscar's interest, in a novel under his review:

The most delightful character in the whole book, however, is a girl called Hilary Marston. . . . Hilary is like a little woodland faun, half Greek and half gipsy; she knows the note of every bird, and the haunt of every animal; she is terribly out of place in a drawing-room, but is on intimate terms with every young poacher in the district; squirrels come and sit on her shoulder, which is pretty, and she carries ferrets in her pockets, which is dreadful; she never reads a book, and has not got a single accomplishment, but she is fascinating and fearless, and wiser, in her own way, than any pedant or bookworm.

Oscar's lifelong partisanship for the higher wisdom of self-assertion is figured in Peter Keegan as in Hilary Marston. Keegan refuses to take conventional part in what one stage direction calls the "narrow, strainless" life of Rosscullen, and he refuses to become like Doyle's father, Cornelius, in whom such a life has left an "almost total atrophy of any sense of enjoyment" and an innate habit of greed.

Shaw allows Keegan to dominate the play's final scene, when Broadbent erupts in one final burst of plans for turning Rosscullen into "a Garden city" with its own cricket club, Polytechnic, and a nicely restored round tower. After heaping sarcasm upon Broadbent's "efficient . . . service of Mammon," this fairy tale of a play ends—just as many of Oscar's fairy tales end—with a marvelous air of the sacramental. Like Oscar, the apostle of inaction and of dreaming, Keegan takes his leave to dream, saying "I am better alone, at the Round Tower, dreaming of heaven." His anglicized countryman Doyle reacts furiously and chides him, "Aye, that's it! there you are! dreaming! dreaming! dreaming! dreaming!"

Broadbent pipes up and says his boyhood dreams of heaven involved "a sort of pale blue satin place." Then, just as Cyril once asked his father what he dreamed, Broadbent asks Keegan what heaven is like in his dreams. The answer comes in Keegan's last speech before vanishing in the direction of the round tower. The dream he tells of would surely have been applauded by Oscar:

> It is a country where the State is the Church and the Church the people: three in one and one in three. It is a commonwealth in which work is play and play is life: three in one and one in three. It is a temple in which the priest is the worshipper and the worshipper the worshipped; three in one and one in three. It is a godhead in which all life is human and all humanity divine: three in one and one in three. It is, in short, the dream of a madman.

"We poets and dreamers are all brothers," wrote Oscar, and Keegan, though a fiction, is one of Oscar's brothers.

MICHAEL HOLROYD HAS BEEN much taken by the character of Keegan, calling him "the first and most convincing of Shaw's mystical sages." Holroyd views him as a part of the Shavian personality: "Keegan is the man Sonny [Shaw's childhood nickname] might have grown into if he had been able to endure the anguish of living in the Land of Dreams; Larry Doyle is the man Shaw has become." Keegan, one might further venture, voices the Oscarian part of Shaw's personality, the part that was (as Beerbohm said of Oscar) "elaborately fantastic." It is the part that Shaw eventually chose, for the most part, to isolate in a kind of round tower. Holroyd's image for this renunciation of his darkly witty and pessimistic alter ego is more extreme: "Keegan was buried alive in Shaw, but from time to time, prompted by unconscious will, we hear his accents mocking the pragmatic program of G.B.S."

Peter Keegan, thus, is the perfect embodiment for the "secret affinity" that has made the Wildeshawshow such an enduring entertainment for posterity. He tells us much about the Oscarian al-

ter ego in Shaw and the Shavian alter ego in Oscar. This is
worthwhile knowledge, because the gifts and abilities they shared
go far to explain their successes. This serious jester, this fellow
who wryly admits he's "cracked" but quite "harmless" (yet isn't),
this joker with the truth: he is clearly intended as Shaw's homage
to the most worthy element in the Irish spirit. In his long preface
to the play, Shaw asserted that the Irish imagination differs from
the English in being "far subtler and more fastidious"—largely because the Irishman "has one eye always on things as they are."
That Oscar had such an eye, I think, accounts for the remarkable
and unexpected gravity that can so often be discerned behind his
inspired foolery.

Could Shaw have thought of Oscar as he created Keegan?
One is tempted to think so, if only because we learn that Keegan
has also received his education at Oxford. But perhaps the real
proof lies in how often Keegan reminds one of the dark side of
the Oscar we have come to know. The likeness is especially
strong at the very end of the play. Keegan's dream sails well over
the head of Broadbent, whose daft response is simply, "What a
regular old Church and State Tory he is! He's a character: he'll be
an attraction here." How like the "character" Oscar, who became
such a delighting "attraction" in London in the 1880s and early
1890s. In the final speech of the play, Shaw gave Broadbent a few
more words about Keegan that, as usual, are far truer than he is
able to imagine: "I feel sincerely obliged to Keegan: he has made
me feel a better man: distinctly better."

How true that is, too, of our acquaintance with both the famous and the stranger Wilde.

Chapter Eighteen

☆ ☆ ☆ ☆ ☆ ☆ ☆ ☆ ☆ ☆ ☆ ☆ ☆ ☆ ☆ ☆

OSCAR TODAY

A dreamer is one who can only find his way by moonlight, and his punishment is that he sees the dawn before the rest of the world.
—"THE CRITIC AS ARTIST"

Every dream is a prophecy: every jest is an earnest in the womb of Time.
—KEEGAN, IN SHAW'S *JOHN BULL'S OTHER ISLAND*

IN HER MEMOIR A *New England Girlhood*, Nancy Hale wrote of her gentle, pink-cheeked bachelor uncle Paul, who had lived in Paris throughout the 1890s, studying at the Beaux-Arts:

> My Uncle Paul ... used to see Whistler and Monet, and once he saw Wilde, who was then in the evil days before his death. Uncle Paul said that later in Paris there was a society formed of people who had admired Wilde's work and who claimed that he was not dead but living somewhere still. They claimed that no one had seen him in his coffin and that what Lord Alfred Doug-

375

las said did not count. When I knew my Uncle Paul first, it was at least 1915, and he used to say then and later that perhaps Wilde was still not dead.

The fantasy of a charismatic celebrity who "still lives" has its obvious appeal, as witness, most spectacularly, the posthumous life of the King of R&R, Elvis Presley. One can imagine especially easily the appeal of such a fantasy for the society—surely a homosexual one—mentioned by Uncle Paul. In the repressive decades-long aftermath of Oscar's fall, he was bound to be the focus of much nostalgia for what, in the first years of the twentieth century, must have seemed like a kind of miniature golden—or at least brilliantly Yellow—age. ("What a number of Urnings [homosexuals] are being portrayed in novels now!" wrote John Addington Symonds amazedly to Edmund Gosse in 1891.) Resurrecting Oscar's proud, salient spirit would have been a perfect compensatory emotional strategy for dealing not only with the loss of his courageous example but also with the considerable loss of momentum in the movement toward gay liberation itself.

In any event, Uncle Paul sets the imagination off down a pathway of whimsy. What, he excites one to wonder, if Oscar were alive today? How much in the terrain of his *fin de siècle* would he recognize in our own? What "progress" would delight him; what appalling evidence of century-long stasis would disgust? What exquisite follies would elicit the inimitable laughter that Helena Sickert said she would hear till she died? Would he look upon the world and be moved to recycle—for he was not above recycling his *bons mots* and aphorisms—what he wrote in 1891: "The evolution of man is slow. The injustice of men is great"? Tantalizing questions, to which this chapter will venture some imaginary answers.

From what cathedra might he utter his clever, devastating *facetiae* . . . and from which happy metropolis would they resound? My best, or at least most cherished, guess is San Francisco. After all, does not Lord Henry remark to Dorian on this city's strange attraction to the vanished? "It is an odd thing, but everyone who disappears is said to be seen at San Francisco. It must be a delightful city, and possess all the attractions of the next world." I picture him ensconced high on one of the city's hills. For Oscar was his mother's son, and she said she was an eagle in her youth and craved high places. California, a state in which, as it was quipped in the last century, all the cities are named after saints and all the people are sinners would be ideal for a man who insisted that, without Sin, "the world would stagnate, or grow old, or become colourless." And a city often referred to then as the Hoodlum City would seem the perfect home for this magnificent trespasser. Oscar was also much taken by the Northern California landscape, referring to the "eternal summer here, groves of orange trees in fruit and flower, green fields, and purple hills, a very Italy, without its art."

San Francisco certainly proved the most successful of his sojourns in more than 130 American and Canadian cities in the course of his lecture tour. He told the local *Examiner*, "The further West one comes, the more there is to like," and the already large metropolis was as far West as one could go. Indeed, in one letter from "Frisco" he sent greetings "from the uttermost end of the great world." San Francisco was by 1882 an enormous city; with 235,000 inhabitants, it was twenty times larger than Los Angeles, which Oscar skipped even though offered a private car on a special train to travel there. The area sustained more Oscarian performances than any other he visited: four in the City, plus four more in nearby Stockton, Oakland, and San Jose. Finding his audiences so cordial, he concluded, "Western people are much more genial than those of the East," and he gave them some of his most relaxed performances. "I am really appreciated," he reported, "by the cultured classes."*

Oscar particularly delighted in a tour, led by the mayor no less, through Chinatown, with its opium parlors, "houses" (broth-

---

* There were some dissenters: the *San Jose Daily Morning Times* (31 March 1882) opined that "Wilde's reasoning is like his frowzy hair, parted in the middle" and that "as a poet he is obscene." The *San Jose Mercury* (4 April 1882) found him "a most grotesque, boyish-looking young man" and noted "the most atrociously ugly suit of wearing apparel that could well be devised by man."

els), and "persons" (prostitutes). He regretted that London did not also have such a quarter. Later, in the "Impressions of America" lecture he delivered around England, he called San Francisco "a really beautiful city," singling out Chinatown as "the most artistic town I have ever come across." In a Chinese restaurant he found himself drinking tea "out of china cups as delicate as the petals of a rose-leaf," whereas at the gaudy hotels—notably the grandiose Palace, where he stayed—he was "supplied with a delft cup an inch and a half thick. When the Chinese bill was presented it was made out on rice paper, the account being done in Indian ink as fantastically as if an artist had been etching little birds on a fan." Members of the city's recently founded Bohemian Club, perceiving him to be "a Miss Nancy," invited him to a drinking bout, but he ended up leaving all his hosts drunk under the table. So impressed were they the next day that, after sobering up, they sent a deputation to ask him to sit for a portrait for the Club's walls. Taking the when-in-Rome approach, he likewise showed his skills at poker. But he also felt free enough to single out to the *Examiner* reporter as his "most finished and perfect" work the poem "Charmides," which had so scandalized Canon Miles.

All in all, Oscar was much taken with the town's inhabitants. The *Examiner* reported him as objecting to the city being called the Hoodlum City: "No, it is the city of fine men and beautiful women." And he was also quite taken by the local geography. The prairies of the Midwest reminded him "of a piece of blotting paper," but, as he later told a reporter for the Montreal *Daily Witness*, "San Francisco has the most lovely surroundings of any city except Naples."

Picture Oscar, then, perched in some high place, before him a panoramic view of Baghdad-by-the-Bay. He is smoking, of course . . . perhaps some of the hashish he found so appealing on his visit to Algiers. In fact, let us imagine the room decorated after the manner of Oscar's smoking room in Tite Street, which, though "very dark and gloomy," inspired such awe in his son Vyvyan. The decor was North African, a style very popular in the

Haight-Ashbury days and not uncommon now. There was William Morris wallpaper of dark red and dull gold; glass-bead curtains hung before the windows; and divans, ottomans, Moorish hangings and lanterns filled the room. "My father used to sit in this room for hours," Vyvyan wrote, "smoking and talking to his friends. . . . Twilight and mystery were the dominant notes in the smoking room, which smelled exquisitely of tobacco-smoke."

Thus laid back and speaking from on high at the uttermost end of the great world, what would Oscar have to say about the madding crowds down below?

IN THE LAST PARAGRAPH of his biography, Richard Ellmann leaves us with the provocative assertion that Oscar "belongs to our world more than to Victoria's." That statement is perhaps the truest of many true statements Ellmann made about Oscar in the course of his long book. For Oscar was extraordinarily forward-looking. It was, he wrote in 1891, the duty of the artist to look forward: "The past is of no importance. The present is of no importance. It is with the future that we have to deal. . . . The future is what artists are." He was such an artist, and this is the principal reason why so much of the essential personality and perception and philosophy in his writings have refused to date, even where (as in his poetry and most of his plays) the literary styles and genres he employed do show their age.

It is thus an irony but not a coincidence that his description and praise of Walt Whitman should at the same time be description and praise of himself: "The chief value of his work is in its prophecy, not in its performance. He has begun a prelude to larger themes. He is the herald of a new era. As a man he is the precursor of a fresh type." Oscar was thus placing Whitman (and himself) firmly among the greatest artists who, as he explained to Gide, "brought answers to questions that had not yet been asked." Those who do bring answers without precedent questions are bound to seem to the age in which they live to be jesters, sinners, outlaws, dreamers, rebels, or teachers (as George Ives put it) of "things which cannot be held." In his day, Oscar was called on countless occasions—and often was happy to call himself—by all of these epithets.

It is certain that, from his San Francisco aerie, Oscar would have laced his observations with many an "I told you so" and many a reiteration of his grim remark that "the present is what man ought not to be." He might even be moved to conclude, from a late-twentieth-century vantage point, that the evolution of man is not merely slow but nonexistent. For countless of his pronouncements—in which drollery and acerbity are blended in equal measure—seem as accurate today as when they were uttered a century ago. Many of them being if anything more true now than when first uttered, they tend to urge the mind into an apocalyptic, *fin du globe* mood. Oscar, for instance, might cast his eye on the imploding metropolises of the world and repeat what he once told Ross: "Civilizations continue because people hate them. A modern city is the exact opposite of what everyone wants." He might glance at the plethoric advances in technology and repeat his observation in "The Soul of Man" that "there is something tragic in the fact that as soon as man had invented a machine to do his work he began to starve." Would he stroll through our appliance stores and be moved to repeat, from *Dorian Gray*, "We live in an age when unnecessary things are our only necessities"? He would certainly find no reason to alter his view that we live in "a thoroughly selfish . . . a thoroughly grasping age"—and in but one more century that worships Mammon: "The God of this century is wealth. To succeed one must have wealth. At all costs one must have wealth." Much there would be for Oscar to say about what he called "the strange poverty of the rich."

For the political scene and its inhabitants today he would need to alter his old scorn very little. He could insist again, "What we want is a little more reality and a little less rhetoric"—a modest if hopeless wish that sounds particularly desirable after an election year. His view of politicians in concert was admirably succinct: "The Lords Temporal say nothing, the Lords Spiritual have nothing to say, and the House of Commons has nothing to say and says it." Not a bad précis of the U.S. Congress, either. He would probably repeat the remark that Lord Henry often makes to Dorian Gray, namely, "It is personalities, not principles, that move the age." Oscar in 1891 imagined a brighter future for the poor and homeless in countries that boasted great wealth:

> There will be no people living in fetid dens and fetid rags, and bringing up unhealthy, hunger-pinched children in the midst of impossible and absolutely repulsive surroundings. . . . If a frost comes we shall not have a hundred thousand men out of work, tramping about the streets in a state of disgusting misery, or whining to their neighbours for alms, or crowding round the doors of loathsome shelters to try and secure a hunch of bread and a night's unclean lodging.

If he were to travel about London, Washington, New York City, and many another metropolis today, it is doubtful he would be surprised to find the grim scene he sketched unchanged, in fact exacerbated, and governments seemingly paralyzed in their efforts to improve it.

Oscar's badinage in the privacy of his gay circle might run to the misogynistic, but there can be little doubt that he would show himself staunchly PC and fully in accord with the feminist agenda. His editorship at *Woman's World*, we have seen, was notably enlightened. Among treatises on hoops, methods of copying ancient needlework, and "The Ethics of Tidiness," he also included essays on "Woman's Work in Politics," on Vassar College in America, on "The Fallacy of the Superiority of Man," and on "Woman's Suffrage"—its author wondering at "the exclusion of all women, except one, from direct political power."

When a young woman won a scholarship in literature at the Royal University in Ireland, Oscar editorialized, "It is pleasant to be able to chronicle an item of Irish news that has nothing to do with the violence of party politics or party feeling, and that shows how worthy women are of that higher culture and education which has been so tardily and, in some instances, so grudgingly granted to them." In another short editorial he quoted a passage from Daniel Defoe's *Essay upon Projects* (1697) that begins, "I have often thought of it as one of the most barbarous customs in the world that we deny the advantages of learning to women." Defoe's essay goes into great detail about his scheme for the foundation of women's colleges, among his proposals being the penalty of death for any man proposing marriage to "any of the girl students during term time." Oscar's conclusion about the essay is, "In its anticipation of many of our most modern inventions it shows how thoroughly practical all dreamers are."

Oscar held up America, in his day, as a beacon of progress on women's issues: "Nothing in the United States struck me more than the fact that the remarkable intellectual progress of that country is very largely due to the efforts of American women, who edit many of the most powerful magazines and newspapers, take part in the discussion of every question of public interest, and exercise an important influence upon the growth and tendencies of literature and art." Unfortunately, one prediction about women in the workplace has not quite been realized. "In a recent article in *La France,*" Oscar reported, a Monsieur Sarcey said that "the further we advance . . . the more apparent does it become that women are to take their share as bread-winners in the world. The task is no longer monopolised by men, and will, perhaps, be equally shared by the sexes in another hundred years." (Oscar also suggested a sartorial consequence of this trend, unisex fashions: "It is probable that dress of the two sexes will be assimilated, as similarity of costume always follows similarity of pursuits.") Finally, in a brilliant short piece countering the argument that the admission of women to political life would mean the imposition of their "ethics of the family" on government, Oscar replied, "The family ideal of the State may be difficult of attainment, but as an ideal it is better than the [present] policeman theory. It would mean the moralisation of politics. The cultivation of separate sorts of virtues and separate ideals of duty in men and woman has led to the whole social fabric being weaker and unhealthier than it need be." And, for good measure, he further urged the compulsory service of physically able women in military service (as nurses). Thus, one imagines Oscar would find the increased numbers of women now in elected political office and in military service—though appallingly belated—one of his few causes for rejoicing.

Gloom, however, would roll in like summer fog through the Golden Gate if our back-to-the-future Oscar were to turn his attention to the vociferous puritanical moralists of the present. His choicest eruptions would need no altering for the 1990s:

> The intellect of the race is wasted in the sordid and stupid quarrels of second-rate politicians or third-rate theologians. It was reserved for a man of science [Darwin] to show us the supreme example of that 'sweet reasonableness' of which Arnold spoke so wisely, and, alas! to so little effect. . . . If one contemplates the ordinary pulpits and platforms of England, one can but feel the contempt of Julian, or the indifference of Montaigne. We are dominated by the fanatic, whose worst vice is his sincerity. Anything approaching to the free play of the mind is practically unknown amongst us. People cry out against the sinner, yet it is not the sinful, but the stupid, who are our shame. There is no sin except stupidity.

The ignominious downfall of many a supposedly God-fearing evangelist and politician in recent years would have delighted him. Though, as his Mrs Cheveley suggests, these moral collapses would not surprise him in the least. "Nowadays, with our modern mania for morality," she observes, "everyone has to pose as a paragon of purity, incorruptibility, and all the other seven deadly virtues—and what is the result? You all go over like ninepins— one after the other. Not a year passes in England without somebody disappearing. Scandals used to lend charm, or at least interest, to a man—now they crush him." Just weeks after Mrs Cheveley first spoke these acerbities on the stage of the Theatre Royal, the "mania for morality" crushed Oscar himself.

The way journalists abetted the moralists' mania evoked some of Oscar's most sulfuric scorn. Here is one castigation that—with the ascendancy of television journalism—still sounds as if it could have been written yesterday. Written in 1891, it also held some ominous portent for Oscar himself and the way the press treated him at his fall:

> In centuries before ours the public nailed the ears of journalists to the pump. That was quite hideous. In this century journalists have nailed their own ears to the keyhole. That is much worse. . . . The harm is done by the serious, thoughtful, earnest journalists, who solemnly . . . drag before the eyes of the public some incident in the private life of a great statesman. . . . [They] invite the public to discuss the incident, to exercise authority in the matter, to give their views, and not merely to give their views, but to carry them into action, to dictate to the man upon all other points, to dictate to his party, to dictate to his country, in fact to make themselves ridiculous, offensive, and harmful. The private lives of men and women should not be told to the public. The public have nothing to do with them at all.

Allied to the right of privacy, in Oscar's mind, was the right of free artistic expression. The censorious uproar over exhibition of the brilliant photographs of Robert Mapplethorpe would doubtless have infuriated him. He might have reminded the world, as he said in "The Soul of Man," that when people "describe a work as grossly immoral, they mean that the artist has said or made a beautiful thing that is true." The Mapplethorpe uproar might also have reminded Oscar of the first attacks in the press on *Dorian*

Gray, which eventually made him rise up and lecture the editor of the *Pall Mall Gazette* sternly, "Believe me, sir, Puritanism is never so offensive and destructive as when it deals with art matters. It is there that its influence is radically wrong. It is this Puritanism ... that is always marring the artistic instinct of the English." Oscar would also find the religious fundamentalism that has effectively incarcerated Salman Rushdie equally disgusting: of the disappearance of the great African universities at Fez he observed, "Freedom of thought has been killed by the Koran." Though Oscar would surely be bemused at how many decades it took for the censorship of the stage and films to be (more or less) abandoned, he would still say that the world has not yet learned the lesson that "there is very little use in airing one's moral sense at the expense of one's artistic appreciation." And he might also express his old preference—which he emphasized with sarcastic italics—for the French *modus operandi* of his day: "In France ... they limit the journalist, and allow the artist almost perfect freedom. *Here we allow absolute freedom to the journalist, and entirely limit the artist.*"

What other grand pontifications might Oscar be moved to recycle as the moon glides over the hills of the East Bay? He might meditate on the spectacular vulgarities of celebrity today and recall that he wrote once, "Formerly we used to canonize our heroes. The modern method is to vulgarize them." The eyes of the man who said it was always Judas who writes the biography would have narrowed to slits at the current raft of tattling life stories. Of their authors, Oscar observed, "They are the mere body-snatchers of literature. The dust is given to one, and the ashes to the other, and the soul is out of their reach." A visit to a magazine and newspaper shop would leave him stunned at how much worse the "foolish habit of reading periodicals" has become. Such publications "chronicle, with degrading avidity, the sins of the second-rate, and ... give us accurate and prosaic details of the doings of people of absolutely no interest whatsoever." He would view the Everest of printed matter inundating the planet and perhaps even be moved to dig up for republication his witty letter to the editor of the *Pall Mall Gazette*, which had been running a series of columns on "The Best Hundred Books" to read. Oscar suggested that the mission of telling what *not* to read was the one "eminently needed in this age of ours, an age that reads so much that it has no time to admire, and writes so much that it has no time to think. Whoever will select out of the chaos of our modern curricula 'The Worst Hundred Books,' and publish a list of them, will confer on the rising generation a real and lasting benefit." Finally, Oscar might look at the busyness and business down below and think that one other aspect of the new age has not changed an iota—has surely worsened: "We live in the age of the overworked, and the under-educated; the age in which people are so industrious that they become absolutely stupid."

Bosie called Oscar, "more or less, a prophet," and the accuracy of some of his prophecies would probably evoke, between languid puffs, some gloatful preening. His prediction to Arthur Conan Doyle about future wars—"A chemist on each side will approach the frontier with a bottle"—presaged the strategic importance of chemical warfare in World War I and as recently as the Iran-Iraq conflict. The rise of Communism would have horrified him, but its fall he did predict: "It is clear, then, that no Authoritarian Socialism will do. For while under the present system a very large number of people can lead lives of a certain amount of freedom and expression and happiness, under an industrial-barrack system, or a system of economic tyranny, nobody would be able to have any such freedom at all. . . . *It is only in voluntary associations that man is fine.*" Oscar might also be amused by the recent fashion in academia for deconstructive literary theory, which declares the author and his intentions irrelevant and man the pawn of language. To theorists in this mode he could justly remark, "I not only follow you, I precede you" . . . by about a hundred years. He declared the highest form of criticism is that which "does not confine itself . . . to discovering the real intention of the artist and accepting that as final." For a finished work "has an independent life of its own, and may deliver a message far other than that which was put in its lips to say." Oscar's insistence that language is "the parent, and not the child, of thought," that conscious aim "is worse than a delusion," and that men "are the slave of words" made him a pioneering deconstructionist. Incidentally, Oscar had a warning for eager followers of the latest fashion, in literary theory as elsewhere. "Nothing is so dangerous as being too modern," says Lady Markby in *An Ideal Husband*. "One is apt to grow old-fashioned quite suddenly."

Surely the prophecy Oscar would be happiest and proudest of is the one he made about the future of gay liberation. Oscar was not normally sanguine of temperament, so it was characteristic of him to give Gerald, the naive, untutored ingenue in *A Woman of No Importance*, the line about justice being slow but coming in the end. However, this optimistic sentiment—which resembles strikingly the assertion of Martin Luther King, Jr., that "the arc of the moral universe is long, but it bends toward justice"—does parallel the one prophecy he made about the future liberation of the Love that dare not speak its name. It came in a letter to George Ives written from Nice in 1898: "Yes: I have no doubt we shall win, but the road is long, and red with monstrous martyrdoms. Nothing but the repeal of the Criminal Law Amendment Act would do any good. That is the essential. It is not so much public opinion as public officials that need educating." Perhaps Ives remembered this letter when, two years later, Oscar's death plunged him into misery. For he wrote in his diary on 1 December, "Oscar Wilde, victim and martyr, died yesterday in Paris," and on 2 December, thinking no doubt of the reaction of England's gay population: "The land is full of tears I know: we must leave to time and evolution and then our day will come."

The world took its time, though, and a proper "evolution" did not commence in earnest until the 1960s. As late as 1967, Croft-Cooke could describe the terrible experiences of Oscar in the mid-1890s as having "a harrowing comparability with . . . our own decades." Nor can one say that evolution in the following decades has been inexorably forward. There have been periods of decided devolution, of which the most notable and recent was the presidential election of 1992. The rhetoric of this campaign demonstrated how vulnerable to attack the gay movement still is—and how long (and occasionally reddened by "monstrous martyrdoms") the road may yet be. An eagerness to condemn and ostracize irrupted most disagreeably—at exactly the historical moment for the country when the ecumenical, all-embracing spirit of Walt Whitman (whom Edward Carpenter called "the inaugurator . . . of a new world of democratic ideals") and Oscar Wilde would seem to have been most desperately needed. "To know anything about oneself," Oscar wrote, "one must know all about others. There must be no mood with which one cannot sympathise, no dead mode of life that one cannot make alive." The spectacle of a vice president still clinging to the notion that homosexuality is a matter of choice reminded one gloomily of how far we still are from succeeding at the practical goal Oscar insisted on pursuing, namely, the education of "public officials." As early as 1895, Edward Carpenter could assert, "It would seem almost certain that there must be some physiological basis for the [homosexual] desire." Oscar today would wonder in stupefaction and disgust that uncertainty on this point has persisted in high places for an entire century.

Would Oscar have been gratified to find himself such an iconic figure for the Cause? In "The Critic as Artist" there is a lovely, mordant passage on the delusion of conscious intention in this benighted and inscrutable world:

> If we lived long enough to see the results of our actions it may be that those who call themselves good would be sickened with a dull remorse, and those whom the world calls evil stirred by a noble joy. Each little thing that we do passes into the great machine of life which may grind our virtues to powder and make them worthless, or transform our sins into elements of a new civilization, more marvellous and more splendid than any that has gone before.

Of all Oscar's unwitting prophecies about his own life that we have encountered, this, I believe, is the most poignant. For in the fullness of time his "sins" became elements of a new civilization that *is* more marvelous and splendid in its attitudes toward the Love that once dared not speak its name. His "gross indecency" led to one of the "monstrous martyrdoms" that he predicted lay in the future of the gay liberation movement: perhaps its first enduringly famous one. He whom the world once called evil might well feel now "stirred by a noble joy" in contemplation of the place of honor he now occupies in the movement. Oscar's remark to Frank Harris in his darkest hour—that some are called upon to suffer as an example to humanity and be (in Shelley's phrase) "an echo and a light unto eternity"—may have sounded oddly inflated then, but time has vindicated it brilliantly.

Punch magazine made fun of Oscar in one of its last skits on him in the personage of a Guy Fawkes doll named Fustian Flitters. He is uncontrollably given to paradoxes, and in one of them he opines, "Only failures ever *do* succeed." A century has transformed this send-up into the truest and most agreeable of all Oscarian truisms. Though the progress he envisioned is by no means complete, he might still permit himself to preen a bit, boast that he was right about justice being slow but coming in the end.

What, by the way, would Oscar have had to say about AIDS and the human (and governmental) response to the crisis? Something caustic, to be sure. Perhaps he would simply have quoted the harsh assessment of human nature made by his Celtic soul mate Bernard Shaw in 1894: "No fact is ever attended to by the average citizen until the neglect of it has killed enough of his neighbors to thoroughly frighten him."

☆ ☆ ☆

ONE FINAL WHIMSICAL QUESTION might be asked about "Oscar today." What gainful employment—one would not want to say "useful profession," since he deplored such a concept—might have supported a domicile with a fine prospect of San Francisco

Bay, gold-tipped cigarettes, the occasional dinner of ortolans wrapped in grape leaves, and bottles of Pommery or Perrier-Jouet when the spirit moved? He would make a splendid late-night talk-show habitué or host, a mesmerizing blend of Gore Vidal and Truman Capote, but I suspect his real forte would be in the realm of "book-chat," which, as Ellmann suggested, he practically invented.

Oscar often proved himself a gallant and generous-spirited reviewer, especially in covering the literary scene as editor of *Woman's World*. But the real charm of his book-reviewing skills lay in his delectably barbed manner of expressing dismay or disgust. On run-of-the-mill English novelists he opined, "They lead us through a barren desert of verbiage to a mirage that they call life." Then he added, with Oscarian *noblesse oblige*, "However, one should not be too severe on English novels: they are the only relaxation of the intellectually unemployed." Of a novel by one Mrs Chetwynd he allowed, "The book can be read without any trouble and was probably written without any trouble also." Of the novels of Rhoda Broughton, he observed, "She at least possesses that one touch of vulgarity that makes the whole world kin."

No friend of biographers as a race, when they fell short Oscar could cut to the quick. Of a feckless life of Dante Gabriel Rossetti, he concluded, "It is just the sort of biography Guildenstern might have written of Hamlet." Of a hopelessly pedantic life of Wordsworth he waxed thus wroth: "Carlyle once proposed in jest to write a life of Michael Angelo without making any reference to his art, and Mr Caine has shown that such a project is perfectly feasible. He has written the life of a great peripatetic philosopher and chronicled only the peripatetics." Oscar adds for good measure, "So mediocre is Mr Caine's book that even accuracy could not make it better."

His "briefly noted" fillers could also reek of vinegar:

The accomplished authoress of *Soap* was once compared to George Eliot by the *Court Journal*, and to Carlyle by

the *Daily News*, but we fear that we cannot compete
with our contemporaries in these daring comparisons.
Her present book is very clever, rather vulgar, and contains some fine examples of bad French.

And, of course, his book-chat left many an incisive quip in its
wake. For instance, his aggravation at cheap literature that is "always making demands on our credulity without ever appealing to
our imagination" or his squelch of an author who tried to pre-
empt negative criticism: "We would earnestly beg Mr Winter not
to write foolish prefaces about unappreciative critics; for it is only
mediocrities and old maids who consider it a grievance to be misunderstood." Oscar clearly would have been quite at home on the
present-day cut-and-thrust literary scene: "There is always something peculiarly impotent," he knew, "about the violence of a literary man."

The only event of recent years that one can imagine causing
our San Francisco–based Oscar genuine apoplexy perhaps deserves mention. In the mid-1980s, a group of entrepreneurs conceived the idea of marketing beer for a gay clientele. Naturally,
inevitably, they concluded that the ideal brand name for the bev-
erage should be "Wilde's." *Beer*, for heaven's sake! ("Beer, the Bible, and the seven deadly virtues have made our England what it
is" is among Oscar's unpublished aphorisms.) One can say with
confidence that the great lover of champagne would either have
spun in his Père-Lachaise grave on learning about this appropri-
ation of his name—or pealed hysterical, derisive laughter from his
San Francisco penthouse.

Just a month before the arrest, *Punch* asked, "Will the elaborate Wildean paradoxes have to a future generation the freshness
and the laughter-provoking qualities of [Sheridan's] Mrs Malaprop?... Will a Doctor of Letters towards the end of the next
century be seen to smile over Oscar's inversions?" *Punch* concluded, "I doubt it." But now it seems clear that the answer to
these questions is a most emphatic yes, and not only for Litt.D.'s
but for all of us.

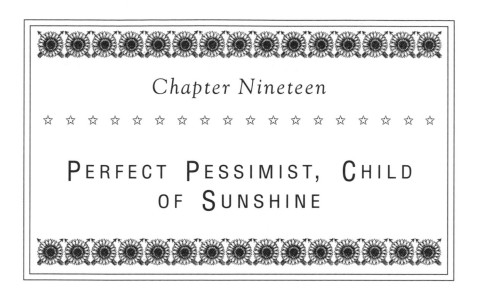

Chapter Nineteen

☆ ☆ ☆ ☆ ☆ ☆ ☆ ☆ ☆ ☆ ☆ ☆ ☆ ☆ ☆

PERFECT PESSIMIST, CHILD OF SUNSHINE

I'll laugh and cry at the same time.
—FIGARO, IN BEAUMARCHAIS'S *LE MARIAGE DE FIGARO*

In Falstaff there is something of Hamlet, in Hamlet there is not a little of Falstaff.
—"THE DECAY OF LYING"

CONSTANTINE CAVAFY BEGINS HIS fine poem "Che fece . . . il gran Rifiuto" (titled after Dante):

> For some people the day comes
> when they have to declare the great Yes
> or the great No . . .

The man with the "Yes" in him readily utters it and goes "from honor to honor, strong in his conviction." But

> He who refuses does not repent. Asked again,
> he'd still say no. Yet that no—the right no—
> drags him down all his life.

Most of us in this world go through life uttering very modest yeas and nays, usually in dithering juxtaposition. When we are "great" it is merely in uttering a heaven-storming Maybe. It is the fiercely courageous sayers of the great No's and the great Yes's who stand out. In Shakespeare, one thinks immediately of all the memorable naysayers like Lear ("No, no, no life!"), Iago ("Demand me nothing"), and Antony ("No, no, no, no, no" he says to Cleopatra). This is no surprise: for every "yes" in Shakespeare's plays, there are seventeen "no's"—No being the stuff of drama and, as Oscar also well recognized, the stuff of all Art. On the affirmative other hand, one thinks of Nietzsche's *Dawn,* which its author called a "Yes-saying book," and of Molly Bloom's *Ulysses*-ending monologue, which begins with a Yes and ends: "I put my arms around him yes and drew him down to me so he could feel my breasts all perfume yes and his heart was going like mad and yes I said yes I will Yes." Such words inviting sexual license Oscar—his heart also beating madly, perhaps—was no doubt eager to hear on many a forbidden occasion.

Virtuosos who can utter both the great Yes and the great No to equally spectacular effect—as divas in the opera house do, their Yes's and No's often coinciding with deafening high C's—are very seldom encountered, and one of the chief fascinations and puzzlements about Oscar is that he was of this rare breed. Somehow the great Yes and the great No managed to coexist in him, undiminished in their utterly discrete (but by no means discreet) power. As we have seen in the "Closet Philosopher" chapter, his Yes was uttered, as Cavafy says, by one "strong in his conviction." This was his Nietzschean "Yes to life even in its strangest and hardest problems" and the Yes of *homo ludens,* of man at play. But as the *"amor fati"* chapter also suggested, a potent No—both courageous and reckless—was ever at the ready within him as well, the No of the "fatalist and stoic" one Parisian acquaintance thought him to be. This was, in Cavafy's phrase, the right No . . . the No he would not repent of, the No that dragged him down all his life.

Two observations—one by the Comtesse de Brémont, the

other by Oscar himself—capture this extraordinary coexistence of the affirming and negating spirits. The Comtesse shrewdly summarized about Oscar, "There is nothing so weak and, at the same time, so powerful as genius. Nothing so helpless and yet so helpful as genius." The seemingly paradoxical coexistence in Oscar's personality of weakness and power, helplessness and helpfulness, is in part explained by the great Yes and No. Perhaps it is not too fanciful to imagine the Yes and No being symbolized in the two rings that Stuart Merrill noticed he always wore: one brought him good fortune, the other bad. "For unlike most people," Oscar the ex-convict explained to Merrill, "I have never mixed my shares of fortune and misfortune. For a long time I was the happiest of men, now I well deserve to be the most unhappy. At the moment I am under the influence of my evil ring." This anecdote captures the poignant discreteness of the Oscarian Yes and No and encourages further meditation on Oscar's two great and supremely contradictory masks.

First, the mask of Hamlet, which he wore under the influence of his ring of "outrageous fortune." Second, the mask of the "goodly portly" Falstaff, which he wore under the ring of benign influence. In this guise he appeared as Beerbohm remembered him: a great "talker" who "had all—poetry, wit, humour, anecdote, repartee" . . . and a man not only brilliantly witty in himself but the cause of wit in others. For Beerbohm also recalled him as a "good host" who "brought people out" and made "dull wine bright"—an emphatically Falstaffian compliment.

One of these masks has always been—and still is—far more popular and comfortable as a definer of his public image, but the other mask was always very near to hand, often worn but rarely in public. Finally, one cannot understand Oscar without seeing him in both of these masks. He asserted, "Man is least himself when he talks in his own person. Give him a mask, and he will tell you the truth." The astonishment, in his own case, is that so much of what seems "the truth" about his personality and writings is uttered from behind two masks so unlike each other as those of Hamlet and Falstaff.

The Stranger Wilde

☆ ☆ ☆

TOWARD THE END OF the first act of *The Importance of Being Earnest* this dialogue passes between Algy and his manservant:

> ALGERNON: I hope to-morrow will be a fine day, Lane.
> LANE: It never is, sir.
> ALGERNON: Lane, you're a perfect pessimist.
> LANE: I do my best to give satisfaction, sir.

Oscar was notorious for putting his quite undisguised alter egos on stage: Lane, though a very small role, must be counted among them. For there runs through Oscar's life, correspondence, and published works a vein of pessimism worthy of Hamlet, that most famously perfect of all pessimists who, so far as the play tells us, also never experiences "a fine day."

Oscar observed once, "There are as many Hamlets as there are melancholies"; there are also many kinds of melancholies in Oscar. Polonius's remark to Claudius about Hamlet—"There's something in his soul/O'er which his melancholy sits on brood"—suits Oscar perfectly when his ring of misfortune is in the ascendant. Conversely, Hamlet's "life" on stage is effectively summarized in a fine musical image that Oscar employed to describe his own life in *De profundis*: "My life . . . had all the while been a real Symphony of Sorrow, passing through its rhythmically-linked movements to its certain resolution, with that inevitableness that in Art characterises the treatment of every great theme." Though Oscar the *arbiter elegantiarum* deplored the "customary suits of solemn black" favored by Hamlet and many nineteenth-century men, Hamlet's "inky cloak" of melancholy was an oft-worn part of his intellectual wardrobe.

One obvious shared source of such melancholy is the sense one has of two essentially extrovert personalities concealing ultimate truths behind masked personas. Both Oscar and the Prince could admit, as the artist Basil Hallward does in *Dorian Gray*,

"I have grown to love secrecy." Both are constantly flirting with revelation in virtuoso fashion, hinting, as Hamlet says, at "that within which passes show." Both also suffer palpably from the recognition Oscar expressed in a letter just a year before the denouement of his tragedy: "It is not wise to show one's heart to the world." It is especially unwise (and makes masks especially necessary) when, as in Hamlet's case, "the time is out of joint" or when, as in Oscar's case, the times were merely vulgar: "In so vulgar an age as this we all need masks."

And so Hamlet plays the madman, Oscar the dilettante and dandy—but both with a "method in't." Oscar might well have been speaking of Polonius when he said, "Seriousness of manner is the disguise of the fool," and of himself and Hamlet when he added, "Folly in its exquisite modes of triviality and indifference and lack of care is the robe of the wise man." He once jested to Ross that his next book would be "a discussion as to whether the commentators on *Hamlet* are mad or only pretending to be," but that he never produced an Oscarian commentary on the play is a matter for serious rue.

The melancholy shared by Hamlet and Oscar also derives from their high order of intellectual distinction and power of imagination. Hamlet is of course the English theater's archetype of the mind-sick *isolé*. Oscar, in his Hamlet guise, also presents an extraordinary figure of isolation—isolated in part by his sexuality, but also by the exercise of that supreme instrument of liberation, the imagination. The power to create by oneself "a fiction, a dream of passion," as the players at Elsinore do, and then live within this dream is the power of imagination; exploiting this gift, Oscar believed, was the only truly "useful" profession in life. Though Hamlet inveighs against the man who is "passion's slave," he to his eternal fame is such a slave. For him, as for Oscar, passion seems the only way. As Lord Henry says in *Dorian Gray*, "Life is a question of nerves and fibres, and slowly built-up cells in which thought hides and passion has its dreams." The imaginative power to create and inhabit these dreams is given to the few: to criminals and artists, trespassers and poets, rebels and immoralists—with all of whom Oscar frequently identified himself. Hamlet, Oscar felt, was of the same party. The Prince, he asserts in *De profundis*, "is a dreamer" and has "the nature of a poet." He is, in short, Oscar's brother: "We poets and dreamers are all brothers," he had written in a letter several years earlier.

The profound apartness of Oscar and Hamlet—like that of Shaw's Peter Keegan—distances them from their fellow man and makes possible their withering soliloquies. Access to fearful knowledge sets Hamlet apart from the rest of the cast in his playworld, and Oscar was likewise set apart from the *dramatis personae* of his Victorian age. He was profoundly aware of this dissociation, admitting once that the doomed painter Hallward in *Dorian Gray* "is what I think I am." In one of the most informative autobiographical passages Oscar ever wrote, he has Hallward express a sense of the isolating effect of any special gift from the gods:

> There is a fatality about all physical and intellectual distinction, the sort of fatality that seems to dog through history the falterings steps of kings. It is better not to be different from one's fellows. The ugly and the stupid have the best of it in this world. They can sit at their ease and gape at the play. If they know nothing of victory, they are at least spared the knowledge of defeat. They live as we all should live, undisturbed, indifferent, and without disquiet. . . . Your rank and wealth, Harry; my brains, such as they are—my art, whatever it may be worth; Dorian Gray's good looks—we shall all suffer for what the gods have given us, suffer terribly.

Hallward's grim discourse reminds one of *Hamlet* several times: the allusion to the "faltering steps" of kings (and princes); the stupid, indifferent gaping of an audience like, say, the one watching *The Mousetrap;* and all the distinguishing qualities of rank, brains, art, and good looks that make Hamlet such a splendid tragedy hero.

One other gift of the gods, too, Oscar shared with Hamlet:

a golden tongue. Hamlet is unanimously accounted Shakespeare's Lord of Language, and this Oscar called himself on more than one occasion: "I was a Lord of Language, and had myself the soul of a poet." This gift made it possible for him—when the ring of melancholy ruled—to paraphrase time and again Hamlet's devastating speech that begins, "I have of late . . . lost all my mirth." With no trouble at all, one could patch together from Oscar's own aphorisms and paradoxes a version of Hamlet's crushing putdown of the world as a "sterile promontory," the heavens a "pestilent congregation of vapors," and man a "quintessence of dust."

This vein of fierce derision manifested itself early. Indeed, in a letter written to a college classmate while on summer holiday, Oscar suggests he may have inherited this penchant for pessimism from his mother, who sometimes let the world's slings and arrows cause her to turn cynic:

> She has a very strong faith in . . . the divine intelligence of which we on earth partake. Here she is very strong, though of course at times troubled by the discord and jarring of the world, when she takes a dip into pessimism.
>
> Her last pessimist, Schopenhauer, says the whole human race ought on a given day, after a strong remonstrance *firmly but respectfully* urged on God, to walk into the sea and leave the world tenantless, but of course some skulking wretches would hide and be left behind to people the world again I am afraid.

There is undergraduate insouciance here, befitting a twenty-year-old, but it marks the beginning of a great theme on which Oscar was to compose ever more bitter variations. Sometimes they resound in serious or melodramatic contexts, as when Lady Windermere asserts, "Actions are the first tragedy in life, words are the second. Words are perhaps the worst. Words are merciless." Or when Mrs Allonby—who sees clearly a world that is out of joint—observes in *A Woman of No Importance* that life is "simply a *mauvais quart d'heure* made up of exquisite moments." Sometimes Oscar's fatalism appears like a shaft of darkness in a comic context, as when Jack admonishes Algy in *Earnest*, "For heaven's sake, don't try to be cynical. It's perfectly easy to be cynical."

In the late 1880s and early 1890s, Oscar found it easier and easier to be cynical. Perhaps his first real burst of destructive energy came in 1889, with the publication of "The Decay of Lying." In this brilliant attack upon the Poloniuses of his day he praises the Whim (also fundamental in Hamlet's personality) and discourages, as fatal to the imagination, any consort with the "aged and well-informed." He also admires Maupassant for how, Hamlet-like, the French author's "keen mordant irony . . . strips life of the few poor rags that still cover her, and shows us foul sore and festering wound." Oscar's remark about Falstaff and Hamlet in the epigraph occurs here by way of preparation for his assertion that the most drastic differences in personality cannot conceal a grim truth about human nature: "Where we differ from each other is purely in accidentals. . . . The more one analyses people, the more all reasons for analysis disappear. Sooner or later one comes to that dreadful universal thing called human nature."

In the following year's "Critic as Artist," Oscar donned again Hamlet's sable thoughts. He in effect "defies augury," asserting that the notion of "conscious aim" is "worse than a delusion": our powerlessness over the consequences of our acts is complete. His insistence that "each little thing that we do passes into the great machine of life, which may grind our virtues to powder . . . or transform our sins into elements of a new civilization," curiously echoes Hamlet's own "Since no man, of aught he leaves, knows what is't to leave betimes, let be." Perhaps the best and most succinct summary we have of the "philosophy" of Shakespeare's bottomless play comes a few pages later in the essay, where Gilbert says simply, "When a man acts he is a puppet. When he describes he is a poet. The whole secret lies in that."

The month before "The Critic as Artist" appeared, Oscar wore his "inky cloak" to shocking effect in the pages of *Dorian Gray*. The Hamlet figure here, of course, is Lord Henry Wotton, for whom there are also no more "fine days": thunderheads, rather, with no silver linings. "Something tragic" is found lying behind every exquisite thing; every effect that one produces "gives one an enemy"; all ways end at the same point: "Disillusion." Toward the end of the novel occurs this touch of fatalism:

> "*Fin de siècle,*" murmured Lord Henry.
> "*Fin du globe,*" answered his hostess.
> "I wish it were *fin du globe,*" said Dorian, with a sigh.
> "Life is a great disappointment."

Such profound gloom is present, though not always readily apparent, in virtually all of Oscar's writings, whether one accosts him in his flippant, cheeky vein or in his more refrigerated, cankered mood. But the Victorian public was happily besotted with the former Oscar, the seemingly harmless and blithe childish spirit. Very few observers at the time were shrewd enough to guess at the existence of the darker side or hear Hamlet's inflection in his utterances; they could not get close enough to their delightful Harlequin to notice the tear of Pierrot painted under his eye. One of the few who did was Percival Almy, who in 1894 offered this amazed estimation of Oscar: "His veracity is terrible . . . and all the more terrible because it is implied rather than direct. He leaves us not a lie to cover us. . . . Oh, he is a grim physician!"

The awesome strength of the No in Oscar, however, only becomes apparent in the more private and unguarded pages of his private conversations and letters. One thinks, for instance, of Vincent O'Sullivan remembering that one of Oscar's "favourite sayings" was that "there is something vulgar in all success. The greatest men fail—or seem to the world to have failed." This is as pertinent a comment on Hamlet's own response to the challenge of his father's ghost as one could wish. There is perhaps even something of Hamlet's profound bleakness in Oscar's rueful remark from a letter of 1886: "Sometimes I think the artistic life is a long and lovely suicide, and am not sorry that it is so." This confession is but one more of the tragic foreshadowings that filled

Oscar's life. Much that he wrote—like Salome's request for the head of Jokanaan—possessed an element of the suicidal.

Oscar in England, like Hamlet in Denmark, was finally, as he morosely concluded to his friend More Adey, "a problem for which there was no solution."

☆ ☆ ☆

UNDER THE INFLUENCE OF his ring of misfortune, Oscar was driven toward introversion and misanthropy, which flavor almost all of his writings, even the fairy tales. Under the influence of his ring of happy fortune, on the other hand, he became the Player—or Playful—King. He became the brilliantly sociable, extroverted child at heart who is usually conjured today at the mention of his name. This is the Oscar who led Borges to say that "the pleasure we derive from his company is irresistible and constant" and who led Helena Sickert to call him "a child of sunshine" and single out "joyousness" as one of his two great features (kindness the other). This is the Falstaffian Oscar: shamelessly and carelessly idle, naively self-vaunting, incessantly flippant.

Such exhilarating company was very hard to resist or relinquish, as Frank Harris made movingly clear near the end of his book on his long-dead friend:

> When to the sessions of sad memory I summon up the spirits of those whom I have met in the world and loved, men famous and men of unfulfilled renown, I miss no one so much as I miss Oscar Wilde. . . . I would rather have him back now than almost anyone I have ever met. I have known more heroic souls and some deeper souls; souls more keenly alive to ideas of duty and generosity; but I have known no more charming, no more quickening, no more delightful spirit.

Harris's tone is here not that of Hamlet's detached, ironic "Alas, poor Yorick" eulogy for a long-gone jester, but one of genuine affection and nostalgia. This wistful tone is encountered very often in reminiscences of those contemporaries who heard the chimes at midnight with Oscar. Doubtless the same kind of affection and nostalgia for Falstaff's character among Shakespeare's Globe Theater clientele (and with Elizabeth, too, if the famous story of her command to resurrect is true) caused him to bring Falstaff back as the star of *The Merry Wives of Windsor*.

That Oscar was perfectly attuned to Falstaff's world of outrageous playfulness is perhaps most efficiently captured by a perusal of the "Phrases and Philosophies for the Use of the Young" that he contributed to *The Chameleon* in 1894. Several of these aphorisms, taken together, virtually lay out the premises of Shakespeare's characterization of his "huge hill of flesh":

Pleasure is the only thing one should live for. Nothing ages like happiness.

One should always be a little improbable.

Any preoccupation with ideas of what is right or wrong in conduct shows an arrested intellectual development.

The condition of perfection is idleness.

To love oneself is the beginning of a life-long romance.

Such are the commandments that govern Falstaff's every move.

Many of Oscar's most notorious character traits are also reminiscent of Falstaff. For instance, his admitted laziness and invariable desire to linger at his recreations and ignore the great, busy world. This tendency to truancy from the real world Oscar expressed in a letter about leaving his first great playpen, Oxford University. Straitened family finances, he told Bouncer Ward, might mean "leaving Oxford and doing some horrid work to earn bread. The world is too much for me." Oscar also possessed a hugely expansive personality that, as Samuel Johnson said of Falstaff, made him "inimitable." The *Cleveland Herald* put it well, when it editorialized in advance of Oscar's arrival that he deserved "decent treatment even though he be so utterly *et cetera* that the American mind cannot grasp him." A related part of Falstaff's "utterly *et cetera*" character is the agility, unexpectedness, and surprise of his utterances, and these qualities, too, were noted by many witnesses to be abundant in Oscar's conversation. Beerbohm recalled him never uttering a commonplace—there was "always some twist" in his phrasing. He also thought Oscar's jollity (like Falstaff's) sometimes "overdone," but could not deny that there was "real vitality" in it.

But what finally made Oscar so charismatic behind his Falstaffian mask was simply the irresistible and constant instinct to laugh. By most all accounts he was, to borrow the phrases of the Master of the Revels in *A Midsummer Night's Dream*, a man of "merry tears" and "the passion of loud laughter." Though his intellect beckoned him toward the chilly Scandinavian cynicism of Elsinore, his temperament drew him toward sunnier and warmer climes. Hence his devotion to Mediterranean haunts. Mrs Allonby observes in *A Woman of No Importance*, "Nothing is serious except passion. The intellect is not a serious thing, and never has been." If there is any autobiographical truth in this view, perhaps one can then say Oscar's Falstaffian "passion" for laughter finally won out over his Hamlet-like intellect.

Indeed, in a letter written in 1898 he declared, "Laughter is the primaeval attitude towards life—a mode of approach that survives only in artists and criminals." This remark about laughter occurred during a discussion of the response of children to literature and how their humor vanishes as they grow up. But the happy, primeval instinct to laugh persists in Falstaff into very old age. Robert Ross insisted that it also survived in Oscar—even through the trauma of his trials and imprisonment: "That Wilde suffered at times from extreme poverty and intensely from social ostracism I know very well; but his temperament was essentially a happy one, and I think his good spirits and enjoyment of life far outweighed any bitter recollection or realisations of an equivocal and tragic position. No doubt he felt the latter keenly, but he concealed his feeling as a general rule, and his manifestations of it only lasted a very few days." Ross would have us believe that Oscar's heart was not fatally broken as Falstaff's was by the trauma of Hal's rejection; it would be pleasant and comforting to think so.

Two stories told about Oscar, if true (and they have the distinct ring of truth), do capture the man's unsinkable, Falstaffian exuberance and refusal to wear the inky cloak in public. These stories lend some credibility to Ross's optimistic view. The first, my favorite of all the hundreds of anecdotes retailed about Oscar, took place after the Queensberry charges became public, threatening, among many other sad consequences, the closing of Oscar's two plays then running, *An Ideal Husband* and *Earnest*. Lewis Waller (the actor playing Chiltern in the former) and Allan Aynesworth (playing Algy in the latter) were walking down Piccadilly deep in conversation about the man who seemed likely to end their employment when suddenly, to their horror, Oscar hailed them cheerfully from a hansom cab. The story, as Max Beerbohm told it, continues:

They returned his greeting pallidly, hoping Wilde would ride on, but he didn't. He got out and came up to them. "Have you heard," he inquired, "what that swine Queensberry has had the effrontery to say?" Writhing with embarrassment, they both protested that no rumor of the Marquis's allegation had reached their chaste ears. "Since you haven't heard it, I'll tell you," said Wilde, with the eagerness of a tutor avid to fill in a gap in folklore. "He actually had the effrontery to say"— and he fixed his eye on Waller—"that *The Importance of Being Earnest* was a better-acted play than *An Ideal Husband!*" He smiled radiantly, waved, got back into his hansom, and rode off down Piccadilly, leaving his victims gasping.

The imp of the playful had not abandoned Oscar even at this devastating time.

The other little narrative comes in Ross's letter to More Adey describing Oscar's last few days. The letter is as rich in pathos as the Hostess's description of the death of Falstaff in *Henry V*, but one brief passage suggests that Falstaffian spirit accompanied him to the grave. Ross reported that, shortly after Reggie Turner arrived for a visit, "Oscar told us that he had had a horrible dream the previous night—'that he had been supping with the dead.' Reggie made a very typical response, 'My dear Oscar, you were probably the life and soul of the party.' This delighted Oscar, who became high-spirited again, almost hysterical."

☆ ☆ ☆

A FEW DAYS AFTER Oscar was released from prison, he received an eagerly awaited letter from Bosie at the Hôtel de la Plage in Berneval-sur-Mer. Three young friends were visiting him, and he could only glimpse the letter's last three lines. "I love the last words of anything," he wrote in a brief note the next day; "the end in art is the beginning."

The last words about Oscar, however, are very hard to compose, most obviously because Hamlet and Falstaff are so inextricably bound together in his nature. He was a man who sometimes lost all his mirth, at other times none of it. This makes it hard for the mind to grasp him. The judgment as to whether the dark side or the sunshine side of the man is dominant—or whether an astonishing equilibrium is achieved—will therefore probably depend on the temperament one brings to him.

His ending was, if not tragic, at the very least profoundly sad. In many ways it was a result of the metastasis of exactly the Falstaffian traits that made him such an exhilarating public celebrity to behold: his love of pleasure, his delight in improbability, his insouciance, and his lifelong romance of perfectly requited self-love. This last trait may be what led Shaw to assert that Oscar was (indeed, like Falstaff) "utterly selfish" and "incapable of friendship" . . . though Shaw added that he was capable of "the most touching kindness." Shaw also observed, "Many of our worst habits are acquired in an imaginary world," and we have noticed that this is exactly where Yeats thought Oscar lived his life. In a similar vein, Walt Whitman expressed his qualms about Oscar, saying he could "never completely make Wilde out—out for good or bad. He writes exquisitely—is as lucid as a star on a clear night—but there seems to be a little substance lacking at the root." These not implausible assessments of an imperfect character, as well as the mortification of the great fall itself, make it far too easy to end this long look at the stranger Wilde on a disheartening note . . . to end, in the phrase of Oscar's Duchess of Paisley, with the conclusion that the man was not "quite right."

But this would be to take sides, and, as Lord Illingworth observes, taking sides leads inexorably to earnestness and boredom. Besides, when the Duchess of Paisley remarks that there is something not "quite right" about palmistry, Lady Windermere utters the perfect Oscarian riposte: "Nothing interesting ever is." No, the only proper last words on this most extraordinarily interesting man must mingle tears and laughter, in the manner of Beaumarchais's probing but ebullient ex-barber, Figaro.

And I can think of no better way to evoke the potent amalgam of sadness and joy in Oscar's life, by way of an *envoi*, than to end with a picture of his own ending: the scenes at his deathbed and funeral. For, in the almost perfect equipoise of tears and smiles in these scenes, nothing in Oscar's life became him like the leaving of it. Robbie Ross's letter to More Adey describing these scenes is full of touches of drollery and pathos—and of events that spark reminiscences both happy and sad.

In addition to his famous jests about not outliving the century and spoiling the Paris Exhibition and the black humor of his last-minute entry into the Roman Catholic church, amusement insinuated itself in many other respects. Ross's remark, "Dying in Paris is really a very difficult and expensive luxury for a foreigner," calls to mind a life of spendthrift luxuriating—and Algy's huge £762.14s.2d. bill in the Gribsby scene of *Earnest*. A lifetime of travel under assumed identities resonates in the farcical uproar that occurred just after his body was washed and placed in a winding-sheet: "The excellent [hotelier] Dupoirier lost his head and complicated matters by making a mystery over Oscar's name." For Oscar had been, Ross explained, "registered under the name of Melmoth at the hotel, and it is contrary to the French law to be under an assumed name in your hotel."

That the Hôtel d'Alsace was at the time besieged mainly by two of Oscar's least favorite kinds of people—journalists and creditors—would have elicited some choice squelches from him, no doubt. (A *Chameleon* maxim of his has it that only by not paying one's bills can one "hope to live in the memory of the commercial classes.") The picture of poor Ross scouring Paris, a city very well supplied with ecclesiastics, to find nuns to watch the body also raises a smile: "It was only after incredible difficulties I got two Franciscan sisters." If Ross had had the presence of mind to employ men in drag, Oscar's soul might have rested much more easily. A District Doctor made an official visit and insisted that Oscar must have committed suicide or been murdered. The revolting prospect of a trip to the morgue was narrowly avoided by bribery: "After a series of drinks and unseasonable jests [which Oscar might in fact have relished], and a liberal fee, the District Doctor consented to sign the permission for burial." Another bureaucrat soon arrived to inventory Oscar's belongings; he asked how many collars Oscar had and the value of his umbrella. (Ross felt he must assure Adey this idiocy took place: "This is quite true, and not a mere exaggeration of mine.")

After the legal formalities, many visitors paid their respects and were allowed to view the body after signing a register. Oscar would have had some choice words for the "various English people, who gave assumed names." Sadly, an anonymous person came by with flowers on behalf of Cyril and Vyvyan, though the boys were surely not told then of their father's death. Ross arranged for Maurice Gilbert to take a deathbed photograph. As with the cows Oscar photographed in the Borghese gardens, there would be no worry about the subject moving and spoiling the picture. But Ross said "the flashlight did not work properly" and thought the session a failure, though a reasonably good picture was salvaged by Gilbert.

The description of the funeral had its whimsical, romantic touches, too. Of course, it is impossible to think of it without recalling the passage in *The Importance of Being Earnest* in which Jack Worthing announces that his brother Earnest has died in Paris. Dr Chasuble asks whether the interment will take place in England:

> JACK: No. He seemed to have expressed a desire to be buried in Paris.
>
> CHASUBLE: In Paris! *(Shakes his head.)* I fear that hardly points to any very serious state of mind at the last.

Ross recorded that fifty-six persons were present, including five women in deep mourning. He had avoided publicity to keep the service small and was taken aback by the turnout, having ordered only three coaches. Still, the first one in the procession was occupied, Oscar-like, solely by Father Cuthbert and an acolyte. Ross counted twenty-two floral wreaths. Fittingly, many of the names of those responsible for them bring memories of laughter to mind: Max Beerbohm, Reggie Turner, the divine Adela Schuster, and even poor, benighted Harold Mellor.

Turner wrote to Beerbohm afterward, "Oscar's coffin was covered with really beautiful flowers. We got one wreath of laurels which we placed at the head and tied all the cards to it." This wreath, which Ross arranged, bore the inscription, "A tribute to his literary achievements and distinction," and on it he listed the names "of those who had shown kindness to him during or after his imprisonment." The list included his publisher Arthur Humphreys, the artists and designers (and lovers) Charles Ricketts and Charles Shannon, More Adey, Will Rothenstein, Alfred Douglas, Frank Harris, Mellor, Turner, Dal Young, Beerbohm, the Lady of Wimbledon, and his beloved Sphinx, Ada Leverson.

One wreath, Ross noted, was not made of real flowers. This was "a pathetic bead trophy" proffered by the owner of the Hôtel d'Alsace, inscribed simply "*À mon locataire*." Still, it was, in a way, the most poignant of all the mortuary tributes. For Ross ended his long narrative to Adey by remarking that he could "scarcely speak in moderation of the magnanimity, humanity and charity of Dupoirier"—and these are precisely the epithets one is inclined to use, if not of Oscar himself, certainly of the spirit of what he has left us.

Chronology

☆ ☆ ☆ ☆ ☆ ☆ ☆ ☆ ☆ ☆ ☆ ☆ ☆ ☆ ☆ ☆ ☆ ☆

1854   16 October: OW born in Dublin to William (1815–76) and Jane Francesca Wilde (1821–96; née Elgee)

1864–71 Student at Portora Royal School, Enniskillen

1873   Wins scholarship to Trinity College, Dublin

1874   June: takes examination at Oxford, wins scholarship in classics at Magdalen College
        October: matriculates

1875   Summer: travels to Italy, France, Ireland

1877   March–April: travels to Genoa, Ravenna, Greece, Naples, Rome; arrives back at Oxford, from which he has been temporarily expelled for absence

1878   June: final examinations at Oxford; wins Newdigate Prize for poem "Ravenna"
        July: awarded a Double First for his examinations
        November: takes his Oxford B.A. and moves to London

1879 Begins writing occasional journalistic essays and publishing poems

May: mother and brother, William (1852–99), move permanently from Dublin to London

1880 *Punch* magazine begins fifteen-year period of satirizing OW

Summer: rooms with Frank Miles at 1 Tite Street, Chelsea

20 November: *Where's the Cat,* a satire on the Aesthetic Movement including a character like OW, opens in London

Fall–winter: Gilbert and Sullivan preparing *Patience* for 23 April 1881 premiere

1881 May: meets Constance Mary Lloyd (1858–98) at her grandmother's Dublin house; OW's *Poems* published

October–November: presentation copy of *Poems* requested by the Oxford Union; after debate, vote to accept it is defeated

December: plans for performance of OW's first play, *Vera,* canceled

24 December: sails for New York City for a yearlong lecture tour of America and Canada sponsored by Richard D'Oyly Carte; among the more than 130 cities he visits are Washington, Philadelphia, Boston, Chicago, San Francisco, St. Louis, Cleveland, Cincinnati, Montreal, and Toronto

1883 January: returns to London from New York City

February–April: stays in Paris, meeting several French celebrities, among them Verlaine, Hugo, Mallarmé, Edmond de Goncourt; works on play *The Duchess of Padua*

May: returns to London; resumes relations with Constance Lloyd

August: sails for New York City for production of *Vera*, which opens on the 21st to mixed reviews, closing in one week

September: returns to London and begins heavy lecture schedule

25 November: becomes engaged to Constance

1884   29 May: marriage takes place at St. James's Church, Paddington, followed by a honeymoon in Paris

December: couple moves into house at 16 Tite Street

1885   Lecturing and occasional writing continue

5 June: first son, Cyril, born at Tite Street

1886   Meets Robert Ross; begins regular writing for *Pall Mall Gazette*

Early November: second son, Vyvyan Oscar Beresford, born

1887   27 March: story "The Canterville Ghost" appears in *New York Tribune*

11 May: story "Lord Arthur Savile's Crime" begins to appear in *Court and Society Review*

18 May: signs agreement to become editor of *Woman's World*; first issue under his supervision appears in November; edits magazine for two years before resigning in October 1889

1888   May: collection of children's stories, *The Happy Prince and Other Tales*, published

October: proposed for membership in the Savile Club (supported by Henry James, Edmund Gosse, Rider Haggard) but not elected

1889 Meets John Gray at about this time

January: "Pen, Pencil and Poison" appears in *Fortnightly Review*; "The Decay of Lying" appears in *Nineteenth Century*

July: "The Portrait of Mr W.H." appears in *Blackwood's Magazine*

December: engaged in writing *The Picture of Dorian Gray*

1890 20 June: *Dorian Gray* appears in the July issue of *Lippincott's Magazine*; derisive review of it, titled "A Study in Puppydom," appears in *St. James's Gazette*, eliciting a lengthy exchange of letters

July: first part of an essay later retitled "The Critic as Artist" appears in *Nineteenth Century* (second part appears in September)

1891 26 January: *The Duchess of Padua* opens in New York, runs three weeks

February: essay "The Soul of Man Under Socialism" appears in *Fortnightly Review*

April: revised version of *Dorian Gray* published in book form

May: *Intentions*, a collection of essays, published

June: first meeting with Lord Alfred Douglas probably takes place

November: second volume of tales, *A House of Pomegranates*, published

November–December: stays without family for two months in Paris

Late December: finishes *Salomé* while staying at Torquay

1892 January: begins residing in the West End (Albemarle Hotel); has met Edward Shelley, office boy at his publisher's, by this time

20 February: first London premiere, of *Lady Windermere's Fan*, takes place, St. James's Theatre

June: performance of *Salomé* banned by censor

1893 February: French version of *Salomé* published

19 April: *A Woman of No Importance* opens at the Haymarket Theatre

October: begins renting rooms in St. James's Place (stays there until the end of March 1894)

1894 1 April: Marquess of Queensberry sees OW and Lord Alfred Douglas lunching together at Café Royal

April–May: travels to Paris, then to Florence for rendezvous with Douglas

30 June: Queensberry makes threatening visit to Tite Street

August: with family at Worthing, writing *Earnest*

December: only issue of *The Chameleon*, scandalous Oxford undergraduate magazine, appears; it contains some maxims by OW

1895 January: *Oscariana*, Constance's collection of OW aphorisms, published privately

3 January: *An Ideal Husband* opens at the Haymarket Theatre

17 January: OW and Douglas leave for trip to Algiers, OW returning at month's end (meets Gide on the 27th)

14 February: premiere of *Earnest* at the St. James's Theatre; OW now living at the Avondale Hotel, Piccadilly

18 February: Queensberry leaves insulting calling card at OW's club, the Albemarle (OW actually receives it ten days later)

early March: OW sues Queensberry for libel; latter committed for trial on the 9th and enters Plea of Justification on the 30th

7 March: OW attends *Earnest* with Constance and Douglas

about 13–20 March: OW and Douglas away on trip to Monte Carlo

3 April: libel trial begins, collapses on the 5th; OW arrested later that day, charged at Bow Street station, then moved to Holloway Prison

26 April: first trial of OW (and Alfred Taylor) begins; ends in hung jury on 1 May

7 May: granted bail and released pending retrial; stays at first with mother in Chelsea, then, secretly, with Ada and Ernest Leverson in Kensington

20 May: retrial begins, ends on the 25th in conviction and sentence to two years' hard labor; OW removed to Holloway, later to Pentonville, Wandsworth, and finally Reading Prison

Fall: Constance and sons, name changed to Holland, now living in Switzerland; later move to Heidelberg for schooling

1896   3 February: mother dies (Constance travels from Genoa to break the news to OW—their last meeting)

7 July: hanging of C. T. Wooldridge at Reading Prison inspires *The Ballad of Reading Gaol*

1897   January–March: writes long letter to Douglas, later called *De profundis*

19 May: released from penal custody in London, travels immediately to the Continent, commencing three years' irregular travel in France, Italy, and Switzerland

1898   February: *The Ballad of Reading Gaol* published with considerable success

7 April: Constance dies, aged forty, in Genoa, shortly after two spinal operations; buried in the Protestant cemetery there

1899   February: first edition of *Earnest* published (OW's name not on title page)
May: now staying in Paris at the Hôtel d'Alsace

1900   30 November: dies at 1:50 p.m., aged forty-six, at Hôtel d'Alsace; buried at cemetery in Bagneux (remains removed to Père-Lachaise cemetery in 1909)

Notes

ABBREVIATIONS

Editions

C   *The Complete Works* (1966; 1989, HarperCollins)
L   *The Letters of Oscar Wilde* (1962, Harcourt, Brace)
P   *Wilde: The Complete Plays* (1988, Methuen)
M   *Miscellanies* volume of *The First Collected Edition* (1908; 1969 reprint)
R   *Reviews* volume of *The First Collected Edition* (1908; 1969 reprint)
MK E. H. Mikhail, *Oscar Wilde: Interviews and Recollections* (1979)

Wilde's Main Works

Fan	*Lady Windermere's Fan*
Woman	*A Woman of No Importance*
Ideal	*An Ideal Husband*
Earnest	*The Importance of Being Earnest*
Dorian	*The Picture of Dorian Gray*
"Critic"	*"The Critic as Artist"*
"Soul"	*"The Soul of Man Under Socialism"*
"Decay"	*"The Decay of Lying"*
"Pen"	*"Pen, Pencil and Poison"*

Note: The most accessible editions of Wilde's dramatic and nondramatic works have been chosen for the following citations. However, all quotations have been reproduced exactly as they appeared in first editions; hence there are a number of minor discrepancies between quotations here and the text in the HarperCollins and Methuen editions. Since so many editions of *The Picture of Dorian Gray* are available, chapter numbers from the novel are also included in parentheses.

FOREWORD

xi **It is a popular superstition:** "Impressions of America," ed. Stuart Mason (1906), p. 27.

odd elephantine gait: Robert Ross, in an unpublished preface to a projected collection of Wilde's letters, wrote of "that odd elephantine gait which I have never seen in anyone else" (ms. Clark, quoted L564).

I find Cromer: 1 September 1892 (L320). Oscar is also known to have golfed while visiting Lady Queensberry at Bracknell; his son Vyvyan says that Ross remembered him as "enthusiastic, if somewhat inefficient," at the game (*Son of Oscar Wilde*, p. 200).

the unspeakable: *Woman* (P312).

a bully boy: to Mrs Bernard Beere, 17 April 1882 (L112).

excellent sandcastles: Vyvyan tells of his father's architectural skills in *Son of Oscar Wilde*, p. 55.

Can you photograph cows: to Ross, 12 April 1900 (L824).

leaning over: The event was reported by Gustave Le Rouge (MK462–63).

xii **it hangs:** The Library, affiliated with UCLA, houses the world's most important and extensive collection of material on Wilde and his circle. The painting fetched £14 at the sheriff's sale.

xiii **Sin is a thing:** C117(12). Ellmann (p. 444) and Hyde (*The Annotated Wilde*, p. 24) both assert Lautrec's visit as a fact. But according to Herbert Schimmel, "There is no positive evidence that Lautrec was in London in 1895" (*The Letters of Henri de Toulouse-Lautrec* [1991], p. 271), and some have suggested that the portrait derived from a meeting in Paris. In all, seven figures of Wilde by Lautrec exist. At least one of Oscar's friends, Vincent O'Sullivan, did not think the portrait resembled him (*Aspects of Wilde*, p. 155).

He was a frank: *Men and Memories* (1937), p. 64.

a colour-sense: "Critic" (C1058).

Never trust a woman: *Dorian*, C85(8).

xiv **the most famous pederast:** Rupert Croft-Cooke, *Feasting with Panthers*, p. 176.

the greatest talker: preface to Sherard, *Bernard Shaw, Frank Harris, and Oscar Wilde*, p. xiii.

If, with the literate: "A Pig's-Eye View of Literature," *Collected Poetry* (1959), p. 109.

As people recede: p. 175.

The degree and kind: *Beyond Good and Evil*, #75, *Portable Nietzsche*, p. 444.

xv **the relationship:** Wendell Harris, in *Victorian Prose: A Guide to Research*, ed. David DeLaura (1973), p. 461.

We have had: p. 259.

in an age: *Love in Earnest*, p. xxi. Just one example of the "explosion": in 1992 a book by Allan Cuseo titled *Homosexual Characters in Young Adult Novels, 1969–1982* was published; it was 516 pages long.

In Ellmann's account: "Nothing Wilde," *Nation*, 13 February 1988, p. 204; Patricia Behrendt presses a more caustic and extreme attack, concluding that Ellmann's view of homosexuality "panders, frankly, to the homophobic reader" (*Oscar Wilde: Eros and Aesthetics*, pp. 94–100).

xvi **still largely excluded:** p. 70. See also pp. 6–18, 64–78, and Dollimore's extensive bibliography, pp. 359–81; likewise, Ian Small concludes even more recently that "serious analysis" of Wilde's homosexuality "has been conspicuous by its absence" (*Oscar Wilde Revalued*, p. 161).

an unattractive form: review of the *Memoirs of Wilhelmine, Margravine of Baireuth*, *Woman's World*, November 1887 (R191).

proper occupation: "Critic" (C1015).

We cannot re-write: "Pen" (C1008).

xvii **I wish he was *not*:** to Reginald Harding, 28 November 1879 (L61).

a great big, splendid boy: *Philadelphia Press*, 19 January 1882 (MK47).

O. Wilde!: reported by Richard Le Gallienne, *The Romantic '90s*, p. 93.

the most charming: *circa* February 1892, *More Letters*, p. 115.

Yes. I always: H. M. Hyde, *The Trials of Oscar Wilde*, p. 125.

I am in the public press: to Ada Leverson, 1 June 1897 (L588). Many years earlier, he signed off a letter, "I like my friends to call me OSCAR" (to W. Graham Robertson, early 1888, L217).

The story told by his son: reported in Holland, *Son of Oscar Wilde*, pp. 19–20. Ellmann, however, could find no Swedish records of the operation or the godfathering (p. 11).

Wilde ... operated: in Frank Harris, *Oscar Wilde*, p. 330.

1 SEEING OSCAR

1 **His detractors:** *Finnegans Wake* (1939 ed.), p. 33.

Before I first met Oscar: *Letters to the Sphinx*, pp. 31–32.

Oscar was: "My Memories of Oscar Wilde," in Frank Harris, *Oscar Wilde*, p.

334. Hart-Davis reports Lady Campbell's phrase as "The Great White Slug" (L222n).

2   **bright-coloured linings:** 2 February 1891 (L284).

colourless, moon-like: G. T. Atkinson, *Cornhill Magazine* (1929), p. 559 (MK16).

were heavy: Reminiscences (1926), p. 85.

unashamedly curled: *The Romantic '90s*, p. 243.

3   **I took my *coiffeur*:** *Twenty Years of My Life* (1925), p. 80.

something grotesquely excessive: *The Romantic '90s*, pp. 243–44.

The best tailor: *Aspects of Wilde*, pp. 154–55.

a great ungainly crane: circa 6 March 1882, quoted in Lloyd Lewis and Henry Smith, *Oscar Wilde Discovers America*, p. 216.

a rich yet ungainly fruit: letter of 30 November 1900 (British Library, quoted by Ellmann, p. 35).

He was by then: A. Hamilton Grant, *Cornhill Magazine* (1931; MK223).

rather badly shaped mouth: *To Tell My Story* (1948; MK266).

slow episcopal gestures: *Aspects of Wilde*, p. 155.

M. Joseph-Renaud: in Stuart Mason's 1906 edition of Wilde's "Impressions of America" lecture (p. 40).

his courteous eyes: *Works and Days from the Journal of Michael Field* (1933; MK199). Field was the pseudonym of Katharine Bradley.

4   **The plainness of his face:** *The Days I Knew* (1925), p. 86.

the eyes smiled: Henri de Régnier, "Souvenirs sur Oscar Wilde," *Figures et caractères* (1901; MK165).

pure blue light and **Exquisitely musical:** Jean Joseph-Renaud, "Preface," *Oscar Wilde: Intentions* (1905; MK167).

wonderful golden voice: p. 141.

one of the most alluring: *The Days I Knew*, p. 86.

low, musical voice: C29(2).

His appearance: *Without Prejudice* (1936), p. 211.

a strange, almost *macabre* element: *Melodies and Memories* (1925), p. 74.

He had not: *Aspects of Wilde*, p. 154.

5   **His clean-shaven face:** 27 March 1882 (MK67).

An unbiassed: "Critic" (C1047). In an essay on Pater, he wrote: "It is only about things that do not interest one, that one can give a really unbiassed opinion; and this is no doubt the reason why an unbiassed opinion is always valueless" (R539).

half-fatuous ... wholly charming: *Letters to Reggie Turner*, p. 286. Max Beerbohm used both phrases in the same sentence in his first published essay, "Oscar Wilde by an American."

6   **a contented ogre:** Gedeon Spilett, *Gil Blas*, 22 November 1897 (MK354).

I have a kind of: reported in L. B. Walford, *Memories of Victorian England* (1912), p. 232.

Our life is lazy: ms. letter to Lionel Johnson, 8 February 1893 (L868).

7   You are quite delightful: C1015.

Everything you have said: *Woman* (P352).

the dim idea: P348.

English society: letter to Frank Harris, 4 November 1900 (2CL193).

used to entertain: Merrill wrote this just after Oscar died in *La Plume*, 15 December 1900 (MK466).

made dying Victorianism: *The Romantic '90s*, p. 270.

8   Oscar *meant* well: John Stokes, "Wilde at Bay," p. 185.

9   Doubtless, he was weak: *The Romantic '90s*, p. 257.

prime specimen etc.: in Harris, pp. 329–41.

If I craved: *News Chronicle*, February 1948, quoted in Hesketh Pearson, *GBS: A Postscript* (1951), p. 132.

serious playboy: *Partisan Review* (1950), p. 39.

genuine counterfeiter: Jean Delay, *The Youth of André Gide*, p. 291.

He was . . . a man: "Prefatory Dedication," *De profundis* (1905; reprint 1969), pp. xv–xvi.

a love letter: p. 515.

10   no other Irishman: "Oscar Wilde," *Neue Freie Presse* (Vienna), 23 April 1905, in *The Matter with Ireland*, ed. David Greene, Dan H. Laurence (1962), p. 29.

The gibbet: to More Adey, 28 September 1896 (L410).

The pleasure we derive: "About Oscar Wilde" (1946), in *Borges: A Reader*, ed. E. Monegal, A. Reid (1981), p. 178.

I was all wrong: to Will Rothenstein, 9 June 1897 (L605).

apart from his: "Oscar Wilde and the Theatre," *The Masque* (1947), p. 6. Agate *did* write: "Wilde's plays are, apart from their wit, the purest fudge" (p.7).

There is something *outré*: "The Unimportance of Being Oscar," *Partisan Review* (1947), p. 302.

Now, of Oscar Wilde: Colin MacInnes, "The Heart of a Legend: The Writings of Ada Leverson," *Encounter* (1961), p. 46.

prone to suppose: *The New Organon* (1620), *Francis Bacon: A Selection*, ed. Sidney Warhaft (1965), p. 337.

11   I must tell you: "A Wilde 'Tag' to a Tame Play," p. 113.

12   It still seems perfect: *Around Theatres* (1930), I, p. 240.

It was by way: *Last Theatres 1904–1910* (1970), p. 102.

As a matter of fact: quoted in Holroyd, II, p. 147.

Is there another life story: *Partisan Review* 17 (1950), p. 390.

There is a great deal: *Pall Mall Gazette*, 5 June 1889 (R509).

as soon as the interest: C85 (8).

13 **Life is terribly deficient:** "Critic" (C1034).

My tragedy: to Ross, circa November 1896 (L413).**Imagine a wilderness:** I. Zangwill, quoted in *Westminster Review,* 27 May 1895.

the conversationalist: *Partisan Review* 17 (1950), p. 390.

The best of his writing: quoted by Adolphe Retté, *Le Symbolisme* (1903; MK191).

his personality: to Adela Schuster, 23 December 1900 (L862).

You could not tell: "A Note of Explanation," posthumously published as a preface to Ada Leverson, *Letters to the Sphinx,* p. 16.

14 **You talk books away:** C45(3).

an astonishment: *Autobiography,* p. 113. Yeats also called Oscar "the greatest talker of his time" (p. 121).

monologue man: *Memories and Adventures* (1924), p. 78.

I suppose: *Adam International Review* (1954), pp. viii–ix (MK273).

15 **quicker in repartee:** *Letters to the Sphinx,* p. 24.

Many, many times: MK215.

Nowadays everybody: to Ross, 31 May 1897 (L584).

I stayed with him: ms. letter (Hyde collection), 23 December 1900 (L862).

unfailing gaiety: *The Romantic '90s,* p. 258.

16 **no purpose in life:** *The Eighteen Nineties,* p. 87.

After all, nothing: review of 24 May 1893, *Music in London 1890–1894* (reprint 1973), II, p. 331.

passion for paradox: 23 April 1893.

It was natural: quoted in L565.

All Americans etc.: P311, P310, P308.

17 **You fence divinely:** P320.

cheeky paradoxical wit: to Mrs Hugh Bell, 23 February 1892, *Letters,* ed. Leon Edel (1980), III, p. 373.

Consistency is: "The Relation of Dress to Art," *Pall Mall Gazette,* 28 February 1885 (M69). He elsewhere phrased his championship of inconsistency in the form of a paradox: "We are never more true to ourselves than when we are inconsistent" ("Critic," C1045).

But you don't mean: C982.

The way of paradoxes: C43(3).

18 **As I once said:** *The Romantic '90s,* p. 257.

a counter-glitter: *The Theatre,* March 1894 (MK233).

I am proud to say: *Selected Plays,* tr. Evert Sprinchorn (1986), p. 207.

A good circus: "London Models," *English Illustrated Magazine,* January 1889 (M127–28).

19 **serious letters:** *If It Die,* p. 299 (Gide's ellipses).

Oscar is so pathetic: to Carlos Blacker, 20 March 1898 (L718n).

When you are alone: *Letters to the Sphinx*, p. 42.

totally lacking: "An Improbable Life," *The New Yorker*, 9 March 1963, in *Forewords and Afterwords* (1974), p. 321.

Man is least himself: C1045.

Anybody can act: 19 February 1892 (L311).

20   **The distinction of Phipps:** P169.

never allows us: MK233.

I thought life: *De Profundis* (L444).

Mr James Payn: "Decay" (C973).

21   **Your letter:** late February 1894 (L353).

Wilde covered over: p. 296.

22   **The book that poisoned:** 12 February 1894 (L352). Incidentally, two years earlier Oscar answered the same question by saying the book was "partly suggested by Huysmans' *À Rebours*" (I.313).

23   **intellectual impressionist:** "Mr Pater's *Imaginary Portraits*," *Pall Mall Gazette*, 11 June 1887 (R174).

I like persons: C23(1).

One should never: *Woman* (P311).

Men of conviction: *The Antichrist*, #54, *Portable Nietzsche*, p. 638.

24   **an acute political awareness:** *Sexual Dissidence*, p. 73.

a wicked place: *Immaturity*, *Works* (1930), I, pp. 73–77.

Alhambra ballets: letter to Stewart Headlam, 26 December 1922 (*Collected Letters: 1911–1925*, p. 802).

25   **Are you very much:** C155(18).

wild adoration: C160(19).

wild longing: C105(11).

I used to be: to Reggie Turner, 21 June 1897 (L616).

One feels about it: "*The Picture of Dorian Gray*: Wilde's Parable of the Fall," *Critical Inquiry* 7 (1980), p. 421.

26   **Only the shallow:** C1204.

made themselves *publick*: Boswell's *Life of Johnson* (1953 Oxford ed.), p. 351.

a method by which and **realise himself:** "Critic" (C1048).

Everybody's been so: *With Walt Whitman in Camden*, Vol. 2 (1908), p. 289 (emphasis added). The conversation took place on 7 September

2   TRESPASSER

27   **His writing:** *Cornhill Magazine* (May 1929), p. 560 (MK16). Atkinson was a contemporary of Oscar's at Magdalen College, Oxford.

much beauty: to More Adey, March 1899 (L784).

28 **My father:** *Son of Oscar Wilde*, p. 45.

the conduct of others: "Phrases and Philosophies for the Use of the Young," *The Chameleon*, December 1894 (C1205).

He had a way: *I Have Been Young* (1935; published under her married name, H. M. Swanwick), p. 65.

One took all: *Autobiography*, p. 122.

29 **You seem to me:** letter of 5 August 1891, quoted by Ian Small, "Oscar Wilde as a Professional Writer," *Library Chronicle of the University of Texas at Austin* 20 (1993), p. 38.

a Heresiarch: preface to Robert Sherard, *Bernard Shaw, Frank Harris, and Oscar Wilde*, p. 12.

usually in direct opposition: "Decay" (C991).

supreme scoundrel: "Critic" (C1009).

They seemed: "Impressions of America," p. 31.

Yeats's remark: *Autobiography* (1938), p. 172.

There is danger: C1099.

30 **I can't travel:** 6 July 1882 (L122).

two favourite characters: quoted in L493n.

really the greatest monument: *Pall Mall Gazette*, 13 September 1886 (R77).

Whoever contributes: R78.

all Balzac's heroes: to W. M. Fullerton, 25 June 1899 (L804).

You must really: to Leonard Smithers, 24 May 1898 (L744).

31 **Rodin's statue:** to Ross, 1 May 1898 (L732).

an astonishing masterpiece: to Turner, 11 May 1898 (L738).

the great Celtic school: 9 May 1893 (L339).

a school of truancy: *Bernard Shaw* (1991), III, p. 200.

The dons are 'astonied': to William Ward, 20 July 1878 (L53).

the prigs and **Morality, insofar:** "Morality as Anti-nature," #6, *Twilight of the Idols, Portable Nietzsche*, pp. 491–92.

32 **The comic thing:** ms. letter to Ross, 27 June 1898 (Clark Library). The friend was Carlos Blacker; this is one of three passages censored by Hart-Davis from the 1962 *Letters* to "avoid giving pain to descendants."

always trying and **saying he was:** quoted in Jean Delay, *The Youth of André Gide*, p. 291 (original italics). Delay summarized, "Wilde's influence on Gide was above all that of an immoralist"; on Wilde as a profoundly "anti-credal" herald of the modern age, see Philip Reiff's powerful essay, "The Impossible Culture," in *Salmagundi* 58–59 (1982–83), 406–25.

Great Irresponsible: letter to the editor, *Pall Mall Gazette*, 1 July 1892 (L317n).

Your husband: *Ideal* (P163).

perhaps the one pursuit: *Saturday Review*, 13 May 1899, in *Pen Portraits and Reviews* (1932), p. 218.

33   **likes Ford and Marlowe:** Percival Almy, *The Theatre*, March 1894 (MK229).

inclined to say: review of an Irving–Terry performance of *Hamlet*, *Dramatic Review*, 9 May 1885 (R18).

Dickens has influenced and **admirable . . . undoubtedly:** *Woman's World*, January 1888 (R260–61).

our first authority: "Critic" (C1055).

the mountains of California: *Denver Tribune*, 13 April 1882 (MK77).

that disappointing Atlantic Ocean: "I hope that some time will elapse before he [Henry Irving] and Miss Terry cross again that disappointing Atlantic Ocean" (*Dramatic Review*, 9 May 1885; R20).

The Queen is *not*: Lady Randolph Churchill, *Reminiscences* (1908), p. 216.

Comedy: the criticism: in Harris, *Oscar Wilde*, pp. 336–37.

seven deadly virtues: *Dorian*, C147(17).

domestic virtues: "Pen" (C1007).

tragic . . . perfect profiles: "Phrases and Philosophies" (C1206).

34   **We live in an age:** "Critic" (C1042).

On this point: *Earnest* (P276).

You should study: *Woman* (P347).

the desire to do good: C1042–43.

Philanthropic people: C40(3).

In an evil moment: "A Chinese Sage," *Speaker*, 8 February 1890 (R531).

Morality is: P164. Mrs Cheveley also says in *An Ideal Husband*: "Philanthropy seems to me to have become simply the refuge of people who wish to annoy their fellow creatures" (P116).

interfering with the individual: "A Chinese Sage" (R531).

35   **to be moral:** quoted in Delay, p. 295.

An altruistic morality: "Skirmishes of an Untimely Man," #35, *Twilight*, *Portable Nietzsche*, p. 535. Elsewhere Nietzsche virtually paraphrases Oscar on philanthropic work: "I find . . . behind the praise of impersonal activity for the public benefit: fear of everything individual" (*The Dawn*, #173).

I have a distinct recollection: P115.

Fortunately, in England: "Decay" (C971).

The English public: C1009.

the native land: C118(12).

Isn't it comic: *Contemporary Portraits*, p. 124.

The English type: to Ross, 1 June 1898 (L752).

36   **He had a reputation:** appendix in Vyvyan Holland, *Son of Oscar Wilde*, p. 219.

had always thought: *The Romantic '90s*, p. 78.

I never could make out: *Aspects of Wilde*, p. 84.

that fortifying body: in Harris, *Oscar Wilde*, p. 335.

I think that Wilde: *Journal* for 1 January 1892, quoted in Delay, p. 294.

37   **"Know Thyself" was written:** "Soul" (C1085).

    Mr Terriss's Squire Thornhill: *"Olivia* at the Lyceum," *Dramatic Review*, 30 May 1885 (R30–31).

    perverse and impossible person: to Ross, 31 May 1898 (L750).

    No crime is vulgar: "Phrases and Philosophies" (C1205).

    All art is immoral: "Critic" (C1039)

38   **[The] abnormal:** "A Few Maxims for the Instruction of the Over-Educated" (L869).

    How different: "Decay" (C971).

    Never attempt: quoted by Almy (MK233).

    To have been: *Woman* (P349).

    loves true ignorance: quoted by Almy (MK233).

    to say Mr. Wilde is not: "Oscar Wilde by an American," *Letters to Reggie Turner*, p. 290.

    When Oscar Wilde: *Memories and Impressions* (1911), p. 166.

    The years from 1885 and **His philosophy:** *George Bernard Shaw* (1911), pp. 255–56, 28.

39   **An idea that is not dangerous:** C1044.

    fine thinker: C1087.

    Art is Individualism: C1091.

    Disobedience: C1081.

    agitators are: C1082.

40   **for the English:** "Skirmishes," #5, *Twilight of the Idols, Portable Nietzsche*, p. 516.

    To be good: C69(6). This philosophy is discussed more fully in Chapter 15, "Closet Philosopher."

    There is no country: C1042.

    extremely artistic temperament: C933.

    Believe me: quoted by Gedeon Spilett, *Gil Blas*, 22 November 1897 (MK355).

41   **Wickedness is a myth:** "Phrases and Philosophies" (C1205).

    There is one thing: P319.

    myself: quoted in Hesketh Pearson, *Beerbohm Tree: His Life and Laughter* (1956), p. 65.

    most glaring fault: *Woman* (P352).

42   **making himself too much at home:** "The Unimportance of Being Oscar," *Partisan Review* (1947), p. 302.

3 *PUNCH* V. OSCAR I

43   **Oscar Wilde!:** *A Peep into the Past* (1923), p. 9. Beerbohm uses "crank" in the now archaic sense of a fantastic whim or clever conceit.

45 **Which of you two:** O'Sullivan, *Aspects of Wilde*, p. 174.

The drowse: "From the Philistine Point of View," 18 October 1879, p. 169.

Racine, with the chill off: 16 July 1892, p. 24.

46 **Is that mayonnaise:** 15 July 1893, p. 13.

48 **Oscar knew no more:** in Harris, *Oscar Wilde*, p. 336.

most dramatic event: Michael Levey, *The Case of Walter Pater* (1978), p. 204.

50 **That I'm limp:** 30 April 1881, p. 201.

52 **my days with Heliogabalus:** to Ross, 20 February 1898 (L705). Oscar wrote later of a boy he had met at an American bar in Paris: "One beautiful boy of bad character . . . goes there too, but he is so like Antinous, and so smart, that he is allowed to talk to poets" (to Turner, 3 December 1898, L768).

I find it harder: quoted in Ellmann, p. 45.

full of blue china: 7 September 1878, p. 98.

54 **most Aesthetic line:** 28 May 1881, p. 229.

the tender companionship: "Fleur des Alpes; or, Postlethwaite's Last Love," 25 December 1880, p. 293.

56 **Swelldom is friends:** "The Rise and Fall of the Jack Spratts," Part III, 21 September 1878, p. 124.

57 **very low spirits:** 18 October 1879, p. 169.

58 **I do not say:** from the Queensberry libel trial transcript, quoted in Ellmann, p. 447.

a Professor of Aesthetics: p. 81. There are some striking premonitions of the future in Burnand's play. We learn, for instance, of Streyke and his nephew Basil Giorgione running up a huge bill "for all sorts of luxuries at a neighbouring restaurant, while they pretend to live on the contemplation of lilies"—shades of Oscar's lavish spending at Willis's, Kettner's, and the Café Royal in the 1890s. After the performance a furious Maudle "glided homewards, and comforted himself with cold lily and Mr Pater."

59 **a volume of echoes:** 23 July 1881, p. 26.

60 **Life *is* nought:** 20 August 1881, p. 84.

Mr Oscar Wilde's Play: 1 September 1883, p. 99.

63 **We've just seen:** 24 November 1883, p. 249.

4 ARBITER ELEGANTIARUM

65 **Fashion is:** P169.

I hope you: 6 September 1900 (L835).

two kinds of characters: *Aspects of Wilde*, pp. 18–19.

66 **throw his characters:** *The Old Drama and the New* (1923), p. 126.

flawless dandy: P117.

dressed in the height of fashion: P140.

Enter Lord Goring: P169.

Reaching London: 9 March 1892.

67   **a magnificent floral bed:** 12 January 1882, p. 5.

    smoking suit: article appended by Robert Ross to his 1906 edition of Wilde's "Impressions of America" lecture (p. 38).

68   **A dark purple velvet sack-coat:** *Impersonations* (1891), p. 197.

    He was dressed: *Letters to the Sphinx*, pp. 33–34.

    withered bouquet: Smith and Lewis, *Oscar Wilde Discovers America*, p. 245.

    The little note: 2 February 1891 (L283).

    A really well-made buttonhole: C1205.

69   **Lillie Langtry remembered:** *The Days I Knew* (1925), p. 84.

    possessed a walking-stick: *Memories and Impressions* (1911), p. 167.

    in constant service: 2 February 1891 (L284).

    He had that curious love: C996.

    Style largely depends: P279.

70   **The essential thing:** *Woman* (P345).

    Dandyism is: "A Few Maxims for the Instruction of the Over-educated," *Saturday Review*, 17 November 1894 (L870)

    a certain taint: to Wemyss Reid, 5 September 1887 (L203). Oscar added in this letter, "This is not merely my view, but is undoubtedly the view of those whom we want to contribute. In writing to the various women whose names stand now on the contributors' list I carefully avoided mentioning the name of the magazine, but in certain cases I have been obliged to tell it, and on every occasion of this kind the name has met with the strongest opposition."

    a most vulgar trivial production: to William Sharp, November 1887 (L212).

    on Concord: letter of 6 December 1887 (L213).

    the right of woman: Arthur Fish, "Memories of Oscar Wilde," *Cassell's Weekly*, 2 May 1893 (MK152).

72   **one great genius:** *Woman's World*, January 1888 (R260).

    Why didn't you name me: quoted in Mrs Claude Beddington, *All That I Have Met* (1929), p. 41.

    Lady Wilde's translation: *Woman's World*, January 1889 (R388).

    overdone, loaded: *Aspects of Wilde*, p. 38.

    too cumbrous: *Woman's World*, January 1889 (R375).

    one of the finest: *Woman's World*, November 1887 (R207).

73   **is fond of airing:** This review appeared in the *Pall Mall Gazette*, 17 May 1889 (R499), but did not discourage Ouida from contributing to *Woman's World* for Oscar.

    dainty sleeve-links: L507.

    I am anxious: to Ross, 1 April 1897 (L517).

74   with coloured borders: 6 May 1897 (L534–35).
75   One should either be: C1206.
      In the mode: holograph ms., Berg Collection, New York Public Library.
      one thing needful: *The Gay Science*, #290, *Portable Nietzsche*, pp. 98–99.
      He recognised: C995.
      In all unimportant matters: C1205.
      In matters of grave importance: P274.
76   The costume in question: 2 February 1891 (L283).
      ease and liberty and strangling stock: *Pall Mall Gazette*, 14 October 1884
          (M48, M50).
      I hope he consults: *Pall Mall Gazette*, 11 November 1884 (M52).
77   A man is called affected: C1101.
      There is no general rule: *Contemporary Portraits*, p. 114.
      by which what and in his inmost heart: C103–4.
78   was so in love: in Harris, *Oscar Wilde*, p. 338.
      As his hand moved: "Souvenirs sur Oscar Wilde," *Figures et caractères* (1901;
          MK166).
79   After all: "Soul" (C1086).

5 "MOTHERS ARE DARLINGS"

81   Fathers should: P192.
      People's mothers: P335.
82   Is that clever: P237.
      strange, peculiar: 5 February 1896.
83   the nemesis of character: to More Adey, 27 November 1897 (L685).
      Oscar O'F.: 15 June 1875 (L6).
      Sir William: 26 June 1875 (L11).
      To love oneself: P170.
      in married life: P225.
84   large pretentious house etc.: *Some Victorian Women* (1923), pp. 1–2.
85   high character: P204.
      I told him: P56.
      I don't play accurately: P217.
86   All the characters: 20 June 1863, p. 810.
      verbose and turgid style: Horace Wyndham, *Speranza: A Biography of Lady
          Wilde*, p. 162.
      grand, misty: quoted by Ellmann, p. 17.
      tries to make passion: review of *Guilderoy*, *Pall Mall Gazette*, 17 May 1889
          (R494–95).
      of the heavy type: *Aspects of Wilde*, p. 156.

sort of caricature **Dionysus:** *The Romantic '90s*, p. 243.

a Roman emperor: *Letters to the Sphinx*, p. 32.

87 **I express the soul:** quoted by Wyndham, p. 64.

I want to live and **longed always:** *Autobiography*, p. 120.

never had her eyes: White, p. 147.

queened it always: White, *The Parents of Oscar Wilde*, p. 210.

made her surroundings: *Oscar Wilde and His Mother*, p. 47.

she might have been a queen: *Adventures of a Novelist* (1932), p. 182.

88 **one of the London curios:** p. 181.

lying on the sofa: anecdote reported by Sherard, *The Life of Oscar Wilde*, p. 31.

You must never: quoted by Wyndham, p. 70.

in the fatal intimacy: quoted by White, p. 147.

89 **The best chance:** quoted by Henriette Corkran in White, pp. 147–48.

Let all genius: quoted by Wyndham, p. 129.

very companionable: Anne Clark Amor, *Mrs Oscar Wilde*, pp. 65–66.

as Lady Wilde: *The Trials*, p. 47.

thoroughly womanly woman: *Oscar Wilde and His Mother*, p. 83.

For six thousand years and following quotations: *Essays and Stories*, pp. 196–217.

90 **revolts against social usages:** "American Women," *Essays and Stories*, p. 11.

latter-half-nineteenth-century woman: "Venus Victrix," *Essays and Stories*, pp. 153–55.

fatal tendency and **Middlemarch especially:** *Notes on Men, Women, and Books* (1891), pp. 176, 171.

As a rule: Henriette Corkran, *Celebrities and I* (1902), quoted in White, p. 253.

91 **since Oscar wrote:** David Bispham reported her saying this to a friend of his in *A Quaker Singer's Recollections* (1920), p. 150.

the most wonderful piece: ms. letter, June 1890 (Clark).

Literary dress: "Suitability of Dress," *Essays and Stories*, p. 96.

A woman . . . should: "Venus Victrix," *Essays and Stories*, p. 159.

92 **securely fixed:** White, p. 230.

Oscar revered his mother: p. 158.

All poets love: to W. E. Henley, October 1888 (L230).

The best book: *Woman's World*, February 1889 (R406–7).

strong, splendid souls: reprinted in *Essays and Stories*, p. 261.

The despair and misery: 2 July 1896 (L403).

93 **You knew:** L458.

intellectually . . . with: L496.

of senseless pleasure: to Michael Davitt (May–June 1897; L587).

Woman is no coward: *Essays and Stories*, p. 263.

94 **prison would do him good:** quoted in White, p. 269.
    I thought that Oscar: 29 August 1895 (L398n).
    You have missed: P344.
95 **She looks on me:** ms. in Clark, reproduced in Small, *Oscar Wilde Revalued*,
        p. 145.
    moods of rage: 28 May 1897 (L576–77).
    in echoes: to Frances Forbes-Robertson, June 1899 (L803).
    Her talk: *Celebrities and I* (1902), quoted by Wyndham, p. 194.
96 **Thou wilt pass:** *Poems,* p. 197.
    We are all heart: *Woman* (P364).
    I thought: P97.
    son lived with: *Autobiography,* pp. 120–21.

6   A WIFE'S TRAGEDY

97 **Leading a double life:** ms. in Clark, reproduced in Small, *Oscar Wilde Reval-*
    ued, p. 145.
    The Cloister: 14 May 1900 (L828).
98 **Of course I love:** Rodney Shewan has carefully edited *A Wife's Tragedy* (*The-*
    atre Research International 7 [1982], 75–131) and discussed its dating and
    ramifications for Wilde's biography (*Theatre Research International* 8
    [1983], 83–94). His view that 1887–89 "in many respects seems the more
    likely" fits very agreeably with the view of the Wilde marriage set forth
    in the present chapter. Shewan, too, is inclined to view the draft as one
    of Wilde's autobiographically "premonitory" scenarios.
    a very noble: R419.
99 **a provincial little Artemis:** 17 May 1889 (R495).
100 **violet-eyed little Artemis:** 16 December 1883 (L154).
    horrid ugly Swiss governess: letter to Bosie, August 1894 (L360).
    What do you think etc.: August 1894 (L360–62; original italics). After his re-
    lease from prison Oscar, desperate for money, sold rights to this scenario
    several times over; it was eventually made into the play *Mr and Mrs*
    Daventry by Frank Harris.
101 **That, too:** Wilfred Chesson, "A Reminiscence of 1898," *Bookman* (New
    York), December 1911, Appendix B, in *More Letters,* p. 200.
102 **O. W. came:** quoted in Page, *An Oscar Wilde Chronology,* p. 16.
    as interesting as: 24 November 1883 (L153).
    I was disappointed: "Impressions of America," ed. Stuart Mason (1906), p. 25.
    My dearest Otho: 26 November 1883 (L153).
    Her **name is Constance:** to Waldo Story, 22 January 1884 (L155).
103 **I am not in favour:** P280.

She scarcely ever speaks: *Twenty Years of My Life, 1867 to 1887* (1925), p. 79.

rich creamy satin dress: Sherard, *The Life of Oscar Wilde*, p. 255.

Fear I may not: quoted in Anne Clark Amor, *Mrs Oscar Wilde*, p. 44.

104   **Dear and Beloved:** 16 December 1884 (L165).

I can write: "To My Wife" (C809).

a youthful: *Oscar Wilde and His Mother*, pp. 88–89.

105   **in spite of its:** 18 November 1885 (R36–38).

Like government: *How to Be Happy Though Married* (1886), p. 2.

Satiety follows quickly: p. 57.

A married pair: p. 5.

Yes! my dear Waldino: to Waldo Story, 22 January 1884 (L155).

106   **comradeship or:** *Walt Whitman: A Study* (1893), p. 54; the footnote mentioned is on pp. 78–79. Symonds wrote that "the intense delight which he derives from the personal presence and physical contact of a beloved man finds luminous expression in 'A Glimpse,' 'Recorders ages hence,' 'When I heard at the Close of Day,' 'I saw in Louisiana a Live-Oak growing,' 'Long I thought that Knowledge alone would suffice me,' 'O Tanfaced Prairie-Boy,' and 'Vigil Strange I kept on the Field one Night' " (pp. 73–74).

    grew increasingly discreet: Michael Levey, *The Case of Walter Pater* (1978), p. 19. Levey has written that Pater's mostly banal letters convey "such a painful suppression of personality as to suggest [Pater] was haunted by the dangers for him of betraying direct emotion of any kind" (p. 21).

To this day: *Psychopathia Sexualis* (7th ed., 1893), p. 261.

[Krafft-Ebing] goes on: "Homogenic Love," pp. 333–34.

107   **The first year:** p. 207.

When first married: *Letters to the Sphinx*, p. 44.

108   **I, who at the sight:** p. 261.

In married households: P218.

When I married: *Oscar Wilde*, pp. 186–87.

109   **a long conversation:** *Human, All-Too-Human*, #406, *Portable Nietzsche*, p. 59.

Mrs Wilde was: *The Romantic '90s*, p. 250.

110   **The world is surely unjust:** 11 November 1883 (letter in the Hyde collection, quoted in Ellmann, p. 244).

The fact of a man: "Pen" (C1007).

111   **I am not a champion:** C66(6).

    "Mrs Oscar Wilde at Home": This article is reproduced in full in Joyce Bentley, *The Importance of Being Constance*, pp. 105–8.

I always hear: C47(4).

The Ideal Husband: P325–26.

Don't you realize: *The Romantic '90s*, p. 251.

112   **good women:** P344.

You married a man: P156.

Modern women: P160.

I am quite as fond: to William ("Bouncer") Ward, March 1877 (L32; original italics). "Kitten" was Reginald Harding (see illus. p. 171).

113   The book is: to Arthur Humphreys, late November 1894 (L378). Some commentators have found in Constance's letters to Humphreys reason to think that, having finally seen the truth about her husband, she had fallen in love with him (see Ellmann, p. 425).

My wife does not understand: 1 April 1897 (L512).

114   a proper basis for marriage: "Lord Arthur Savile's Crime" (C172).

The one charm of marriage: C20(1).

If ever I get married: P219.

Constance, from Oscar: copy in the Berg Collection, New York Public Library.

A few days before: *If It Die*, p. 295.

115   When I come back: August 1894 (L364).

the truth became: Bentley, p. 100.

Mrs Wilde said: *An Idler's Impression* (1917), p. 22.

I am so sorry: ms. letter, Clark.

as long as you will: ms. letter, Clark.

outlawed noblemen: 9 July 1890 (L265n).

are quite monstrous: early July (L264).

nothing but harm: *Journal* (1925), for 1 January 1892 (p. 28). In December 1891, Gide wrote to Paul Valéry, "Wilde is religiously contriving to kill what is left of my soul" (quoted in Delay, p. 289).

116   Do you think: W. H. Leverton, *Through the Box-Office Window* (1932), p. 67.

117   Most of the smart young men: *Letters to the Sphinx*, p. 27.

One should always: P347.

shred into the mixture: "Stray Thoughts on Play-Writing," 29 April 1893, p. 193.

118   Don't make scenes: P44.

You are just the same: P64.

It is because men feel: R498.

she makes no row: C20(1).

Women have a wonderful instinct: P140.

How alone I am: P64.

119   I don't know Oscar's address: ms. letter, 12 March 1895, in Clark.

120   My dear Mrs Robinson: 19 April 1895 (L389n).

It is so terrible: to Emily Thursfield, 25 June 1895, ms. in Clark.

121   an absolute wreck: letter to Otho Holland Lloyd (L399n).

The Stranger Wilde

The interview took place: "The Story of Oscar Wilde's Life and Experience in Reading Gaol, By His Warder," *Bruno's Weekly*, 22 January 1916 (reprint 1963), p. 17.

If she had treated him properly: *Without Apology*, p. 220.

122 **come back, slightly damaged:** P44.

Women are not meant: P207.

I have again: 26 March 1897 (L515n).

123 **Whether I am married:** 1 April 1897 (L516).

One can always be kind: ms. Clark, in Small, *Oscar Wilde Revalued*, p. 141.

There is one thing worse: P209.

first really heartless play: in Harris, *Oscar Wilde*, pp. 332–33.

124 **get Mrs Marshall:** 1 April 1897 (L513).

My poor misguided husband: to Hannah Smith, 15 October 1895 (Ellmann, p. 492).

All possibility of our living together: 4 March 1898 (L714n).

I know that: 10 March 1898 (L716–17n).

a very nice letter: L727 (her letter has not survived).

Try not to feel: quoted by Holland, *Son of Oscar Wilde*, p. 130.

125 **Come tomorrow** etc.: 12 April 1898 (L729–30).

You will have heard: to Leonard Smithers, 17 April 1898 (L729n).

He really did not understand: to Adela Schuster, 23 December 1900 (L862).

The cemetery is a garden: circa 1 March 1899 (L783).

126 **On my way:** to Reggie Turner, 20 March 1899 (L787).

Is it my fault: letter of 4 January 1884, catalogue for the John B. Stetson sale (1920), p. 73 (copy in the Morgan Library).

7 "MY GOOD PAPA!"

127 **I remember:** *Oscar Wilde: An Idler's Impression*, p. 15.

pillage of an unprotected house: *The Life of Oscar Wilde*, p. 361.

128 **For months afterwards:** *Son of Oscar Wilde*, p. 62.

129 **I never heard:** *The Real Oscar Wilde*, pp. 372, 365.

I have brought: 10 March 1896 (L399).

I could not bear: L453. The Shakespearean allusion here is to Othello's reference to his dead Desdemona: "If heaven would make me such another world / Of one entire and perfect chrysolite, / I'd not have sold her for it" (5.2.144–46).

As regards my children: 8 March 1897 (L422).

130 **secret visits:** *La Plume*, 15 December 1900 (MK467).

after 1895: p. 52.

The baby is wonderful: to Norman Forbes-Robertson, early June 1885 (L177).

early childhood was as happy: p. 40.

131 **Most small boys:** p. 52.

as a parent: p. 88.

Grown-up people: pp. 49–50. Vyvyan and Cyril also generally preferred Oscar's Irish relations to the Scottish ones on his mother's side; those relatives' "disapproval" of Oscar and his circle Cyril and Vyvyan often felt "overflowing on to ourselves."

With children: *Mrs J. Comyns Carr's Reminiscences* (1926), p. 86.

Oscar made himself: *I Have Been Young* (1935; under her married name, H. M. Swanwick), p. 64.

He was a real companion etc.: pp. 52–57.

132 **The kitten:** circa 1888, ms. Clark, in Small, *Oscar Wilde Revalued*, p. 45.

133 **Wilde looked:** *Autobiography*, p. 119.

It is the duty: *The Romantic '90s*, pp. 252–54.

134 **A horrid, ugly Swiss governess:** August 1894 (L360).

135 **Is the world a dust-heap:** 16 November 1885, *More Letters*, p. 59. See also pp. 58–63 and L175–80 for other letters to Marillier.

modes of erotomania: to the Home Secretary, 2 July 1896 (L403).

subdued, meditative: Page, *Chronology*, p. 33.

Oscar's star: 16 September 1887.

My dearest Cyril: 3 March 1891 (L288).

136 **the drains:** to Arthur Clifton, 17 February 1892, *More Letters*, p. 114.

I required rest: *De profundis* (L432).

137 **with pigeons and children:** letter of Campbell Dodgson to Lionel Johnson, 8 February 1893 (L868).

And do you know: *Melodies and Memories* (1925), p. 75.

quite repelled: 19 August 1893, *Letters to Reggie Turner*, p. 53.

I am very anxious: to Arthur Humphreys, September 1894 (L370).

It is the first: Hyde, *The Trials*, p. 121.

The said Oscar: Hyde, p. 326.

138 **I can see my brother now:** p. 94.

With regard to my children: to More Adey, 25 September 1896 (L409).

139 **She sends me photographs:** to Ross, 29–30 May 1897 (L582).

I am greatly disappointed: 6 September 1897 (L639).

I must remake: 23 September 1897 (L647).

140 **expression of great kindness** etc.: Holland, *Time Remembered: After Père Lachaise*, pp. 11–12.

141 **the hackneyed expression:** pp. 61–63.

the more convinced I became: quoted by Holland, *Son of Oscar Wilde*, p. 140.

142 **never mentions:** *Mrs Oscar Wilde*, p. 63.

good-natured to a fault: 25 June 1895, ms. Clark.

certainly the best: letter to Ross, ca. 1888, ms. Clark, in Small, *Oscar Wilde Revalued*, p. 45.

143 **Children begin:** P340, P376.

Time . . . has convinced me: p. 203.

He was the kindest: p. 199.

Many deeply religious people: pp. 203–4.

base their religion: p. 11.

It [was] constantly and I have learnt: p. 201.

8 TALES OF A PRODIGAL BABY

145 **In a real man:** *Thus Spoke Zarathustra, Portable Nietzsche*, p. 178.

It will be: C1084.

a sort of adopted prodigal baby: reported by William Rothenstein in *Men and Memories 1892–1900* (1931), p. 362.

I give myself: Jean Joseph-Renaud, 6 December 1891 (MK171).

146 **The whim:** Bouncer Ward, "An Oxford Reminiscence," in Holland, *Son of Oscar Wilde*, p. 250.

had a superb vitality: *Letters to the Sphinx*, p. 32.

an easy-going sort: *Chiaroscuro: Fragments of Autobiography* (1952), p. 54.

haunting the nursery: Anne Clark Amor, *Mrs Oscar Wilde*, p. 88.

fat—fat not: *Anglo-American Times*, 25 March 1893, appendix A, *Letters to Reggie Turner*, p. 286.

enormous dowager: ms. notes, Berg Collection, New York Public Library.

he made one think: *The Romantic '90s*, p. 244.

face has an air: MK90.

fond of children: to Leonard Smithers, 25 May 1898 (L744).

He was like: *The Romantic '90s*, p. 270.

147 **The Ranee:** 26 March 1897 (L515n).

dramatized endlessly: Isobel Murray, *The Complete Shorter Fiction* (1979), p. 9.

O'Sullivan preferred: "I have never cared much for Wilde's writings taken as a collection. What I do care for among them, his *Fairy Tales* and *The Sphinx*, are neglected by most of his admirers" (*Aspects of Wilde*, p. 10).

The whole, too brief, book: 12 June 1888 (L219n). O'Sullivan on Pater: "He, too, seemed to prefer Wilde's *Fairy Tales* to the rest of his production" (p. 13).

the gods bestowed: reported by O'Sullivan, p. 78.

elaborately fantastic spirit: *Saturday Review*, 26 November 1904, *Last Theatres 1904–1910*, pp. 102–3.

dangerously near: 20 October 1888, p. 472.

148 **a sadness unusual:** p. 299.

Yet ruled he not long: "The Star-Child" (C284).

strolling round: L475.

149   **They are quite beautiful:** quoted by Murray, p. 9.

   Modern realistic art: "Literary and Other Notes," *Woman's World*, December 1887 (R235).

   really a form of exaggeration: "Decay" (C978).

   are doomed: "Decay" (C989).

   the Wilde who: Murray, p. 9.

   All art is: *Dorian*, C17 (Preface).

150   **Is the story** etc.: C301–4.

   likes things to be explained: letter to the editor, *Scots Observer*, 13 August 1890 (L271).

151   **solid stolid British intellect:** "Decay" (C990).

   meant partly for children: to G. H. Kersley, 15 June 1888 (L219).

152   **an attempt to treat:** 1 July 1888 (L221).

   He is so loud: "Decay" (C973). He said this of Hall Caine.

   an attempt to mirror: to Amelie Chanler, January 1889 (L237).

   Ordinary critics: to Ross, 3 December 1898 (L767).

153   **The mind of a child:** *The Romantic '90s*, p. 252.

   are brought to a recognition: p. 299. "Discovering who they really are is the pursuit of most of Wilde's principal characters" (p. 13).

154   **What a charming day:** 22 June 1889, *More Letters*, p. 83.

   Dear Clyde: September 1890 (L275).

   Clyde Fitch: L275n. On 10 October 1890 Fitch wrote to a friend from aboard the S.S. *Fulda*, "I am bringing you . . . Oscar Wilde's book of short fairy-tales, *The Happy Prince*, and I got him to write in it, as if it were my own, and now I send it to you." (Montrose Moses and Virginia Gerson, *Clyde Fitch and His Letters* [1924], pp. 56–57).

   only not quite so useful etc.: C285–91. Robert Martin touches on the sexual allegory of this tale in "Oscar Wilde and the Fairy Tale: 'The Happy Prince' as Self-Dramatization,' *Studies in Short Fiction* 16 (1979), 74–77.

157   **I am a very remarkable Rocket** etc.: C310–18.

   When people talk: C1010.

158   **too obviously free:** Dalhousie Young, *Apologia pro Oscar Wilde* (1895), p. 22.

   with soft green grass etc.: C297–300. The Christian aspects of this story and other Wilde works are discussed by G. Wilson Knight in *The Christian Renaissance* (1962), pp. 287–300; see also Joyce Carol Oates's "*The Picture of Dorian Gray*: Wilde's Parable of the Fall," *Critical Inquiry* 7 (1980), 419–28: "Wilde's great theme is the Fall," Oates concludes (p. 425).

   Selfishness always aims: C1101.

160   **Christ as a little boy:** "Soul" (C1102).

   he who would lead: "Soul" (C1087).

Perfect . . . Perfect: ms. circa 1890, in Clark (original ellipses).

161 **wild-eyed and open-mouthed** etc.: C248–71.
The mountains of Kabylia: to Ross, 25 January 1895, *More Letters*, p. 129.
nights with Antinous: to Ross, 20 February 1898 (L705).

162 **white and delicate** etc.: C273–84.
endless hunger: letter to Will Rothenstein, 9 June 1897 (L605).
idle in his boat etc.: C248–72.

166 **in few cases:** *Partisan Review* (1950), p. 392.
stumbled a little: 20 October 1889, p. 472.
No doubt: "Decay" (C981).

167 **The writer of this review:** December 1891 (L301–2).

9   ASS-THETE: LOVER OF YOUTH

169 **I have never learned:** 8 November (L181).
Failure is: L430. Pushkin expressed a similar idea in *Eugene Onegin:* "Habit is Heaven's own redress/It takes the place of happiness" (2.31; Arndt translation, 1963).

170 **ersewild:** *Finnegans Wake* (1939 ed.), p. 314.
The Bugger's: program note for *Feasting with Panthers*, Trinity Square Repertory Company Providence, Rhode Island (1973).
Wild 'Oscar': reproduced from Lewis and Smith, *Oscar Wilde Discovers America*, p. 157. Lewis and Smith include another advertisement in which "Hoss-Car Wilde" is used to sell "the Very latest 'To[o] Utter' Styles for Railroad Men."

171 **A man who walked about:** *Adventures of a Novelist* (1932), p. 183.
loathsome modes of erotomania: 2 July 1896 (L403).

172 **insanity of perverted sensual instinct:** 10 November 1896 (L411).
dismissed with opprobrious epithets: "Homogenic Love," p. 335.
"bastard" word: "Homogenic Love," p. 325.
most who have speculated: See the discussion in Hyde, *The Trials of Oscar Wilde*, p. 58. All following quotations from trial transcripts are from Hyde.

173 **while lying in bed:** 10 July 1876 (L15).
I want to ask: 6 August 1876 (L23; original italics).

174 **Did I tell you:** 14 March 1877 (L34). Oscar's collegiate reputation for forbidden tastes is surely in play in the promise made by a friend two years later, in 1879, to propose him for membership in the Savile Club, on the assumption that Oscar would "outgrow Pessimism and all morbid nonsense" and become "a clear-headed, vigorous, healthy manly writer" (let-

ter to Wilde from Charles Leland, in Small, *Oscar Wilde Revalued*, p. 75).
Nine years later, the Savile turned Oscar down.

If a man: 17 November 1881, quoted by Ellmann, p. 147.

175   **separation for a time:** ms. letter in Clark, quoted by Ellmann, p. 148.

the first boy: quoted by Hyde, p. 58. Hyde has noted that Arthur Ransome, who derived much of his information for *Oscar Wilde* (1912) from Ross, tends to confirm Ross's assertion: "In 1886 he began that course of conduct that was to lead to his downfall." Ross is among the most reputable and honest commenters on Oscar, so it seems plausible to accept his statement.

the region of horrible snow: January–February 1886 (L184–85).

176   **Frequenting the society:** C973. Oscar varied the idea the next year in "The Critic as Artist": Gilbert says to Ernest, "I am afraid that you have been listening to the conversation of someone older than yourself. That is always a dangerous thing to do, and if you allow it to degenerate into a habit you will find it absolutely fatal to any intellectual development" (C1015).

most marvellous youth: C31(2).

The old believe everything: M178.

delightful and immortal: 26 February 1892 (M168).

177   **gather their harvest:** C55–56(4).

Is it five years ago: to H. C. Marillier, 5 November 1885 (L180).

Twenty-three!: *The Romantic '90s*, p. 185.

He is not: 7 June 1897 (L601).

velocity with young men: *Feasting with Panthers*, p. 274.

mocking and enamored: *The Gay Science*, Book IV, #340, tr. Walter Kaufmann (1974), p. 272.

178   **emotionally hero-worshipping:** L275n.

You precious: This and all following quotations from ms. letters in Clark. Among Fitch's English homosexual acquaintances were Robert Hichens (author of the notorious *Green Carnation*) and John Gray's friend André Raffalovich ("A jolly visit I had with Raffalovich," he wrote on 18 September 1888); Aubrey Beardsley met Fitch and thought him "really quite pleasant" (letter to Raffalovich, 19 May 1897, *The Letters of Aubrey Beardsley* [1970], p. 320). Somerset Maugham knew Fitch, the first American dramatist to become a millionaire, and called him "the most brilliant conversationalist of this period" (quoted in Archie Bell, *The Clyde Fitch I Knew* [1909], p. 25).

Fitch never married and was, like Oscar, very close to his mother. Indeed, he wrote in a letter of 16 May 1902, "My mother has been the one great love of my life" (*Clyde Fitch and His Letters*, p. 13). Also like Oscar, he had a penchant for "eccentric apparel" (Bell, p. 2), an "antipathy to early rising" (p. 22), and a taste for lavish interior decoration (at his Greenwich house one room was "fitted out like the apartment of a Persian prince"—p. 101). In the Oscarian manner, Fitch made a very colorful and memorable collegian: at Amherst he was known for his collection of dolls, the floral frieze he painted on the walls of his Chi Psi fraternity room, his taste for china (whether *blue* is not reported), and his brilliant performances of female roles in fraternity and College theatricals. Even a Hartford high school classmate, William Lyon Phelps, recalled Fitch in ways eerily reminiscent of Oscar. In odd gait: "His gait was strange, the motive power seeming to dwell exclusively in the hips; if you can imagine a gay sidewheel steamer, with the port and starboard wheels moving in turn instead of together, you will obtain a fair idea of the approach of William C. Fitch" (clever image for what is now termed the "swish"!). In attire: "No other youth would have dared to wear such clothes ... the radiance of those glossy garments almost hurt the unprotected eye." In fearless assertion of personality: "We thought he was effeminate, a mollycoddle, a sissy; we did not know that he had the courage of his convictions, and was thus the bravest boy in school" (*Essays on Modern Dramatists* [1921], pp. 142–44).

Later in life, Fitch was famed for the brilliant female impersonations he performed in the process of rehearsing actresses for their roles in his plays. One actress declared, "Not a woman of us could approach him in look, manner, and, above all, voice." (See Kim Marra, "Clyde Fitch: Transvestite *Metteur-en-scène* of the Feminine," *New England Theatre Journal* 3 [1992], 15–37.) Fitch was a great opera lover and was once approached by Puccini to write a libretto for an American opera (before going to David Belasco for *La Fanciulla del West*).

A cache of about sixty letters in the New York Public Library from Fitch to another gay friend, Dewitt Miller, sheds further interesting light on the relationship with Wilde. In June 1892 Fitch lodged several weeks at the Albany in London (the residence of George Ives and of Ernest Worthing in *The Importance of Being Earnest*) and wrote, "When Whistler and Wilde quarrelled I stuck to the Wildes." In a postscript to another letter, Fitch wrote, "Yes, I *have* read 'Dorian.' I have a copy w^h Wilde gave me. I will take your volume over with a great deal of pleasure. I will ask Wilde to write something in it." A most fascinating letter, dated 2 January 1891, does not mention Oscar but tells much of Fitch's view of homosexuality and the Closet. Over lunch at Delmonico's, it seems, Miller had spoken of "certain temperaments of men for the not ordinary sexual enjoyment," mentioned several names, and then expressed a desire "to write up the subject." Fitch continued, "Thinking it over afterward, I felt that it was something I did not at all approve of. I felt and feel you could have no right to do this, to expose what would ruin the reputation of many men living and dead who had fought hard against their temptations and done all in their power to make up for their secret life. . . . I believe this temperament belongs to them, and they are answerable for it to God (who perhaps is <u>also</u> answerable to them) and not to the world who would condemn and damn them. Their family, their <u>mothers</u>, should be remembered." Fitch added at the end, "I ask that you will <u>answer</u> <u>but</u> destroy this letter." Here, it seems, is a very early debate, in miniature, on the propriety of "outing."

181 **a rather nice man:** 9 April 1895, *Letters*, p. 8.

the most lord: unpublished notes, quoted in Delay, p. 392.

Women kneel: P317.

The future: P345.

prey to [the] absolute madness: 10 November 1896 (L411).

cheeky little street rats: p. 271.

then Victorian society: *Wilde's Devoted Friend*, p. 41.

182 **Your brother is lucky:** Hyde, p. 178.

I have a weakness: Hyde, p. 204.

a walking stick: Hyde, p. 204.

perfect type: C70(6).

the Roman age: "Homogenic Love," p. 327.

183 **Just now:** *The Poems of Catullus*, tr. Peter Whigham (1966), p. 116.

When you say: I.46 (A.D. 85–86), *Martial: The Epigrams*, tr. James Michie (1973).

If from the baths: IX.33 (A.D. 94), tr. Michie.

Natta calls: XI.72, tr. Anthony Reid, *Epigrams*, p. 445.

was born to be: letter to his mother, 30 January 1895, quoted in Delay, *The Youth of André Gide*, p. 392.

Roman emperor of the decadence: *The Real Oscar Wilde*, p. 365.

184 **of Moors:** "A Ride through Morocco," *Pall Mall Gazette*, 8 October 1886 (R93).

boys as beautiful: quoted by Gide, *If It Die*, p. 297.

There is a great deal: circa 25 January 1895, *More Letters*, pp. 128–29.

To those who are preoccupied: "Pen" (C993).

It was a dreadful thing: C1006.

Men always look so silly: P176.

good looks: P248.

unsexed blackguards: 26 May 1895.

185 **adored a young man:** Hyde, p. 112. Hyde is the source for all quotations from the trials.

The pleasure to me: p. 127. Curiously, Oscar was here echoing Samuel Johnson: "Sir, I love the acquaintance of young people; because, in the first place I don't like to think of myself as growing old. In the next place, young acquaintances must last longest, if they do last; and then, Sir, young men have more virtues than old men; they have more generous sentiments in every respect. I love the young dogs of this age: they have more wit and humour and knowledge of life than we had." But he added, "The young dogs are not so good scholars" (Boswell, *Life of Johnson*, p. 315).

red rose-leaf lips: p. 117.

Do you think: p. 202.

Why did you: pp. 202–3. At the Queensberry trial Oscar retorted to a similar question in like wise: "To me youth, the mere fact of youth, is so wonderful that I would sooner talk to a young man for half-an-hour than be—well, cross-examined in Court!" (p. 129).

186   **marred and maimed:** to George Alexander, February 1895 (L384).

Rather a rough neighborhood: p. 203.

I make no social distinctions: p. 248.

You deny: p. 252.

young men: p. 189.

187   **a moment of fatal folly:** p. 133.

calculated to subvert morality: the plea is reproduced in full by Hyde, pp. 323–27.

188   **His conduct:** p. 60. Taylor was charged with *pedicatio*, but this charge was eventually dropped.

190   **look more like an equal:** p. 122.

Did you know: p. 127.

poetry and art: p. 173.

Did any of these men: p. 129.

191   **stained in a peculiar way:** p. 188.

boy of sixteen: p. 194.

Oscar at bay: John Connell, *W. E. Henley* (1949), p. 298.

Sin is an essential element: C1023.

Self-denial is simply a method: C1024.

The basis of every scandal: C154(18).

wreck the soul: to Selwyn Image, 3 June 1897 (L594).

192   **I knew Oscar well:** quoted by Desmond Chapman-Huston, *The Lost Historian* (1936), pp. 237–38.

193   **the terrible alchemy of egotism:** *De profundis* (L437).

without grace: *De profundis* (L428).

rather charming: 7 and 13 May 1893, *Letters to Reggie Turner*, p. 39.

a difficult character: John Stokes, "Wilde at Bay," p. 178.

burning candles: *The Real Oscar Wilde*, p. 348.

warned Lord A: Stokes, p. 178.

Don't be afraid: P343–44.

194 **hissing, withering, savage voice:** *If It Die*, p. 299. The credibility of Gide's views about Oscar has been much debated (see James Griffin's "The Importance of Being Spurious: Gide's 'Lies,' A Forged Letter, and the Emerging Wilde Biography," *Journal of Modern Literature* 10 [1983], 166–72), but it is worth remembering what Oscar's soberest and most knowledgeable close friend, Ross, thought: "The only *personal* reflections" published about Oscar "to which any importance or belief can be attached are those by Monsieur André Gide and Ernest La Jeunesse" (in Leverson, *Letters to the Sphinx*, p. 14).

    When he saw me: *If It Die*, pp. 300–1.

195 **£5,000 on Bosie:** *De profundis* (L428).

    At twelve o'clock: *De profundis* (L426).

    Time after time: November 1896 (L413).

196 **My heart:** 3.11.57–59.

    The basis of character: L429–30.

    all ways: C155(18).

    Boys, brandy, and betting: 29 June 1900 (L831). Boys apparently ceased to monopolize Bosie's attention, for he eventually married (unhappily and briefly) and converted to Catholicism; he remained a gambler, though, placing two losing bets on horses the day he died. He became ferociously litigious, served some time in prison for libeling Winston Churchill about the Battle of Jutland, and wrote much silly stuff. The choicest silliness, to my mind, is his review of Shaw's play *Getting Married*. He accused Shaw of not possessing "a masculine intellect," and with magnificent priggishness complained of "Mr Shaw's impertinent treatment of serious subjects." The *pièce de résistance*, however, is the monumental hypocrisy of his concern for family values: "Mr Shaw . . . is beginning to make serious inroads on the British home, and if he had his own way he would break it up altogether" ("For Shame Mr Shaw," *The Academy*, 23 May 1908, p. 806).

197 **O sweetest of all boys:** 20 May 1895 (L398).

10 *PUNCH* V. OSCAR II

200 **He both pleases men:** 2.1.141–42.

    a rather De Quincey-ish article: p. 12.

    that artistically got-up Magazine: 5 October 1889, p. 160.

    People as a rule: *Letters to the Sphinx*, p. 29.

201 **an effeminate, invertebrate:** 7 January 1882, p. 12. "Charmides" and "Rosa Mystica" are the titles of two Wilde poems.

    Oscar Wilde's Wildest: 19 July 1890, p. 25.

202 **every motor:** 20 September 1890, p. 135.
203 **No; let [Oscar]:** 30 May 1891, p. 257.
     The license for: 9 July 1892, p. 1.
204 **wearisome tirades:** 6 May 1893, p. 213.
205 **not getting on:** 30 December 1893, pp. 304–5.
206 **I invented:** 1 October 1894 (L373).
     "Two Decadent Guys": 10 November 1894, p. 225.
208 **We are the real:** 6 April 1895, p. 157.
209 ***Ars longa est:*** 13 April 1895, p. 171.
     When Adam: 27 April 1895, p. 203.
210 **At last!:** 11 May 1895, p. 222.
     When society is aware: *Pall Mall Gazette,* 17 May 1889 (R498).
211 **His admirers:** MK234.

11 THE MAN WILDE: HIS CRIME

213 **Blackstone described:** *Bowers v. Hardwick,* 478 U.S. 198, p. 2847 (opinion concurring with the majority; original emphasis).
214 **For as much as:** 25 Henry 8, c. 6.
     sodomites came: quoted by Cohen, p. 189.
215 **I will not:** *Commentaries,* Vol. IV, pp. 215–16 (the Latin phrase: "the horrible sin not to be named among Christians"). The *University of Miami Law Review* note cited below asserts that Blackstone's views provided "the basis for most U.S. sodomy laws," which were passed mainly between 1830 and 1870 (p. 526).

On the subject of English legislation concerning homosexuality, several studies may be consulted: H. M. Hyde, *The Trials of Oscar Wilde* (1948; reprint 1973) . . . notably the preface by Sir Travers Humphreys and appendix E, "The Prevalence of Male Homosexuality in England"; H. M. Hyde, *The Love that Dared Not Speak Its Name* (1970); the first chapter of Jeffrey Weeks, *Coming Out: Homosexual Politics in Britain, from the Nineteenth Century to the Present* (1977); Alan Bray, *Homosexuality in Renaissance England* (1982); Louis Crompton, *Byron and Greek Love: Homophobia in Nineteenth Century England* (1985); Ed Cohen, *Talk on the Wilde Side* (1992), especially the chapter "Legislating the Norm," pp. 103–25.

It doesn't matter: recorded in Daphne Fielding, *The Duchess of Jermyn Street* (1964), p. 37.

witty and cultured writer: Lewis and Smith, *Oscar Wilde Discovers America,* p. 26.

Labouchere is the best writer: circa 25 February 1882, quoted in *Oscar Wilde Discovers America,* p. 209.

216 **Weary of being asked:** to Mrs George Lewis, circa 20 March 1882 (L105).

217 **Any male person:** *Law Reports, The Public General Statutes, 1884–1885,* Vol. 21, Chap. 69, p. 362.

first legal classification: Cohen, p. 203.

Humphreys . . . emphasized: Hyde, p. 12.

No one having experience: Hyde, p. 13.

The purity of the households: quoted in Cohen, p. 204.

218 **in a fantastic female garb:** Christopher Millard (a.k.a. Stuart Mason), quoted in Croft-Cooke, *Feasting with Panthers,* p. 277.

The prosecution of Oscar Wilde: p. 121.

219 **The homogenic passion:** "Homogenic Love" (1895), p. 345 (original italics).

I know *for an absolute fact*: typescript of the article in the Clark Library (p. 9). Ellmann has discussed why the article was never published (p. 488).

220 **While in London:** *Echo de Paris,* 6 December 1891 (MK170).

If Oscar: *Aspects of Wilde,* p. 59.

That terrifying man: Delay, *The Youth of André Gide,* p. 391.

221 **Sir, I am sorry:** *Collected Letters 1874–1897,* ed. Dan H. Laurence (1965), pp. 230–31.

224 **It has to be remarked:** Carpenter, pp. 346–47 (original italics).

227 **it is revolting:** All *Bowers v. Hardwick* quotations are from 478 U.S. 198, pp. 2848–55; for a recent overview of sodomy statutes and the right to privacy, see "Survey on the Constitutional Right to Privacy in the Context of Homosexual Activity," *University of Miami Law Review* (1986), pp. 521–687.

228 **fallen from fifty to twenty-four:** States banning homosexual and heterosexual sodomy: Alabama, Arizona, Florida, Georgia, Idaho, Louisiana, Maryland, Massachusetts, Michigan, Minnesota, Mississippi, North Carolina, Oklahoma, Rhode Island, South Carolina, Utah, Virginia, District of Columbia; states banning only homosexual sodomy: Arkansas, Kansas, Missouri, Montana, Nevada, Tennessee, Texas.

Summarizing then: pp. 339–40.

229 **senseless pleasure:** to Michael Davitt, late May or early June 1897 (L587).

Great men: "Skirmishes of an Untimely Man," #44, *Twilight of the Idols, Portable Nietzsche,* p. 547.

Wilde was arrested: *My Days and Dreams* (1916), p. 19.

230 **the chief of whom** etc.: pp. 319–20 (1895—6th New York edition).

Dear Sir: to Leo Maxse, *More Letters,* p. 123.

apparently admires immorality: p. 320. This view doubtless derived from Oscar's praise of the murderer Wainewright in "Pen" (1889) and *The Picture of Dorian Gray* (1890).

231 **upon the homosexual passion:** 29 December, *The Letters of John Addington Symonds* (1969), III, p. 799.

233   **A man of genius:** quoted in Boswell, *The Life of Johnson* (1953), p. 270.
Nothing should: C1084.
so-called Gribsby scene: The scene, together with an explanatory note by H. Montgomery Hyde, is included as an afterpiece to *Earnest* in *The Complete Plays* (P291–99); it is incorporated, as originally written, in *The Complete Works* (C349–52).

234   **I am not a scrap:** 28 May 1897 (L581).
that fatal Friday: L442.

235   **I don't know:** Hyde, p. 130.
I have no books etc.: L390–95.
Poor Oscar: 9 April 1895, *Letters of Max Beerbohm*, p. 8.
Knowing English custom: *Oscar Wilde*, p. 137.

236   **I hoped and expected:** Hyde, p. 145.
If you wish it: p. 140.
Wilde was given: Sir Travers Humphreys, in Hyde, p. 9.
If the country: Hyde, p. 149.
more than five hundred: Henry Harland's report to Edmund Gosse, letter of 5 May 1895 (quoted by Ellmann, p. 457).
All the conditions: P103.

237   **the truth is rarely pure:** P224.
Why don't you withdraw: reported by Hyde, p. 93.

238   **Oscar is an Irish gentleman:** Pearson, *Oscar Wilde*, p. 271.
buy letters of mine: p. 174.
the intrepid young woman: *Daily News*, 5 February 1896.
If you stay: Pearson, p. 271.
O my mother: *Coriolanus*, 5.3.185–89.

239   **A mother's love:** P344.
I have never known: Harris, p. 210.
I have given my word: Hyde, p. 224.
Wilde was told: Hyde, pp. 10–11.
You can pay: *Oscar Wilde*, p. 168.
too ill: *The Real Oscar Wilde*, p. 371.

240   **thinner and consequently fine:** David Cecil, *Max: A Biography*, p. 122.
The only thing: July 1894 (L358).
We have been: 25 March 1895 (L385).
With what a crash: 9 April 1895 (L389).
extremely optimistic: *Letters to the Sphinx*, p. 41.
I see a very brilliant life: L358n.
the impenetrable blank wall: *Contemporary Portraits*, p. 104.

241   **thought he had:** *Autobiography*, p. 112.

nine out of twelve jurors: 3 May 1895, *Letters to Reggie Turner*, p. 102.

A year, Frank: p. 178.

dead to all sense of shame: Hyde, p. 272.

Oh, Frank: pp. 171–77.

242 **On a yacht:** C154(18).

I was consumed: p. 175. Harris had been present the previous month when Oscar refused his lawyers' offer to drag the case out to cover his flight: "Robert Ross urged him to accept Matthews' offer; but he would not. Why? I am sure he had no reason, for I put the question to him more than once, and even after reflecting, he had no explanation to give" (p. 140).

a beaten Eastern gong: Arthur Symons, quoted in Philippa Pullar, *Frank Harris*, p. 157.

One does not: W. L. George, quoted in E. Merrill Root, *Frank Harris*, p. 86.

243 **You were more:** in Harris, p. 340.

Frank Harris is: to Reggie Turner, 3 February 1899 (L778).

Surely it is better: p. 173 Augustus John wrote: "He showed . . . sound judgment when in his greatest dilemma he chose to sit tight (in every sense) and await the police, rather than face freedom in the company of Frank Harris" (MK373).

To be called on: Harris, p. 340.

a very touching letter: *Autobiography*, p. 112.

244 **Only love:** P368.

A slim thing: 9 April 1895 (L389).

Nothing but Alfred Douglas's: 16 April 1895 (L391).

From your silken hair: 20 May 1895 (L398).

Every great love: May 1895 (L397).

245 **She stood up:** *Oscar Wilde*, pp. 209–10.

246 **For God's sake:** Harris, p. 338.

Don't be witty: p. 154.

His ornate and gushing language: 26 May 1895.

247 **Have no fear:** quoted in Brian Roberts, *The Mad Bad Line*, p. 217.

This little earnest or posing world: *Memories and Impressions*, p. 164.

The force of: Harris, p. 335. Ada Leverson analyzed Oscar's class appeal differently, but she too isolated the "jury class" as hostile to him: "With his extraordinary high spirits and love of fun he appealed to the lower class; his higher gifts enchanted the artistic and such of the great world as love to amuse themselves. . . . But the lower middle-class never liked him, always distrusted him and disliked his success" (*Letters to the Sphinx*, p. 29).

The public are now familiar: 26 May 1895.

mentally stunned: p. 168.

248 **I couldn't think:** p. 154.

The scene that evening: *Letters to Reggie Turner*, p. 104.

He says things: C54(4).

It is to do nothing: C1039.

I am afraid: to Mrs Allhusen (L255).

Mr Wilde's *dramatis personae*: 6 May 1893, p. 213.

Plot continues to be: 15 February 1895.

249   born actor: letter to Carlos Blacker, 20 March 1898 (L718n).

I'm caught: p. 173.

You reveal Wilde: Harris, p. 337.

I can't see myself: Robert Sherard, *The Real Oscar Wilde*, p. 371.

A false name: 20 May 1895 (L398).

Many people were kind: letter to Adela Schuster, 23 December 1900 (L862).

grand seigneur: quoted in Leverson, p. 39.

look of immovable obstinacy: *Letters to the Sphinx*, pp. 41–42.

250   There was an extraordinary calm: *The Real Oscar Wilde*, p. 372.

imperious mask: p. 113.

You have a splendid position: P129.

On the whole: "Soul" (C1093).

It often happens: C84(8).

had a pathetic belief: Hyde, p. 11.

251   Mary McCarthy shrewdly observed: "The Unimportance of Being Oscar," *Partisan Review* (1947), pp. 302–4.

mocking and enamored monster: *The Gay Science*, #340, *Portable Nietzsche*, p. 101.

to asphyxiate: 13 April 1895, p. 177.

If he had lived: *Anglo-American Times*, 25 March 1893, in *Letters to Reggie Turner*, p. 290.

Socrates would not: *Contemporary Portraits*, p. 124.

252   as Ellmann observed: p. 435.

As a man sows: P295.

Sooner or later: P129.

At the great moment: L430.

I have been: *If It Die*, pp. 301–2.

253   The thing has always seemed: p. 167.

There are moments: P63.

It is that deep, spiritual affection: Hyde, p. 201.

254   simply wonderful: David Cecil, p. 121.

the great of the earth: John Stokes, "Wilde at Bay," p. 181.

Whenever a man does: *Dorian*, C66(6).

13 TRAGEDIAN: *AMOR FATI*

255 **Most men:** C174.

My formula: *Ecce Homo*, II, #10 (1968 tr. Walter Kaufmann). The passage continues: "that one wants nothing to be different, not forward, not backward, not in all eternity. Not merely bear what is necessary, still less conceal it . . . but *love* it." See, in this regard, chapters five and six of Alexander Nehamas's *Nietzsche: Life as Literature* (1985).

without a trace: Le Rouge's reminiscence appeared in *Nouvelles litteraires* of 3 and 10 November 1928 (MK461).

257 **behind every exquisite thing:** C41(3).

You must always: quoted in Ellmann, p. 429.

the exaggeration: *Dramatic Review*, 6 June 1885 (R32).

vowed to disaster: *Aspects of Wilde*, p. 46.

Is there anything: L478.

St. Helena was necessary: *Aspects of Wilde*, p. 46.

258 **Life then is a failure:** C1035.

I do not pose: Hyde, *The Trials*, p. 117.

revolting and repellent: *De profundis* (L444).

one of the tragedies: "A Lord of Language," *Vanity Fair*, 2 March 1905, appendix in H. M. Hyde, *Oscar Wilde: The Aftermath*, p. 207.

the greatest tragedy: John Stokes, "Wilde at Bay," p. 184.

He walked: "Sebastian Melmoth" (1905), *Selected Prose* (1952), p. 303.

You see types: letter of 30 January 1895, Delay, *The Youth of André Gide*, p. 392.

259 **I'll never:** 5.3.34–37.

A spirit: "Skirmishes of an Untimely Man," #49, *Twilight of the Idols, Portable Nietzsche*, p. 554. Nietzsche was also devoted to the philosophy of *amor fati*. Carl Pletsch wrote in *Young Nietzsche* that he "preached the gospel of loving one's own fate (*amor fati*)" and from about 1865 "was tacitly living by the motto, *amor fati*" (pp. 14, 70); many other parallels between the moral philosophy of Nietzsche and Wilde are discussed below in Chapter 15, "Closet Philosopher."

260 **There is no such thing:** C153(15).

life is as full: p. 130.

the note of Doom: L475.

an excitement: "An Improbable Life," *The New Yorker*, 9 March 1963, in *Forewords and Afterwords* (1974), p. 304. Ian Small, in fact, has expressed regret that the constant reiteration of the "myth" of a tragic fall by biographers—including recent ones like Ellmann and Pine (who has even divided his study into genesis, hubris, nemesis, and catharsis sections)—has seriously arrested Wilde studies (see *Oscar Wilde Revalued*, pp. 2–3,

20–21); Andrew Shelley, reviewing Ellmann, made the same point: "Too much emphasis has been placed on the role of Nemesis in Wilde's life" (*Essays in Criticism* 38 [1988], p. 161).

There goes a man: Hyde, *The Trials*, pp. 30–31.

Nothing that actually occurs: "Phrases and Philosophies" (C1205).

261 **Somehow or other:** David Hunter-Blair, *In Victorian Days* (1939), pp. 121–22.

a man full of wit: holograph ms. in the Morgan Library, pp. 7–9.

If you do mean them: reported in Desmond Chapman-Huston, *The Lost Historian* (1936), p. 73.

Literature always anticipates life: C983.

262 **Looking at him:** C173.

blank wall: L358n.

Of an extremely artistic temperament: "Pen" (C993).

263 **mad hungers:** C103(11).

strange rumours: C102(11).

these hideous things and **Why is your friendship:** C117(12).

If the poor: C1205.

The beggars here: 25 January 1895, *More Letters*, p. 129.

live down anything: *Woman* (P320).

persistently compromise us: *Woman* (P327).

264 **I am amorous:** C558–59.

My sweet rose: 20 May 1895 (L397–98).

terribly dangerous: P141.

To stake all one's life: P144.

The tragic artist: " 'Reason' in Philosophy," #6, *Twilight of the Idols, Portable Nietzsche*, p. 484.

Some of its passages: letter of 20 March 1899 (L787). E. H. Mikhail has examined the autobiographical aspects of this play—"one of the most open 'confessions' of Wilde's soul"—in "Self-Revelation in *An Ideal Husband*," *Modern Drama* 11 (1968), 180–86.

Once a man: P261.

265 **There was a snow-storm:** *Letters to the Sphinx*, p. 26.

distinguished audience: *Letters to the Sphinx*, pp. 27–29.

His expression: "In Memoriam" (written 1901, published 1905), quoted in Delay, *The Youth of André Gide*, p. 290.

266 **The gods had given me:** L466.

that healthy natural vanity: "Decay" (C987).

When people play: to More Adey, 8 March 1897 (L422).

with a capital "I": *Pall Mall Gazette*, 26 January 1889 (R402).

Vanity, like curiosity: "Some Literary Notes," *Woman's World*, January 1889 (R376–77).

267 **I had things:** L466.

subordinate characters: *Private Domain* (1988), p. 331.

totally inadequate: Hyde, pp. 272–73.

Why is it: to Carlos Blacker, 4 August 1897 (L629).

terrible blindness: C235.

the loss even: *Sebastian Melmoth*, p. 673.

268   that one's most glaring fault: *Woman* (P352).

affectations and eccentricities: *The Romantic '90s*, p. 256.

Each man: C144(16).

I let myself: L466.

It is the sin of pride: MK355.

I fear: 4 August 1897 (L629).

269   an unfinished sketch: inscription, dated 1904, in a presentation copy of *The Land of Heart's Desire*, Berg Collection, New York Public Library.

tragedy . . . he bore: *The Romantic '90s*, p. 257.

the protagonist: "A Lord of Language," in Hyde, *Oscar Wilde: The Aftermath*, p. 207.

I am no longer: MK335.

long and lovely suicide: to H. C. Marillier, February 1886 (L185).

14 FALLEN EAGLE: DEVILS AND ANGELS

271   I suppose: to Ada Leverson, 9 April 1895, *Letters of Max Beerbohm*, p. 8.

How fascinating: letter to Julia Ward Howe, 6 July 1882 (L122).

We can have: C149(17).

I need not ask: to More Adey, after 24 April 1895 (ms. Clark).

I never believe: *Letters to the Sphinx*, p. 39.

272   Well, well: W. H. Leverton, *Through the Box-Office Window* (1932), p. 68.

the hatred of Wilde: *Oscar Wilde*, p. 163.

had attempted to steal: *Aspects of Wilde*, pp. 59–60.

the most fatal: *Nebraska State Journal*, 19 May 1895, in *The World and the Parish*, ed. William M. Curtin (1970), p. 153. A few months later she wrote, "Civilization shudders at his name. . . . Cain's curse was light compared with his" (*Courier*, 28 September 1895, p. 265).

At the noble game: p. 109. A few pages later, he summarized: "People who live in this more tolerant (or at any rate less fiercely hypocritical) age can have no conception of the courage required in those days to be seen even speaking to Oscar Wilde or having any association with him" (p. 113).

vitriol-tinted flower: 13 April 1895, p. 177.

273   evils of this kind: 27 May 1895.

There is not a man: 6 April 1895. Hyde (p. 156n) thought one Charles

Whibley wrote the editorial, but "in any event Henley must take the responsibility for it."

It was impossible: *Oscar Wilde*, p. 148.

274   A man who: P257.

name was seldom: Wyndham, *The Sphinx and Her Circle*, p. 53.

at Oscar's own behest: to Leonard Smithers, 1 December 1898, *More Letters*, p. 175.

275   was covered: Wyndham, p. 53.

not have in his drawing-room: letter to Frank Harris, 13 June 1897 (L608–609; original italics).

shameful charge: Beerbohm referred to the case in a letter to Ross, 14 November 1894, *Letters*, p. 7.

It is thine: John Stokes, "Wilde at Bay," p. 180.

I was never: *Aspects of Wilde*, p. 69.

276   knew perfectly well: pp. 58–59.

A night alarm: "The Lord Looks at Peter," *Poems* (1931), p. 37.

Of Oscar Wilde: Horace Wyndham, *This Was the News* (1948), p. 162.

Hurl'd headlong: *Paradise Lost*, Book I, 11. 45–48.

277   It was a genuine: *Oscar Wilde and the Yellow Nineties*, p. 308.

Ellmann stated: p. 305.

lamentable error: *Memories and Impressions*, pp. 169–70.

After going and The great movement: Stokes, pp. 180–81.

278   Yesterday I was: letter to Robert Ross, 27 December 1898 (L772). A friendly letter from Wilde to Alexander in July 1900 (L832) suggests a later reconciliation.

constituted himself: p. 137.

Demmed nuisance: P55.

Quel monstre: *Max and Will: Max Beerbohm and William Rothenstein, Their Friendship and Letters*, ed. Karl Beckson and Mary Lago (1975), p. 21. Beerbohm elsewhere called him "very vulgar and unwashed and inferior" (*Letters to Reggie Turner*, p. 63); for a full overview of the relationship of the two brothers, see Beckson's "The Importance of Being Angry: The Mutual Antagonism of Oscar and Willie Wilde," in Norman Kiell, ed., *Blood Brothers: Siblings as Writers* (1983), pp. 115–36.

279   thoroughly uninteresting: *The Days I Knew* (1925), p. 87.

a blood relation: *Great Expectations*, Chap. 29.

Willie has been writing: to Ada Leverson, 23 April 1895 (L392).

theatrical insincerity: p. 165.

almost melodramatic protestations: *The Life of Oscar Wilde*, p. 366.

maudlin pathos: in Harris, *Oscar Wilde*, p. 333.

My poor brother writes: Yeats reported this remark (L392n).

has been extracting fivers: *Letters to Reggie Turner*, p. 103.

Between him and me: 15 March 1899 (L785).

the mad, bad line: *De profundis* (L435).

I choose my friends: C23(1).

280   fit of canting hypocrisy: preface to Sherard, *Bernard Shaw, Frank Harris, and Oscar Wilde*, pp. xiii–xiv.

My business: L492.

He was a coarse-minded: Sir Travers Humphreys, in Hyde, *The Trials*, p. 9.

noble art of self-pretence: *Ulysses*, p. 589.

some variation and There is no law: "Marriage etc." (n.d. Watts & Co.), pp. 8, 11. The lecture was delivered on 18 January 1893 in Prince's Hall, Piccadilly (copy in the New York Public Library).

We produce our posterity: this lecture was delivered to the fourth annual conference of the British Secular Union, 31 July 1881, and later published without a date by Watts & Co.

somewhat chequered career: *The Trials*, p. 220n.

My intense admiration: p. 2.

281   There are so many sons: P162.

Can't make out: P120.

That is a paradox: P174.

I used to see: L492.

282   like a wounded stag: Willie Wilde, quoted in Pearson, p. 270.

Must congratulate: Hyde, p. 232.

go to the South Sea Islands: *Autobiography*, p. 121.

result ... of: p. 13.

283   I am afraid: *Fan* (P37)

manners before morals!: *Fan* (P93).

I hear that: to Ada Leverson, 17 April 1895 (L392).

I have learnt: to Selwyn Image (original italics) and to Arthur Humphreys (L594–95).

the minor clubs: *Letters to Reggie Turner*, p. 104.

284   one of the mildest-looking: 26 April 1895.

Seldom has a calmer: 2 May 1895.

The severely colourless summing-up: 27 May 1895.

Of Taylor we do not need: 26 May 1895.

Taylor told him: 26 April 1895.

285   I spoke to him: in Harris, p. 333.

286   Sir, Mr Oscar Wilde: reproduced in Hyde, p. 357.

questioned whether: pp. 38–40.

a dear simple nice fellow: postcard to Ross, 10 June 1897 (L605).

288   You are an old: Christopher Millard, *Oscar Wilde: Three Times Tried* (1912), p. 336.

289   that *candidissima anima*: L433.

who demand the right: quoted in F. G. Bettany, *Stewart Headlam: A Biography* (1926), p. 125.

had a narrow escape: 21 September 1904, *Ellen Terry and Bernard Shaw: A Correspondence* (1931), p. 33.

who fled at once and **I knew quite well** and **Isn't this the man:** Bettany, pp. 130–31.

290   **It so enchanted:** all quotations (with original italics) are from ms. letters in Clark.

A very noble and cultured woman: Harris, p. 169.

whatever of remembrance: November 1896 (L415).

291   **As long as he was allowed:** L860.

Miss Schuster objects: 20 November 1916, ms. in Clark.

292   **Of all my old friends:** to Leonard Smithers, L695.

a brilliant and witty writer: *Autobiography*, p. 113.

293   **Mrs Leverson is delighted:** 14 November 1894, *Letters*, p. 6.

I go to bed: Violet Wyndham, *The Sphinx and Her Circle*, p. 26.

I have selected: L381.

Oscar is coming: May 1895, ms. in Clark.

To keep open house: "Skirmishes of an Untimely Man," #5, *Twilight of the Idols, Portable Nietzsche*, p. 530.

in Ada's memoir: *Letters to the Sphinx*, pp. 37–42.

294   **was bright:** *The Story of an Unhappy Friendship*, p. 179.

All his life: Cecil, *Max: A Biography*, p. 121.

15   CLOSET PHILOSOPHER

295   **To speak the truth:** L502.

Permanence of temperament: 18 February 1899 (L780).

He favours: Book I, #96, tr. James Michie, in *Epigrams of Martial Englished by Divers Hands*, ed. J. P. Sullivan and Peter Whigham (1987), p. 91.

296   **practical and external life:** "Critic" (C1040).

It is a great era: 13 August 1898 (L758).

297   **A critic should:** letter to the editor, *St. James's Gazette*, 27 June 1890 (L260).

Mores non: Book XI, #15, *Epigrams*, p. 417.

Autobiography is irresistible: C1010. One of the aphorisms prefixed to *Dorian* is "The highest, as the lowest, form of criticism is a mode of autobiography" (C17).

298   **If one tells the truth:** "Phrases and Philosophies" (C1205).

grubbing in muck heaps and **for none but:** anonymous notice (probably by Charles Whibley), *Scots Observer*, 5 July 1890 (L265n).

portrays the gilded paganism: 3 July 1890, in Stuart Mason, *Oscar Wilde: Art and Morality* (1912; reprint 1971), pp. 137–38.

It seems very brilliant: John Stokes, "Wilde at Bay," p. 176.

299 **He lived alone:** Archie Bell, *The Clyde Fitch I Knew* (1909), p. 51.

The aim of your society: letter to William Harnett Blanch, published in *To-Day*, 13 January 1894 (L349).

300 **He would seek:** C41(5).

Wickedness is a myth: Hyde, *The Trials*, p. 108.

A teacher: Stokes, p. 177.

a man who: p. 185.

301 **untenable propositions:** *In Victorian Days* (1939), pp. 120–21.

it is quite nonsensical: to Charles Mason, August 1894 (L364).

written by a butterfly: to Arthur Humphreys, 12 February 1895 (L382).

302 **I am off:** undated letter (Oscar met Ives in 1892) in the Humanities Research Center, University of Texas at Austin, reproduced in Small, *Oscar Wilde Revalued*, p. 58.

philosophy of individualism: review of George Woodcock, *The Paradox of Oscar Wilde*, in *Partisan Review* (1950), p. 393.

the only thing: C69(6).

Long after Wilde was dead: *Autobiography*, p. 77.

303 **flawless dandy:** P117.

the first well-dressed philosopher: P169.

called nowadays: P206.

pulling himself together: P207.

304 **taking sides:** P311.

She was one: C311.

Man makes his end: The book is in the collection of Mary Hyde, Viscountess Eccles (Somerville, New Jersey).

305 **Egotism itself:** C970.

Art never expresses: C991.

No artist recognizes: December 1891 (L302).

every man kept: "A Chinese Sage," *Speaker*, 8 February 1890 (R530–31).

306 **The longer one studies:** C1021.

Art . . . springs: C1034.

The aim of life: C29(2).

To be good: C69(6).

307 **Man has sought:** C1103–4.

out of reach: C1079.

What a man really has: C1084.

He said to man: C1085–87.

The things people say: C1086.

tainted in its signification: letter probably to Arthur Clifton, 28 January 1891, in Small, *Oscar Wilde Revalued*, p. 47.

Selfishness is: C1101. This sentiment was also included by Constance in *Oscariana*.

308   **Whenever people agree:** P82.

A truth ceases: "Phrases and Philosophies" (C1205).

There are moments: P63.

I usually say: P145.

I would to God: P150.

309   **I am not alluding:** L467.

Still I believe: 1 April 1897 (L512).

Vanity, that great impulse: 19 November 1897 (L676).

When you allude: to Georgina Weldon, 31 May 1898 (L751; Wilde's italics).

310   **Nietzschean son:** in Frank Harris, *Oscar Wilde*, p. 330.

Gide said: Delay, p. 291.

Wilde was a moralist: p. 100.

did not care about Germany: *Aspects of Wilde*, p. 145.

the bulk of them: speech delivered at the Ritz Hotel, 1 December 1908, p. 3, typescript in Clark (it is printed in Margery Ross, *Robert Ross: Friend of Friends* [1952]).

It is love: *Ideal* (P153).

311   **the degree and kind:** *Beyond Good and Evil* (1886), #75 (PN444). NOTE: Most citations from Nietzsche, with his italics only, are from *The Portable Nietzsche*, ed. Walter Kaufmann and here abbreviated (PN). Thomas Mann remarked on the parallels between the two men in his essay "Nietzsche's Philosophy in the Light of Recent History" (*Last Essays* [1958], pp. 157–58). Mann wrote, "The more or less sought-after martyrdom at the end of Wilde's life—Reading Gaol—adds a touch of sanctity which would have aroused Nietzsche's full sympathy." Philip Reiff, in perhaps the most challenging and disconcerting essay on Wilde as a social philosopher, makes the connection as well: "Nietzsche's future philosopher, as a humorist, is not far from Wilde's artist. . . . Freud, Marx, Nietzsche, Wilde: these are some of the chief evangels associated with new ways toward the realization of the self" ("The Impossible Culture," pp. 422–23); see also Lionel Trilling, *Sincerity and Authenticity* (1972), pp. 118–22; the reader may also wish to consult the chapter on Wilde and Nietzsche in Eve Kosofsky Sedgwick's *The Epistemology of the Closet* (1990), pp. 131–81.

the little pastor: Carl Pletsch, *Young Nietzsche* (1991), p. 20. I am indebted to Pletsch for many details of this sketch of Nietzsche and his philosophy.

loneliest thinker: postcard to Overbeck, 30 July 1881 (PN92).

Only thoughts: "Maxims and Arrows," #34, *Twilight of the Idols* (PN471).

No glass of wine: quoted by Pletsch, p. 104.

312   The surest way: *The Dawn*, #297 (PN91).

Nietzsche is certainly not: quoted by Pletsch, p. 110.

Everything about woman: *Zarathustra* (PN178).

Woman is not yet capable: *Zarathustra* (PN169).

newspaper-reading public: *Beyond Good and Evil*, #263, quoted by Philippa Foot, "Nietzsche's Immoralism," *New York Review of Books*, 13 June 1991, p. 18.

By giving us: "Critic" (C1048). In "The Soul of Man Under Socialism" he called the fourth estate "very bad, and wrong, and demoralising" (C1094).

If all alms: *The Wanderer and His Shadow*, #239 (PN70).

The English public: to the editor, *Scots Observer*, 13 August 1890 (L271).

Germans . . . know: *The Dawn* (1881), #193 (PN83).

313   Man does *not* strive: "Maxims and Arrows," #12, *Twilight* (PN468).

to make the individual: *Notes* (1875; PN50).

I have the gift: *Ecce Homo*, Chap. 1, sec. 1 (PN659).

gay kind of seriousness: *The Wanderer and His Shadow*, #86 (PN69).

power of putting: "Nietzsche in England," *Saturday Review*, 11 April 1896, p. 374. Shaw greatly admired Nietzsche and was one of his English popularizers. He called *Zarathustra* "the first modern book that can be set above the Psalms of David" (*Fabian News*, April 1907, p. 38) and once expressed the humble Shavian desire to be known in Germany as "an English (or Irish) Nietzsche (only ten times cleverer)" (quoted by Holroyd, *Bernard Shaw*, II, p. 50).

peaks . . . thin: *Zarathustra* (PN152).

Believe me: *The Gay Science*, #283 (PN97).

a Devil's Advocate: *Saturday Review*, 13 May 1899, in *Pen Portraits and Reviews* (1932), p. 218.

314   malady peculiar: "A custom of the island of Cea," II.3, *The Complete Essays of Montaigne*, tr. Donald Frame (1958), p. 254.

We immoralists: "Morality as Anti-Nature," #6, *Twilight* (PN491). It is worth remarking that several of Susan Sontag's "Notes on Camp" (1964), which were written "for Oscar," align Camp with the Nietzschean and Oscarian philosophy; consider, for example, "Camp is a solvent of morality. It neutralizes moral indignation" (#52); "Camp is generous. It wants to enjoy" (#55); and "Camp taste is a kind of love, love for human nature. It relishes rather than judges" (#56). See *The Susan Sontag Reader* (1982), pp. 118–19. Also Oscarian are some of Philip Core's definitions in his book *Camp: The Lie that Tells the Truth* (1984): "Camp is . . . first of all a second childhood . . . a disguise that fails" (p. 7).

saying Yes: "What I Owe to the Ancients," #5, *Twilight* (PN562).

any concession: "The Problem of Socrates," #10, *Twilight* (PN478). It contains: pp. 131–32.

315 There are moments: C144(16).

in truth: *Letters to the Sphinx*, p. 28.

it is only: *The Birth of Tragedy, The Basic Writings of Nietzsche,* tr. Walter Kaufmann (1968), p. 52.

The fight against purpose: "Skirmishes," #24, *Twilight* (PN529).

Submission to morality: *The Dawn*, #97 (PN81).

316 How naive: "Morality as Anti-nature," #6 (PN491).

I was not naughty: Harris, *Oscar Wilde*, p. 104.

317 Oscar . . . said: Herbert Vivian, 17 November 1889 (MK154).

The best is lacking: "Skirmishes," #35, *Twilight* (PN535–36).

Don't for anything: quoted by Pletsch, p. 186.

whose egoism was superb: in "A Note of Explanation," prefixed to Leverson, *Letters to the Sphinx*, p. 16.

A virtue must be: #11 (PN577).

318 You may be wise: Boswell's *Life of Johnson* (1953 Oxford ed.), p. 1034.

My own feeling: 11 February 1888, original emphasis (ms. Berg Collection, New York Public Library). Stafford was thirty at the time, Whitman seventy. Oscar figured in one of Whitman's most affectionate letters to Stafford: "You see I think I understand you better than any one—(& like you more too)—(You may not fancy so, but it is so)—& I believe, Hank, there are many things, confidences, questions, candid *says* you would like to have with me, and you have never yet broached—me the same—Have you read about Oscar Wilde? He has been to see me & spent an afternoon—He is a fine large handsome youngster—and had the *good sense* to take a great fancy to *me!*" (25 January 1882, *Correspondence*, ed. E. H. Miller [1962], III, p. 264).

Self-culture is the true ideal: "Critic" (C1043).

What he wanted: *Idols,* "Skirmishes," #49, *Twilight* (PN554). This sentiment, I think, lies behind the second epigraph I have chosen for this chapter.

aside to Gide: *If It Die*, p. 302.

a man who was willing: "Subject and Abject: The Vocation of Michel Foucault," *The New Republic*, 15 February 1993, 26–36; see also James Miller, *The Passion of Michel Foucault* (1992), one of the subjects of Nehamas's review essay.

319 One thing is needful: #290 (PN98–99).

320 save me from my friends: *Aspects of Wilde*, p. 139.

something very severe: p. 12.

Was he ever alive: reported in notes of Max Beerbohm (Berg Collection, New York Public Library).

a poor creature: letter to Bernard Shaw, 21 September 1903, *Letters*, p. 38.

timid and exacting soul: *Around Theatres*, I, p. 351.

If the British public: to Horatio Forbes Brown, 22 July 1890, *The Letters of John Addington Symonds* (1969), III, p. 477.

Hosscar Wilde: quoted in Ellmann, p. 179.

It is an odd: to Horatio Forbes Brown, 22 July 1890, *Letters of John Addington Symonds* (1969). III, p. 477.

no living English novelist: quoted in Lewis and Smith, *Oscar Wilde Discovers America*, p. 355.

the repulsive and fatuous Oscar: 23 January 1882, *Letters*, II, p. 372.

321   **the unspeakable one:** letter to Henrietta Reubell, quoted in Ellmann, p. 367.

candid and primitive: letter to Mrs Hugh Bell, 23 February 1892 (Oscar's famous curtain speech after *Fan* did not amuse James), *Letters*, ed. Leon Edel (1980), III, p. 372.

It is a most wonderful: letter to Ross, January 1899 (L776).

Nothing is serious: P313.

Ives . . . suggested: Stokes, p. 179.

sticks to his colours: Stokes, p. 181.

322   **dissertation in praise:** October 1894, p. 356 (L375n).

When the prurient: 22 October 1894 (L375).

You have thrown a bomb: quoted in Ives's diary, Stokes, p. 179.

He is such a good fellow: to Sherard, 26 August 1896 (L407).

And the brute said: *Book of Chains* (1897), p. 91

George Ives has sent: 16 November 1897 (L673).

323   **we disagree:** Stokes, p. 183.

My dear George: 12 February 1900 (L815–16).

324   **I know you *intended*:** 22 February 1900 (L816).

I will be charmed: 6 September 1900 (L835).

325   **I hope you will come:** 8 September 1900 (L835).

a monumental bore: Stokes, p. 184.

Friendship is: "A Few Maxims for the Instruction of the Over-Educated," *Saturday Review*, 17 November 1894 (C1203).

A nice fellow: 27 December 1898 (L772).

Mellor cure: to Ross, 1 September 1900 (L833). One of Mellor's letters from this year pays Oscar a charming compliment: "My new pig house is quite delightful. Eolo is very naughty. And you I suppose are & always will be both. Ever yours Harold" (24 April, ms. Clark).

I don't like Mellor: 15 March 1899 (L785).

The villa is pretty: 20 March 1899 (L786).

326   **I don't like Switzerland:** to Louis Wilkinson (L787).

Mellor carries out: to Leonard Smithers (L788).

There is insanity: L789.

Mellor keeps his own: to Frank Harris (L790).

He really is too insane: to Ross, 29 March 1899 (L791).
327   a young lad: to Ross, 1 April 1899 (L792).
Gland/At the House: to Smithers, 30 March 1899 (L791).
is now in Paris: 1 September 1900 (L833).
morbid: Stokes, p. 184.
often charged etc.: "Homogenic Love," pp. 335–37 (original italics).
328   morbid & perfumed manner: letter to Edmund Gosse, 22 July 1890, *Letters of John Addington Symonds* (1969), III, p. 478.
329   There is one other word: C1093 (original italics).

16 PARIAH-DOG

331   I wish: letter reproduced in Small, *Oscar Wilde Revalued*, p. 63.
I now live: L803.
Ours is certainly: C989.
I am dazed: 15 April 1895, *More Letters*, p. 133.
332   We all felt: *Letters to the Sphinx*, pp. 44–45.
Dear Sphinx: 20 May 1897 (L566).
leaning tower: Gertrude Atherton, *Adventures of a Novelist* (1932), p. 183.
333   the fundamental spirit: "About Oscar Wilde" (1946), in *Borges: A Reader*, ed. E. Monegal, A. Reid (1981), p. 178.
Neither to myself: to Leonard Smithers, 11 December 1897 (L695).
Two things: to Adela Schuster, 23 December 1900 (L862).
I live a very ordinary life: 24 May 1898 (L743).
334   While I can sit: 17 May 1897 (L555).
His face had something: *Le Symbolisme: anecdotes et souvenirs* (1903), p. 213.
the pariah-dog: to Smithers, 11 December 1897 (L695).
I have no note-paper: to Smithers, 22 October 1897 (L666).
a poor little Bohemian hotel: to H. C. Pollitt, 3 December 1898 (L767).
My dear Robbie: 25 November 1898 (L763).
now a strange luxury: to Pollitt, 19 January 1899 (L777).
the exquisite taste: to Reginald Turner, 19 January 1899 (L776).
persons whose origin: P277.
The middle-class English: circa 22 February 1899 (L781).
335   cunning in the art: *Contemporary Portraits*, p. 118.
I never could understand: to Smithers, 17 March 1898 (L717).
I am always worried: to Pollitt, 26 November 1898 (L764).
the most generous man: *Letters to the Sphinx*, p. 47.
"Work!" said Wilde: *The Romantic '90s*, pp. 259–60.
336   one of those tragic beggars: *Aspects of Wilde*, p. 162.
I was walking: *Melodies and Memories* (1925), p. 75.

337 *They* take their punishment: to Turner, 17 May 1897 (L554).
     Among his many fine qualities: L862.
     "was" is not "is": 3.4.28.
     I no longer: to Harris, 13 June 1897 (L607).
     been obliged to decline: 13 September 1897 (L639).
     Why should I: *Contemporary Portraits*, p. 125.
     As regards a comedy: late February 1898 (L708).
338 my *chante de cygne*: 9 March 1898 (L715). The satyr Marsyas challenged
     Apollo to a flute-playing contest; when Apollo was judged the winner he
     had Marsyas tied to a tree and flayed him alive.
     at the drinking suggestion: Bernard Thornton, *Theatre Magazine* (New York,
     June 1918), p. 370.
     unproductive drunkard: in Harris, *Oscar Wilde*, p. 342.
     earnestly idling: to Ross, 2 February 1899 (L778).
     People who repent: 1 June 1898 (L752).
     I enclose: 8 May 1898 (L735).
     I should go: 11 May 1898 (L739).
339 his joyous humor: *Contemporary Portraits*, p. 126. (Harris here reported the
     following anecdote.)
     My wallpaper: quoted in Ellmann, p. 581.
     I am now *neurasthenic*: *More Letters*, p. 184.
     He of course laughed: L860.
340 I was if anything: Father Cuthbert Dunne's ms. narrative (L857).
     no doubt that reformation: "Critic" (C1053).
     the endless hunger: to Will Rothenstein, 9 June 1897 (L605).
     days of gilded infamy: to Ross, 28 May 1897 (L577).
341 A patriot: to Ross, circa 18 February 1898 (L705). "Uranian" was a common
     term of the time for homosexual love; it derives from the speech of
     Pausanias in Plato's *Symposium*: "To this Love, gentlemen, we must hold
     fast, for he is the fair and heavenly one, born of Urania, the Muse of
     heaven" (*The Collected Dialogues of Plato*, ed. E. Hamilton, H. Cairns
     [1961], p. 541); see also Timothy d'Arch Smith, *Love in Earnest* (1970).
     I believe they would like: 18 February 1899 (L780).
     Ah! you are beginning: P41.
     It is quite true: 3 December 1898 (L766).
     Do you remember: to Turner, 26 November 1898 (L765).
     the curves of his mouth: to Ross, July 1898 (L757).
342 The inhabitants: to Pollitt, 31 December 1898 (L774).
     a beautiful young actor: to Turner, 20 March 1899 (L787).
     near Genoa: to Smithers, 30 March 1899 (L791).
     a charming American: 6 June 1899 (L800).
     Casquette is well: to Ross, June 1899 (L801).

I have given up: 21 April 1900 (L823).

I gave a ticket: May 1900 (L827).

My dear Neapolitans: to Smithers, 2 September 1900 (L834).

343 **I wanted a friend:** Wilde related the conversation to Gide; it is recorded in *If It Die* (p. 302).

I shall be very lonely: Harris, *Oscar Wilde*, pp. 210–11.

My companions: to Ross, 14 May 1898 (L740).

I have fallen: 14 May 1900 (L828).

344 **When one looks back:** C1034–35.

gold-haired like an angel: to the Leversons, 9 April 1895 (L389).

madness of kisses: to Bosie, January 1893 (L326).

golden-haired boy: to Bosie, May 1895 (L397).

17   WILDESHAWSHOW

Note: Quotations from Shaw's *Collected Letters*, ed. Dan H. Laurence, are abbreviated 1874–97 (1CL), 1898–1910 (2CL), 1911–25 (3CL), 1926–50 (4CL); quotations from Shaw's *Complete Plays* are abbreviated (PL). Quotations from Michael Holroyd's three-volume biography, *Bernard Shaw*, are abbreviated (1H, 2H, 3H).

345 **Your wildeshaweshowe:** *Finnegans Wake*, p. 256.

Great antipathy: quoted in O'Sullivan, *Aspects of Wilde*, p. 216.

long divided the stage: *Autobiography*, p. 241.

346 **great Celtic School:** letter of 9 May 1893 (L339).

infernal meddlesomeness: to Robert Loraine, January 1920 (3CL652–53).

the mere habit of energy: 2H210.

a writing and talking machine: to Mrs Patrick Campbell, 8 November 1912, 2CL126.

347 **I am lazy:** L339.

I have always said: 28 February 1893, in Shaw, *Theatrics*, ed. Dan H. Laurence (1994).

I don't mind hard work: P239.

Views belong: Hyde, *The Trials*, p. 110.

Every play: "Shaw Looks at Life at 70" (1927; 1H403).

instinctive habit: 2H223.

It is only: *Dorian*, C25(1).

wrote for the stage: *Collected Prose*, I, p. 127.

348 **All through the book:** *Saturday Review*, 2 November 1901, in *Around Theatres*, p. 218.

I am not: 14 February 1910, 2CL900–1.

Many of our novelists: review of Lee's *Faithful and Unfaithful, Woman's World,*
February 1889 (R419).

349 **He does not inspire:** PL372.

the work of helping Life: PL375.

attitude towards life: *Contemporary Portraits* (1915), p. 112. The Irish poetess
Ada Tyrrell knew Wilde and Shaw as young men and offered this suggestive and plausible comparison: "George is a good man *all through* and Oscar had only good *impulses*, though with more sentiment than George;
more romance in fact, which is always a charm to me" (quoted in Harris,
Contemporary Portraits, second series [1919], pp. 42–43).

350 **Socialism . . . is** and **He cares more:** *George Bernard Shaw* (1910), pp. 80, 86.

face of an outlaw: Elinor Huddert to Shaw, 19 November 1891 (1H94).

New York tailor: Alicia Finkel, "A Tale of Lilies . . .", p. 12.

temperance-beverage face: quoted in 2H59.

Exercise! The only: interview in *The Sketch*, 9 January 1895 (MK242).

as if it were: 1H160.

351 **much ridiculed jaegerism:** to Ellen Terry, 31 December 1897 (1CL840).

the Shavian equivalent: 1H160.

the very shabbiest: quoted by the Utah *Herald*, in Lewis and Smith, *Oscar
Wilde Discovers America*, p. 276.

a dud country: 2H57.

literary and artistic society: in Harris, *Oscar Wilde*, p. 331.

My wife insists: 1 March 1906, *Letters to Siegfried Trebitsch* (1986), p. 95.

352 **a demoralizing country:** 2H207.

liberation: "A Note on (towards) Bernard Shaw," in *Labyrinths* (1964), p. 251.

joy: *Borges: A Reader*, p. 178.

I sing my own class: preface to *Immaturity*, p. x.

a snob: letter to Frank Harris, 7 October 1908 (2CL813).

It is utterly: to Rev. Ensor Walters, 16 September 1901, 2CL238. Shaw's belief was that "Effectiveness of assertion is the Alpha and Omega of style"
(1H211); he claimed to have learned this from Handel: "It was from
Handel that I learned that style consists of force of assertion. If you can
say a thing with one stroke unanswerably you have style; if not, you are
at best a *marchand de plaisir.* . . . You may despise what you like, but you
cannot contradict Handel" (*Shaw's Music*, III, p. 640).

made him into: 2H223.

353 **He came and spoke** etc.: in Harris, *Oscar Wilde*, pp. 330–43.

really disliked Wilde: GBS: *A Postscript* (1951), p. 131; in a 1939 letter to
Bosie (Hyde, p. 117), Shaw chose to give a different impression: "I did
not dislike Wilde, and I don't think he disliked me."

owed something to persons: preface to *Immaturity, Works* [1930], I, p. xliv. All
quotations are from this edition. Holroyd also believes Hawkshaw—

whom Holroyd oddly refers to throughout as Hawksmith—"owes something to Oscar" (1H75). Hawkshaw, Holroyd says, "has not strength enough to resist the applause of a society that is, below its glossy surface, uncaring and uncomprehending." This was a prophetic Shavian bull's-eye: Oscar's undiscriminating eagerness for adulation was to be a main source of his vulnerability.

355 **our queer shyness:** in Harris, *Oscar Wilde*, p. 331.

really pleasant afternoon: Shaw's diary indicates this took place on 14 August 1890; Shaw attended hoping to encounter some music (*Diaries*, I, p. 642).

356 **Mr Oscar Wilde:** *Diaries*, I, p. 392.

the first glimpse: *Wales England Weds* (1940), p. 85.

357 **An excellent fellow:** 25 September 1896, *Ellen Terry and Bernard Shaw: A Correspondence* (1931; Theater Arts ed.), p. 76; Luther Munday recalled Oscar saying this also about Whistler (MK178). In a letter of 9 August 1939 to Bosie (Mary Hyde, p. 117), Shaw repeated the *bon mot* and added, "This was true; and so good that he used it several times of different people. He always did." Shaw happily retailed Oscar's witticism because (as he shrewdly observed several years after Oscar died), "This is one of those subtle compliments which most people take for malicious barbs. Only a nonentity has friends who like him unconditionally" (*The Matter with Ireland*, p. 31).

358 **All the long reviews:** letter to David O'Donaghue, 8 May 1889 (1CL210).

Wilde is doing us: 4 May 1893, in Shaw, *Theatrics*, ed. Dan H. Laurence (1994).

You must give up: letter to Golding Bright, 19 November 1894 (1CL459–60).

359 **The only dramatist:** 13 November 1897, p. 402. Shaw also offered the name of the gay apologist Edward Carpenter, whose poems he thought representative of "modern democratic developments in poetry" (20 November issue, p. 432).

Our present-day morality: "Oscar Wilde," 23 April 1905, in *The Matter with Ireland*, ed. David H. Greene and Dan H. Laurence (1962), p. 32.

360 **I never knew:** *Myself and My Friends* (1933), p. 61.

still with such energy: letter to S. Fischer, 19 April 1906, *Selected Letters 1902–1926* (1947), p. 86.

He seemed thoroughly: "The Diner-Out," *Horizon*, October 1941, p. 256.

happiness is not: to Eva Christy, December 1900 (2CL203).

Vanity is: *Letters to Reggie Turner*, p. 289.

There is this to be said: *In Good Company* (1917), p. 192.

Meanwhile a serene friendliness: to Alexander Thompson, 15 November 1916 (3CL436).

361 **I am never wrong:** 15 January 1903 (2CL304).

Everest of Vanity: 2H181.

who is modest: *Shaw's Music*, ed. Dan H. Laurence (1981), I, p. 855.

Life is an adventure: letter to Mrs V. O. Plenazár, 15 July 1929 (4CL154).

lived . . . an imaginary life: *Autobiography*, p. 121.

He does not live: 1H137.

but imperfectly: "The Best Books for Children," *Pall Mall Gazette*, 7 November 1887, in *Shaw Annual* 9 (1989), p. 25.

in a cunning little baby-chair: letter to Clara Rilke, 19 April 1906, *Selected Letters*, p. 88.

362 **an elderly adolescent:** quoted 2H355.

suggests a puppet play: *The Shavian Playground* (1972), pp. 48–49; Holroyd's brilliant comparison of W. S. Gilbert and Shaw makes a similar point: "Gilbert was the child who mimicked the adult world; Shaw was the child who saw through it" (1H304). Oscar was most certainly a child of the Shavian type.

There must be: 2H325.

It is a bad one: review of *Fan*, 22 February 1892.

I have striven: to Vladimir Tchertkoff, August 1905 (2CL551).

363 **that most horrible form:** *Shaw's Music*, II, p. 819.

Most people: to Rosina Filippi, 16 September 1913 (3CL203).

Bad taste: to Mrs Alfred Lyttelton, 25 July 1913 (3CL192).

every genuine religious person: Foreword, "The Revolutionist's Handbook" (*Man and Superman*).

the rarest: "Maxims for Revolutionists" (*Man and Superman*).

When a man: letter to T. Sturge Moore, 25 April 1911, *William Butler Yeats and T. Sturge Moore: Their Correspondence* (1953), p. 19.

My dear fellow: 1H298.

He loses influence: 1H136.

364 **Bassetto was:** *Shaw's Music*, I, p. 58.

a paradox: *George Bernard Shaw* (1910), pp. 19–20.

His laughter: *I Have Been Young* (1935; pseud. H. M. Swanwick), p. 64.

he laughed: 4CL885.

I found: 1H133.

without my veneer: 2H187.

365 **a philosophic humourist:** review, *The World*, 30 May 1905.

England is the land: 23 February 1893 (L332).

a miserable drunkard and **had no comedic impulses:** preface to *Immaturity*, pp. xv, xxiv; "I work as my father drank," said Shaw (p. xxxvi).

Woman's greatest art: *Saturday Review*, 28 May 1895, in *Our Theatres in the Nineties*, I, p. 202.

Mr Tree might: *Saturday Review*, 16 May 1896, in *Our Theatres in the Nineties*, II, p. 131.

funny without being vulgar: Richard Le Gallienne, *The Romantic '90s*, pp. 260–61.

366 **are just so many skeletons:** *Saturday Review*, 21 May 1898.

You must always remember: 24 April 1938 (in Hyde, p. 36).

the scientific principle etc.: C1040–41. The views he expresses again show his affinity with Nietzsche. For Nietzsche, according to Philippa Foot, "Our actions arise not primarily from conscious motivations but rather from physiological and psychological factors beyond our control" ("Nietzsche's Immoralism," *New York Review of Books*, 13 June 1991, p. 20).

367 **When I left Dublin:** preface to *Immaturity*, p. xxxvi.

emigration was: letter to St. John Ervine, 19 November 1937 (1H60).

As long as Ireland: to Charlotte Payne-Townshend, 4 November 1896 (1CL691).

368 **Irish exaggeration:** PL449.

quite civilized: P185. O'Sullivan wrote that Oscar was "very Irish in aspect and methods" and that "the great Irishmen of the eighteenth century who exercised such a fascination on the English—Burke, Congreve, Steele, Sheridan—must have been in many ways like him" (*Aspects of Wilde*, p. 79).

I am an Irishman: to Viola Tree, 5 December 1911 (3CL61). Most of Shaw's boasts of his ancestry were likewise paradoxical: "I am a genuinely typical Irishman of the Danish, Norman, Cromwellian, and (of course) Scotch invasions" (1906 preface to *John Bull's Other Island*, *Collected Plays and Prefaces* [1971], II, p. 811).

irrepressible idiosyncrasy: letter to Shaw, 22 June 1921 (1H136).

most real: *George Bernard Shaw*, p. 18. William Archer thought it the "most delightful" of Shaw's "discussion" plays (*The Old Drama and the New* [1923], p. 353).

369 **Society often forgives:** "Critic" (C1039).

a poetic actor: 2H85.

370 **This world:** PL440.

371 **he always challenges:** *George Bernard Shaw*, p. 28.

372 **The most delightful character:** *Woman's World*, May 1889 (R263).

373 **We poets:** letter to John Barlas, 19 January 1892, *More Letters*, p. 108.

the first and most convincing: 2H85.

elaborately fantastic: *Last Theatres*, p. 103.

374 **far subtler:** *Collected Plays and Prefaces*, II, p. 814.

375   **A dreamer:** C1058.

     Every dream: *The Complete Plays*, p. 452.

     My Uncle Paul: *A New England Girlhood* (1958), p. 109.

376   **What a number:** letter of 22 June 1891, *Letters of John Addington Symonds* (1969), III, p. 586.

     The evolution of man: C1103.

     It is an odd thing: C159(19).

377   **the world would stagnate:** "Critic" (C1023).

     eternal summer: letter to Norman Forbes-Robertson, 27 March 1882 (L109).

     the further West: Lewis and Smith, *Oscar Wilde Discovers America*, p. 243.

     from the uttermost end: L109.

     Western people: Lewis and Smith, p. 243.

     I am really appreciated and **houses . . . persons:** L109.

378   **a really beautiful city:** "Impressions of America," ed. Stuart Mason (1906), pp. 28–29.

     a Miss Nancy: Jerome A. Hart reported in *In Our Second Century* (1931): "Wilde appeared at the Bohemian Club as a dinner guest—not of the club, but of a member. He wore his esthetic togs, and carried a lily. Some of the members therefore considered him a Miss Nancy, and determined to get him tipsy and have some fun with him. But Wilde turned out to be . . . a three-bottle man . . . and those who had looked to see an intoxicated esthete succumbed themselves to the Bottle Goddess" (p. 313).

     most finished and perfect: Lewis and Smith, p. 244.

     being called the Hoodlum City: *The Daily Witness* (Montreal), 15 May 1882 (MK82).

     San Francisco has: *The Daily Witness*, 15 May 1882 (MK82).

     very dark and gloomy: *Son of Oscar Wilde*, pp. 44–45.

379   **belongs to our world:** p. 589; Philip Reiff reiterates this view in his essay "The Impossible Culture": "Nothing is more contemporary than Wilde's imagination" (p. 411) . . . "The genius of modernity is in Wilde's cleverness" (p. 422).

     The past is: "Soul" (C1100).

     The chief value: *Pall Mall Gazette*, 25 January 1889 (R401).

     brought answers: *Journal* (1925), quoted in Delay, p. 293; Gide wrote in "In Memoriam" that Oscar said to him there were "two kinds of artists: one brings answers, and the other questions. . . . There are [also] works which wait, and which one does not understand for a long time; the reason is that they bring answers to questions which have not yet been raised; for the question often arrives a terribly long time after the answer" (pp. 26–27).

380 things which cannot be held: John Stokes, "Wilde at Bay," p. 177.
the present: "Soul" (C1100).
Civilizations continue: 31 May 1897 (L584).
there is something tragic: C1089.
We live in an age: C79(8).
a thoroughly selfish: "Critic" (C1043).
The god of this century: *Ideal* (P142).
the strange poverty: *De profundis* (L476).
What we want: *Pall Mall Gazette*, 4 August 1886 (R76).

381 The Lords Temporal: "Soul" (C1094).
It is personalities: C54(4).
There will be no people: "Soul" (C1080).
the exclusion of all women: March 1889, p. 140.
It is pleasant: "Literary and Other Notes," *Woman's World*, December 1887 (R241).

382 I have often thought: "Literary and Other Notes," *Woman's World*, November 1888 (R266).
Nothing in the United States: "Literary and Other Notes," *Woman's World*, November 1887 (R204); this was the first issue of which Oscar was the editor.
In a recent article: "Literary and Other Notes," *Woman's World*, November 1887 (R205).
The family ideal: "Some Literary Notes," *Woman's World*, May 1889 (R488).

383 The intellect of the race: "Critic" (C1057).
Nowadays, with our modern mania: *Woman* (P128).

384 In centuries before ours: "Soul" (C1095).
describe a work: C1092.

385 Believe me, sir: 27 June 1890 (L261).
Freedom of thought: "A Ride in Morocco," *Pall Mall Gazette*, 8 October 1886 (R94).
there is very little use: "Mr Mahaffy's New Book," *Pall Mall Gazette*, 9 November 1887 (R213).
In France: "Soul" (C1095).
Formerly we used to: "Critic" (C1009).
always Judas and They are: "Critic" (C1010).
foolish habit: "Critic" (C1022).
chronicle, with degrading avidity: "Critic" (C1049).

386 eminently needed: February 1886 (L186).
We live in the age: "Critic" (C1042).
more or less, a prophet: *Autobiography*, p. 77.
A chemist on each side: *Memories and Adventures* (1924), p. 73.
It is clear: "Soul" (C1082).

does not confine itself: "Critic" (C1029).

387   the parent etc.: "Critic" (C1023). That Oscar and Paul de Man—two men with good reason to wish the private life of the author to be ruled out of bounds—should have shared their views of literary criticism is, I suspect, not coincidental.

Nothing is so dangerous: P157.

Justice being slow: P365.

Yes: I have: 21 March 1898 (L721).

Oscar Wilde, victim: Stokes, "Wilde at Bay," p. 184.

a harrowing comparability: Feasting with Panthers, p. 259.

388   the inaugurator: "Homogenic Love," p. 344.

To know anything: "Critic" (C1040).

It would seem almost certain: "Homogenic Love," p. 338.

If we lived: C1023.

389   Only failures: 10 March 1894, p. 225.

No fact: review of 28 January 1894, Shaw's Music, III, p. 98.

390   as Ellmann suggested: "The review was a form that Wilde enjoyed. He made it into a form of chat" (p. 263).

They lead us: "Pleasing and Prattling," Pall Mall Gazette, 4 April 1886 (R76).

The book can be read: Pall Mall Gazette, 4 April 1886 (R75).

She at least: "New Novels," Pall Mall Gazette, 28 October 1886 (R99).

It is just the sort: "A Cheap Edition of a Great Man," Pall Mall Gazette, 18 April 1887 (R148).

Carlyle once: "Great Writers by Little Men," Pall Mall Gazette, 28 March 1887 (R139 40).

The accomplished authoress: "A Batch of Novels," Pall Mall Gazette, 2 May 1887 (R161).

391   always making demands: "Some Novels," Saturday Review, 2 May 1887 (R165).

We would earnestly beg: "Some Novels," Saturday Review, 7 May 1887 (R167).

There is always: "Mr Mahaffy's New Book," Pall Mall Gazette, 9 November 1887 (R209–10); Oscar's review of Mahaffy's book was coruscating, but the Dublin professor of ancient history had his revenge. After the downfall, whenever anyone asked Mahaffy about Oscar, he would reply: "We no longer speak of Mr Oscar Wilde" (Hyde, The Trials, p. 31).

Beer, the Bible: ms. in Clark, reproduced in Small, Oscar Wilde Revalued, p. 127.

Will the elaborate: 2 March 1895, p. 106.

393 **I'll laugh:** Act III, Beaumarchais, *The Barber of Seville and The Marriage of Figaro,* tr. John Wood (1964), p. 178.
 In Falstaff: C975.
 "Che fece . . . : *Collected Poems* (1992), p. 12. The title is from the *Inferno* 3.60.

394 **Yes-saying book:** *Ecce Homo* (1989 ed.), p. 293.
 Yes to life: "What I Owe to the Ancients," #5, *Twilight of the Idols, Portable Nietzsche,* p. 562.
 fatalist and stoic: Stuart Merrill's obituary essay, *La Plume,* 15 December 1900 (MK466); the interviewer Gedeon Spilett was also left feeling that Oscar was "very much the fatalist" (MK355).

395 **There is nothing:** *Oscar Wilde and His Mother,* p. 21.
 For unlike most people: MK466.
 talker . . . good host: ms. notes, Berg Collection, New York Public Library.
 Man is least himself: "Critic" (C1045).

396 **I hope to-morrow:** P241.
 There are as many Hamlets: "Critic" (C1034).
 My life: L436.

397 **I have grown:** C20(1).
 It is not wise and **In so vulgar an age** and **Seriousness of manner:** to Philip Houghton, February 1894 (L353).
 a discussion: Ross, in Harris's *Oscar Wilde: His Life and Confessions* (1918), p. 606.
 Life is a question: C162(19).

398 **is a dreamer:** L504.
 We poets: to John Barlas, 19 June 1892, *More Letters,* p. 108.
 is what I: to Philip Houghton, 12 February 1894 (L352)
 There is a fatality: C19(1).

399 **I was a Lord:** to Ernest Dowson, 5 June 1897 (L597).
 She has a very strong faith: to William Ward, 26 July 1876 (L20).
 Actions are: P89.

400 **simply a *mauvais quart d'heure*:** P324.
 For heaven's sake: P226.
 keen mordant irony: C974.

401 **Something tragic** etc.: C41(3), C149(17), C155(18).
 Fin de siècle: C137(15).
 His veracity: *The Theatre,* March 1894 (MK234).
 there is something vulgar: *Aspects of Wilde,* p. 222.
 Sometimes I think: to H. C. Marillier, February 1886 (L185).

402 **a problem:** 27 November 1897 (L685).

the pleasure we derive: "About Oscar Wilde," *Borges: A Reader*, p. 178.

a child of sunshine and joyousness: *I Have Been Young*, pp. 67–68.

When to the sessions: *Oscar Wilde*, p. 320.

403   Pleasure is etc.: C1205–6.

leaving Oxford: 11 July 1878 (L52).

404   decent treatment: quoted, Lewis and Smith, *Oscar Wilde Discovers America*, p. 182.

always some twist: ms. notes, Berg Collection, New York Public Library.

Nothing is serious: P313.

Laughter is: to Ross, 3 December 1898 (L767).

That Wilde suffered: preface to *De Profundis* (1908 edition), p. xv. Ross was here responding to Robert Sherard's assertion, in his book, that Oscar was very unhappy in his last years.

405   They returned his greeting: *Portrait of Max* (1960), p. 84. Max was repeating the story as told by Waller.

406   Oscar told us: 14 December 1900 (L849).

I love the last words: 4 June 1897 (L595).

utterly selfish and incapable of friendship: in Harris, *Oscar Wilde*, pp. 329, 332.

407   Many of our worst habits: quoted by Holroyd, *Bernard Shaw*, I, p. 207.

never completely make Wilde out: reported by Horace Traubel in *With Walt Whitman in Camden*, Vol. 2 (1908), p. 192. Whitman made the remark on 24 August 1888.

quite right: "Lord Arthur Savile's Crime" (C170).

Dying in Paris etc.: 14 December 1900 (L855–56).

408   hope to live: C1205.

409   No. He seemed: P250.

Oscar's coffin: 8 December 1900 (L858).

Select Bibliography

Oscar Wilde
Editions Cited in the Present Study.

The Complete Works (Collins, 1966; HarperCollins, 1989 rpt.).
The Complete Plays, ed. H. Montgomery Hyde (Methuen, 1988).
Miscellanies volume of *The First Collected Edition of the Works of Oscar Wilde*, ed. Robert Ross (1908; rpt. 1969).
Reviews volume of *The First Collected Edition* (1908; rpt. 1969).
The Prose of Oscar Wilde (Albert & Charles Boni, 1930: for *Sebastian Melmoth* only).
Impressions of America, ed. Stuart Mason (pseud. Christopher Millard; 1906).
The Letters of Oscar Wilde, ed. Rupert Hart-Davis (Harcourt, Brace, 1962).
More Letters of Oscar Wilde, ed. Rupert Hart-Davis (John Murray, 1985).

Other Studies

Included here are books cited in this study that are principally about—or contain important chapters on—Wilde and his circle, as well as some notable recent publications on the history of the homosexual movement that are relevant to Wilde's life, works, and reception.

475

ACKROYD, PETER. *The Last Testament of Oscar Wilde* (1983).

ALTMAN, DENNIS. *Homosexual Oppression and Liberation* (1974).

AMOR, ANNE CLARK. *Mrs Oscar Wilde: A Woman of Some Importance* (1983).

ANONYMOUS. "The Story of Oscar Wilde's Life and Experience in Reading Gaol, By His Warder," *Bruno's Weekly*, 22 January 1916 (rpt. 1963).

AUDEN, W. H. "An Improbable Life," *The New Yorker*, 9 March 1963, in *Forewords and Afterwords* (1974), 302–24.

————. review of George Woodcock, *The Paradox of Oscar Wilde*, *Partisan Review* 17 (1950), 390–94.

BARTLETT, NEIL. *Who Was That Man: A Present for Mr Oscar Wilde* (1988).

BECKSON, KARL. *London in the 1890s: A Cultural History* (1992).

————. *Oscar Wilde: The Critical Heritage* (1970).

BEERBOHM, MAX. *The Letters of Max Beerbohm 1892–1956*, ed. Rupert Hart-Davis (1988).

————. *Letters to Reggie Turner*, ed. Rupert Hart-Davis (1964).

————. *A Peep into the Past* (1923).

BEHRENDT, PATRICIA. *Oscar Wilde: Eros and Aesthetics* (1991).

BENTLEY, JOYCE. *The Importance of Being Constance* (1983).

BORLAND, MAUREEN. *Oscar Wilde's Devoted Friend* (1990).

BRASOL, BORIS. *Oscar Wilde, the Man, the Artist, the Martyr* (1938).

BRÉMONT, COMTESSE ANNA DE. *Oscar Wilde and His Mother* (1911).

CARPENTER, EDWARD. "Homogenic Love and its Place in a Free Society" (1895; rpt. in Brian Reade, *Sexual Heretics* [1970], 324–47).

COHEN, ED. *Talk on the Wilde Side* (1992).

CORE, PHILIP. *Camp: The Lie that Tells the Truth* (1984).

CROMPTON, LOUIS. *Byron and Greek Love: Homophobia in 19th-Century England* (1985).

CROFT-COOKE, RUPERT. *Bosie: Lord Alfred Douglas, His Friends and Enemies* (1963).

————. *Feasting with Panthers* (1967).

DELAY, JEAN. *The Youth of André Gide* (1956).

DELLAMORA, RICHARD. *Masculine Desire: The Sexual Politics of Victorian Aestheticism* (1990).

DOLLIMORE, JONATHAN. *Sexual Dissidence* (1991).

DOUGLAS, LORD ALFRED. *The Autobiography of Lord Alfred Douglas* (1929).

————. *Oscar Wilde and Myself* (1914).

————. *Oscar Wilde: A Summing Up* (1940).

————. *Without Apology* (1938).

ELLMANN, RICHARD. *Oscar Wilde* (1987; see also Horst Schroeder, below).

FINKEL, ALICIA. "A Tale of Lilies, Sunflowers, and Knee-Breeches: Oscar Wilde's Wardrobe for His American Tour," *Dress* 15 (1989), 4–15.

FOUCAULT, MICHEL. *The History of Sexuality* (Eng. ed. 1980).

GAGNIER, REGENIA. *Idylls of the Marketplace: Oscar Wilde and the Victorian Public* (1986).

GIDE, ANDRÉ. *If It Die (Si le grain ne meurt*, 1920; Eng. tr. Dorothy Bussy, 1935).

_____. *Oscar Wilde: A Study* (1910; incl. "In Memoriam").

GOODMAN, JONATHAN. *The Oscar Wilde File* (1988).

HARRIS, FRANK. *Contemporary Portraits* (1915).

_____. *Oscar Wilde: His Life and Confessions* (1930; rpt. 1959).

HOCQUENGHEM, GUY. *Homosexual Desire* (1972; Eng. tr. 1978).

HOFMANNSTHAL, HUGO VON. "Sebastian Melmoth" (1905), *Selected Prose* (1952), 301–305.

HOLLAND, VYVYAN. *Son of Oscar Wilde* (British ed., 1954).

_____. *Time Remembered After Père Lachaise* (1967).

HYDE, H. MONTGOMERY. *The Annotated Oscar Wilde* (1982).

_____. *The Love That Dared Not Speak Its Name: A Candid History of Homosexuality in Britain* (1970; orig. Eng. title: *The Other Love*).

_____. *Oscar Wilde: A Biography* (1975).

_____. *Oscar Wilde: The Aftermath* (1963).

_____. *The Trials of Oscar Wilde* (1948; 1962 rev. ed.).

HYDE, MARY. *Bernard Shaw and Lord Alfred Douglas: A Correspondence* (1982).

JACKSON, HOLBROOK. *The Eighteen Nineties* (1913; rpt. 1966).

JULLIAN, PHILIPPE. *Oscar Wilde* (1968).

KOHL, NORBERT. *Oscar Wilde: The Works of a Conformist Rebel* (1980).

LE GALLIENNE, RICHARD. *The Romantic '90s* (1925).

LEVERSON, ADA. *Letters to the Sphinx from Oscar Wilde, with Reminiscences of the Author* (1930).

LEWIS, LLOYD, AND HENRY JUSTIN SMITH. *Oscar Wilde Discovers America* (1936).

MASON, STUART. *A Bibliography of Oscar Wilde* (1914).

_____. *Oscar Wilde: Art and Morality* (1912; rpt. 1971).

MEYERS, JEFFREY. *Homosexuality and Literature 1890–1930* (1977).

MIKHAIL, E. H. *Oscar Wilde: An Annotated Bibliography* (1978).

_____. *Oscar Wilde: Interviews and Recollections* (1979).

MILLER, JAMES. *The Passion of Michel Foucault* (1992).

NASSAAR, CHRISTOPHER. *Into the Demon Universe: A Literary Exploration of Oscar Wilde* (1974).

NIETZSCHE, FRIEDRICH. *The Portable Nietzsche*, ed. Walter Kaufmann (1954).

OATES, JOYCE CAROL. "*The Picture of Dorian Gray*: Wilde's Parable of the Fall," *Critical Inquiry* (1980), 419–28.

O'SULLIVAN, VINCENT. *Aspects of Wilde* (Eng. ed., 1936).

PAGE, NORMAN. *An Oscar Wilde Chronology* (1991).

PEARSON, HESKETH. *The Life of Oscar Wilde* (1946).

PINE, RICHARD. *Oscar Wilde* (1983).

POWELL, KERRY. *Oscar Wilde and the Theatre of the 1890s* (1990).

READE, BRIAN. *Sexual Heretics: Male Homosexuality in English Literature from 1850 to 1900* (1970).

REIFF, PHILIP. "The Impossible Culture: Wilde as a Modern Prophet," *Salmagundi* 58–59 (1982–83), 406–26.

ROBERTS, BRIAN. *The Mad Bad Line: The Family of Lord Alfred Douglas* (1981).

SALTUS, EDGAR. *Oscar Wilde: An Idler's Impression* (1917).

SEDGWICK, EVE KOSOFKSY. *The Epistemology of the Closet* (1990).

SCHROEDER, HORST. *Additions and Corrections to Richard Ellmann's "Oscar Wilde"* (1989).

SHERARD, ROBERT. *Bernard Shaw, Frank Harris, and Oscar Wilde* (1937 ed.).

————. *The Life of Oscar Wilde* (1906).

————. *Oscar Wilde: The Story of an Unhappy Friendship* (1902).

————. *The Real Oscar Wilde* (1917).

SHEWAN, RODNEY, *Oscar Wilde: Art and Egotism* (1977).

————. "A Wife's Tragedy: An Unpublished Sketch for a Play by Oscar Wilde," *Theatre Research International* 7 (1982), 75–131.

————. "Oscar Wilde and *A Wife's Tragedy*: Facts and Conjectures," *Theatre Research International* 8 (1983), 183–95.

SMALL, IAN. "Oscar Wilde as a Professional Writer," *Library Chronicle of the University of Texas at Austin* 20 (1993), 32–49.

————. *Oscar Wilde Revalued: An Essay on New Materials and Methods of Research* (1993).

SMITH, TIMOTHY D'ARCH. *Love in Earnest: Some Notes on the Lives and Writings of English Uranian Poets from 1889 to 1930* (1970).

SONTAG, SUSAN. "Notes on Camp" (1964), *Susan Sontag Reader* (1982).

STOKES, JOHN. "Wilde at Bay: The Diaries of George Ives," *English Literature in Transition 1880–1920* 26 (1983), 175–86.

"Survey on the Constitutional Right to Privacy in the Context of Homosexual Activity," *University of Miami Law Review* (1986), 521–687.

WEEKS, JEFFREY. *Coming Out: Homosexual Politics, from the Nineteenth Century to the Present* (1977).

————. *Sex, Politics and Society: The Regulation of Sexuality Since 1800* (1981).

WHITE, TERENCE DE VERE. *The Parents of Oscar Wilde* (1967).

WILDE, FRANCESCA JANE, LADY. *Essays and Stories* (1907).

WINWAR, FRANCES. *Oscar Wilde and the Yellow Nineties* (1940).

WOODCOCK, GEORGE. *The Paradox of Oscar Wilde* (1949).

WORTH, KATHARINE. *Oscar Wilde* (1983).

WYNDHAM, HORACE. *Speranza: A Biography of Lady Wilde* (1951).

WYNDHAM, VIOLET. *The Sphinx and Her Circle* (1963).

ZATLIN, LINDA. *Aubrey Beardsley and Victorian Sexual Politics* (1990).

Index

☆ ☆ ☆ ☆ ☆ ☆ ☆ ☆ ☆ ☆ ☆ ☆ ☆ ☆ ☆ ☆ ☆ ☆

A

Adey, More, 27–28, 74, 129, 290–293, 332, 409, 410
Aeschylus, 173
Agate, James, 10, 423
Alexander, George, 100, 233, 237, 260, 274, 278, 454
Alhambra theater, 24
Almy, Percival, 18, 210–211, 401
Amor, Anne Clark, 89, 131, 142
Antinous, 3, 52, 161, 429

Apollo, 127, 463
Archer, William, 32, 66, 361, 363, 364–365, 368, 468
Aristotle, 304–306, 309
Arnold, Matthew, 383
Atherton, Gertrude, 87–88, 171
Atkins, Freddy, 116, 182, 186 (illust.), 188, 191
Atkinson, G. T., 2, 27, 425
Auden, W. H., 9, 12, 13, 19, 166, 260, 302–303
Aynesworth, Allan, 405

B

Babbacombe House, 6, 120, 132, 136–137
Bacon, Sir Francis, 10
Balcombe, Florence, 103, 153
Balzac, Honoré de, 30–31, 72, 222, 250, 309
Baudelaire, Charles, 30
Beardsley, Aubrey, 137, 208
Beaumarchais, Pierre Augustin Caron de, 393, 407
Beckson, Karl, 454
Beerbohm, Sir Max, 2, 4, 11, 14, 19, 38, 43–44, 137, 147, 157, 193, 216, 235, 241, 248, 251, 253, 254, 258, 269, 271, 278, 279, 293, 294, 301, 320, 348, 350, 360, 373, 395, 404, 405, 409
Beethoven, Ludwig van, 305, 356n
Bentham, Jeremy, 224, 310
Behrendt, Patricia, 421
Bernhardt, Sarah, 104, 203
Biron, Chartres, 4
Blacker, Carlos, 124–125, 139, 268, 337, 426
Blackmun, Harry, 226–228
Blackstone, William, 213, 214–215, 446
Borges, Jorge Luis, 10, 333, 352, 361, 402
Borland, Maureen, 181
Bosie. *See* Douglas, Lord Alfred
Boucicault, Dion, 75
Bowers v. Hardwick, 226–228
Bray, Alan, 446
Brémont, Anna, Comtesse de, 87, 89, 104, 106, 394–395
Bright, Reginald Golding, 363
Brontë, Charlotte, 72
Brooke, Lady (Ranee of Sarawak), 147

Brookfield, Charles, 260, 278
Browning, Elizabeth Barrett, 93
Browning, Oscar, xvi-xvii
Buchanan, Robert, 28–29
Burger, Warren, 213
Burnand, Frank, 45, 58, 429
Burne-Jones, Edward, 48, 104, 275, 289

C

Caine, Hall, 390
Campbell, Lady Colin, 1–2, 358
Campbell, Mrs Patrick, 215
Capote, Truman, 390
Carlyle, Thomas, 390–391
Carpenter, Edward, 106, 172, 182, 218–219, 224–229, 231, 277, 328–329, 388, 466
Carr, Mrs J. Comyns, 131
Carson, Sir Edward, 185, 187, 189, 260, 300
Cather, Willa, 272, 453
Catullus, 173, 182–183
Cavafy, Constantine, 393, 394
Cellini, Benvenuto, 29–30, 31
Chameleon, The, magazine, 40–41, 68, 75, 150, 176, 187, 263, 321, 403, 408
Charles, Mr Justice, 284
Chesterton, G. K., 14, 38–39, 350, 368, 371
Chuang-tzu, 305–306
Clark Library (Los Angeles), xii, 97, 178, 420
Clarke, Edward, 236, 274–275, 284
Cleveland Herald, 404
Cleveland Street scandal, 218, 220, 221, 223
Closet, the, 295–329, 443
Cohen, Ed, xv, 446
Coke, Edward, 214

Conway, Alphonse, 137–138, 182, 190

Cooper, Edith, 3

Core, Philip, 459

Corkran, Henriette, 95

Courier Journal (Louisville), 5, 59

Criminal Law Amendment Act (1885), 30, 34, 215–229, 245, 278, 286–287, 387

Croft-Cooke, Rupert, xv, 177, 193, 387

Crompton, Louis, 446

D

Daily Chronicle, 337, 347

Daily News, 82–83, 274

Daily Record-Union (Sacramento), 5

Daily Telegraph, 2, 20, 68–69, 75, 254, 283, 362

d'Arch Smith, Timothy, xv, 463

Davis, Jefferson, 271

Defoe, Daniel, 382

Delay, Jean, 426

de Man, Paul, 471

De Quincey, Thomas, 200

Dickens, Charles, 33, 61, 72, 84, 155, 201, 210, 250, 279

Dodgson, Campbell, 6–7, 31, 136

Dollimore, Jonathan, xv–xvi, 24

Douglas, John Sholto. *See* Queensberry, Marquess of

Douglas, Lord Alfred ("Bosie"), xiv, 3, 6, 21, 29, 44, 100, 113, 115, 116, 119, 121, 134, 137, 162, 185, 189 (illust.), 190, 192–197, 206–207, 219, 221, 237, 243–246, 259, 284, 335, 341, 343, 344, 356, 406, 409; translation of *Salome*, 113, 136; urges libel suit, 234, 304; view of father, 280–281;

view of W, 3, 29, 241, 302–303, 375–376, 386; view of trials, 218, 241, 272, 284; W's view of, 134, 137, 185, 192–197, 207–208, 243–244, 344

Douglas, Percy (brother of Lord Alfred), 239, 280, 282 (illust.), 289

Douglas, Sholto (brother of Lord Alfred), 280

Doyle, Arthur Conan, 14, 386

Drumlanrig, Viscount, 275

Du Maurier, George, 45, 46, 48, 54

Dupoirier, Edouard, xii, 334, 408, 410

E

Echo, The, 49, 66–67, 78

Eliot, George, 72, 390

Ellmann, Richard, xv, 9, 148, 153, 178, 252, 260, 261, 277, 310, 379, 390, 421, 447, 451–452

Emerson, Ralph Waldo, 70

Evening News, The, 282, 284

F

Field, Michael (pseud. Katharine Bradley), 3

Finnegans Wake, 1, 170, 345

Fitch, Clyde, 154–156, 160, 178–181, 179 (illust.), 298–299, 439, 441–443

Fitzroy Street scandal, 218, 221

Flaubert, Gustave, 72, 307

Foot, Philippa, 459, 468

Ford, Ford Madox, 38, 69, 247, 277, 301

Foucault, Michel, 318n

Fuller, Margaret, 70
Furniss, Harry, 84, 85

G

Gide, André, 9, 13, 19n, 21–22, 32, 35, 36–37, 114–115, 177n, 181n, 183, 184, 194–195, 220–221, 252, 258, 310, 318, 379, 426, 435, 445, 469
Gilbert, W. S., 52, 69, 204, 355, 363, 467
Gladstone, William, 153
Goethe, Johann Wolfgang von, 318, 349
Gosse, Edmund, 14, 376
Grainger, Walter, 162, 187
Grant, A. H., 3, 4
Gray, John, 116, 135, 276, 298, 357
Green Carnation, The, 206
Griffin, James, 445
Grundy, Sydney, 283

H

Hale, Nancy, 375
Handel, George Frederick, 465
Harding, Reginald, 112–113, 173 (illust.), 435
Hardy, Rev. E. J., 105
Harris, Frank, 77, 108–109, 113, 116, 117, 175, 194, 235–236, 238–243, 242 (illust.), 245–251, 259, 272, 273, 291, 293, 337, 349, 356, 402–403, 409, 433, 449
Hart-Davis, Rupert, 178, 422, 426
Headlam, Rev. Stewart, 239, 285, 288, 289, 332
Heliogabalus, Roman emperor, 52, 183
Henley, W. E., 191, 260, 273, 277

Henry VIII, King of England, 213
Herald (New York), 60
Hichens, Robert, 206, 441
Hofmannsthal, Hugo von, 258
Holland, Cyril (son), xi, 6, 44, 104, 120, 121, 125–142, 147, 192, 259, 274, 316, 408, 437
Holland, Merlin (grandson), 130n
Holland, Vyvyan (son), xi, xiv, 6, 28, 44, 104, 120, 121, 124, 125–143, 145, 155, 192, 259, 274, 292, 316, 378–379, 408, 420, 437
Holroyd, Michael, 31, 351, 352, 361, 373, 465–466
Home Secretary (Matthew Ridley), 92, 171–172, 181, 192, 196
homosexuality, xiv–xv, 21–23, 49–50, 83, 102, 114–117, 141, 169–197, 231, 252–254, 275, 286–287, 306–307, 309, 318n, 321–322, 327–329, 376, 387–389, 442–443; gay liberation movement, 277, 298–299, 309–310, 387–389, 442–443; humor about, 169–170, 181–183, 295–296; and marriage, 105–109; legislation against, 213–229, 446–447; Victorian attitudes about, 117, 171–172, 181, 209–210, 219–224, 229–231, 235, 286–288, 298, 319–320, 327–328. *See also* Closet, the; Wilde, Oscar, CHARAC-TERISTICS: homosexuality
Hope, Adrian, 121, 138–139, 142
Houghton, Philip, 21–22, 25
Howe, Julia Ward, 30, 70
Humphreys, Arthur, 409, 435

Humphreys, Travers, 217, 220, 234, 239, 250, 280, 446
Hunter-Blair, David, 301
Huysmans, Joris-Karl, 161, 425
Hyde, H. Montgomery, 89, 187, 280, 446

I

Ibsen, Henrik, 260, 358
Irving, Henry, 37, 216, 427
Ives, George, 7–9, 65, 177n, 193, 221, 254, 258, 264–265, 275, 277, 298–302, 321–325, 327, 329, 380, 387

J

Jackson, Holbrook, 15–16
James, Henry, 14, 17, 116, 320–321, 325, 359, 461
Jesus Christ, 37, 160, 257, 307, 317, 344
John, Augustus, 146, 449
Johnson, Samuel, 14, 26, 233, 318n, 403–404, 443–444
Jopling, Louise, 3, 103
Joyce, James, 1, 31, 170, 280, 345, 394

K

Kaufmann, Walter, 319
Keats, John, 251, 307
Kernahan, Coulson, 360
King, Martin Luther, Jr., 387
Kipling, Rudyard, 33, 336
Knight, G. Wilson, 439
Kohl, Norbert, 9
Krafft-Ebing, Richard, 106–107, 108, 172, 328

L

Labouchere, Henry, 215–216, 216 (illust.), 218, 221, 224, 277–278
Lady of Wimbledon. *See* Schuster, Adela
Lady's Pictorial, 67
Le Jeunesse, Ernest, 255–256, 445
Langtry, Lillie, 3–4, 69, 99–100, 104, 116, 134, 278–279
Lee, Margaret, 98–100, 104, 110, 111
Le Gallienne, Richard, 2–4, 7, 15, 18, 36, 86, 109, 111, 116, 133, 146, 153, 177, 268–269, 335, 365n
Le Rouge, Gustave, 255, 269
Leverson, Ada, 1–2, 11, 15, 19, 45–46, 68–69, 107, 117, 128, 146, 181n, 200, 205, 235, 240, 244, 249, 253, 266, 271, 274, 292–294, 315, 332, 335, 409, 449
Leverson, Ernest, 94, 128, 244, 253, 275, 292
Levey, Michael, 434
Lika Joko magazine, 112
Lippincott's Magazine, 40, 201
Lloyd, Otho (brother of Constance), 102, 115, 122, 138, 146–147
Lloyd's Weekly, 273
Louÿs, Pierre, 114–115, 137, 343
Low, Sidney, 192

M

MacInnes, Colin, 10
Mahaffy, John, 471
Mallarmé, Stephane, 135
Mann, Thomas, 314, 458
Mapplethorpe, Robert, 384

Marillier, H. C., 135, 169, 175–176, 177
Marra, Kim, 442
Martial, 173, 182–183, 295–296, 297
Martin, Robert, 439
Mason, Charles Spurrier, 114–115
Mason, Stuart, 286
Maugham, Somerset, 441
Maupassant, Guy de, 400
Mavor, Sidney, 116, 186, 284
McCarthy, Lillah, 360
McCarthy, Mary, 10, 41–42, 251
Melba, Nellie, 4, 15, 137, 336, 340
Mellor, Harold, 27–28, 325–329, 334, 342, 409, 461
Mendès, Catulle, 275–276
Merrill, Stuart, 7, 130, 285, 395
Michelangelo Buonarroti, 253, 390
Mikhail, E. H., 452
Miles, Canon, 102, 175, 378
Miles, Frank, 102, 175
Millard, Christopher. *See* Mason, Stuart
Miller, Dewitt, 442
Miller, James, 460
Milton, John, 225
Milwaukee Sentinel, 3
Molière, 327
Montaigne, Michel de, 313–314, 383
Morgan, Margery, 362
Morris, William, 48, 351
Mount-Temple, Lady, 6, 120, 132
Mull, Martin, 318n
Murray, Isobel, 149, 151

N

Napoleon I, emperor, 257
National Observer, 273

Nehamas, Alexander, 318n, 451, 460
Neue Freie Presse (Vienna), 359
New York Times, 67
Nietzsche, Friedrich, 23, 31–32, 35, 39–40, 75, 109–110, 145, 177, 229, 251, 255, 259, 264, 293, 310–319, 329, 361, 370, 394, 427, 451, 458–459, 468
Nordau, Max, 230, 310

O

Oates, Joyce Carol, 25, 439
Ossian, 61, 86
O'Sullivan, Vincent, 3, 4–5, 30, 36, 65, 72, 86, 147, 220, 240, 257, 272, 275, 276, 310, 320, 336, 401, 420, 438, 468
Ouida (Louise de la Ramée), 72–73, 86, 99–100, 104, 118, 430

P

Pall Mall Gazette, 99, 104, 135, 167, 206, 305, 352, 358, 363, 385
Parke, Ernest, 221, 223, 224
Parker, Charlie, 97, 187 (illust.), 188, 190
Parker, Dorothy, xiv
Parker, William, 187 (illust.)
Partridge, J. Bernard, 46
Pater, Walter, 23, 48, 106, 147, 156, 169, 319–320, 333, 422, 429, 434, 438
Patience, 52, 58, 69, 102
Payn, James, 20
Payne, Ralph, 22, 25
Pearson, Hesketh, 353, 355
Peel, Robert, 214
Pennington, Harper, xii, xiv, 69, 275

Percival, John, 261
Phelps, William Lyon, 442
Plato, 172, 463
Pletsch, Carl, 314, 451, 458
Polycrates, tyrant of Samos,
   256–257
Potter, Helen, 68
Prevôst, Abbé, 357
Punch magazine, 11, 43–63, 71, 84,
   117, 157, 199–211, 248, 251,
   272–273, 292, 354, 389, 391
Pushkin, Alexander, 440

Q

Queensberry, Lady, 6, 280, 420
Queensberry, Marquess of (John
   Sholto Douglas), 10, 17, 40,
   58, 171, 184–185, 208,
   219–220, 236, 237, 245, 247,
   252, 259, 260, 273, 275,
   279–283, 282 (illust.),
   287–288, 346, 369, 405

R

Racine, Jean Baptiste, 45
Raffalovich, André, 441
Ransome, Arthur, 441
Rational Dress Society, 91, 111
Régnier, Henri de, 4, 78
Reiff, Philip, 426, 458, 469
Renaud, Jean-Joseph, 3, 4
Reynolds's Newspaper, 184–185, 220,
   246–247, 284–285
Rhys, Ernest, 356n
Rilke, Rainer Maria, 360, 361–362
Robinson, Mrs (palmist), 120, 240,
   251, 262, 344
Rodd, Rennell, 261
Rodin, Auguste, 30–31, 250, 309,
   351, 360, 361–362

Ross, Robert, 3, 9, 13, 15, 95, 97,
   113, 115, 119–120, 122–126,
   129, 132, 135, 137, 139, 145,
   146, 161, 169, 175, 176, 181,
   259, 291–292, 310n, 333,
   334, 338, 339–340, 341, 356,
   404–410, 441, 449, 473;
   literary executor for W, 113,
   310n
Rossetti, Dante Gabriel, 48, 289
Rothenstein, Will, xiii, 283, 409
Rushdie, Salman, 385
Ruskin, John, 104, 132, 153

S

Saltus, Edgar, 115, 127
Sambourne, Edward, 59
San Francisco Examiner, 378
Saturday Review, 147, 166–167, 168,
   273
Savonarola, Girolamo, 29
Scaurus, M. Aemilius, 261
Schimmel, Herbert, 420
Schopenhauer, Arthur, 399
Schuster, Adela, 15, 259, 290–293,
   409
Schwabe, Maurice, 188, 189 (illust.)
Scots Observer, 115
Sedgwick, Eve Kosofsky, 458
Shakespeare, William, 10, 33, 54,
   253, 258, 277, 289, 296–297,
   362, 365, 394, 403
   PLAYS: *The Merry Wives of
   Windsor,* 403; *A Midsummer
   Night's Dream,* 404; *As You
   Like It,* 337; *Much Ado About
   Nothing,* 104, 135, 200;
   Henry V, 406; *The Winter's
   Tale,* 167
   CHARACTERS: Antony, 196, 394;
   Beatrice, 200; Benedick, 104,

Shakespeare, CHARACTERS (cont.)
200; Caliban, 167, 280;
Celia, 337; Cleopatra, 110,
111, 196, 394; Coriolanus,
238, 258–259; Falstaff, 16,
134, 148, 259, 269, 365, 393,
395, 402–406; Hamlet, 16,
33, 148, 149, 255, 365, 390,
393, 395–402, 406; Horatio,
259; Iago, 394; Juliet, 205,
365; King Lear, 394; Leontes,
259; Mamillius, 167, 259;
Master of the Revels, 404;
Mistress Quickly (Hostess),
259, 406; Octavia, 110;
Ophelia, 33; Othello, 269,
436; Player King, 402;
Polonius, 28, 258, 396, 397,
400; Prince Hal, 255, 405;
Romeo, 126; Rosencrantz
and Guildenstern, 149, 255,
260, 390; Volumnia, 87, 238,
259
Shaw, Bernard, xvii–xviii, 1, 7, 9,
10, 12, 16, 23, 24, 31, 33,
36, 48, 66, 78, 123, 157, 194,
221–224, 226, 243, 246, 247,
249, 285, 289, 338, 345–374,
349 (illust.), 389, 465–466;
affinities with W, 345–374;
attack on Criminal Law
Amendment Act, 221–224;
on Nietzsche, 313, 459; on
Willie Wilde, 279
WORKS: Arms and the Man, 362,
363; Cashel Byron's
Profession, 348; Fanny's First
Play, 353; Immaturity, 24n,
349, 353–355, 465–466; John
Bull's Other Island, 367–375,
398, 468; Pygmalion, 362
Shaw, Charlotte, 352, 364

Shelley, Andrew, 452
Shelley, Edward, 116, 136, 177, 186
(illust.)
Shelley, Percy, 251, 389
Sherard, Robert, 127, 129, 193, 239,
244, 250, 251, 279, 473
Sheridan, Richard, 179, 391, 468
Shewan, Rodney, 433
Sickert, Helena, 28, 364, 376, 402
Sickert, Walter, 333
Small, Ian, 421, 451
Smithers, Leonard, 30–31
Socrates, 29, 31, 177, 251–252, 313,
318n
Somerset, Lord Henry, 298
Sontag, Susan, 459
Sophocles, 258
Speranza. See Wilde, Lady
Spilett, Gedeon, 268, 472
Spinoza, Baruch, 311
Stendhal, 30
Sterne, Laurence, 346
Stevenson, Robert Louis, 150
Stokes, John, 300
Stonewall riot, xv–xvi, 319
Strauss, Richard, 310n
Strindberg, August, 18
Swift, Jonathan, 346
Swinburne, Algernon, 14, 48, 59,
173
Symonds, John Addington,
105–106, 231, 320, 376, 434
Symons, A. J. A., 360

T
Taylor, Alfred, 24, 114, 116, 182,
185n, 186 (illust.), 188,
190–191, 218, 282, 284, 288,
444
Taylor, Mrs John, 266
Taylor, Paul, 267

Terry, Ellen, 37, 104, 149, 283, 289, 357, 427

Theater, The, magazine, 20, 211

Times-Picayune (New Orleans), 146

To-day magazine, 111

Tolstoy, Leo, 348

Toulouse-Lautrec, Henri de, xii–xiii, 2, 3, 420

Tree, Beerbohm, xi, 15, 41, 104, 116, 249, 365

Trilling, Lionel, 458

Trollope, Anthony, 33, 72

Truth (London), 215, 221, 224, 278

Turner, Reggie, 177n, 181, 264, 333, 406, 409

Tyrell, Ada, 465

U

Ulysses, 394

V

Van Gogh, Vincent, 149

Vanbrugh, Irene, 3

Victoria, Queen of England, 33, 70, 272, 285, 379

Vidal, Gore, 390

Vitellius, Roman emperor, 183

W

Wagner, Richard, 130, 159, 358

Wainewright, Thomas, 40, 69, 75, 184, 200, 262–263

Walford, L. B., 6

Walküre, Die, 159

Waller, Lewis, 405

Ward, William ("Bouncer"), 145–146, 172–174, 173 (illust.), 403

Ward, Sam, 67

Washington Post, 339

Weeks, Jeffrey, 446

Wells, H. G., 362

Westminster Review, 219, 273, 284

Whistler, James McNeill, 45, 103, 128, 216, 266, 358, 375, 466

White, Terence, 92

Whitman, Walt, xvii, 26, 105, 146, 172, 173, 318n, 379, 388, 407, 434, 460

Wilde, Constance (wife, née Lloyd), xii–xiii, 6, 19, 70, 88–92, 97–126, 99 (illust.), 128, 136–139, 142, 146–147, 155, 175, 192, 237, 249, 274, 316, 335, 435, 458

Wilde, Cyril (son). *See* Holland, Cyril

Wilde, Isola (sister), 142

Wilde, Lady (mother, "Speranza"), 72, 82–96, 84 (illust.), 85 (illust.), 101, 117, 121, 237–239, 244–245, 259, 279, 353, 354, 365, 399

Wilde, Oscar.

IMPORTANT BIOGRAPHICAL EVENTS *(chronologically):*

Poems published, 101–102, 174

lecture tour of U.S., xvi–xvii, 3, 61, 67–68, 102, 170, 215–216, 377–379

courtship and marriage, 101–104, 130, 155, 175

premiere of first play, *Vera,* 110

two sons born, 104, 130, 134, 175

meets Robert Ross, 175

edits *Women's World,* 70–73, 348

Lady Windermere's Fan opens, 11–12, 116, 461

A *Woman of No Importance* opens, 16

An Ideal Husband opens, 112

Wilde, BIOGRAPHICAL EVENTS *(cont.)*
   Earnest opens, 68, 117, 123, 184,
      248, 265, 272, 281, 301, 321,
      356
   arrest, 138, 157, 208, 229,
      235–236, 271, 272 (illust.)
   sale of Tite St. belongings, xii,
      120, 127–128, 420
   trials, xii, xvii, 12, 128, 185, 191,
      246–247, 250–251, 264, 281,
      284–289
   conviction, 12, 230, 271,
      285–288
   in prison, 73, 92, 121, 129, 138,
      234, 283, 458
   death of mother, 82, 92, 121, 239,
      274
   travels after prison, 12, 95,
      139–140, 255–257, 269, 321,
      332–344
   death of wife, 121, 124–125
   last illness, 291, 406
   death and burial, 145, 292, 387,
      406–410

   WHEREABOUTS:
   Algiers, 21, 152, 161, 163,
      183–184, 194, 237, 240, 252,
      258, 263–264, 351–352, 378
   Babbacombe Cliff, Torquay,
      Devon, 6, 31, 136, 193
   Bad Homburg, 116
   Berneval-sur-Mer, 95, 406
   Courtfield Gardens (Kensington),
      128, 248, 271–272, 275,
      293–294
   Cromer, Norfolk, xi, 115
   Dublin, 101–102, 173, 260, 273
   Edinburgh, 104
   French Riviera, 278, 325,
      341–342, 406
   Genoa, 125–126, 327, 342

Goring-on-Thames, 187
Holloway Prison, 127, 191,
   234–235, 240, 244, 248, 283,
   293, 331
Hôtel d'Alsace, xii, 257, 323–324,
   334, 408–410
Lake Geneva, 27–28, 158,
   325–326
Leadville, Colorado, xi, xvii, 29
Leverson house. *See* Courtfield
   Gardens
Monte Carlo, 119, 237, 264, 334
Morocco. *See* Algiers
Naples, 336, 342
Old Bailey (Central Criminal
   Court), 185, 208, 210, 238,
   245, 251, 258, 288
Oxford (Magdalen College), 36,
   49, 88, 103, 112, 148,
   172–175, 261, 273, 301,
   304–305, 440–441
Paris, 103, 135–136, 139–140,
   155, 182, 188, 255–256, 294,
   323–325, 327, 334, 335, 336,
   341, 342, 343, 406–410, 429
Piccadilly, 44, 116, 119, 136, 155,
   177, 182, 190–191, 194, 301,
   405
Reading Prison, 73, 92, 143, 171,
   240, 321, 337, 458
Rome, xi, 342, 408
San Francisco Bay Area, 68, 171,
   377–379
Sorrento, 256
Tite St., Chelsea, xii, 43–44, 70,
   99–100, 103–104, 108, 118,
   131–134, 136, 146, 175,
   180–181, 188, 190, 378–379
United States, xvi, 3, 61, 67–68,
   102, 170, 215–216, 377–378
Worthing (Sussex), 100, 114,
   134, 137, 181, 190

CHARACTERISTICS:

appearance, 1–6, 9, 54, 86, 103, 146, 265, 278, 311, 350, 377n

behavior as:

actor/concealer, 19–23, 249–250, 298–299, 303, 395–397, 471

aesthete, 46–63, 66–70, 74–79

arbiter of fashion, 65–79, 396

book reviewer, 12, 98–100, 104–105, 371–372, 390–391, 471

conversationalist, 9, 13–15, 72, 192, 261, 294, 301, 376, 402

dandy, 21, 181n, 303

defendant, 185–187, 189–190, 246, 250–252, 253–254, 258, 281, 300, 347, 444

editor, 70–73, 90, 200, 348, 390, 430

enfant terrible, 145–146, 361–362

father, xi, 127–140

golfer, xi, 420

husband, 97–126, 135

iconoclast, 32–33

lover of Lord Alfred Douglas, 100–101, 119–120, 192–197, 243–245

mother's son, 81–82, 85–96

paradoxist, 16–18, 150, 281, 299–301, 313, 368, 424

pariah, 268–269, 321–327, 333–344

photographer, xi, 408

playwright, 10–11, 15, 65–66, 97, 100–101, 116, 176, 203–204, 233–234

risk-taker, xvi, 264, 298, 313

Sebastian Melmoth (pseudonym), 139–140, 249, 257, 332–333

sexual predator, 22–25, 96, 110, 142, 177, 181–182, 184–187, 189–190, 341–343

smoker, 11, 28, 96, 182, 184, 203, 294, 334, 340, 379

snob, 9, 36, 157

Socrates, modern-day, 29, 31, 177, 251–252, 313

storyteller, 107–108, 132–133, 166–168, 255–257, 294, 316–317, 355–356, 404

tragic hero, 12–13, 83, 148–149, 244, 251–252, 255–269, 276–277, 396

trespasser, 28–42, 303

credos expressed, 17, 21–22, 37, 145, 153, 167–168, 259, 265–266, 283, 295, 304–309, 317–318, 388, 404

homosexuality, xiv–xv, 21–25, 83, 102, 105–108, 149, 206–207, 263, 306–307, 378, 421; and W's children's tales, 149, 152–168; first experiences of, 107–108, 148–149, 175; W's gay circle, 116–117, 153–154, 173–175, 181–182, 409; W's liaisons, 110, 114–116, 126, 134–138, 142, 154, 174, 177–188, 301–302, 341–343; how practiced by W, 188–189; references by W to, 135, 162, 171–173, 175, 181, 184, 191–192, 253–254, 326, 327–329, 341–343, 387; in works by W, 149, 152–168, 187, 201–203, 205–206; satirized in *Punch*, 201–203, 206–210

individualism, philosophy of,

Wilde, CHARACTERISTICS *(cont.)*
39–40, 68, 75–79, 157–159,
167–168, 296–297, 301–302
Irish identity, 36, 39, 249,
366–374
his life, reflected in W's works, 4,
19–23, 25, 41, 66, 77–78,
97–101, 112, 115–119,
122–123, 142–143, 148, 150,
152–168, 181, 184, 193–194,
234–235, 248, 250, 252,
256–257, 261–265, 267–268,
281, 297–298, 301–303, 308,
309, 313–319, 331, 340, 344,
401, 404
misogamy of, 111–114, 117–118,
122, 124
misogyny of, 118, 122–124, 312,
365
name of, xvi–xvii, 274, 278,
283–284, 421
Nietzsche, affinities with,
310–319, 451, 468
physique. *See* appearance *above*
portraits of, Pennington, xii, xiv,
69, 275; Toulouse-Lautrec,
xii–xiii, 2, 3, 420
satire on, 170–171, 275; *Colonel,
The,* 58; *Immaturity,*
353–355; *Patience,* 11, 52,
58, 69, 102; *Where's the Cat,*
58. *See also main entry for*
Punch *magazine*
Shaw, affinities with, 345–374
voice of, 4, 65, 155, 259

WORKS *(mentioned and/or quoted):*
Ballad of Reading Gaol, The
(1898), 24, 124, 274,
337–338
children's tales, *See A House of*

Pomegranates and *The Happy
Prince*
"Charmides" (poem), 175, 201,
378
"Critic as Artist, The" (1890),
xiii, 7, 13, 19, 29, 33–35, 37,
39, 40, 157, 191, 202, 248,
258, 296–297, 306, 312, 318,
340, 344, 366–369, 375, 377,
380, 383, 385–388, 395, 396,
400
"Decay of Lying, The" (1889),
17, 20, 29, 38, 149, 151, 152,
166–167, 176, 203, 261–262,
266, 305, 331, 393, 400
De Profundis (1905), 9–10, 20,
92–93, 124, 129, 148, 169,
196, 244, 245, 252, 257,
265–266, 267, 295, 309, 359,
380, 396, 398
"Few Maxims for the Instruction
of the Over-Educated, A"
(1894), 70, 325
Happy Prince, The (1888),
147–160, 167–168, 439
"The Happy Prince," 148,
154–156, 158, 159
"The Nightingale and the
Rose," 166
"The Selfish Giant," 132–133,
158–160
"The Devoted Friend," 34,
150–151
"The Remarkable Rocket,"
147, 156–158
House of Pomegranates, A (1891),
147–150, 161–168
"The Young King," 148, 161
"The Birthday of the Infanta,"
267
"The Fisherman and his Soul,"
162–166

"The Star-Child," 148, 162

"House Beautiful, The" (lecture), 102

Ideal Husband, An 18, 20, 32, 34–35, 65, 66, 81, 83, 84, 98, 112, 118, 122, 123, 184, 204, 250, 252, 264, 278, 281, 303, 308, 310, 368, 380, 383, 405, 427

Importance of Being Earnest, The (1895), xiv, 11–12, 15, 33–34, 69, 75, 81–84, 98, 103, 108, 114, 158–159, 160, 166, 184, 237, 247, 251, 265, 274, 298, 334, 347, 357, 396, 400, 405, 409; first ed., 274; genesis of plot, 302; Gribsby scene, 233–235, 252, 407; premiere, 68, 117, 184, 248, 272, 281, 301, 321, 356; Shaw on, 123

"Impressions of America" (1906), xi, 29, 102, 378

Intentions (1891), 203

Lady Windermere's Fan (1892), xvii, 11, 85, 96, 97, 116, 118, 122, 147, 176, 203, 236, 253, 274, 278, 283, 308, 341, 362, 399, 407, 461

Lord Arthur Savile's Crime and Other Stories (1891), 114, 255, 262, 407

Oscariana (1895), xii–xiii, 19, 119

"Pen, Pencil and Poison" (1889), xvi, 69, 110, 184, 200, 262

"Phrases and Philosophies for the Use of the Young" (1894), 28, 33–34, 37, 41, 260n, 298, 308, 403

Picture of Dorian Gray, The (1890), xii–xiii, 4, 12–13, 14, 16–17, 22–26, 29, 34, 39–40, 46, 77–78, 91, 111, 114, 115, 118, 142, 161–162, 176, 177, 182, 187, 191, 196, 200–201, 205–206, 231, 242, 246, 248, 250, 254, 257, 260, 261, 263, 268, 271, 279, 297–300, 302, 306, 315, 320, 328, 329, 347, 357, 376–377, 380–381, 396–397, 400–401, 425

Poems (1881), 19, 59–60, 101–102, 104, 174–175, 354

"Portrait of Mr W. H., The" (1889), 178

Salome (1893), 7–8, 45, 46, 113, 114, 136, 148, 203, 263–264, 310n, 315, 343, 347, 365, 402

"Soul of Man Under Socialism, The" (1891), 29–30, 37, 39, 77, 78, 158–159, 160, 233, 250, 306–307, 317, 329, 356, 379, 380, 381, 384

Vera, or The Nihilists (1883), 60–61, 110

Wife's Tragedy, A (circa 1887–90), 97–98, 103, 110–111, 113

Woman of No Importance, A (1893), xi, 6–7, 16–17, 23, 34, 41, 46, 81, 94, 96, 98, 111, 112, 116, 142–143, 181, 193–194, 204, 239, 244, 248, 263, 268, 304, 321, 383, 387, 399–400, 404

HIS VIEWS ABOUT:

acrobats, 18–19

art and artists, xvi, 19, 20, 29, 37–39, 68, 70, 75–76, 110, 149–150, 167–168, 250, 258, 305, 306, 315, 329, 347, 379,

Wilde, HIS VIEWS ABOUT (*cont.*)
397–398, 400, 401–402, 406, 469
Atlantic Ocean, 33, 427
autobiography, 297, 306, 456
Balzac, 30
Beerbohm, 19
biographers, 385, 390
book reviewing, 12
Bosie. *See* Douglas, Lord Alfred *below*
British fiction, 34
British public, 20, 150–151, 167, 250–251, 299–300, 312
brother Willie, 238, 279
California, 33, 377–378
children and childhood, 145, 152
children's tales, 133, 152–153
the Closet, 295–329
color, xiii, 40, 69, 78, 206
Communism, 386
his "crime" and mistakes, 10, 171–172, 196
critics and criticism, 296–297, 386–387, 422
Dickens, 33
doctors, 338
Douglas, Lord Alfred, 134, 137, 185, 193–197, 207–208, 243–244, 264, 344
dress. *See* style *below*
fashion. *See* style *below*
father and fatherhood, 81, 83–84
fauns, 161, 163–166, 180, 184
flowers, 67, 68
gay liberation movement, 387
Harris, Frank, 243
heredity, 83, 366–367
history and historians, xvi
Ives, George, 321–325
James, (Henry), 321
journalists, 43, 312, 384–385, 459

Kipling, 33
male beauty, 27–28, 177n, 187
marriage, 97–126
Mellor, Harold, 27, 325–327
missionaries, 111–112, 237
"modern" life, 380–391
morality and moralists, 35, 315–317, 383–385
Morris, William, 351
mother, Speranza, 82–96, 238–239, 244–245
Niagara Falls, 102
occultism, 240, 407
paradoxes, 16–19
Paris, 220
Pater, 320
philanthropists, 34–35, 111–112, 150, 427
politicians, 38, 380–381, 383
popes, 29–30
professions, 33–34, 389
Rodin, 30–31, 250
Ross, Robert, 291–292
San Francisco and Bay Area, 376–378
Shakespeare, 33
Shaw, 346, 357, 365
sin, 191, 377
sons Cyril and Vyvyan, 129–131, 134, 138–140
style, 2, 28, 65–79, 102, 295, 387
superstition, 299
the Swiss, 27, 326
Trollope, 33
Whitman, 379
wife Constance, 101–126, 155
women, 118, 123–124
women of America, 382
women's rights, 381–384
youth, 85, 107–108, 169, 176–177, 185, 193–195, 441, 443–444